COMMON GROUND
DIFFERENT OPINIONS

COMMON GROUND DIFFERENT OPINIONS

LATTER-DAY SAINTS AND
CONTEMPORARY ISSUES

Edited by
Justin F. White and
James E. Faulconer

Greg Kofford Books
Salt Lake City, 2013

Copyright © 2013 Greg Kofford Books
Cover design copyright © 2013 Greg Kofford Books, Inc.
Cover design by Loyd Ericson

Published in the USA.

All rights reserved. No part of this volume may be reproduced in any form without written permission from the publisher, Greg Kofford Books. The views expressed herein are the responsibility of the authors and do not necessarily represent the position of Greg Kofford Books.

Greg Kofford Books
P.O. Box 1362
Draper, UT 84020
www.gregkofford.com
facebook.com/gkbooks

Also available in ebook.

2017   16   15   14   13   5   4   3   2   1

Library of Congress Cataloging-in-Publication Data

Common ground, different opinions : Latter-day Saints and contemporary issues / edited by Justin F. White and James E. Faulconer.
   pages cm
 Includes index.
 ISBN 978-1-58958-573-7
 1. Mormons--Religious life. 2. Mormons--Political activity. 3. Church of Jesus Christ of Latter-day Saints--Doctrines. 4. Mormon Church--Doctrines. I. White, Justin F., editor of compilation. II. Faulconer, James E., editor of compilation.
 BX8656.C54 2013
 289.3'32--dc23
                    2013030366

Contents

Introduction, vii
James E. Faulconer

1. Paradigms, 3
   Robert L. Gleave
2. What Is Our Doctrine? 13
   Robert L. Millet
3. What Do We Mean by "Church Doctrine," 35
   Nathan B. Oman
4. Presiding in Our Homes: Are We Doing Too Much or Too Little? 53
   Larry Wimmer
5. Same-Gender Attraction and Same-Sex Marriage, 61
   Kent R. Brooks
6. Toward a Post-Heterosexual Mormon Theology, 85
   Taylor G. Petrey
7. Making Meaning and Making Families: Evaluating the Assumptive Grounds for Advocacy For or Against Same-Gender Marriage, 109
   Richard N. Williams
8. In Your Patience Possess Ye Your Souls, 129
   Camille S. Williams
9. For Louisa, 145
   Kristine Haglund
10. A Journey through Feminism: Reflections of an LDS Woman, 163
    Marleen S. Williams
11. All God's Children Got a Place in the Choir: Race and the Restored Gospel, 177
    Margaret Blair Young
12. Following Christ in Times of War: Latter-day Saints as Peacemakers, 195
    Bruce W. Young

13 Why We Fight: A Moral and Spiritual Basis
    for Latter-day Saint Military Service Today, 219
    Eric A. Eliason
14 Why I Am a Republican, 243
    Bob Bennett
15 Partisanship and the Gospel of Jesus Christ, 255
    Richard Davis
16 Heaven and Earth: Thinking through Environmentalism, 269
    George B. Handley
17 An Argument against Embryonic Stem Cell Research, 285
    David A. Jensen
18 Becoming a Person: Stem Cells and LDS Teachings, 307
    Sariah Cottrell and *Stephen L. Peck*
19 Evolution: From Naiveté to Understanding, 325
    Daniel Fairbanks
20 Genesis and Darwin: Finding Common and Uncommon Ground, 337
    David Grandy

The Authors, 357

Subject Index, 361

Scripture Index, 364

Introduction

Thinking About Contemporary Issues

James E. Faulconer

Perhaps there were times when Latter-day Saints could ignore much of the world and the problems of that world. Such times would require little attention to the social and political problems "outside." A person could focus on the problems of their family, ward, or local community. However, if there were such times they are gone forever. Today young Latter-day Saints are not confined to a relatively small geographic area, but find themselves scattered all over the world. And the larger world has come into and become part of those places where we were once perhaps able to look only to ourselves. Regardless of where young Latter-day Saints live, they are confronted with one issue after another that demands their thought and decision, and these issues extend far beyond our familial and church boundaries.

For some of these problems, such as abortion, the Church has an already-established statement that answers the question. We know what our answer is, though even knowing what our answer is may not preclude us from thinking about how to give good reasons for that answer. Indeed, we are enjoined by scripture to do so: "Sanctify Christ as Lord in your hearts, always ready to give an answer to anyone who asks you for an account of the hope of the saints, doing so with humility and reverence" (1 Pet. 3:15; my translation). Sometimes our only reason may be that the Church has officially spoken on the issue. That is enough for us—though it is still profitable for us to think about the reasons for the Church's position—but we are almost certain to encounter honest, respectful, and thoughtful people for whom "Because the prophet said so" will not be enough of an answer. They can reasonably ask us to explain *why* we believe what we do. As much as possible, we should be able to articulate additional reasons for them.

For many of the questions we encounter, however, there is no prophetic statement on which we can rely. On some issues, many members of the Church may favor one particular position over another; but since the Church has no position on the issue, we are free to decide for ourselves. Of course, we are free—even obligated—to decide for ourselves even if the Church *does* take a position on some issue, such as abortion or same-sex marriage. We ought to think about and pray about the Church's position and then come to a conclusion for ourselves. But for most Latter-day Saints, where the Church has a position, that position weighs heavily in our decisions. Even where the Church has no position, the fact that many fellow saints stand on one side of the issue rather than another often adds weight to the favored side when we are thinking about it. We pay attention to what others whom we respect believe.

Though authority sometimes gets a bad name, it is necessary in all thought. There are those who have earned our trust in some way that is relevant to the question at hand, no matter what the area of thought in which we engage, from science to literature, and from the arts to religion. Perhaps those people have earned our trust by their education: they have studied the matter at hand and have come to reasonable conclusions; so we trust them when they tell us what is true. Most of us do not have sufficient science education to do the research needed to come to a reasonable conclusion about things like global warming or the disposal of nuclear waste. So we look for scientists whose judgment we can trust, and we accept their conclusions. But science is hardly the only area in which we must depend on someone who has studied more than we have studied. We do so in finance, in buying cars, in cooking, and in many areas of our lives.

But education is not the only way to gain authority. A person can also earn our trust by having relevant experience. When our mountain guide tells us which path is the best for our trip, we accept that advice because the guide has been on this route many times before. The guide knows the ways, the hazards, and our goals, and is able to give us advice we can trust. This is the kind of trust that most of us can put in our parents and many of our leaders: they have experience, and based on that experience they can tell us what conclusions are true. We rely on them when we do not yet have sufficient experience ourselves, and even after we gain that experience we are likely to consult with them, testing our judgment against theirs.

Some authority is given by virtue of the office that a person holds. If a police officer directs me to a detour, I listen because of the person's office. I trust the person by dint of the fact that he or she is a police officer. Likewise, when the bishop or stake president calls me to do some particular work in the Church, I accept that calling because I recognize the authority of his priesthood and calling.

We rely on the judgment of authorities in many areas of our lives. Indeed, it is impossible in one lifetime for a person to have investigated every question without relying on someone with better knowledge. That is not to say that authorities cannot lead us astray—by insufficient investigation, by misunderstanding, and even by malice. But it is to say that we cannot avoid relying on authority in most areas of our lives.

Nevertheless, there are many social, political, and other issues on which the Church has taken no official position; thus, we cannot rely on its authority in those cases. We are left to our own lights. Among such issues are things such as evolution, stem cell research, environmentalism, our relation to peace and war, political partisanship, and feminism. How do we think about these and similar issues? How do we come to reasonable, responsible conclusions? The way we most often take our first positions is to rely on authority. We adopt the answers that our parents and peers have adopted. If my parents have responded to the question of political partisanship by being Republicans, then I too am probably going to be a Republican, at least in the beginning of my political and intellectual life. If most of those in my family are in favor of stem cell research, it is likely that my first opinion on the subject will be the same as theirs. In a discussion of evolution, my earliest reaction is likely to be that which I have learned from my family and fellow church members.

As a first step in thinking about difficult issues, adopting the position of those whom I have been raised by and grown up among is a good step. Presumably they have thought about these matters and they have good judgment, so I accept their conclusions as my own because I trust them. That is both natural and sensible. However, as I grow older, I need to come to my own conclusions on matters like these. Like my testimony, my positions on these kinds of issues ought not always remain something only garnered from trusted others. I may eventually come to the same conclusion that my parents or peers came to, but nevertheless, it ought to be *my* conclusion. And if my conclusion turns out to be different than theirs, I ought to be able to give a reasonable explanation of why I think differently. Part of being a good member of a family, a ward, a church, a community, or a nation is talking civilly and lovingly about things over which we may disagree and explaining our reasons for what we think. One of the things we discover when we think carefully about issues is that thoughtful, good people sometimes come to different conclusions. Good members of the Church may differ on important political and social issues. But even when they disagree, they ought to be able to talk to one another about those disagreements and to explain themselves.

The gospel requires that we be one. The Savior has made that point many times. For example, in the upper room where he instituted the ordinance of the Sacrament, he prayed, that his disciples might "be one, even as we are" (John 17:11). In the latter days, he has made that unity our goal, promising that those who believe on him "May become the sons of God, even one in me as I am one in the Father, as the Father is one in me, that we may be one" (D&C 30:2). And he has warned us that if we are not one, then we are not his (D&C 38:27).

We sometimes meet people who have thought about an issue, perhaps the environment, politics, or something else, and we come to a conclusion that is different than that of their parents or the majority of other saints whom they know. Then, unfortunately, they come to the further conclusion that if they disagree with members of the Church about that issue, they must also disagree about the truth of the gospel and the Church. "Mormons do not—or even cannot—believe as I do," they incorrectly assume. Tragically they believe that because the Church must be one, their difference of opinion has put them outside the Church. That is not only bad reasoning (the fact that we disagree about one thing does not mean that we disagree about another), it is a false conclusion.

The truth is that our spiritual unity does not preclude disagreement about many things. It dictates that we agree on the gospel, which Jesus defined in his visit to the Nephites as faith, repentance, baptism, the gift of the Holy Ghost, and endurance to the end (3 Ne. 27:13–16). These are matters in which agreement means less "intellectual agreement" than it does "being in harmony." The agreement required by the gospel dictates that we support one another, sharing our burdens, mourning together, giving strength to one another, and standing together always as witnesses of the Father and the Son (Mosiah 18:8–9). The gospel does not require that our ideas be the same.

Our disagreements over questions for which there is no revealed answer must not create a break between us. It must not cause us to break our baptismal covenant as Alma describes. If we cease to be brothers and sisters in the gospel because we disagree, treating one another as inferior or as enemies, or if we dispute about matters central to the gospel—not agreeing on the word (D&C 41:2)—then our disagreement is sinful and can become tragic. But loving brothers and sisters can disagree, even on important matters, and continue to love, respect, support, and comfort one another. They can disagree about many things yet stand together as witnesses of God.

In this volume you will find brothers and sisters who do not agree about some things, but they do agree about the gospel—the good news of Jesus Christ. They remain brothers and sisters, and often they are and remain friends. These people, committed to the gospel of Jesus Christ and its latter-day Restoration, provide us with models for both how we might think about certain issues and how we might disagree with those whom we love.

Most of us learn how to come to conclusions regarding the questions we have by modeling what we see others do, rather than taking formal lessons in critical reasoning or in the relevant subject matters. Indeed, absent models whom we observe and imitate, I suspect that formal lessons are rarely very effective. We observe how a trusted confidant has come to a conclusion, and we then imitate that person's ways of reaching answers to questions. We see when they can supplement the revealed words of the prophets with reasoning and when they cannot. We see them thinking and coming to thoughtful conclusions about issues to which the prophets have given no answer. We see how our models place an issue in context. We see what kinds of evidence they use in thinking about the issue. We learn how they use their powers of reason to either come to a conclusion or decide that there is not yet enough evidence to warrant anything more than a tentative conclusion, if that.

The authors and editors of these essays offer their writings to you as models for thinking about these issues more than as answers that they are trying to persuade you to accept. Though perhaps you will agree with a particular author after reading an essay, it is more important that you understand how a person carefully thinks about issues than it is that you adopt the particular points of view taken by any of the authors. The issues addressed in this volume represent only a small sampling of the issues that a person may be confronted with. They can, however, provide models for thinking about other issues, and it is our hope that they do so.

Some of the twenty essays collected here are paired in a pro and con fashion, with two or more people taking more-or-less opposing views on the same issue. Even when their views are not opposed to one another, the authors do not necessarily take the same approach. Robert Gleave invites us to consider the paradigms we use for understanding things, suggesting that sometimes maturity means adopting a new paradigm. Robert L. Millet and Nathan Oman take different perspectives on the question of what we mean when we refer to church doctrine. Larry Wimmer thinks about the question of what it means to preside in the home. Kent R. Brooks and Richard N. Williams deal with the question of how to explain the Church's position on the issues of same-sex attraction and same-sex marriage, while Taylor Petrey offers a thought experiment for how we might think about same-sex relationships differently than we presently do. The essays of Camille S. Williams, Marleen S. Williams, and Kristine Haglund approach the questions of Mormon feminism from three very different perspectives.

Margaret Blair Young thinks critically about the pre-1978 restriction of the priesthood from black church members and wrestles with the implications of how to make sense of what we do not understand. Bruce W. Young and Eric A. Eliason look at the problem of war from very different perspectives, and Bob Bennett and Richard Davis approach the question of political party affiliation from equally different perspectives. George Handley shows us one way to be an LDS environmentalist. David Jensen, on the one hand, and Steven Peck and Sariah Cottrell, on the other, consider the knotty question of stem cell research from opposing positions. Daniel Fairbanks takes up the question of how a Latter-day Saint can integrate scientific learning and faith by looking at the issue of evolution, while David Grandy looks for common ground between theists and nontheists on the same issue.

Readers of these essays will find themselves invited to think more deeply about these and other issues. More important, they will find themselves invited to not allow the honest differences we have on these and other issues to disrupt the unity we feel as sisters and brothers in the gospel of Jesus Christ.

In "Paradigms," Robert Gleave explores his journey through several different spiritual paradigms. Gleave explains how certain aspects of his early understanding of the gospel limited his growth until he explored new paradigms, or ways of seeing the world. As he explored and embraced these new possibilities, he found them richly rewarding. He closes his essay by inviting readers to explore ways of thinking and experiencing life that might be initially frightening, but that might lead toward increased understanding, a more satisfying self expression, and ultimately the rich rewards of eternal life.

One

Paradigms

Robert L. Gleave

I descend on both sides of my family from several generations of Utah Mormons. I was born in Provo, Utah, while my father was finishing his studies at Brigham Young University. When he graduated, my father entered employment with the Church Educational System. As a result of this employment, we moved frequently. I have spent all but a few years of my life living in Utah, from Ogden to St. George. My father's father spent his entire life farming land that he inherited from his father. The summers of my youth were spent on that family farm in Sevier County, Utah. I am intimately familiar with the culture of Utah Mormonism and have been exposed from an early age to the academic examination of mainstream LDS doctrine.

My earliest recollections are shaded with expectations that the most important thing was "doing" what is right. In my youthful exuberance, I accepted that task with full purpose and energy. Those were good and simple years with a finite set of expectations and a fairly high degree of success. I felt comfortable in the mainstream of Utah society and the Church. It is only in retrospect that I become aware that I was building a cage that would soon imprison me. I recall innumerable primary, Sunday school, and later priesthood lessons, all with a common theme: "do your duty." Although there was variability in the commandment spoken of or in the particular teacher's delivery, what remained constant was the underlying assumption that if one were to learn one's duty and then do it without flaw, everything would be fine (which I was sure meant that there would be no sadness or losses). I remember repeatedly asking myself what was the right thing to do and then trying very hard to do it. Of course, with a youthful mind and experience, my answer to what was right left much to be desired. As an example, conflict reduction was a high priority for me. I remember multiple instances of accepting responsibility for things that I did not do—anything to reduce the tension in the home. As a direct result of injunctions to not be angry, I suffered victimizations without setting limits. All the while I had the expectation that, by doing such "good" things, blessings would follow and things would turn out all right in the end.

In spite of my misguided interpretations of what was right and wrong, the concept of right and wrong was clear. It should be easily distinguishable; good and bad, right and wrong were held out to be as easy to identify as angels and devils. While I occasionally had to adjust my conception of how to see right and wrong, still the basic structure—that right and wrong was an on-off switch—persisted. Like the silver threads of a spider's web, my world was built lesson upon lesson, event upon event, conversation upon conversation. When things did not turn out well, the attribution was quickly made that somehow something had not been done correctly. When things turned out well, attributions were again made that—yes, indeed behaviors had been in line and things had turned out well as a result.

Two unfortunate conclusions were drawn by me. First of all, when things did not turn out well it was experienced as failure. Somehow my behavior had fallen short. Guilt was easily attached, and it was a short step to decrease my sense of personal value as a result. Successes were equally damaging, since positive attribution was just as quickly made to my own value as a result of having chosen well. Expectations of ultimate salvation were now placed into a fragile balance—"if" I could behave well, then salvation was a possibility. However, the probability became more and more distant as I grew older and my awareness of my failures increased. The fragility around my own salvation also began to extend to fragility in other aspects of life. Any potential achievement at school or enjoyment in social relationships would be determined by the success, or more likely failure, of my choices or performance. A very damaging implication that flows from such thoughts (and which further bound me with silken threads) was that "my" behaviors were the predominant determinant of outcome. I was able to control (not only able but also required to control) events and outcomes. My choices became the prime movers of the universe. (I did not miss the clear implication that the responsibility was also mine and that much depended on me "getting it right.") The influences of others were minimized and the responsibility for my choices was accentuated. The circle became complete when guilt was easily found in failure.

During this time I remember many discussions about the Savior, but words like "Redeemer" and "Atonement" had very little meaning. Christ's purpose, it was clear to me at the time, was to provide us an example so that we could follow his way of doing things and then control the universe to turn out "right." The world seemed to make very clear sense. The rules were supposed to be easy to follow and understand. Looking back, in spite of many enjoyable moments, the overall feeling is one of constriction, failure, and limited options. There was no room for preferences or personal choosing to any significant degree. The only personal choices available were to do what was "right, expected, and one's duty" or to cause catastrophe in the world around you and suffer for your irresponsibility. There was little room for taking enjoyment either in the expression of one's personal preferences or in the creativity and diversity of personal relationships. The prison was complete. All action was pre-scripted by a code of conduct that may as well have been chiseled into granite. The Savior's life had proven beyond doubt that the task was possible. All personal expression and creativity could be thrown aside and one need only ask, "What would Jesus do?"

As I entered high school, I became increasingly aware of different ways that people behaved. Different families had different systems and different priorities. People seemed to interpret commandments and ways of being very differently than I. The question of who was right presented puzzles. Still, I was able to keep basic structures intact, and as I entered the mission field, the structure of the Language Training Mission felt familiar. Focusing on the "doings" of learning a language and memorizing missionary discussions drove the relationship issues of living with a companion into the background. On arriving in the mission field, such pursuits became less effective at drowning out the dilemmas faced in interpersonal relationships. I am extremely grateful to one of my companions, with whom I labored for nearly six months. He was from England, and cultural differences along with personal differences set the stage for me to learn that preferences play a very large role in this mortal life. In this companionship I encountered multiple differences, which when argued could not be founded on right and wrong. It became important to negotiate, not just defer or dominate. This was the beginning of the unraveling of the spider's engulfing web and the opening of possibilities that would take many years to unfold.

Those months with my companion taught me much about agency. As we explored our many differences and negotiated a way to live together, I began to see that many things happen for two reasons. First, the world is just the way that it is and second, people have an influence on each other. For the first time, the idea entered my head that I could not control all outcomes by perfect adherence to immutable law. There were others in the universe with preferences, hopes, dreams, and fears which could not be easily placated and subdued by an appeal to ultimate truth. I became increasingly aware that my own ideas, preferences, hopes, and fears had been crushed under the weight of this oppressive paradigm. As I became aware that I had preferences independent of trying to do what was right and began to express those preferences in even minor ways, the joy of living life as a free and independent entity dawned on my soul. I will be forever grateful to my friend for this immeasurable gift.

The tenderness of this budding blossom, however, was nearly snuffed out on my return from my mission. My return to Utah brought with it a return of the high expectation for perfect choosing and the resulting helplessness, depression, and guilt. Along with this came a discounting of my personal preferences, and I again found myself deferring to "duty" and "right." My involvement in the Institute program and religion classes at BYU seemed to confirm what I had always, except for a brief moment, known: behavior was what mattered most and outcome was the ultimate decider of "right."

My parents' divorce in my mid-twenties caused deep consternation and shook this brittle foundation. It seemed that the rules did not hold: they were righteous people well-versed in gospel doctrine, life-time active members of the Church, regular temple-attendees who on the surface seemed to be doing everything "right," but they were unable to maintain a relationship. My foundation was shaken with the force of a volcanic eruption. What I had thought to be bedrock shifted and shook as though liquefied by an earthquake. As the dust settled, I applied Herculean efforts to re-strengthen my foundation and to rebuild broken walls, but peace was nowhere to be found. No matter what I tried, the walls would not stand straight on the jagged foundation that remained. After a few years, which felt to me like "wandering in the wilderness," the notion that personal expression and attention to individual preferences, hopes, and fears was important began again to surface with the help of another friend. Once again, the fresh air of agency brought life and peace into my world.

With the return of agency and the rekindling of the spark that had begun on my mission came an increased sense of independence and competence. My career took a major jump forward. There was an increase of stability in my home and family. My testimony became stronger, and interestingly, my performance on religious criteria improved. It surprised me at first that paying less attention to doing what was right and more attention to doing what I wanted resulted in better performance. Things that had previously come with some difficulty now seemed to be simply part of who I was and became as natural as breathing. This time, the joy of life and expanded sense of conceptual freedom was more lasting. Yet, without specific ways to ground these ideas, and without conceptual structures that had anchor points in scripture, there was erosion. Over time I began to drift back into oppression as the prison of "doing" began to return as my primary objective.

Then in 1990 I participated in a faculty seminar at Brigham Young University sponsored by the Philosophy Department and led by James

Faulconer and others, in which we examined the writings of Emmanuel Levinas. Experientially, I immediately resonated with the concepts presented and found myself having conceptual structures enlarged to anchor the feelings I had previously experienced. Here was language that could express in rational, cohesive ways what I had felt but had been unable to articulate. Here was a call to principle without the specifics being dictated in rigid ways. Here was complexity, preference, desires, fears, and yearnings of the heart attended to with reverence and assigned a significant value. I could hardly contain the expansion of my mind and soul. The increase of joy and the clarity of thought that accompanied this experience were also confirmed to me by the Holy Ghost as important for my life. At the time, I found it curious that it was not confirmed to me as a universal truth that should be spread with evangelical zeal to everyone. Rather, it was confirmed as important to *me*. In retrospect, I see this faculty seminar as an important step in personally moving beyond merely offering lip-service to personal revelation. The idea that something could be true for me and not necessarily for others was extremely freeing. The message seemed to be that each of us could move at our own pace and in our own unique sequence, acquiring the essential qualities of Godhood with individualized tutoring.

Discussions regarding Jesus as the Redeemer and the Savior began to have personal meaning. For me "being" became a more legitimate goal than simply "doing." My home with the crooked walls and jagged foundation began to feel tight and inadequate. I felt a strong desire to move. I felt I needed a residence that had a better view of human complexity, a place that was more accessible to the human condition, especially the fears, pains and sufferings of God's children. I found that I was disinclined to turn a blind eye of conceptual simplicity toward the realities of the struggles of the souls of men, women, and children. As we discussed the call of ethical obligation as expressed by Levinas, I found freedom in the complexity and compassion of his expression and in the inevitability of failure to completely control any given event. I found the concept of infinite obligation and finite resources extremely descriptive of the struggles in myriad arenas as I encountered them in my daily work. Interestingly it was in the concept of constant failure that I found the freedom to succeed. Finally there was room to accept efforts as "good enough" and as worthy of merit and reward in spite of a clearly imperfect performance.

Since that initial encounter with powerful postmodern ideas over two decades ago, I have continued to find language and conceptual grounding that I now recognize to have been present in the gospel all along. My blindness to its presence was in my own tenacious hold on youthful conceptions that were powerfully taught. I recognize as well that those conceptual structures were easily maintained by fear. It seemed, when constrained by the paradigm of "doing," that to leave it would be to leave a sure foundation—exchanging it for uncertainty and lack of grounding. There was also a loss of arrogance which was hard to give up. It was difficult to leave the confidence of being right for the uncertainty of being shaped by the hurts and fears of others. The uncertainty of complexity seemed frightening at best. What I didn't know early in the process was that such a move, while grounded differently, actually provided more solid footing. As the Holy Ghost became more prominent in my life and played a more influential role in understanding and decision making than did universal edict, he also became more personal to me.

I would like to share with you an insight that came to me one day when I was reading in the book of Moses chapter 6, verse 60. It reads: "By the water ye keep the commandment, by the Spirit ye are justified, by the blood ye are sanctified." As I read this scripture, it leapt off the page at me. Here seemed to be an explanation for what had puzzled me so deeply. It seemed to be saying that there were *three* paradigms which grounded truth for someone in the Gospel of Jesus Christ or *three* different ways to look at the commandments and examine life. To me it seemed that he was clearly talking about members of the church since he started with water, which I took to symbolize baptism. I began to imagine hundreds, perhaps thousands of paradigms that might exist in the world. But here were *three* intended for members of the Church. There seemed to be no privileging of one over another, simply a statement that there were three. I recognized that the blessings promised by each were consistent with the teachings of modern prophets and scriptures: keeping the commandment, being justified, and being sanctified. I found that I could fairly easily comprehend the water and spirit paradigms. The blood paradigm, however, seemed vague and unclear. I could recognize, however, my movement from the water paradigm to the spirit paradigm as I left behind the shaken foundation from my parents' divorce and moved into the complexity of being guided more by the Spirit. I learned to allow context and judgment to have more sway in decision-making. My previous rejection of the water paradigm was softened, though, as I saw it was essential in the kingdom of God. I began to be aware of how important it had been in my early years to have a simple foundation that was clear. It put my feet on the path and taught me principles of baptism, tithing, and the Word of Wisdom. I avoided errors that would have caused me significant grief and acquired habits that have been useful. I recognized that the bars of my cage and the silver strands of the spider's web, although in some ways restricting movement and enjoyment, had given me enough structure to at least survive my parents' divorce. While the foundation had broken and the walls were no longer straight, the house still stood in some measure.

The water paradigm alone, however, was not adequate for long-term living. The necessity of the move to the spirit paradigm was precipitated precisely by the inability of the water paradigm to hold up long term, especially under duress. It became important for me to understand that there *are* times when commandments are in conflict; one of them must be broken in order to keep another and that the spirit can justify the breaking of one in the service of keeping another (e.g., Nephi and Laban.) As I have spent more time living in the spirit paradigm, in addition to an increase in joy, agency, freedom, and personal expression, I have found greater access to compassion for the individual son or daughter of God who struggles with the limitations of the veil and all that it means to live in mortality. With the availability of complexity and a welcoming of conflicting positions, along with a rejection of quick fixes and premature closure, there is added room for understanding and empathy. I have found an increased ability to "sit with" human suffering, including my own, accepting it as part of the mortal condition. That which used to be tragedy to me, I can now begin to experience as the refiner's fire with the expectation of ultimate triumph. No longer in the face of hardship do I look for answers chiseled in granite. There is much more comfort and power in the quiet whisperings of the Spirit. Ultimate judgment on the effectiveness of a particular choice no longer rests with the proximate outcome. The context is much broader, including effects yet to be shown in life beyond the veil. There is much that remains unknown; and since final chapters cannot yet be written, much of judgment must remain suspended. Still the direction for how to proceed in any given circumstance is clear. It is not that final outcomes are visible, nor that even the immediate effects of choices and behaviors can be inferred, but the principle involved and the important action to take are made evident. There is much faith required, but I have found my faith in Faith as a principle of action to feel very solid and not at all uncertain.

The spirit paradigm, with its tolerance of ambiguity and willingness to suspend final judgment, seems to call for increased attention to justice. As my interests collide with those of others, I am aware that our interests are often mutually exclusive and that neither can be dismissed. Each of us has a claim on that which we find important, simply on the basis that we find it important.

The spirit paradigm, with its resplendent attention to individual value has some difficulty responding to such mutually exclusive claims. It appears that this is at least one principle for which the spirit paradigm provides an inadequate response.

For this reason, and for a few others, the spirit paradigm recently has begun to feel inadequate as well. I have started to feel a desire to give away my claim on justice as a gift to those around me about whom I care a great deal. It occurs to me that blood is chosen as the metaphor for this third paradigm purposefully. As I explore the edges of the blood paradigm, I notice that the word *longsuffering* is present in many scriptural definitions of charity. The sacrifice called for here appears to be more, or qualitatively different at least, than the sacrifice of money or worldly goods required by the water paradigm. Here the suffering asked for seems to have qualities of soulful and ideational loss and sacrifice. I find myself wanting to give away what previously felt to be emotional necessities. The reason for such sacrifice is not duty but rather a strong desire for the well-being of another. I find myself again wanting to accept responsibility for things that I did not do (I *want* to accept the burden of recovering losses I did not create). This time, however, there is no feeling of victimization. This is not something stolen from me in the service of an external demand. Such sacrifice now begins to feel like a free gift, still given at the cost of significant pain and sacrifice, and yet it is being given to someone whose well-being matters a great deal to me. On the surface, these behaviors—seen only with an objective eye (like a TV camera) and without an understanding of the heartfelt motivations—look very much like victimization—like weakness and passivity. Yet the entire experience of this paradigm bears no resemblance to victimization.

I'm sure this move is not yet complete for me, but I am beginning to have an awareness of where to look for land. As I search out a building lot I am infused with a feeling of stability and inner strength. If house hunting in a paradigm can be this richly rewarding, I'm anxious to move.

While my experience is not typical of all, I encourage a willingness to explore other paradigms and ways of seeing the world. Some may pass through one paradigm or another more quickly. Some may find the order reversed. Some may find themselves in a pattern of repeating paradigms, as I have often done on occasions needing refresher courses, or on other occasions simply finding one paradigm more adequate to deal with the circumstances at hand. Whatever your course, I invite you, the reader, to open your heart and mind and allow yourself to be led into ways of thinking and experiencing life that might be initially frightening but lead toward increased understanding, more satisfying self expression, and ultimately the rich rewards of eternal life.

In "What Is Our Doctrine?" Robert Millet argues that our doctrine should be understood by teachings found in the standard works, in official declarations or proclamations, in current handbooks or curricular materials, or in doctrinal expositions on the subject delivered in General Conference today. Attempts to understand Church doctrine solely by studying the statements of past Church leaders, he argues, are fundamentally misguided and cause many doctrinal misunderstandings among Latter-day Saints and those of other faiths seeking to understand the LDS Church. These approaches fail to understand the consequences of a living church. In short, Millet writes, "Doctrine means teaching. If we do not teach something today, it is not part of our doctrine today." The fact that something does not fall within the doctrine of the Church does not mean, however, that it is necessarily false. There are truths that do not qualify as doctrine, simply because they are not emphasized by current LDS leaders. Quoting Elder Maxwell, Millet concludes by stating that "Deeds do matter as well as doctrines, but the doctrines can move us to do the deeds, and the Spirit can help us to understand the doctrines as well as prompt us to do the deeds."

Two

What Is Our Doctrine?[1]

Robert L. Millet

We have been charged to "teach one another the doctrine of the kingdom. Teach ye diligently," the Lord implores, "and my grace shall attend you, that you may be instructed more perfectly in theory, in principle, in doctrine, in the law of the gospel, in all things that pertain unto the kingdom of God, that are expedient for you to understand" (D&C 88:77–78). But what exactly are we to teach? What is doctrine?

Before beginning, let me affirm that I understand implicitly that the right and authority to declare, interpret, and clarify doctrine rest with living apostles and prophets. This chapter will thus only speak *about* doctrine and in no way attempt to reach beyond my own stewardship.

Doctrine: Its Purpose, Power, and Purity

Doctrine is "the basic body of Christian teaching or understanding (2 Tim. 3:16). Christian doctrine is composed of teachings which are to be handed on through instruction and proclamation. . . . Religious doctrine deals with the ultimate and most comprehensive questions."[2] Further, "Gospel doctrine is synonymous with the truths of salvation. It comprises

---

1. Based on an address to BYU Religious Education Faculty; September 12, 2003, and published as "What Do We Really Believe? Identifying Doctrinal Parameters within Mormonism," in *Discourses in Mormon Theology: Philosophical and Theological Possibilities*, ed. James M. McLachlan and Loyd Ericson (Salt Lake City: Greg Kofford Books, 2007). For a continued discussion of Millet's arguments, see Loyd Ericson, "The Challenges of Defining Mormon Doctrine," *Element* 3, no. 1–2 (Spring & Fall 2007), 69–90; Robert L. Millet, "Defining Doctrine: A Rejoinder to Loyd Ericson," *Element* 5, no. 1 (Spring 2009), 1–7; Nathan B. Oman, "Truth, Doctrine, and Authority," *Element* 5, no. 1 (Spring 2009), 9–18; and Loyd Ericson, "Is It Mormon Doctrine that Mormon Doctrine Is True: A Rejoinder," *Element* 5, no. 1 (Spring 2009): 21–26.

2. *Holman Bible Dictionary*, ed. Trent C. Butler (Nashville: Holman Bible Publishers, 1991), 374.

the tenets, teachings, and true theories found in the scriptures; it includes the principles, precepts, and revealed philosophies of pure religion; prophetic dogmas, maxims, and views are embraced within its folds; the Articles of Faith are part and portion of it, as is every inspired utterance of the Lord's agents."[3]

The central, saving doctrine is that Jesus is the Christ, the Son of God, the Savior and Redeemer of humankind; that he lived, taught, healed, suffered and died for our sins; and that he rose from the dead the third day with a glorious, immortal, resurrected body (1 Cor. 15:1–3; D&C 76:40–42). It was the Prophet Joseph Smith who spoke of these central truths as the "fundamental principles" of our religion to which all other doctrines are but appendages.[4] Elder Boyd K. Packer taught: "Truth, glorious truth, proclaims there is . . . a Mediator. Through Him mercy can be fully extended to each of us without offending the eternal law of justice. *This truth is the very root of Christian doctrine. You may know much about the gospel as it branches out from there, but if you only know the branches and those branches do not touch that root, if they have been cut free from that truth, there will be no life nor substance nor redemption in them.*"[5]

Such counsel really does point us toward that which is of most worth in sermons and in the classroom, that which should receive our greatest emphasis. There is power in doctrine, power in the word (Alma 31:5), power to heal the wounded soul (Jacob 2:8), and power to transform human behavior. "True doctrine, understood, changes attitudes and behavior," Elder Packer explained. "The study of the doctrines of the gospel will improve behavior quicker than a study of behavior will improve behavior. That is why we stress so forcefully the study of the doctrines of the gospel."[6] Elder Neal A. Maxwell also pointed out that "[d]octrines believed and practiced do change and improve us, while insuring our vital access to the Spirit. Both outcomes are crucial."[7]

We are under obligation to learn the doctrines, teach them properly, and bind ourselves to speak and act in harmony with them. Only in this way can we perpetuate truth in a world filled with error, avoid deception, focus on what matters most, and find joy and happiness in the process.

---

3. Bruce R. McConkie, *Mormon Doctrine*, 2nd ed. (Salt Lake City: Bookcraft, 1966), 204.

4. Joseph Smith, *Teachings of the Prophet Joseph Smith*, comp. and ed. Joseph Fielding Smith (Salt Lake City: Deseret Book, 1976), 121.

5. Boyd K. Packer, "The Mediator," *Ensign*, May 1977, 55, emphasis added.

6. Boyd K. Packer, "Little Children," *Ensign*, November 1986, 18.

7. Neal A. Maxwell, *One More Strain of Praise* (Salt Lake City: Bookcraft, 1999), x.

"I have spoken before," President Gordon B. Hinckley stated, "about the importance of keeping the doctrine of the Church pure, and seeing that it is taught in all of our meetings. I worry about this. Small aberrations in doctrinal teaching can lead to large and evil falsehoods."[8]

How do we "keep the doctrine pure"? What might we do? Five things seem important:

1. We can teach directly from the scriptures, the standard works. The scriptures contain the mind, will, voice, and word of the Lord (D&C 68:3–4) to men and women in earlier days and thus contain doctrine and applications that are both timely and timeless. "And all scripture given by inspiration of God, is profitable for doctrine, for reproof, for correction, for instruction in righteousness; that the man [or woman] of God may be perfect, thoroughly furnished unto all good works" (JST, 2 Tim. 3:16–17).

2. We can present doctrine in the same way the prophets in our own day present it (D&C 52:9, 36), in terms of both content and emphasis. Mormon wrote: "And it came to pass that Alma, having authority from God, organized priests; . . . and he commanded them that *they should teach nothing save it were the things which he had taught*" (Mosiah 18:18–19, emphasis added). "Therefore, they did assemble themselves together in different bodies, being called churches; every church having their priests and their teachers, and *every priest teaching the word according as it was delivered to him by the mouth of Alma*. And thus, notwithstanding there being many churches they were all one church, yea, even the church of God" (Mosiah 25:21–22, emphasis added).

3. We can pay special attention to the scriptural commentary offered by living apostles and prophets in General Conference addresses, cross reference the same into our scriptures, and teach this commentary in conjunction with the scripture. For example, we can study the teachings of

- Elder Jeffrey R. Holland concerning the Parable of the Prodigal Son in the April 2002 General Conference;
- Elder Robert D. Hales concerning the covenant of baptism in October 2000;
- Elder Joseph B. Wirthlin concerning the principles of fasting in April 2001;
- Elder Dallin H. Oaks concerning conversion and "becoming," as well as his thoughtful commentary on the Parable of the Workers in the Vineyard in October 2000;

---

8. Gordon B. Hinckley, *Teachings of Gordon B. Hinckley* (Salt Lake City: Deseret Book, 1997), 620.

- Elder M. Russell Ballard concerning "Who is my neighbor?" and the "doctrine of inclusion" in October 2001.

And so forth.

4. We can teach the gospel with plainness and simplicity, focus on fundamentals, and emphasize what matters most. We do not tell all we know, nor do we teach on the edge of our knowledge. The Prophet Joseph Smith explained that "it is not always wise to relate all the truth. Even Jesus, the Son of God, had to refrain from doing so, and had to restrain His feelings many times for the safety of Himself and His followers, and had to conceal the righteous purposes of His heart in relation to many things pertaining to His Father's kingdom."[9]

5. We can acknowledge that there are some things we simply do not know. President Joseph F. Smith declared: "It is no discredit to our intelligence or to our integrity to say frankly in the face of a hundred speculative questions, 'I do not know.' One thing is certain, and that is, God has revealed enough to our understanding for our exaltation and for our happiness. Let the Saints, then, utilize what they already have; be simple and unaffected in their religion, both in thought and word, and they will not easily lose their bearings and be subjected to the vain philosophies of man."[10]

Doctrinal Parameters

In recent years I have tried to look beneath the surface and discern the nature of the objections that so many in the religious world have toward the Latter-day Saints. To be sure, the phenomenal growth of the Church poses a real threat to many; more specifically, the Christian groups resent the way we "steal their sheep." We are not in the line of historic Christianity and thus are neither Catholic nor Protestant. We believe in scripture beyond the Bible and in continuing revelation through apostles and prophets. We do not accept the concepts concerning God, Christ, and the Godhead that grew out of the post-New Testament church councils. All of these things constitute reasons why many Protestants and Catholics label us as non-Christian. We have tried, with some success I think, to speak of ourselves as "Christian but different." There is another reason we are suspect, however, one that underlies and buttresses large amounts of anti-Mormon propaganda, namely, what they perceive to be some of our "unusual doctrines," many of which were presented by a few Church leaders of the past.

---

9. Smith, *Teachings*, 392.
10. Joseph F. Smith, *Gospel Doctrine* (Salt Lake City: Deseret Book, 1971), 9.

Let me illustrate with an experience I had just a few months ago. A Baptist minister was in my office one day. We were chatting about a number of things, including doctrine. He said to me, "Bob, you people believe in such strange things!" "Like what?" I asked. "Oh, for example," he said, "you believe in blood atonement. And that affects Utah's insistence on retaining death by a firing squad." I responded: "No we don't." "Yes you do," he came right back. "I know of several statements by Brigham Young, Heber C. Kimball, and Jedediah Grant that teach such things." "I'm aware of those statements," I said. I then found myself saying something that I had never voiced before: "Yes, they were taught, but *they do not represent the doctrine of our Church*. We believe in the blood atonement of Jesus Christ, and that alone." My friend didn't skip a beat: "What do you mean they don't represent the doctrine of your Church? They were spoken by major Church leaders."

I explained that such statements were made, for the most part, during the time of the Mormon Reformation, and they were examples of a kind of "revival rhetoric" in which the leaders of the Church were striving to "raise the bar" in terms of obedience and faithfulness. I assured him that the Church, by its own canonical standards, does not have the right or the power to take a person's life because of disobedience or even apostasy (D&C 134:10). I read to him a passage from the Book of Mormon in which the Nephite prophets had resorted to "exceeding harshness, . . . continually reminding [the people] of death, and the duration of eternity, and the judgments and the power of God, . . . and exceedingly great plainness of speech" in order to "keep them from going down speedily to destruction" (Enos 1:23).

This seemed to satisfy him to some extent, but then he said: "Bob, many of my fellow Christians have noted how hard it is to figure out what Mormons believe. They say it's like trying to nail green Jell-O to the wall! What *do* you people believe? How do you decide what *is* your doctrine and what is not?" I sensed that we were in the midst of a very important conversation, one that was pushing me to the limits and requiring that I do some of the deepest thinking I had done in a long time. His questions were valid. They were in no way mean-spirited. They were not intended to entrap or embarrass me or the Church. He simply was seeking information. I said: "You've asked some excellent questions. Let me see what I can do to answer them." I suggested that he consider the following three ideas:

1. The teachings of the Church today have a rather narrow focus, range, and direction; central and saving doctrine is what we are

called upon to teach and emphasize, not tangential and peripheral teachings.

2. Very often what is drawn from Church leaders of the past, like the matter of blood atonement mentioned above, is misquoted, misrepresented, or taken out of context. Further, not everything that was ever spoken or written by a Church leader in the past is a part of what we teach today. Our doctrine is a living constitution, a living tree of life, a dynamic Church (D&C 1:30). We are commanded to pay heed to the words of living oracles (D&C 90:3–5).

3. In determining whether something is a part of the doctrine of the Church, we might ask: Is it found within the four standard works or within official declarations or proclamations? Is it taught or discussed in General Conference or other official gatherings by general Church leaders today? Is it found in the general handbooks or approved curriculum of the Church today? If it meets at least one of these criteria, we can feel secure and appropriate about teaching it. We might also add that included within the category of "all that God does reveal" would be certain matters that fall under our injunction to maintain "sacred silence." For example, the content of the temple endowment today would certainly be considered a part of the doctrine of the Church.

A significant percentage of anti-Mormonism focuses on statements by previous Church leaders that dealt with peripheral or non-central issues. No one criticizes us for a belief in God, in the divinity of Jesus Christ or his atoning work, in the literal bodily resurrection of the Savior and the eventual resurrection of mankind, in baptism by immersion, in the gift of the Holy Ghost, in the sacrament of the Lord's Supper, etc. But we are challenged regularly for statements in our literature on such matters as the following:

- God's life before he was God;
- how Jesus was conceived;
- the specific fate of sons of perdition;
- teachings about Adam as God;
- details concerning what it means to become like God hereafter;
- plural marriage is essential to one's exaltation;
- why blacks were denied the priesthood prior to 1978, etc.

In that spirit, we must never allow a person not of our faith to teach us—to insist upon—what *we* believe. If as an active, practicing member of The Church of Jesus Christ of Latter-day Saints I do not have the right to introduce or declare doctrine, why should someone from outside my faith be allowed to do so?

Loyalty to Men Called as Prophets

While we love the scriptures and thank God regularly for them, we believe that one can have sufficient confidence and even reverence for holy writ without believing that every word between Genesis 1:1 and Revelation 22:21 is the word for word dictation of the Almighty. Nor do we have to firmly believe that the Bible now reads as it has always read. Indeed, our own scriptures attest that plain and precious truths and many covenants of the Lord were taken away or kept back from the Bible before it was compiled (1 Ne. 13:20-29; Moses 1:40-41; A of F 8).[11] However, we still cherish the sacred volume, recognize and teach the doctrines of salvation within it, and seek to pattern our lives according to its timeless teachings.

In like manner, we can sustain with all our hearts the prophets and apostles without believing that they are perfect or that everything they say or do is exactly what God wants said and done. In short, we do not believe in apostolic or prophetic infallibility. Moses made mistakes, but we love and sustain him and accept his writings nonetheless. Peter made mistakes, but we still honor him and study his words. Paul made mistakes, but we admire his boldness and dedication and treasure his epistles. James pointed out that Elijah "was a man subject to like passions as we are" (James 5:17), and the Prophet Joseph Smith taught that "a prophet [is] a prophet only when he [is] acting as such."[12] On another occasion the Prophet declared: "I told them I was but a man, and they must not expect me to be perfect; if they expected perfection from me, I should expect it from them; but if they would bear with my infirmities and the infirmities of the brethren, I would likewise bear with their infirmities."[13] "I can fellowship the President of the Church," said Lorenzo Snow, "if he does not know everything I know. . . . I saw the . . . imperfections in [Joseph Smith]. . . . I thanked God that he would put upon a man who had those imperfections the power and authority he placed upon him . . . for I knew that I myself had weakness, and I thought there was a chance for me."[14]

---

11. Compare with Smith, *Teachings*, 9-10, 61, 327.
12. Ibid., 278.
13. Ibid., 268.
14. Cited in Neal A. Maxwell, "Out of Obscurity," *Ensign*, November 1984, 10.

Every member of the Church, including those called to guide its destiny, has the right to be wrong at one time or another—to say something that simply is not true. They also have the right to improve their views, to change their minds and correct mistakes as new light and new truth become available. The Prophet Joseph once remarked: "I did not like the old man [a brother Pelatiah Brown] being called up for erring in doctrine.... It does not prove that a man is not a good man because he errs in doctrine."[15] Elder Bruce R. McConkie stated that "I do not get very troubled about an honest and a sincere person who makes a mistake in doctrine, provided that it is a mistake of the intellect or a mistake of understanding, and provided it is not on a great basic and fundamental principle." He also explained that "If you err in some doctrines, and I have, and all of us have, what we want to do is get the further light and knowledge that we ought to receive and get our souls in tune and clarify our thinking."[16]

As we have been reminded again and again, whom God calls, God qualifies. That is, God calls his prophets. He empowers and strengthens the individual, provides an eternal perspective, loosens his tongue, and enables him to make known divine truth. But being called as an apostle or even as President of the Church does not remove the man from mortality or make him perfect. President David O. McKay explained that "when God makes the prophet He does not unmake the man."[17] Joseph Smith stated

> I was this morning introduced to a man from the east. After hearing my name, he remarked that I was nothing but a man, indicating by this expression, that he had supposed that a person to whom the Lord would see fit to reveal his will, must be something more than a man. He seemed to have forgotten the saying that fell from the lips of James, that [Elijah] was a man subject to like passions as we are, yet he had such power with God, that he, in answer to his prayers, shut the heavens that they gave no rain for the space of three years and six months.[18]

---

15. Joseph Smith, et al., *History of the Church of Jesus Christ of Latter-day Saints*, ed. B. H. Roberts, 7 vols. (Salt Lake City: Deseret Book, 1957), 5:340.

16. Bruce R. McConkie, "The Foolishness of Teaching," address to Church Educational System, September 1981, in Salt Lake City. Available at http://emp.byui.edu/marrottr/FOOLISHNESS.htm (accessed May 20, 2013).

17. David O. McKay, April 5, 1907, *Report of the Semi-Annual Conference of the Church of Jesus Christ of Latter-day Saints* (Salt Lake City: Church of Jesus Christ of Latter-day Saints, semi-annual), 11–12 (hereafter cited as *Conference Report*). See also October 1912, 121; April 1962, 7.

18. Smith, *Teachings*, 89.

"With all their inspiration and greatness," Elder McConkie declared, "prophets are yet mortal men with imperfections common to mankind in general. They have their opinions and prejudices and are left to work out their problems without inspiration in many instances."[19] "Thus the opinions and views, even of a prophet, may contain error, unless those opinions and views were inspired by the Spirit."[20]

Elder Harold B. Lee pointed out:

> There have been times when even the President of the Church has not been moved upon by the Holy Ghost. There is, I suppose you'd say, a classic story of Brigham Young in the time when Johnston's army was on the move. The Saints were all inflamed, and President Young had his feelings whetted to fighting pitch. He stood up in the morning session of General Conference and preached a sermon vibrant with defiance at the approaching army, declaring an intention to oppose them and drive them back. In the afternoon he rose and said that Brigham Young had been talking in the morning but the Lord was going to talk now. He then delivered an address the tempo of which was the exact opposite of the morning sermon. Whether that happened or not, it illustrates a principle: that the Lord can move upon his people but they may speak on occasions their own opinions.[21]

In 1865 the First Presidency counseled the Latter-day Saints:

> We do not wish incorrect and unsound doctrines to be handed down to posterity under the sanction of great names, to be received and valued by future generations as authentic and reliable, creating labor and difficulties for our successors to perform and contend with, which we ought not to transmit to them. The interests of posterity are, to a certain extent, in our hands. Errors in history and in doctrine, if left uncorrected by us who are conversant with the events, and who are in a position to judge of the truth or falsity of the doctrines, would go to our children as though we had sanctioned and endorsed them. . . . We know what sanctity there is always attached to the writings of men who have passed away, especially to the writings of Apostles, when none of their contemporaries are left, and we, therefore, feel the necessity of being watchful upon these points.[22]

President Gordon B. Hinckley stated: "I have worked with seven Presidents of this Church. I have recognized that all have been human. But

---

19. McConkie, *Mormon Doctrine*, 608.
20. Bruce R. McConkie, "Ordinary Men, Extraordinary Callings," *New Era*, January 2007, 13.
21. Harold B. Lee, *The Teachings of Harold B. Lee*, ed. Clyde J. Williams (Salt Lake City: Bookcraft, 1996), 542.
22. Brigham Young, Heber C. Kimball, Daniel H. Wells, in *Messages of the First Presidency*, 6 vols., comp. James R. Clark (Salt Lake City: Bookcraft, 1965–1975), 2:232.

I have never been concerned over this. They may have had some weaknesses. But this has never troubled me. I know that the God of heaven has used mortal men throughout history to accomplish His divine purposes."[23] On another occasion President Hinckley pleaded with the Saints that

> as we continue our search for truth . . . we look for strength and goodness rather than weakness and foibles in those who did so great a work in their time. We recognize that our forebears were human. They doubtless made mistakes. . . . There was only one perfect man who ever walked the earth. The Lord has used imperfect people in the process of building his perfect society. If some of them occasionally stumbled, or if their characters may have been slightly flawed in one way or another, the wonder is the greater that they accomplished so much.[24]

Prophets are men called of God to serve as covenant spokesmen for His children on earth, and thus one should never take lightly what they say. The early Brethren of this dispensation were the living prophets for their contemporaries, and much of what we believe and practice today rests upon the doctrinal foundation they laid. But the work of the Restoration entails a gradual unfolding of divine truth in a line upon line fashion. Some years ago my colleague, Joseph McConkie, remarked to a group of religious educators, "We have the scholarship of the early brethren to build upon; we have the advantage of additional history; we have inched our way up the mountain of our destiny and now stand in a position to see things with greater clarity than did they. . . . We live in finer houses than did our pioneer forefathers, but this does not argue that we are better or that our rewards will be greater. In like manner our understanding of gospel principles should be better housed, and we should constantly be seeking to make it so. There is no honor in our reading by oil lamps when we have been granted better light."[25] Thus it is important to note that ultimately the Lord will hold us responsible for the teachings and direction and focus provided by the living oracles of our own day, both in terms of their commentary upon canonized scripture, as well as the living scripture that is delivered through them by the power of the Holy Ghost (D&C 68:3–4).

---

23. Gordon B. Hinckley, "Believe His Prophets," *Ensign*, May 1992, 54.

24. Gordon B. Hinckley, "The Continuous Pursuit of Truth," *Ensign*, April 1986, 5.

25. Joseph Fielding McConkie, "The Gathering of Israel and the Return of Christ," the Sixth Annual Church Educational System Religious Educators' Symposium, August 1982, Brigham Young University, typescript, 3, 5.

Facing Hard Issues

My experience suggests that anti-Mormonism will probably continue to increase in volume, at least until the Savior returns and shuts down the presses. Because we believe in the apostasy and the need for a restoration of the fullness of the gospel, we will never be fully accepted by those who claim to have all the truth they need in the Bible. But I want to note two things about anti-Mormonism: First, anti-Mormon material affects both those who are not Latter-day Saints as well as those who are. Not only does it in some cases deter or frighten curious or interested investigators, but it also troubles far more members of the Church than I had previously realized. I must receive ten phone calls, letters, or e-mails per week from members throughout the Church asking hard questions that have been raised by their neighbors or by some propaganda they read. A short time ago a young man (married, with a family) phoned me in the late afternoon, excused himself for the interruption, and then proceeded to tell me that he was teetering on the edge of leaving the Church because of his doubts. He posed several questions, and I responded to each one and bore my testimony. After about a half-hour chat, he offered profound thanks and indicated that he felt he would be okay now. Such an experience is not uncommon; antagonistic materials are here to stay and are adversely affecting the attitudes of both Latter-day Saints and those of other faiths.

My second point about anti-Mormonism is that very often the critics of the Church simply use our own stuff against us. They do not need to create new material; they simply dig up and repackage what some of our own Church leaders have said in the past that would not be considered a part of the doctrine of the Church today. Latter-day Saints are eager to sustain and uphold their leaders. Consequently, we are especially hesitant to suggest that something taught by President Brigham Young or Elders Orson Pratt or Orson Hyde might not be in harmony with the truth as God has made it known to us "line upon line, precept upon precept" (Isa. 28:10; 2 Ne. 28:30).

Some time ago a colleague and I were in southern California speaking to a group of about 500 people, both Latter-day Saint and Protestant. During the question-and-answer phase of the program, someone asked the inevitable: "Are you really Christian? Do you, as many claim, worship a different Jesus?" I explained that we worship the Christ of the New Testament, and that we believe wholeheartedly in his virgin birth, his divine Sonship, his miracles, his transforming teachings, his atoning sacrifice, and his bodily resurrection from the dead. I added that we also believe in the teachings of and about Christ found in the Book of Mormon and modern revelation.

After the meeting an LDS woman came up to me and said: "You didn't tell the truth about what we believe!" Startled, I asked: "What do you mean?" She responded: "You said we believe in the virgin birth of Christ, and you know very well that we don't believe that." "Yes we do," I retorted. She then said with a great deal of emotion: "I want to believe you, but people have told me for years that we believe that God the Father had sexual relations with Mary and thereby Jesus was conceived." I looked her in the eyes and said: "I'm aware of that teaching, but that is not the doctrine of the Church; that is not what we teach in the Church today. Have you ever heard the Brethren teach it in conference? Is it in the standard works, the curricular materials, or the handbooks of the Church? Is it a part of an official declaration or proclamation?" I watched as a 500-pound weight seemed to come off her shoulders, as tears came into her eyes, and she simply said: "Thank you, Brother Millet."

Not long ago, Pastor Greg Johnson and I met with an evangelical Christian church located outside Salt Lake City. The minister of the church asked us to come and make a presentation ("An Evangelical and a Latter-day Saint in Dialogue") that Greg and I have made several times before in different parts of the country. The whole purpose of our presentation is to model the kind of relationships people with differing religious views can have. This kind of presentation has proven, in my estimation, to be one of the most effective bridge-building exercises in which I have been involved.

On this particular night, the first question asked by someone in the audience was on DNA and the Book of Mormon. I made a brief comment and indicated that a more detailed (and informed) response would be forthcoming soon in a journal article from a BYU biologist. There were many, many hands in the air at this point. I called on a woman close to the front of the church. Her question was: "How do you deal with the Adam-God doctrine?" I responded: "Thank you for that question. It gives me an opportunity to explain a principle early in our exchange that will lay the foundation for other things to be said." I took a few moments to address the questions, "What is our doctrine? What do we teach today?" I indicated that if some teaching or idea was not in the standard works, not among official declarations or proclamations, not taught currently by living apostles or prophets in General Conference or other official gatherings, or not in the general handbooks or official curriculum of the Church, it is probably *not* a part of the doctrine or teachings of the Church.

I was surprised when my pastor friend then said to the group: "Are you listening to Bob? Do you hear what he is saying? This is important! It's time for us to stop criticizing Latter-day Saints on matters they don't even teach today." At this point in the meeting, two things happened: first, the number of hands of questioners went down, and second, the tone of the meeting changed quite dramatically. The questions were not baiting or challenging ones, but rather efforts to clarify. For example, the last question asked was by a middle-aged man. He stood up and said: "I for one would like to thank you, from the bottom of my heart, for what you have done here tonight. This thrills my soul. I think this is what Jesus would do. I have lived in Utah for many years, and I have many LDS friends. We get along okay; we don't fight and quarrel over religious matters. But we really don't talk with one another about the things that matter most to us, that is, our faith. I don't plan to become a Latter-day Saint, and I'm certain my Mormon friends don't plan to become evangelical, but I would like to find more effective ways to talk heart to heart. Could you two make a few suggestions on how we can deepen and sweeten our relationships with our LDS neighbors?"

These experiences highlight for me the challenge we face. I have no hesitation telling an individual or a group "I don't know" when I am asked why men are ordained to the priesthood and women are not, or why Blacks were denied the blessings of the priesthood for almost a century and a half, and several other matters that have neither been revealed nor clarified by those holding the proper keys. The difficulty comes when someone in the past *has* spoken on these matters, *has* put forward ideas that are out of harmony with what we know and teach today, and when those teachings are still available, either in print or among the everyday conversations of the members, and have never been corrected or clarified. The questions underlying all of this are simply "What is our doctrine? What are the teachings of the Church today?" If we could somehow help the Saints (and the larger religious world) know the answer to those questions, it would no doubt enhance our missionary effort, our convert retention, our activation, and the image and overall strength of the Church. If presented properly, it need not weaken faith or create doubts. It could do much to focus the Saints more on the central, saving verities of the gospel.

It is inevitable that some persons, either Latter-day Saints or those of other faiths, who are told that not everything stated by an LDS prophet or apostle is a part of the doctrine of the Church and of what we teach today, will be troubled and ask follow-up questions: "Well then, what *else* did this Church leader teach that is not considered doctrine today? How can we confidently accept anything else he taught? What other directions taken or procedures pursued by the Church in an earlier time do we not follow in our day?" The fact is that one need not take such an approach. This is like throwing the baby out with the bath water. We must never allow ourselves to overgeneralize and thus overreact, nor must we be guilty of discounting all that is good and uplifting and divinely given because of an aberration. After all, a prophet once expressing an opinion or perhaps even putting forward a doctrinal view that needed further clarification or even correction does not invalidate all else he has done or said. I would certainly hate to be judged that way and have no desire to be guilty of doing the same to the Lord's anointed. God calls his prophets, and God corrects them. He knows their strengths, and he knows their weakness.

Those of other faiths who are quick to criticize the Church and question its truthfulness because of past teachings from Church leaders that are not accepted as doctrine today would do well to ask themselves if they are prepared to apply the same standards of judgment to their own tradition, their own prominent speakers, or their own past. This is like asking someone, "Would you like to better understand Roman Catholicism today? Then study carefully the atrocities of the Crusades or the horrors of the Inquisition." Or, "Would you like a deeper glimpse into the hearts of Lutherans today? Then make it your business to study the anti-Semitic writings of Martin Luther." Or, "Would you care to better understand where Southern Baptists are coming from? Then simply read the many sermons of Baptist preachers during the time of the Civil War who utilized biblical passages to justify the practice of slavery."

There is one final matter that follows from the above. True doctrine has what might be called "sticking power"—it is taught and discussed and perpetuated over time, and with the passing of years seems to take on greater significance. Time, experience, careful and ponderous thought, and subsequent revelation through prophets—these all either reinforce and support, or bring into question and eventually discount a particular idea. To the Latter-day Saints the Lord Jesus declared: "And I give unto you a commandment, that ye shall forsake all evil and cleave unto all good, that ye shall live by every word which proceedeth forth out of the mouth of God. For he will give unto the faithful line upon line, precept upon precept; and I will try you and prove you herewith" (D&C 98:11–12; compare Isa. 28:9–10; 2 Ne. 28:30).

For example, in the early days of the restored Church, an idea was perpetuated by some that sons of perdition would eventually be restored and allowed to experience mortality again. Not only did Joseph Smith denounce the idea, but modern revelation concerning the inseparable union of body and spirit in the resurrection defies it.[26] On the other hand, doc-

---

26. Smith, *Teachings*, 24; see also D&C 93:33; 138:17.

trines such as the proper relationship between the grace of God and the good works of man, the redemption of the dead, exaltation through eternal marriage, and the overall significance of temples—have been discussed and clarified and reinforced by those holding the keys of the kingdom. We not only fully accept these matters fully as true and from God, but we also grasp their profundity even more than when they were first made known. Falsehood and error will eventually be detected and dismissed by those charged to guide the destiny of the kingdom of God, but truth, as Joseph Smith observed, "will cut its own way."[27]

Further Illustrations

We discussed earlier that one of the ways to keep our doctrine pure is to present the gospel message the way the prophets and apostles today present it. Similarly, our explanations of certain "hard doctrines" or "deeper doctrines" should not go beyond what the prophets believe and teach today. Let's take two illustrations. The first is an extremely sensitive matter, one that does now affect and will yet affect the quantity and quality of convert baptisms in the Church. I speak of the matter of the blacks and the priesthood. I was raised in the Church, just as many of you were, and I was well aware of the priesthood restriction. For as long as I can remember, the explanation for why our black brethren and sisters were denied the full blessings of the priesthood (including the temple) was some variation of the theme that they had been less valiant in the premortal life and thus had come to earth under a curse—an explanation that has been perpetuated as doctrine for most of our Church's history. I had committed to memory early on the article of our faith that states that men and women will be punished for their own sins and not for Adam's transgression (A of F 2) and later read that "the sins of the fathers cannot be answered upon the heads of the children" (Moses 6:54), but I had assumed that these principles somehow did not apply to blacks.

In June of 1978 everything changed—not just the matter of who could or could not be ordained to the priesthood, but also the nature of the explanation for *why* the restriction had been in place from the beginning. Elder Dallin H. Oaks, in a 1988 interview, was asked:

> As much as any doctrine the Church has espoused, or controversy the Church has been embroiled in, this one [the priesthood restriction] seems to stand out. Church members seemed to have less to go on to get a grasp of

---

27. Ibid., 313.

the issue. Can you address why this was the case, and what can be learned from it?

In response, Elder Oaks stated that

> If you read the scriptures with this question in mind, "Why did the Lord command this or why did he command that," you find that in less than one in a hundred commands was any reason given. It's not the pattern of the Lord to give reasons. We can put reason to revelation. We can put reasons to commandments. When we do we're on our own. Some people put reasons to the one we're talking about here, and they turned out to be spectacularly wrong. There is a lesson in that. The lesson I've drawn from that [is that] I decided a long time ago that I had faith in the command and I had no faith in the reasons that had been suggested for it.

Then came a follow-up question: "Are you referring to reasons given even by general authorities?" Elder Oaks answered:

> Sure. I'm referring to reasons given by general authorities and reasons elaborated upon that reason by others. The whole set of reasons seemed to me to be unnecessary risk-taking. . . . Let's don't make the mistake that's been made in the past, here and in other areas, trying to put reasons to revelation. The reasons turn out to be man-made to a great extent. The revelations are what we sustain as the will of the Lord and that's where safety lies.[28]

In other words, we really do not know why the restriction on the priesthood existed. When we are asked "Why?" the correct answer is "I don't know." The priesthood was restricted "for reasons which we believe are known to God, but which he has not made fully known to man."[29] I have come to realize that this is what Elder McConkie meant in his August 1978 address to the Church Educational System when he counseled us to

> Forget everything that I have said, or what President Brigham Young or President George Q. Cannon or whosoever has said in days past that is contrary to the present revelation. We spoke with a limited understanding and without the light and knowledge that now has come into the world.
>
> We get our truth and our light line upon line and precept upon precept. We have now had added a new flood of intelligence and light on this particular subject, and it erases all the darkness and all the views and all the thoughts of the past. They don't matter any more. . . . It is a new day and a new arrangement, and the Lord has now given the revelation that sheds light out into the world on

---

28. Dallin H. Oaks, Interview with Associated Press, *Provo Daily Herald*, June 5, 1988, 21.

29. David O. McKay, Hugh B. Brown, N. Eldon Tanner, First Presidency Message, January 1970.

this subject. As to any slivers of light or any particles of darkness of the past, we forget about them.[30]

It seems to me, therefore, that we as Latter-day Saints have two problems to solve in making the restored gospel available more extensively to people of color. First, we need to have our hearts and minds purified of all pride and prejudice. Second, we need to dismiss all previous explanations for the restriction and indicate that while we simply do not know why the restriction existed before, the fullness of the blessings of the restored gospel are now available to all who prepare themselves to receive them. Elder M. Russell Ballard observed that "We don't know all of the reasons why the Lord does what he does. We need to be content that someday we'll fully understand it."[31]

Now to the second illustration. I think that I have never opened myself to questions before a group of persons not of our faith where I have not been asked about our doctrine of God and the Godhead, particularly concerning the teachings of Joseph Smith and Lorenzo Snow. I generally do not have too much difficulty explaining our view of how through the Atonement man can eventually become like God. For that matter, Orthodox Christianity, a huge segment of the Christian world, still holds to a view of theosis or human deification. The Bible itself teaches that men and women may become "partakers of the divine nature" (2 Pet. 1:4), "joint heirs with Christ" (Rom. 8:17), gain "the mind of Christ" (1 Cor. 2:16), and become perfect, even as our Father in heaven is perfect (Matt. 5:48). The Apostle John declared: "Beloved, now are we the [children] of God, and it doth not yet appear what we shall be: but we know that, when he shall appear, we shall be like him; for we shall see him as he is" (1 Jn. 3:2). Perhaps more important, this doctrine is taught powerfully in modern revelation (D&C 76:58, 132:19–20).

The tougher issue for many Christians to deal with is the accompanying doctrine set forth in the King Follett Sermon[32] and the Lorenzo Snow couplet[33]—namely, that God was once a man. Latter-day scriptures state unequivocally that God is a man, a Man of Holiness (Moses 6:57) who possesses a body of flesh and bones (D&C 130:22). These concepts are clearly a part of the doctrinal restoration. We teach that man is not of a lower order

---

30. Bruce R. McConkie, "The New Revelation on Priesthood," in *Priesthood* (Salt Lake City: Deseret Book, 1981), 132.

31. Spoken at Elijah Abel Memorial Service; reported in *LDS Church News*, October 5, 2002, 12.

32. Smith, *Teachings*, 345–46.

33. Lorenzo Snow, *Teachings of Lorenzo Snow*, ed. Clyde J. Williams (Salt Lake City: Bookcraft, 1996), 1.

or different species than God. This, of course, makes many of our Christian friends extremely nervous (if not angry), because it appears to them that we are lowering God and thus attempting to bridge the Creator/creature chasm.

I suppose all we can respond is that we know what we know as a result of modern revelation, and that from our perspective the distance between God and man is still tremendous, almost infinite. Our Father in Heaven is indeed omnipotent, omniscient, and, by the power of his Holy Spirit, omnipresent. He is a gloried, exalted, resurrected being, "the only supreme governor and independent being in whom all fullness and perfection dwell; . . . in him every good gift and every good principle dwell; . . . he is the Father of lights; in him the principle of faith dwells independently, and he is the object in whom the faith of all other rational and accountable beings center for life and salvation."[34] Modern revelation attests that the Almighty sits enthroned "with glory, honor, power, majesty, might, dominion, truth, justice, judgment, mercy, and an infinity of fullness" (D&C 109:77).

And what do we know beyond the fact that God is an exalted Man? What do we know of his mortal existence? What do we know of the time before he became God? Nothing. We really do not know more than what was stated by the Prophet Joseph Smith, and that is precious little. Insights concerning God's life before Godhood are not found in the standard works, in official declarations or proclamations, in current handbooks or curricular materials, nor are doctrinal expositions on the subject delivered in General Conference today. This topic is not what we would call a central and saving doctrine, one that must be believed (or understood) in order to hold a temple recommend or be in good standing in the Church.

This latter illustration highlights an important point: Doctrine means teaching. If we do not teach something today, it is not part of our doctrine today. This does not, however, mean that it is untrue. A teaching may be true and yet not a part of what is taught and emphasized in the Church today. Whether it is true or not may in fact be irrelevant, if indeed the Brethren do not teach it today or if it is not taught directly in the standard works or found in our correlated curriculum. Let's take another question: Was Jesus married? The scriptures do not provide an answer. "We do not know anything about Jesus Christ being married," President Charles W. Penrose stated. "The Church has no authoritative declaration on the subject."[35] So whether Jesus was married is not part of the doctrine of the Church. It would be well for us to apply the following lesson from President Harold

---

34. *Lectures on Faith* (Salt Lake City: Deseret Book, 1985), 2:2.
35. "Editor's Table," *Improvement Era* (September 1912): 1042.

B. Lee: "With respect to doctrines and meanings of scriptures, let me give you a safe counsel. It is usually not well to use a single passage of scripture [or, I would add, a single sermon] in proof of a point of doctrine unless it is confirmed by modern revelation or by the Book of Mormon. . . . To single out a passage of scripture to prove a point, unless it is [so] confirmed . . . is always a hazardous thing."[36]

Conclusion

There is a very real sense in which we as Latter-day Saints are spoiled. We have been given so much, have had so much knowledge dispensed from on high relative to the nature of God, Christ, man, the Plan of Salvation, and the overall purpose of life here and the glory to be had hereafter, that we are prone to expect to have *all* of the answers to the questions of life. Elder Neal A. Maxwell pointed out that

> the exhilarations of discipleship exceed its burdens. Hence, while journeying through our Sinai, we are nourished in the Bountiful-like oases of the Restoration. Of these oases some of our first impressions may prove to be more childish than definitive. . . . In our appreciation, little wonder some of us mistake a particular tree for the whole of an oasis, or a particularly refreshing pool for the entirety of the Restoration's gushing and living waters. Hence, in our early exclamations there may even be some unintended exaggerations. We have seen and partaken of far too much; hence, we "cannot [speak] the smallest part [which] we feel" (Alma 26:16).[37]

We have much, to be sure, but there are indeed "many great and important things pertaining to the kingdom of God" yet to come forth (A of F 9). The Lord stated to Joseph Smith in Nauvoo: "I deign to reveal unto my church things which have been kept hid from before the foundation of the world, things that pertain to the dispensation of the fulness of times" (D&C 124:41; compare 121:26, 128:18). As Elder Oaks observed, we have been given many of the commands but not all of the reasons why, many of the directives but not all of the explanations. I state to my classes regularly that it is as important for us to know *what we do not know* as it is for us to know what we know. Far too many things are taught, discussed, or even argued about that fit into the realm of the unrevealed and thus the unresolved. Such matters, particularly if they do not fall within that range

---

36. Lee, *Teachings*, 157.
37. Neal A. Maxwell, "Becometh as a Child," *Ensign*, May 1996, 68–69.

of revealed truth we teach today, do not edify or inspire. Often, very often, they lead to confusion and sow discord.

This does not in any way mean that we should not seek to study and grow and expand in our gospel understanding. Peter explained that there needs to be a reason for the hope within us (1 Pet. 3:15). Our knowledge should be as settling to the mind as it is soothing to the heart. Elder Maxwell taught that some "Church members know just enough about the doctrines to converse superficially on them, but their scant knowledge about the deep doctrines is inadequate for deep discipleship (See 1 Cor. 2:10). Thus uninformed about the deep doctrines, they make no deep change in their lives."[38] President Hugh B. Brown once observed:

> I am impressed with the testimony of a man who can stand and say he knows the gospel is true. But what I would like to ask is "But, sir, do you know the gospel?"... Mere testimony can be gained with but perfunctory knowledge of the Church and its teachings.... But to retain a testimony, to be of service in building the Lord's kingdom, requires a serious study of the gospel and knowing what it is.[39]

On another occasion President Brown taught that we are only required to

> defend those doctrines of the Church contained in the four standard works. ... Anything beyond that by anyone is his or her own opinion and not scripture.... The only way I know of by which the teachings of any person or group may become binding upon the Church is if the teachings have been reviewed by all the Brethren, submitted to the highest councils of the Church, and then approved by the whole body of the Church.[40]

Again, the issue is one of focus, one of emphasis—where we choose to spend our time when we teach the gospel to both Latter-day Saints and to those of other faiths.

There is a valid reason why it is difficult to "tie down" Latter-day Saint doctrine, one that derives from the very nature of the Restoration. The fact that God continues to speak through His anointed servants; the fact that He, through those servants, continues to reveal, elucidate and clarify what has already been given; and the fact that our canon of scripture is open,

---

38. Neal A. Maxwell, *Men and Women of Christ* (Salt Lake City: Bookcraft, 1991), 2.
39. Personal correspondence to Robert J. Matthews, 28 January 1969; cited in Matthews, "Using the Scriptures," *1981 Brigham Young University Fireside and Devotional Speeches* (Provo: BYU Publications, 1981), 124.
40. Edwin B. Firmage, ed., *An Abundant Life: The Memoirs of Hugh B. Brown* (Salt Lake City: Signature Books, 1988), 124.

flexible, and expanding—all of this militates against what many in the Christian world would call a systematic theology.

It is the declaration of sound and solid doctrine—the doctrine found in scripture and taught regularly by Church leaders—that builds faith and strengthens testimony and commitment to the Lord and his kingdom. Elder Maxwell explained that "Deeds *do* matter as well as doctrines, but the doctrines can move us to do the deeds, and the Spirit can help us to understand the doctrines as well as prompt us to do the deeds."[41] He also noted that "When weary legs falter and detours and roadside allurements entice, the fundamental doctrines will summon from deep within us fresh determination. Extraordinary truths can move us to extraordinary accomplishments."[42]

The teaching and application of sound doctrine are great safeguards to us in these last days, shields against the fiery darts of the adversary. Understanding true doctrine and being true to that doctrine can keep us from ignorance, error, and sin. The Apostle Paul counseled Timothy: "If thou put the brethren [and sisters] in remembrance of these things, thou shalt be a good minister of Jesus Christ, nourished up in the word of faith and of good doctrine whereunto thou hast attained. . . . Till I come, give attendance to reading, to exhortation, to doctrine" (1 Tim. 4:6, 13).

---

41. Neal A. Maxwell, *That My Family Should Partake* (Salt Lake City: Deseret Book, 1974), 87.

42. Neal A. Maxwell, *All These Things Shall Give Thee Experience* (Salt Lake City: Deseret Book, 1979), 4.

In "What Do We Mean by 'Church Doctrine'?" Nate Oman employs legal theory to examine several possible ways to understand the term "church doctrine." Starting with natural law, then moving to the rule of recognition, and finishing with law as integrity, Oman argues that law can profitably be used to help understand what we mean by church doctrine. Although natural law and rule of recognition have similarities with how we understand church doctrine, they both fail to account for the many ways church doctrine is understood. Law as integrity, or "telling the best possible story," drawing from a variety of sources, including previous statements, cases, historical context, and so on, best reflects the way we understand church doctrine. Oman concludes by examining two safeguards—one, the moral injunction to avoid contention; the other, the institutional hierarchy of the Church—that should guide us when disagreements about church doctrine arise.

Three

What Do We Mean by "Church Doctrine"?[1]

Nathan B. Oman

As Latter-day Saints, we frequently refer to "church doctrine" in our theological discussions. For example, Sister Smith might express her belief that the earth is no more than five or six thousand years old and that the theory of evolution is a Satanically inspired plot. Brother Young responds by noting, "Those are just your opinions. That is not church doctrine." Whatever else the term "church doctrine" might mean in this exchange, it clearly functions as some sort of theological authority, delineating the beliefs that have a claim on Brother Young from those that do not. Like most Mormons, Brother Young seems to think of church doctrine as a set of authoritative teachings taught by the Church. The precise nature of their authority is not clear, but Brother Young does seem confident that we can identify them. Indeed, he may well think that church doctrine is obvious. His assumption about the ease of identifying church doctrine, however, is deeply problematic. Simply stated, it raises the question, "How can we differentiate between church doctrine and mere opinion?" I think it is helpful to address that problem by using the analogous question, "What is the law?" Ultimately, I am going to argue that, *as we normally use the term,* "church doctrine" is best thought of as a particular kind of interpretation.

The Problem of Church Doctrine

Before I can make my argument, however, I need to show that the question, "What is church doctrine?" is problematic because it is mysteri-

---
1. A scholarly version of this paper was published as "Jurisprudence and the Problem of Church Doctrine," *Element* 2, no. 2 (Fall 2006): 1–19. For a continued discussion of Oman's arguments, see Loyd Ericson, "The Challenges of Defining Mormon Doctrine," *Element* 3, no. 1–2 (Spring/Fall 2007): 69–90; Robert L. Millet, "Defining Doctrine: A Rejoinder to Loyd Ericson," *Element* 5, no. 1 (Spring 2009): 1–7; Nathan B. Oman, "Truth, Doctrine, and Authority," *Element* 5, no. 1 (Spring 2009): 9–18; and Loyd Ericson, "Is It Mormon Doctrine that Mormon Doctrine Is True: A Rejoinder," *Element* 5, no. 1 (Spring 2009): 21–26.

ous. Consider a comparison: the Roman Catholic Church. Like the LDS Church, Roman Catholicism is a unified institution with a strong emphasis on authority. In that regard we are similar, but we differ as to what we mean by "church doctrine." Someone interested in the "church doctrine" of Roman Catholicism could consult the *Catechism of the Catholic Church,* an 864-page volume setting forth the official doctrine of the Roman Catholic Church. The LDS Church has nothing like that.

Nevertheless, we seem to have an easy solution to define church doctrine: church doctrine is simply material that is published by the Church, perhaps subject to the caveat that it has been properly correlated. Let us call this "the correlation argument." This is where our first analogy from the philosophy of law appears. During the first half of the twentieth-century, a group of American thinkers known as the legal realists adopted a similar answer to the question, "What is the law?" As one member of the movement wrote:

> Doing something about disputes . . . is the business of law. And the people who have the doing in charge, whether they be judges or sheriffs or clerks or jailers or lawyers, are officials of the law. *What these officials do about disputes is, to my mind, the law itself.*[2]

I hope that the analogy to the correlation argument is clear: law is simply what the judges do; church doctrine is simply what the correlation program says. But, of course, this will not do. We cannot say that the law is simply what judges do because the judges themselves look up the law and try to follow it in rendering their decisions. In the same way, those on the correlation committees (and others who speak for the Church) look to church doctrine as the governing standard of what they are doing. This assumes, however, that church doctrine exists as some body of identifiable, authoritative teachings *independent of correlation committees or whoever else is expounding it.*

My point is not that church doctrine does not exist or that it somehow lacks authority, nor is it my point that we cannot identify clear instances of church doctrine. The claims that Jesus Christ is the Savior of mankind and that Latter-day Saints in good standing should not drink coffee are both uncontroversial instances of church doctrine. My point is that identifying the full contours of church doctrine presents a puzzle: apart from those clear instances, when we refer to church doctrine or argue with one another over it, what are we talking about?

---

2. Karl Llewellyn, *The Bramble Bush: On Our Law and Its Study* (New York: Oceana Publications, Inc., 1930), 3; emphasis added.

Authority and the Analogy of Law

Readers may have some misgivings about using the law to think about church doctrine. Generally speaking, the word "legalistic" implies a kind of thinking that is rigid and unprofitably formal. Given this fact and the harsh treatment that lawyers receive in the scriptures (see, for example, Luke 11:46 and Alma 10:27), I need to justify the analogy between church doctrine and the law that I am proposing. The most important point of similarity lies in the concept of authority. According to the philosopher Joseph Raz, the key feature of the concept of authority is that it implicitly claims to give us reasons for acting apart from any other reasons. Though we often deride "blind belief," Raz points out that to recognize authority is always, in a sense, to agree to follow blindly. He says:

> There is a sense in which if one accepts the legitimacy of an authority one is committed to following it blindly. One can be very watchful that it shall not overstep its authority and be sensitive to the presence of non-excluded considerations. But barring these possibilities, one is to follow the authority regardless of one's view of the merits of the case (that is blindly). One may form a view on the merits but so long as one follows the authority this is an academic exercise of no practical importance.[3]

This does not mean, of course, that authority is without its reasons. For something to be a valid authority, there must be good reasons for it to be an authority. Rather, the point is that authority purports to offer a particular kind of reason for acting, one that excludes reasons that we would otherwise find compelling.

By definition, following authority is not a matter of weighing the individual merits of the authority's position against our own beliefs and then choosing to accept or reject the authority's position. Following authority always carries at least the possibility of ignoring some reason or reasons that we would otherwise find compelling. If an authority that I recognize tells me I ought not to go swimming in the lake, even if I would otherwise have reasons to go—it is hot, I am on vacation, I enjoy swimming, I am a good swimmer and I have a swim-buddy—I don't go swimming. I exclude or ignore my reasons for going in favor of the authority's command not to do so.

---

3. Joseph Raz, *The Authority of Law: Essays on Law and Morality* (Oxford: Oxford University Press, 1979), 24–25. I take that in the quoted paragraph Raz is using "practical" in its philosophical sense of "relating to action" rather than in its more general sense of useful. Nothing about Raz's theory suggests that thinking about authority is useless.

As a result, claims of authority are always at least partially independent of their substantive content. We must know the border where authority's claims begin, at which point we ignore some of our reasons. Yet it is circular to define the border in purely substantive terms as the point at which we find an authority's position independently compelling. The reason is that we look to authority to discover which of our substantive beliefs ought to be excluded. It is circular to look to our substantive beliefs to discover which of our substantive beliefs to exclude. Rather, we must have some formal criterion independent of our substantive beliefs to identify the limits of authority. In this sense, authority will always require some level of formalism to define its contours.

Both the law and church doctrine are defined at least in part by their claim to authority. Writing in the nineteenth century, John Austin argued that the law is simply a set of general commands backed by threats and issued by the person whom a community generally obeys.[4] The key concepts in Austin's definition of law are command, threat, and obedience. He says that law is simply a special combination of these three concepts at a very general level. The problem with this definition is that it provides no way of differentiating between the operation of law and the mugger who demands, "Your money or your life." Both are cases of commands, threats, and obedience. Yet crime is not a subspecies of law; it is its opposite.

The defect in Austin's theory flows from his failure to recognize law's claim to authority. As subsequent philosophers have pointed out, one of the key differences between law and the mugger is that law makes an additional claim, namely that we are morally obligated to obey it. In other words, from the internal point of view, law always contains a claim to authority. The claim may be mistaken—for example the anti-Semitic Nuremberg Laws of Hitler's Germany are not in fact entitled to any substantive moral respect—but the presence of that claim is part of what marks off law from mere force.[5]

Obviously, church doctrine also contains a claim to authority. Consider for example, the following exchange: Brother Young says, "I think that as a Latter-day Saint I ought to be able to drink coffee. After all there are many things that are far worse for a person than caffeine." Sister Smith responds by saying, "True enough, but it is church doctrine that the Word of Wisdom requires Latter-day Saints to refrain from drinking coffee." Notice

---

4. See generally John Austin, *The Province of Jurisprudence Determined* (London: John Murray, 1832).

5. See H.L.A. Hart, *The Concept of Law*, 2nd ed. (Oxford: Clarendon Press, 1997); and especially Raz, *The Authority of Law*. 37–38.

that Sister Smith does not attempt to refute Brother Young's reason—"there are many things that are far worse for you than caffeine." Indeed, she agrees with it, yet her response suggests that Brother Young's reason does not matter. The authority of church doctrine excludes it. Brother Young might respond by disagreeing with her about the meaning of church doctrine. He might refuse to acknowledge the legitimacy of its authority, suggesting for example that it is oppressive or that religious authority ought to be confined to non-dietary matters. He might suggest that authority is inherently wrong, and that people ought to always follow what they determine to be the best course. Those responses, however, recognize that to say something is church doctrine is to claim that certain reasons against church doctrine are excluded and that the saints are required to assent to it, even in situations where they might otherwise come to different conclusions. This does not mean that church doctrine is the sinister manifestation of a megalomaniac cult, any more than the notion that one ought to stop at a red light is evidence that the United States is a totalitarian dictatorship. It does mean that both church doctrine and the law claim authority.[6]

Jurisprudential Solutions to the Problem of Church Doctrine

Over the centuries, legal philosophy has struggled to find ways of identifying the law. Because these theories try—with greater or lesser degrees of success—to take into account the authority of law, they can serve as useful analogies for thinking about church doctrine. For my purposes, however, their usefulness lies not in the various accounts that they offer for *why* the law has authority, but rather in their concern for the form of that authority. In particular, these theories of law claim to offer us a way to identify the boundaries of the law—not in the sense of the extent of its moral justification but rather to the extent of its claimed authority. In other words, these theories are concerned with figuring out what is or is not the law, rather than the extent to which we must follow the law. Looking at how jurisprudential theories have tried to answer this question, we can construct and evaluate analogous approaches to church doctrine.

---

6. This does not mean, of course, that they claim to be exactly the same kind of authority or that they claim authority over the same things. It does mean that within their respective spheres—whatever they may be—both the law and church doctrine claim to offer exclusive reasons for the claims they make.

The first theory I turn to is natural law. Forced to hazard a brief definition, I think that the core of natural law can be stated as the claim that law is defined in terms of what is morally justified. Perhaps more importantly, natural law involves a very strong negative claim, namely that a command or rule that is immoral, no matter how official looking, is not law. Suffice it to say, this definition is a gross over-simplification; natural law does not simply identify law and morality. Natural law thinkers acknowledge that law has certain social and institutional aspects—for example, enforcement—but they deny that it can be defined purely in terms of its social aspect.

What would an analogous theory of church doctrine look like? Joseph Smith once declared, "One of the grand fundamental principles of 'Mormonism' is to receive truth let it come from whence it may."[7] Also, Brigham Young taught, "'Mormonism' embraces all truth that is revealed and that is unrevealed, whether religious, political, scientific, or philosophical."[8] President Young, I take it, is making a claim about the contours of Mormonism properly understood, rather than about the status of the society of Deseret in the nineteenth century (or the society of the Wasatch Front in the twenty-first century, for that matter). On this view, Mormonism is co-extensive with truth. Applying this notion to church doctrine, we would say that church doctrine is that which is true. In other words, truth acts as our criterion for identifying church doctrine. Just as natural law identifies law with morality, a natural law approach to the question of what is church doctrine identifies it with truth. The audacity and expansiveness of this approach is appealing, but unfortunately it suffers from some basic problems.

Saying that church doctrine is simply coextensive with what is true cannot make sense of some very basic ways in which the concept is used. Imagine that while discussing the Word of Wisdom, Sister Smith says, "You shouldn't eat chocolate. It has caffeine and is bad for you." Brother Young responds, "That is just your opinion. It is not church doctrine." Suppose, however, that his reaction is prompted by the fact that he is uncertain about whether he should eat chocolate. There would be nothing shocking about Brother Young's invocation of church doctrine in such a situation. Faced with a doubtful situation, he is using the term "church doctrine" to confirm the legitimacy of his doubt. The authority of church doctrine does not re-

---

7. Joseph Smith, *Teachings of the Prophet Joseph Smith*, comp. and ed. Joseph Fielding Smith (Salt Lake City: Deseret Book, 1976), 313.

8. Brigham Young, *The Discourses of Brigham Young*, ed. John A. Widtsoe (Salt Lake City: Deseret Book, 1925), 2.

quire him to assent to Sister Smith's position. Furthermore, it is precisely because Brother Young seems to know the contours of church doctrine that he knows that he is under no obligation to accept Sister Smith's claims. Yet if church doctrine were truth, in identifying its contours he would necessarily have laid to rest any doubts as to Sister Smith's position. Indeed, placing it outside of church doctrine would be tantamount to claiming that it was false. Yet this is precisely what our doubtful Brother Young refuses to do. He does not say it is false that one should not eat chocolate; he says that it is not church doctrine that one should not eat chocolate.

The equation of church doctrine with truth is further undermined if we believe—as I think we are required to do—that there are issues for which church doctrine is silent. For example, I take it to be fairly uncontroversial that there is no church doctrine on the precise location of Williamsburg, Virginia. Somewhat more controversially, one can plausibly (and correctly, in my view) claim that there is no church doctrine on the truth or falsity of the theory of evolution. No one could plausibly argue, however, that because of this, no statement about the location of Williamsburg, Virginia (or the theory of evolution) could be true or false. The statement that "Williamsburg, Virginia is located on the banks of the Potomac River" is clearly false, the silence of church doctrine notwithstanding. Nor does it make sense of our ordinary usage of the term "church doctrine" to say, "It is church doctrine that Williamsburg, Virginia is on the York-James Peninsula."

A second possible analogy is called "legal positivism." Legal positivists reject natural law's claim about the necessary connection between law and morality. For them law is always a matter of social fact. For example, a legal positivist might say that one does not discover the law of the United States by discovering what is morally justified. Rather one simply reads a copy of the *United States Code*. What is or is not included in the *United States Code*, however, is not a moral fact but a social one. Legal positivists nevertheless disagree among themselves about what sorts of social facts one should look to in defining the boundaries of law. According to H. L. A. Hart, an influential legal positivist, law is a system of rules. Some rules govern human behavior, including, for example, the rule that murder is prohibited. Some rules govern the promulgation and validity of other rules. On this view, law is ultimately defined by what Hart called a "rule of recognition."[9] This is a rule that allows us to differentiate those rules that are law from other rules, such as rules of manners or the rules of golf, which are not law: for example, in the United States a statute passed by both houses of Congress

---

9. See Hart, *Concept of Law*, 100–110.

and signed by the President is law. This rule, called "the rule of bicameral passage and presentment," is a rule of recognition. The existence of such a rule is a matter of social fact. Hence, if a hermit living in a remote corner of Texas declares himself supreme legislator of the world and begins issuing complex civil codes, his work is not law. This is because there is no socially accepted rule stating that the rules laid down by the wild hermit are to be recognized as law.

The rule of recognition provides a seemingly elegant solution to the problem of what is church doctrine. On this view church doctrine is whatever is propounded as church doctrine *by the appropriate authority in the appropriate way*. Suppose that I was called as a gospel doctrine teacher and began teaching that Jesus Christ was not in fact the Savior of mankind. Or perhaps I began teaching that it was permissible for Latter-day Saints to drink coffee. My calling as gospel doctrine teacher gives me some standing to speak for the Church, but no one would claim that my teachings become church doctrine by virtue of the fact that I uttered them. Whatever else being a gospel doctrine teacher may confer, it does not confer the ability to promulgate church doctrine. The second qualifier—that doctrine be propounded "in an appropriate way"—is equally important. Elder Bruce R. McConkie neatly illustrates this point in his book, *Mormon Doctrine*. Latter-day Saints recognize that an Apostle has the authority to declare church doctrine. We would nevertheless not want to say that everything an Apostle says is church doctrine. First, there are things said by Apostles before they were ordained—Elder McConkie was an Assistant to the Quorum of the Twelve when *Mormon Doctrine* was published. Second and more importantly, even ordained General Authorities can express views that they explicitly state represent their personal opinions—in his preface, Elder McConkie stated that he was solely responsible for *Mormon Doctrine*. That would not be true if anything a General Authority said was church doctrine. Hence, any rule of recognition for church doctrine will require that we identify both who may announce church doctrine as well as the situations under which these persons' statements are accepted as church doctrine.

The problem is that we do not appear to have any such rule of recognition. One might look to the statements of General Authorities as providing a clear rule of recognition for church doctrine. Joseph Smith, however, taught that a prophet is only a prophet when speaking as a prophet.[10] This suggests that even among the highest councils of the Church—the First

---

10. See Smith, *Teachings*, 278.

Presidency and the Quorum of the Twelve—not every statement is entitled to the authority of church doctrine. What we lack, however, is a clear criterion for identifying when a prophet is speaking as a prophet. For example, should we assume that everything uttered in General Conference is church doctrine? If so, is it because the speakers in General Conference are careful to make sure that they don't say anything that contradicts church doctrine, or because church doctrine simply is what is said in General Conference? Furthermore, is church doctrine confined to some set of *public* statements by high Church leaders? Suppose, for example, that the General Handbook of Instructions were modified so that abstinence from coffee was no longer necessary to qualify as worthy for a temple recommend. Would that change constitute a shift in church doctrine, even if it was not announced from the pulpit in General Conference? The fact that we do not have clear answers to these questions suggests to me that we lack a clear rule of recognition for what constitutes church doctrine.

It is tempting to look to the scriptures and the idea of canonization as a rule of recognition. On this view, church doctrine would consist of whatever the scriptures say. There are at least two problems with this approach. First, it is massively over- and under-inclusive. There are certain things that are very clearly church doctrine that cannot really be found in the scriptures. For example, our current understanding of the Word of Wisdom goes beyond the text of the Doctrine and Covenants itself. The very fact that the Word of Wisdom is regarded today as a commandment is at odds with the text, which clearly states that it is not given by way of commandment (see D&C 89:2). Another example of the under-inclusiveness of the scriptures as a sole source for church doctrine would be the current ecclesiastical structure of the Church. It is very clear that the Bishop is the presiding priesthood authority in his ward, yet this is not something that one can find in the scriptures and was not even settled until at least the 1870s.

The scriptures, however, are not simply under-inclusive. They are also over-inclusive in the sense that they contain many teachings that are not church doctrine. For example, the intricate rules of the Law of Moses found in the Pentateuch are not binding as church doctrine. Certain aspects of the text of the Word of Wisdom—such as the prohibition on meat except in winter or time of famine—do not have the same status as the prohibition of coffee (see D&C 89:12–13). Likewise, Christ's prohibition of divorce in the Gospel of Mark does not seem to be church doctrine (see Mark 10:6–9).

The second problem with looking only to the scriptures for church doctrine is the problem of interpretation. Mormonism began by rejecting the sufficiency of scriptural interpretation alone. After finding himself caught up in a war of words between the rival evangelists in Palmyra, the young Joseph Smith turned to the Bible. He later wrote:

> While I was laboring under the extreme difficulties caused by the contests of these parties of religionists, I was one day reading the Epistle of James, first chapter and fifth verse, which reads: *If any of you lack wisdom, let him ask of God, that giveth to all men liberally, and upbraideth not; and it shall be given him.*
>
> Never did any passage of scripture come with more power to the heart of man than this did at this time to mine. It seemed to enter with great force into every feeling of my heart. I reflected on it again and again, knowing that if any person needed wisdom from God, I did; for how to act I did not know, and unless I could get more wisdom than I then had, I would never know; for the teachers of religion of the different sects understood the same passages of scripture so differently as to *destroy all confidence in settling the question by an appeal to the Bible.* (JS–H 1:11–12; emphasis added)

The new revelation of the Restoration came only after the sufficiency of scripture had been rejected. As it now stands, Mormons regularly invoke the concept of church doctrine as an aid to the interpretation of scripture. For example, should someone teach that the text of Doctrine and Covenants 89 requires that Mormons become vegetarians, the standard response would be "That is just your interpretation; it is not church doctrine." This points, however, to an important function of church doctrine: it is something that we frequently use to identify which interpretations of scripture are authoritative and which are not. This means, however, that church doctrine necessarily exceeds the standard works by themselves.

If an agreed upon rule of recognition existed for church doctrine, then a model of church doctrine along the lines of legal positivism would work. Such a rule would avoid the difficulties involved in the natural law approach to church doctrine that I sketched above. For better or for worse, however, we seem to lack any agreed upon set of social understandings about the contours of the rule of recognition. This does not mean, of course, that the words of scripture, prophets, apostles, and other General Authorities are without authority. It simply means that a statement does not become church doctrine by virtue of being uttered by any particular Church leader or even by virtue of being printed in the standard works. Nor does it mean that the various potential rules of recognition that we might propose are wrong per se. All of these rules can help to orient us toward church doctrine. However, they cannot provide a foolproof way of identifying church doctrine in every case.

Law as Integrity and Church Doctrine

The final theory I want to consider is referred to as "law as integrity" and was put forward by philosopher Ronald Dworkin. According to Dworkin, we have any number of cases where what the law consists of and what it demands is more or less clear and obvious. For example, we know that the US Constitution's requirement that the President be at least thirty-five years of age can be identified as the law without recourse to any elaborate theory of what law is. On the other hand, in certain situations we are faced with what Dworkin calls "hard cases." In these situations the scope of the law is unclear and we are hard pressed to identify its demands. Dworkin imagines how a perfect judge, whom he names Hercules, would decide such a case.[11] According to Dworkin, Hercules would survey the vast mass of clear and easy law relating to the issue. He would then construct a story that makes sense of all of that material. In constructing his story, Hercules seeks to provide an account of the law that sets it in the best possible light. Using a metaphor that has since become famous, Dworkin argued that the judge is like the most recent author of a long chain novel whose previous chapters have been written by others.[12]

> Law as integrity asks a judge deciding a common-law case . . . to think of himself as an author in the chain of common law. He knows that other judges have decided cases that, although not exactly like his case, deal with related problems; he must think of their decisions as part of a long story he must interpret and then continue, according to his own judgment of how to make the developing story as good as it can be.[13]

Dworkin gives the example of the English case of *McLaughlin v. O'Brian*. The case involved a woman who sued a negligent driver for damages for emotional distress. The woman was not in the car accident and had not been physically injured in any way. Rather, she was called to the hospital where she learned that her husband and daughter had been killed.

---

11. Ronald Dworkin, *Law's Empire* (Cambridge: Harvard University Press, 1986), 239–40.
12. See Ronald Dworkin, "Law as Interpretation," *Critical Inquiry* 9, no. 1 (September 1982): 179–200.
13. Dworkin, *Law's Empire*, 238–39.

Previous English cases had awarded damages for emotional distress, but only in cases where the plaintiff had actually witnessed the injury or had come upon a loved one's corpse at the scene of the accident. The question presented by *McLaughlin* was whether these cases authorized damages in a situation when emotional distress was removed from the scene of the accident to the more antiseptic setting of the hospital. The lower court held that McLaughlin could not recover for her distress. On appeal the House of Lords (the British equivalent of the US Supreme Court) reversed the lower court's ruling.

In deciding a case like *McLaughlin*, Hercules does not simply decide whether he believes, all things considered, that recovery for emotional distress in this situation is a good idea. Rather he begins with the earlier cases. Suppose, for example, that Hercules believes that any recovery for emotional distress would be misguided. He thinks that it is a bad policy and that the moral arguments in favor of compensating emotional distress are weak. He cannot, however, simply apply this judgment to McLaughlin's case, because the previous decisions, by which he is bound, clearly reject his position by awarding damages for emotional distress. Nor can he simply hold that the previous decisions were mistaken and that from now on no damages for emotional distress will be awarded. (I am oversimplifying, of course, but not so much as to ruin the point.) Rather, Hercules must look at the previously decided cases and construct the best possible argument he can that justifies them. In justifying them, he looks not only at the outcomes in the cases, but also to the reasons offered by the previous judges. He must also account for these reasons, although in constructing the best possible justification for the previous cases he will necessarily recharacterize the reasoning of previous judges. There are two reasons for this. First, Hercules must make sense of the previous cases in a new context. Second, he is telling a story about both the past case and the current one that tries to make the whole of the law as good as possible. Thus the arguments in support of the holdings by the courts evolve over time.

In *McLaughlin*, Hercules would first draw on the best possible understanding that he has of policy and political morality to justify the conclusion that those who witness the death of a loved one should be compensated. Then he would decide if those arguments justify giving the wife and mother of accident victims compensation when she learns of their deaths in a hospital. In this way, although Hercules's interpretation involves normative judgments, it is not simply a matter of *his* normative judgments. Rather, discovering what the law requires in a particular case is a matter of recognizing the force of the judgments made in previous, controlling precedents. Put another way, a judge creates a story that makes sense of the clearly established cases and then fits the new case into that story in a way that places the whole in the best possible light.

In my view, thinking of church doctrine as a kind of Dworkinian interpretation provides the best account of what we mean by the term. The advantage of Dworkin's view is that it does not require that we have any clear idea about the rule of recognition, nor do we necessarily need to know whether something is true. Rather it requires that we have some easily identifiable core cases of church doctrine from which we can reason.

This is precisely the situation in which we find ourselves. We can easily imagine that Brother Young and Sister Smith have very different opinions about the rule of recognition for church doctrine. For example, Brother Young might believe that church doctrine consists only of texts formally canonized by a vote in General Conference, while Sister Smith might regard any public sermon by a member of the Quorum of the Twelve as church doctrine. Both of them agree, however, that it is church doctrine that Jesus Christ is the Savior of mankind and that Latter-day Saints should not drink coffee. When faced with a new question about church doctrine, rather than trying to determine which of them has the correct rule of recognition they can simply reason on the basis of clear cases, fitting the new question into a story that will place things in their best possible light.

More importantly, I think that this is how most Mormons actually use the concept of church doctrine. To be sure, Latter-day Saints make claims about the truth of church doctrine, and they point to authoritative statements in support of their claim that a proposition or rule of conduct is church doctrine. However, all of these claims are made in a vast context of teachings, experiences, and texts within the Church, which the members seek to accommodate and charitably characterize in their minds. It is their interpretation of the totality that produces their conclusions about what is or is not church doctrine.

The question of whether Diet Coke is prohibited by the Word of Wisdom provides an example of how church doctrine as integrity works in practice. We start with the brute fact that we all agree that the Word of Wisdom is church doctrine, and it forbids drinking coffee, tea, and alcohol. What would be the best story that one could tell about this? One story would be to say that it is a health code designed to prohibit the ingestion of bad substances. Thus we look at alcohol and caffeine and use them as touchstones for Word of Wisdom compliance. According to this view, chocolate and Diet Coke, both of which contain caffeine, are out. There are, however, a number of problems with this interpretation. For example, alcohol is not necessarily bad, and small quantities can actually be good for you. Furthermore, the list of prohibited substances seems to be strangely random from a purely health-oriented point of view. Why condemn excessive meat consumption but not excessive sugar consumption? Why explicitly include relatively harmless substances like tea or coffee but not narcotics? One might offer the argument that in the nineteenth century, when section 89 was given, they did not have drugs. This, however, is historically inaccurate. The nineteenth century was well acquainted with narcotics like opium. Furthermore, the current interpretation of "hot drinks" as meaning tea and coffee (but not herbal tea) did not gel until the twentieth century, so it is not clear why nineteenth-century practice should control our interpretation. Given these difficulties, one could conclude that the interpretation of bad-substances does not provide the best account of the rules.

A better explanation is that the prohibition is meant as a reminder or symbol of the covenant that I make with God and an open-ended admonition to be healthy. This explains the seemingly arbitrary selection of prohibited substances. As symbols they are arbitrary in the same way that using the shape "A" to designate the sound "ahhh" is arbitrary. It also explains the rise of the Word of Wisdom as a central part of Mormon identity in the 1930s. As outward reminders of Mormons' status as a "peculiar people" in the form of things like polygamy or the United Order retreated in the face of intense outside pressure to assimilate, the Word of Wisdom provided a workable mark of the covenant. On this reading, the prohibition of hot drinks cannot be reduced to a prohibition of caffeine that then extends to Diet Coke. The text of the Word of Wisdom itself, as well as widespread teachings in the Church, however, does link it to health (see D&C 89:18). Accordingly, the symbols are not entirely arbitrary, but are rather linked to a general injunction to avoid consumption of substances—including Diet Coke—that are bad for one's health.

There are obviously important ways in which church doctrine as integrity is different than law as integrity. In modern courts a judge faced with a case does not have the luxury of not resolving the question presented. Once the parties have concluded the litigation, the judge is required to choose one of the parties. Accordingly, Dworkin's theory of the law requires that it be complete in the sense of providing some definitive answer to any case that can be posed to it. Even in hard cases there are answers, and the law is not without gaps. Church doctrine, however, does not labor under the same requirements as the law. Sometimes—or often—the best interpretation of Mormon texts, practices, and history is "We simply don't know." Even here, however, the process of interpretation will discipline our ignorance. Mormon texts, practices, and history will foreclose certain answers even while they make other answers more likely, all the while not definitively laying the matter to rest. Hence, on some questions—such as the location of towns in the Virginia tidewater—Church doctrine is simply silent. On other questions, however, the answer might be something like, "Well, under church doctrine there are a couple of possible answers."

For example, the precise meaning of the term "intelligence" as it is used in the scriptures is notoriously vague. Elder McConkie suggested that "intelligence" consisted of some sort of pre-sentient stuff from which spirits are organized.[14] B. H. Roberts thought that "intelligences" were the eternal, self-existent, self-aware core of the spirit that could neither be created nor destroyed.[15] Perhaps most esoterically, Orson Pratt suggested that "intelligence" was an elemental fluid of divinity that pervaded to a greater and lesser extent the entire universe.[16] I take it that none of these positions can be identified as the authoritative approach of church doctrine to the question. They all fit and justify Mormon texts, practices, and history to some extent. On the other hand church doctrine *does* foreclose certain theories of intelligence. For example, the consistent rejection of the doctrine of *ex nihilo* creation by Mormon scriptures and authorities would foreclose the idea that church doctrine can accommodate the view that "intelligence" refers to some spirit substance created from nothing by God through an act of divine fiat.

Some Implications of Church Doctrine as Integrity: Obedience and Personal Judgment

Church doctrine as integrity provides a more nuanced understanding of the relationship between individual judgment and following church doctrine. To see how, we must understand that on this view church doctrine is inherently contestable. This does not mean that the question of whether a claim is church doctrine is without a correct answer.[17] Indeed, church doctrine as integrity necessarily assumes that many aspects of church doc-

---

14. See Blake Ostler, "The Idea of Pre-existence in Mormon Thought," *Dialogue: A Journal of Mormon Thought* 15, no. 1 (Spring 1982): 59, 72.

15. See B. H. Roberts, "The Immortality of Man," in *B. H. Roberts Scrapbook*, vol. 2, comp. Lynn Pulsipher (Provo, Utah: Pulsipher Publishing, 1991), 21, 26.

16. See Orson Pratt, "The Holy Spirit," in *The Essential Orson Pratt*, ed. David Whittacker (Salt Lake City: Signature Books, 1991).

17. Ronald Dworkin, "Is There Really No Right Answer in Hard Cases," in *A Matter of Principle* (Cambridge: Harvard University Press, 1985), 119.

trine are clear. It does mean that we are always likely to have disagreements about certain aspects of what church doctrine requires and that the only way of doctrinally settling these disagreements will be by resorting to complex arguments about the best possible story to be told. It is important to understand that when I say that church doctrine is inherently contestable, I am not talking about disagreements over whether church doctrine is true or whether it should be followed. Rather I am talking about disagreements over the *content* of church doctrine itself: we can always disagree about some parts of church doctrine. We cope with those disagreements morally and institutionally.

Morally, we are to discuss church doctrine with charity and unity, avoiding "contention." In the Book of Mormon, the risen Christ teaches:

> And there shall be no disputations among you, as there have hitherto been; neither shall there be disputations among you concerning the points of my doctrine, as there have hitherto been. For verily, verily I say unto you, he that hath the spirit of contention is not of me, but is of the devil, who is the father of contention, and he stirreth up the hearts of men to contend with anger, one with another. (3 Ne. 11:28–29)

This scripture is not a philosophical Rosetta stone that allows us transparently to identify authoritative church doctrine. Rather we are given a moral injunction—not to "contend with anger"—for coping with the inevitable disagreements about the scope of the authority of church doctrine. This suggests that the primary danger of the contestability of church doctrine is not that we will be mistaken about what is doctrine and what it is not. Rather, the danger is social. It is the danger of rancor, discord, and a loss of unity. The solution to disagreements about doctrine takes the form of a moral injunction about our social interactions—in this case doctrinal discussions—instead of an intellectual method for resolving doctrinal disputes.

In addition to a morality of doctrinal discussion, we have institutional solutions to the practical difficulties of doctrinal disagreements. Return once again to the initial disagreement between Sister Smith and Brother Young about evolution and the age of the earth. Imagine that Sister Smith is called as a gospel doctrine teacher and begins vociferously teaching her anti-evolution views during class, replacing the whole of the Genesis curriculum with a prolonged screed against Darwinism. Brother Young suggests to her that she should stop teaching her opinions as church doctrine. Sister Smith indignantly replies that her views on the age of the earth and the source of the theory of evolution *are* church doctrine, insisting that she holds them precisely for this reason. Both parties take their dispute to their bishop. He asks that Sister Smith confine her lesson more closely to the text of the assigned scriptures. Such a solution to Sister Smith and Brother Young's doctrinal disagreement is entirely institutional. Indeed, it needn't take a doctrinal position at all on the resolution of the dispute. The bishop's decision controls in this situation not because he has privileged access to church doctrine per se, but simply because he is the bishop. In this sense, the hierarchy of the Church, with its accompanying notions of stewardship and jurisdiction, serves as a substitute for a theory that incontestably identifies church doctrine.

The success of the ethical and institutional methods of coping with doctrinal disagreement underscores the inherent contestability of church doctrine. If there were some way of indubitably discovering the precise contours of church doctrine, it would solve at least some of the problems to which the injunction against contention and notions of institutional stewardship address themselves. However, given the proper attitude and institutional structure, the inherent contestability of church doctrine seems to be something that we can live with quite nicely. Nevertheless, the contestability remains.

Conclusion

Church doctrine is an important but mysterious concept. We use it as a way of referring to authoritative beliefs and practices, but it is not clear how we go about identifying it. Like the law, church doctrine purports to offer exclusive, authoritative reasons for belief and action within its sphere. Building on this analogy, we can draft theories from the philosophy of law to help us conceptualize church doctrine. Canvassing some of the most prominent theories suggests that law as integrity provides the best model for church doctrine. On this view, authoritative church doctrine consists of the best possible story that can be told about the totality of Mormon scripture, teachings, practices, and history.

In "Presiding in Our Homes: Are We Doing Too Much or Too Little?" Larry Wimmer explores the oft mentioned but perhaps frequently misunderstood principle of presiding. As the title infers, Wimmer suggests presiding can fail in two different ways. Fathers sometimes, "under the guise of priesthood authority, are coercive and exercise too much control over the lives and decisions of their wives and children." This inappropriate behavior may result, in part, from incorrectly applying understandings of "preside" common in business and governmental settings, and reflects a general misunderstanding of the principle of equal partnership between husband and wife. On the other end of the spectrum, however, some fathers fall short of proper presiding because they fail to lead the family in certain activities such as family scripture reading or family prayer. They may not be guilty of heavy-handedness, but they fail to set proper examples for their families.

Four

Presiding in Our Homes: Are We Doing Too Much or Too Little?

Larry Wimmer

For forty-five years I have observed dedicated Latter-day Saint women, including my wife, wrestle with issues surrounding what it means for their husbands to be the presiding authority in their homes. It may be tempting to conclude that the problem always involves husbands exercising too much control, though it is unfortunately true that this occurs far more commonly than it should. From my experience, however, it is also possible for a wife to feel that her husband performs too little leadership and guidance for the family. I hope I can respond to these diverging views and reconcile them with counsel from our Church leaders.

One of my early encounters with strong feelings about this issue happened when a leader in our ward reminded the congregation that "every ship can have one and only one captain." My wife's response was to ask me afterward if she needed permission to swab the deck. During this same period of time, I confess that in our home my wife was keenly aware of how often the captain was away from the bridge; whether my excuse was my profession, Church assignments, or the need to relax among my hobbies, I was often distracted, leaving far too much responsibility on her strong shoulders. Of course, it seems difficult for a father to preside effectively when he is not home; but even when a father is home, how can he better fulfill this important responsibility? The question of presiding seems something we very often get wrong by going too far in either direction. In hopes of helping us consider this important responsibility, I want to explore two related questions: What does it mean for husbands to preside, and how do we know when we have it right?

Let me first address what seems to have become one of our most serious concerns: our husbands, under the guise of priesthood authority, are coercive and exercise too much control over the lives and decisions of their wives and children. From the most common or standard definitions of the word "preside," it is easy to understand how one might draw the conclusion that whoever is called to preside is required to exercise ultimate authority and control. According to the *Oxford English Dictionary* (OED) "to preside" implies that one:

1. exercise authority or control;
2. occupy the chair or seat of authority;
3. govern, rule, or reign supreme;
4. occupy the seat of authority or act as president;
5. exercise direction, control, or superintendence (to overlook or supervise).

It would also seem to follow from these definitions that others within the same organization or family must necessarily play a secondary, subsidiary, or even inferior role. These definitions comfortably fit many of our governmental, business, and even Church administrative settings. We understand this hierarchical structure, and accept the notion of one president, one governor, one CEO, one bishop, and one captain. I will argue, however, that these standard definitions do not apply to the relationship that should exist between a husband and a wife in a family setting and will support this conclusion with counsel received from our Church leaders.

A reading of Church documents may seem at first to support the notion that the husband should indeed be in charge and act as chairman. In 1973, a "Message from the Church of Jesus Christ of Latter-day Saints" declared that: "A father is the presiding authority in his family."[1] Similarly, twenty-two years later the Church's "Family: A Proclamation to the World" forcefully states: "fathers are to preside over their families." However, on further reading, both documents place explicit *requirements and conditions* on the husband's role that differentiate presiding in a Latter-day Saint home from any of the standard dictionary definitions. The 1973 statement declares that a husband must have unity with his wife, insisting that "it is not a matter of whether you are most worthy or best qualified," and concludes that a husband should not "act without counsel [or] without assistance." The Proclamation on the Family declares that the husband must preside only "*in love and in righteousness*" and ends with the injunction that "in these sacred responsibilities, fathers and mothers are obligated to help one another as *equal partners*."[2] The requirement that a husband and wife be unified, not acting without counsel or assistance but rather in love and righteousness as equal partners, does not correspond to the standard definitions of one who presides as the ultimate authority. A husband is not superior, not in intellect, morals, or authority. He

---

1. Reprinted as "Father, Consider Your Ways," *Ensign*, June 2002, 12.
2. "The Family: A Proclamation to the World," *Ensign*, Nov. 1995, 102.

is not the president. He does not control or preponderate. To see clearly the distinction between a father and other leaders, notice that no one would argue that a president, chairman, governor, or bishop is an equal partner with any other person in an organization. But, we are told explicitly that a father should have an equal partner.

In the spirit of these two documents, Church leaders have repeatedly emphasized the role and responsibility of fathers to preside in their families, and with equal frequency and emphasis they have added conditions that specify a fundamental difference between the LDS concept of "presiding in love and righteousness" versus that of "presiding as president or chairman with ultimate control."

In 1977, President N. Eldon Tanner declared:

> *Together* the couple should determine that they will pray together regularly, that they will have and show love and respect for each other, that they will read and study the scriptures together, and that they will keep the commandments of God and the covenant they made at the time of their marriage vows.
>
> Every Latter-day Saint home should be a model home, where the father is the head of the household, but *presiding with love and in complete harmony with the righteous desires of the mother. Together* they should be seeking the same goals for the family.... We cannot emphasize too often that part of the 121st section of the Doctrine and Covenants which refers to unrighteous exercise of the powers of the priesthood and which every father needs to heed (D&C 121:39, 41–43).[3]

In 1987, President Ezra Taft Benson warned:

> We sometimes hear accounts of men, even in the Church, who think that being head of the home somehow puts them in a superior role and allows them to dictate and make demands upon their family....
> [Y]ou cannot demean [your wife], criticize her, find fault with her, or abuse her by words, sullen behavior, or actions.
>
> Husbands, *recognize your wife's intelligence and her ability to counsel with you as a real partner* regarding family plans, family activities, and family budgeting.[4]

Notice the stark difference between this counsel and the earlier definitions from the OED.

---

3. N. Eldon Tanner, "Fatherhood," *Ensign*, June 1977, 2; emphasis added.
4. Ezra Taft Benson, "To the Fathers in Israel," *Ensign*, Nov 1987, 48; emphasis added.

In 1994, President Howard W. Hunter instructed:

> A man who holds the priesthood *accepts his wife as a partner* in the leadership of the home and family *with full knowledge of and full participation in all decisions* relating thereto.[5]

In 2002, President Gordon B. Hinckley addressed this topic before the General Priesthood instructing those present that

> The wife you choose will be your equal. . . . *In the marriage companionship there is neither inferiority nor superiority.* The woman does not walk ahead of the man; neither does the man walk ahead of the woman. They walk side by side as a son and daughter of God on an eternal journey.
>
> She is not your servant, your chattel, nor anything of the kind.
>
> How tragic and utterly disgusting a phenomenon is wife abuse. Any man in this Church who abuses his wife, who demeans her, who insults her, who exercises unrighteous dominion over her is unworthy to hold the priesthood.[6]

And recently while addressing the Priesthood on the topic of "Fatherhood, an Eternal Calling," Elder L. Tom Perry recently declared:

> Since the beginning, God has instructed mankind that marriage should unite husband and wife together in unity. Therefore, *there is not a president or a vice president in a family.* The couple works together eternally for the good of the family. They are united together in word, in deed, and in action as they lead, guide, and direct their family unit. *They are on equal footing.*[7]

Again, it is clear that the LDS understanding of "presiding in love and righteousness" does not fit under any of the common definitions of "presiding." The only authorized relationship between a husband and a wife is one in which they are working together, united as equal partners, with no one superior to the other in authority. Apparently the fact that a ship has only one captain has *nothing* to do with the priesthood, our home, or our relationships.

Does this incongruity between "presiding" as commonly understood versus how we are counseled to apply it in our LDS homes imply that as

---

5. Howard W. Hunter, "Being a Righteous Husband and Father," *Ensign*, Nov 1994, 49; emphasis added.

6. Gordon B. Hinckley, "Personal Worthiness to Exercise the Priesthood," *Ensign*, May 2002, 52; emphasis added.

7. L. Tom Perry, "Fatherhood, an Eternal Calling," *Ensign*, May 2004, 69; emphasis added.

members of the Church we have a unique meaning or usage of the word? If so, might we be better served by finding a different word to describe what we mean by "preside"? Having searched many dictionaries, including that closest to Joseph Smith's day, Noah Webster's 1828 Dictionary, I find little help in alternative definitions of the word "preside."

The etymology of the word may take us a long way toward clarifying this apparent contradiction. The original root of "preside" comes from the Latin word *praesidere*, and one of the meanings of this root word is "to guard." The word "to guard" means to defend, to preserve, to secure, or implies a state of caution or vigilance. This root meaning takes us a long way toward clarifying an apparent confusion or contradiction. The same sentence of the Proclamation on the Family that declares it the responsibility of husbands to "preside in love and in righteousness," counsels that it is their duty *"to provide the necessities of life and protection for their families"* (emphasis added). That husbands and fathers should guard their families against moral, financial, and physical assault is supported by counsel given Joseph Smith as early as 1833 (see Doctrine & Covenants 101). In order that the Lord's vineyard, possibly Zion and her families, might be protected, the Lord's servants are instructed to build a tower

> that one may *overlook* the land round about, to be a *watchman upon the tower*, that mine olive trees may not be broken down when the enemy shall come to spoil and take upon themselves the fruit of my vineyard. (D&C 101:45, emphasis added)

This interpretation of "preside," "to watch over" or "to guard" supports and clarifies our understanding of what it means for LDS husbands to preside in their homes: husbands are required to "guard / protect / provide leadership and guidance."

Surely it is the responsibility of both fathers *and* mothers to guard, protect, provide leadership and guidance (on the one hand), and to nurture (on the other). Nevertheless, God has apparently created men and women with different strengths, or at least different responsibilities. Mothers are principally charged with the responsibility to nurture; fathers are instructed to accept primary responsibility for the daily necessities and to watch over and guard against those influences that might destroy their families. Both husbands and wives should act in love, righteousness, and unity as they seek counsel from the other.

Section 121 of the Doctrine and Covenants strengthens the notion of *shared* responsibilities and the need for *joint* counsel in all major decisions, warning that if we "exercise control or dominion or compulsion upon the souls of the children of men [including, presumably, wives or husbands], in any degree of unrighteousness, behold the heavens withdraw themselves and the Spirit of the Lord is grieved" (v. 37). This warning is in direct contrast to the blessings promised if husbands "preside in love and in righteousness." This contrast should cause us to pause, and perhaps err on the side of caution in our relationships. Apparently, in the gospel, to preside on the one hand, and to exercise control or compulsion on the other hand are not synonyms—as has sometimes been assumed. Instead, they are antonyms. God has not ordained that males must have the last word. The sooner we begin to understand and respect each other's different but equally sacred gifts and our obligation to assist one another as equal partners, the sooner we will begin to develop happier, more productive, and more meaningful relationships. Clearly we have not addressed the exceptions that exist within specific families or the increasingly prevalent existence of single-parent families. We are addressing, as does the Proclamation itself, general principles and different responsibilities.

Wives may need to be patient with their husbands. Some husbands have come from homes where fathers or grandfathers never did "women's work." Dad and his sons often left the dinner table to watch a ball game while Mom and the daughters cleaned up after them. Other husbands have come from countries where women have been expected to obey their husbands. However, let me make it clear—these traits and types of behavior are *social customs* and *traditions*, not the righteous exercise of priesthood. It may take time, perhaps counsel, and a lot of love to show that there is a better way. Similarly, we need to be reminded that both men and women can exercise control, dominion, or compulsion. And in such cases, not only do the heavens withdraw themselves, it will also be the end of equal partnering and the loss of mutual respect. Love can not survive in the suffocating environment of ongoing criticism even when one partner feels spiritually justified.

I have purposefully mostly discussed the charge that Mormon men as priesthood holders are somehow acting within their right when exercising heavy-handed control and domination in their homes; such acts are granted them so they can properly preside over their families. I hope that I have been able to dispel the belief that that kind of self-justification is authorized by the Proclamation or counsel from Church leaders.

"Spiritual presiding" is about love and compassion; it is about serving those we love as watchmen on the tower—as a guard and as a shield. It is about respecting others and allowing them their divine agency. It is about listening without interruption, and engaging in calm and helpful discussion. It is about resolving disputes by mutual agreement rather than by the husband's edict. Ultimately, presiding in an LDS home is about following the example of the Savior.

In conclusion, I wish to raise the possibility of a very different concern, one that is less intense and less commonly voiced publicly, but which may far outnumber the charge of abuse. From personal experience, I believe a more common concern of Latter-day Saint wives is their wish that their husbands would exercise more priesthood leadership in their homes, not less. Many wives express the feeling that their husbands are providing insufficient spiritual leadership; they hope for a more conspicuous role by their husbands through the priesthood examples and standards they set in their homes.

Too often as husbands and priesthood holders, we seem to define "exercising the priesthood" to mean little more than attending meetings and doing our home teaching (on the last day of the month). Too many of us leave it for our wives to remind us of family prayer or family home evening; our wives remind the children (and sometimes us) that it is time to get ready for Church; our wives ask when we are going to read the scriptures together; it is commonly our wives who remind us that we have not been to the temple recently; and sometimes our wives even remind us of our home teaching responsibilities.

What is my evidence for this concern? First, I have often found myself in that place. Second, I have heard this plea from wives far more than complaints of abusive or domineering behavior. In our stake we often concluded a temple recommend interview by asking "Is there anything we can do for you as a Stake Presidency?" There were not a lot of requests, but the most common was "Please talk to our husbands about *setting examples* in our homes." "Please, ask them to *take more responsibility* for Family Home Evening or reading scriptures together."

Once again these responsibilities are properly shared, but concern over imbalance seems to be heavily a wife's issue. These women were not demanding a right or even a desire to hold the priesthood. They were pleading with us to help their husbands recognize their role and take a more active responsibility to *preside* in their homes—to be their watchmen on the tower; to protect and guard their families against the influences that can weaken and even destroy; and to serve as examples by exercising the powers of the priesthood for the blessing of their family.

The topic of same-gender attraction and same-sex marriage has created fierce debate in our society. In "Same-Gender Attraction and Same-Sex Marriage," Kent Brooks approaches these issues from a LDS perspective, drawing repeatedly from the teachings of Church leaders. He outlines principles that he has found helpful as he has counseled with individuals seeking answers to these and similar issues, including the importance of having the courage to ask questions, remaining patient while waiting for greater understanding, and not losing faith in what you do know because of what you do not know. He writes, "In addition to the testing common to all mortal beings, some trials are of a more personal nature and represent the individualized tutoring an omniscient God knows we need for adequate proving and growing." Then, quoting Elder Oaks, he adds, "All of us have some feelings we did not choose, but the gospel of Jesus Christ teaches us that we still have the power to resist and reform our feelings (as needed) and to assure that they do not lead us to entertain inappropriate thoughts or to engage in sinful behavior. . . . We did not choose these personal susceptibilities either, but we do choose and will be accountable for the attitudes, priorities, behavior, and 'lifestyle' we engraft upon them." He then emphasizes the Savior's role in our lives, specifically outlining the unique redemptive and enabling powers of the Atonement, which allow us to respectively be forgiven for our sins and rise above the susceptibilities of the natural man. These susceptibilities, without the Savior's help, might prevent us from achieving our potential to become like God. And it is only when we are sealed as families—built upon a marriage between man and woman—that we can receive that gift of eternal life.

Five

Same-Gender Attraction and Same-Sex Marriage

Kent R. Brooks

Same-Gender Attraction

For decades, scientists have debated the influence of nature (biological or genetic factors) and nurture (environmental or socio-cultural factors) upon personality and behavior. In recent years, the debate has frequently centered on the issue of homosexuality. Is homosexuality an inherited, inborn condition over which an individual has no control and no choice? Is it the result of socio-cultural experience, the by-product of the environment in which one is raised? Or is it a conscious choice made by thinking, reasoning beings with the capacity to weigh and choose from various alternatives? The complexity of the issue becomes even more apparent when proponents of each viewpoint cite evidence (including empirical research) that seems to support their positions.

The conflicting data are often confusing to the honest seeker of truth, especially when the conclusions drawn from scientific research seem to contradict the teachings of latter-day prophets and revealed truth. Many are left with questions. Some do not know where to go for answers. Others are hesitant even to ask because they fear the judgment, rejection, or reproof of others—especially when their questions deal with issues as sensitive and potentially divisive as same-gender attraction and same-sex marriage. As I have counseled individuals seeking answers to these and other difficult questions, I have found it helpful to begin with four foundational principles.

Four Foundational Principles

First, do not be afraid to have questions, but do have the courage to ask and use wisdom regarding who you ask. Questions, particularly when motivated by an honest desire for truth, invite revelation. We are repeatedly commanded in scripture to ask and are promised we will receive answers if we do (see 3 Ne. 27:29; D&C 4:7, 49:26, 88:63). Much of our canonized scripture came because a prophet had a question and had the faith to believe an answer would be given if he were willing to ask. It is always our privilege, as beloved sons and daughters of God, to ask our Father for answers. "If *any* of you lack wisdom, let him ask of God, that giveth to *all* men liberally, and upbraideth not; and it shall be given him. But let him ask in faith" (James 1:5–6; emphasis added). Part of asking in faith is to carefully study out our questions. That should include identifying those around us to whom we might go for help. It is always wise to look to those we sustain as prophets, seers, and revelators. The Lord counseled us to "seek learning, even by study and also by faith" (D&C 88:118). The individuals most likely to give sound answers to our questions are those who are both learned (who have themselves studied and gained an understanding of the issue) *and* who are faithful (whose first and highest allegiance is to God and who are living so as to have the companionship of the Holy Ghost in their lives).

Second, be patient as you await greater understanding. Truth is given "line upon line and precept upon precept, here a little and there a little" (2 Ne. 28:30) and comes in the Lord's "own *time*, and in his own *way*, and according to his own *will*" (D&C 88:68; emphasis added). The Lord's *timing* is influenced by how we exercise our agency. In other words, answers will be given when we have proven we are ready to receive and act in faith upon those answers. The Lord's *way* of answering our questions can be direct through personal revelation or through the teachings of living prophets and others positioned to help. Our will should be swallowed up in the *will* of God. The more we want what God wants, the more he will trust us with his sacred truths. "If thou shalt ask," He promised, "thou shalt receive revelation upon revelation, knowledge upon knowledge, that thou mayest know the mysteries and peaceable things—that which bringeth joy, that which bringeth life eternal" (D&C 42:61). The answers to some questions come easily and with comparatively little effort. Other questions require great effort, time, faith, prayer, and perhaps fasting. We cannot expect great understanding without great effort and sacrifice. It is a process—a process that requires, at times, great patience.

Third, do not lose faith in what you do know because of what you do not know. While teaching the inhabitants of Gideon, Alma sought to focus the attention of the people on the "*one thing which is of more importance than they all*—for behold, the time is not far distant that the Redeemer liveth and cometh among his people. Behold, I do not say that he will come among us at the time of his dwelling in his mortal tabernacle; for behold, the Spirit hath not said unto me that this should be the case. Now as to this thing I do not know; but this much I do know, that the Lord God hath power to do all things which are according to his word" (Alma 7:8; emphasis added). Each of us must resist the temptation to be distracted from what we *do* know by what we *do not* know. We must anchor our faith and our conduct in the truths we know to be "of more importance than they all," such as knowing God lives, that we are His children, and that His Son, Jesus Christ is the Savior and Redeemer of the world. Then, we must hold on to the answers we paid a price to obtain in the past while we seek for answers to the questions we now have in the present.

Fourth, everything in our Heavenly Father's plan is designed to help us reach our full potential and to increase our happiness. "All things are given them which are *expedient* unto men" (2 Ne. 2:27; emphasis added). That is, while God will not give us everything *we* might deem important to our current happiness or grant every capacity *we* might desire, *He* knows what is *expedient* to our growth and happiness. If we will recognize what He gives us and will embrace it, happiness is always available. Expedient to our happiness throughout our lives are His commandments. Every commandment, every law, and every covenant He gives us is evidence of *God's* love for us. Nephi testified that God "doeth not anything save it be for the benefit of the world; for he loveth the world" (2 Ne. 26:24). Every commandment, every law, and every covenant we keep—or desire to keep—is evidence of *our* love for God. To keep His commandments is to "live after the manner of happiness" (2 Ne. 5:27). Accepting and remembering God's divine motive brings peace even when we, like Nephi, may not "know the meaning of all things" (1 Ne. 11:17) in our lives or in the world around us.

The Great Plan of Happiness

Our Heavenly Father's plan is a "plan of happiness" (Alma 42:8, 16). To deal with difficult issues such as same-gender attraction and same-sex marriage and to experience the happiness available within God's plan, it is essential to understand the important elements of that plan. Before coming to this earth, we existed as individual spirits—male or female—in a premortal world. Begotten by a Heavenly Father and a Heavenly Mother, "each [one of us] is a beloved spirit son or daughter of heavenly parents." Gender was then, is now, and will always be "an essential characteristic of [our] individual . . . identity and purpose."[1] Our mortal bodies take the same form, male or

---

1. "The Family: A Proclamation to the World," *Ensign*, Nov. 1995, 102.

female, as the premortal spirits they house. Gender did not originate with mortal birth and is not the result of accident or chance.[2] Gender is part of our divine nature and is closely linked to our divine destiny. Because of our "exceeding faith and good works" and because we learned to "choose good over evil" (Alma 13:3) while in premortality, we were foreordained, according to our gender, to become husbands and fathers or wives and mothers. Exaltation in the celestial kingdom (our divine destiny) is predicated upon our faithfulness (in mortality) to those foreordained callings.

Eventually, we reached the point in premortality where we could not progress any further without a physical body and the earthly experiences that would enable us to "progress toward perfection" and eventually become "an heir of eternal life."[3] We were taught, we understood, and we accepted Heavenly Father's plan and were prepared for mortality (see D&C 138:56). We understood there would be "opposition in all things" (2 Ne. 2:11) and that we would be subject to the effects of the Fall of Adam and Eve—including disease, physical pain, temptations of the flesh, and death. Mortality was to be a probationary period—a time of testing—in which we would be required to prove our willingness to keep the commandments of God at all times and in all circumstances. We knew Satan would do everything in his power "to oppose the great plan of happiness, to corrupt the purest, most beautiful and appealing experiences of life: romance, love, marriage, and parenthood."[4]

Elder Melvin J. Ballard spoke this way of the adversary's strategy:

> All the assaults that the enemy of our souls will make to capture us will be through the ... lusts, the appetites, [and] the ambitions of the flesh. All the help that comes ... from the Lord to aid us in this struggle will come to us through the spirit that dwells within this mortal body.... Our weak [point] is in the flesh ... and when [the devil] undertakes to capture a soul he will strike at the weak point.... It is not bodies, it is immortal spirits that the devil wants. And he tries to capture them through the body, for the body can enslave the spirit, but the spirit can keep the body a servant and be its master.[5]

To become like our heavenly parents, we must learn to "yield to the enticings of the Holy Spirit and [to] put off the natural man" (Mosiah 3:19), no matter what form or fashion the natural man may take in our lives.

---

2. James E. Talmage, "The Eternity of Sex," in *The Essential James E. Talmage*, ed. James P. Harris (Salt Lake City: Signature Books, 1997), 600.

3. "The Family," 102.

4. Boyd K. Packer, "For Time and All Eternity," *Ensign*, Nov. 1993, 21.

5. Melvin J. Ballard, "The Struggle for the Soul," in *Crusader for Righteousness* (Salt Lake City: Bookcraft, 1966), 178–79, 181.

Mortality gives us the opportunity to refine our ability to exercise the God-given gift of agency—to learn, by earthly experience, to choose good instead of evil (see 2 Ne. 2:16, 27). Only by seeking to know and do the will of God, can we become like God and experience a fullness of joy. "Happiness is the object and design of our existence," said Joseph Smith, "and will be the end thereof, if we pursue the path that leads to it; and this path is virtue, uprightness, faithfulness, holiness, and keeping all the commandments of God."[6] Satan entices us to seek happiness outside of those parameters, often in ways that undermine sexual purity, obscure our eternal identity, detract from our divine nature, or divert us from our eternal destiny.

In addition to the testing common to all mortal beings, some trials are of a more personal nature and represent the individualized tutoring an omniscient God knows we need for adequate proving and growing. One thing the Lord may perhaps see fit to inflict upon us (Mosiah 3:19) or allow as a natural result of the Fall is a "thorn in the flesh" (2 Cor. 12:7), a specific weakness or susceptibility to one kind of temptation or another. "I give unto men *weakness* that they may be humble" the Lord declared (Ether 12:27; emphasis added). Some of those weaknesses or susceptibilities surface at an early age (for example, physical deformities or mental deficiencies) and appear to be inborn—the product of nature, rather than the result of individual choice. Some would place same-gender attraction in this category. Other weaknesses seem to arise from the influence of nurture—the result of how we are raised, the kind of environments to which we are exposed, or the experiences we have. Whether we attribute those susceptibilities to divine design (God made me that way), genetic inheritance from earthly parents (including inherited physical or mental weaknesses), or environmental or socio-cultural factors (how or where I was raised), the question of personal accountability arises. Am I accountable for something I did not choose? Am I responsible for or even capable of harnessing my weaknesses? Am I being untrue to myself or to what I really am if I resist them? Won't the failure to respond to my natural susceptibilities simply invite frustration and unhappiness?

Responding to these questions, Elder Dallin H. Oaks answered:

> All of us have some feelings we did not choose, but the gospel of Jesus Christ teaches us that we still have the power to resist and reform our feelings (as needed) and to assure that they do not lead us to entertain inappropriate thoughts or to engage in sinful behavior.

---

6. Joseph Smith, et al., *History of the Church of Jesus Christ of Latter-day Saints*, ed. B. H. Roberts, 7 vols. (Salt Lake City: Deseret Book, 1948 printing), 5:134–35.

Different persons have different physical characteristics and different susceptibilities to the various physical and emotional pressures we may encounter in our childhood and adult environments. We did not choose these personal susceptibilities either, but we do choose and will be accountable for the attitudes, priorities, behavior, and 'lifestyle' we engraft upon them. . . .

Some people seem to be unusually susceptible to particular actions, reactions, or addictions. Perhaps such susceptibilities are inborn or acquired without personal choice or fault. . . . One person may have feelings that draw him toward gambling. . . . Another person may have a taste for tobacco and a susceptibility to its addiction. Still another may have an unusual attraction to alcohol. . . . Other examples may include [pornography], a hot temper, a contentious manner, a covetous attitude, and so on.

In each case . . . the feelings or other characteristics that increase susceptibility to certain behavior may have some relationship to inheritance. But the relationship is probably very complex. The inherited element may be nothing more than an increased likelihood that an individual will acquire certain feelings if he or she encounters particular influences during the developmental years. But regardless of our different susceptibilities or vulnerabilities . . . we remain responsible for the exercise of our agency in the thoughts we entertain and the behavior we choose. . . .

We need to learn how to live so that a weakness that is mortal will not prevent us from achieving the goal that is eternal. . . .

Beware the argument that because a person has strong drives toward a particular act, he has no power of choice and therefore no responsibility for his actions. This contention runs counter to the most fundamental premises of the gospel of Jesus Christ. . . .

A person who insists that he is not responsible for the exercise of his free agency because he was "born that way" is trying to ignore the outcome of the War in Heaven. We *are* responsible, and if we argue otherwise, our efforts become part of the propaganda effort of the Adversary.[7]

The Role of the Savior

We have the power to choose good instead of evil and are responsible to live in harmony with the laws of God. Still, even though we are beloved

---

7. Dallin H. Oaks, "Same-Gender Attraction," *Ensign*, Oct. 1995, 9–10; emphasis in original. In this article, Elder Oaks is quoting a talk he previously gave at Brigham Young University: "Free Agency and Freedom," *Brigham Young University 1987–88 Devotional Fireside Speeches* (Provo, Utah: BYU Publications, 1988), 46–47. The edited version from which he quotes is found in *The Book of Mormon, The Doctrinal Structure*, ed. Monte S. Nyman and Charles D. Tate Jr. (Provo, Utah: BYU Religious Studies Center, 1989), 13–15.

sons and daughters of God, are endowed with a divine nature, and exercise our agency in righteousness, we are incapable of achieving our divine destiny by our merits alone. "We know that it is by grace that we are saved, after all we can do" (2 Ne. 23:25). "There is no flesh that can dwell in the presence of God, save it be through the merits, and mercy, and grace of the Holy Messiah" (2 Ne. 2:8). Whether weaknesses and sins result from nature, nurture, or a combination of both, the Savior's promise to the humble is the same: "My grace is sufficient for all men that humble themselves before me; for if they humble themselves before me, and have faith in me, then will I make weak things become strong unto them" (Ether 12:27). Therefore, "come unto Christ and be perfected in him, and deny yourselves of all ungodliness; and if ye shall deny yourselves of all ungodliness, and love God with all your might, mind and strength, then is his grace sufficient for you, that by his grace ye may be perfect in Christ" (Moro. 10:32).

The Redemptive Power of the Atonement

After being driven from the Garden of Eden for partaking of the forbidden fruit, Adam and Eve were taught repentance and the role of the Savior. They were counseled: "Wherefore, thou shalt do all that thou doest in the name of the Son, and thou shalt repent and call upon God in the name of the Son forevermore" (Moses 5:8). Adam and Eve heeded that counsel and came to know "the joy of [their] redemption and the eternal life which God giveth unto all the obedient" (Moses 5:11). As it did for our first parents, the Atonement of Jesus Christ has the power to redeem each of us from the effects of the Fall. That "great and last sacrifice" (Alma 34:13) overcame physical death and brought the blessings of resurrection and immortality to every man, woman, and child born on this earth. The Atonement also made it possible for us to be forgiven of our sins and to overcome spiritual death. Even if we act upon a weakness, or in any way violate a law of God and thereby commit sin, we can still become clean again. As we exercise faith in Jesus Christ and sincerely repent, the Savior and his Atonement can remit our sins. Even though they "be as scarlet, they shall be white as snow; though they be red like crimson, they shall be as wool" (Isa. 1:18). Elder Boyd K. Packer testified:

> In the battle of life, the adversary takes enormous numbers of prisoners, and many who know of no way to escape and are pressed into his service. Every soul confined to a concentration camp of sin and guilt has a key to the gate. The adversary cannot hold them if they know how to use it. The key is la-

beled Repentance. The twin principles of repentance and forgiveness exceed in strength the awesome power of the adversary.

I know of no sins connected with the moral standard for which we cannot be forgiven.[8]

The Enabling Power of the Atonement

The Atonement also offers an enabling power to us. The enabling power can increase our capacity to resist temptation, help us rise above all the weaknesses and susceptibilities of the natural man, and empower us to become "partakers of the divine nature" (2 Pet. 1:4). Like the redemptive power of the Atonement, the enabling power is activated by faith in Christ and acceptance of and obedience to his laws. The enabling power is a gift of compensation that makes up the difference when we do our best and still fall short. It is the power that magnifies our abilities, allowing us to do things beyond our own natural capacity. It is the power that enables us to keep trying even when we feel like giving up. It is the power that completes us or makes us perfect, thus making exaltation possible. Only through the Savior are we enabled to overcome all things and to experience a fullness of joy.

One way to access the enabling power of the Atonement is by qualifying for and earnestly seeking the gifts of the Spirit. Elder Dallin H. Oaks taught:

> We should seek after spiritual gifts. They can lead us to God. They can shield us from the power of the adversary. They can compensate for our inadequacies and repair our imperfections. . . . President George Q. Cannon taught . . . "if any of us are imperfect, it is our duty to pray for the gift that will make us perfect. . . . No man ought to say, Oh I cannot help this; it is my nature. He is not justified in it, for the reason that God has promised to give strength to correct these things, and to give gifts that will eliminate them. . . . God wants the saints to be perfected in the truth. For this purpose He gives these gifts, and bestows them upon those who seek after them."[9]

Our Heavenly Father's plan is perfect. Regardless of the temptations we face, the deprivations we experience, or the susceptibilities we may have, He has provided *a* way—obedience to the laws and ordinances of the gospel, and *the* Way—a Savior by whom we can be redeemed and enabled to return to the presence of the Father and enjoy eternal life and exaltation. Within that plan, each of us is "free to choose liberty and eternal life

---

8. Boyd K. Packer, "Our Moral Environment," *Ensign*, http://www.lds.org/ensign/1992/05/our-moral-environment (accessed Sept. 10, 2013).

9. Dallin H. Oaks, "Spiritual Gifts," *Ensign*, Sept. 1986, 82.

through the great Mediator of all men, or to choose captivity and death, according to the captivity and power of the devil; for he seeketh that all men might be miserable like unto himself" (2 Ne. 2:27).

Same-Sex Marriage

One of the most controversial and hotly debated issues of our day is same-sex marriage. Some who have experienced same-gender attraction have chosen to act upon those attractions, to enter into same-sex relationships, and to press for the right to a legal marriage. To deny them that privilege, they claim, is a violation of their civil rights. Others argue that marriage should be defined solely as a relationship between a man and a woman. They oppose same-sex marriage and view it as a moral, rather than a civil or political matter. Some Latter-day saints who oppose same-sex marriage still wonder why the Church, which maintains a strict policy of political neutrality, has been so outspoken on this particular issue and why it has taken such a proactive approach against the legalization of same-sex marriage.

One answer to that question is found in the role and responsibility of prophets. In the Doctrine and Covenants, prophets, seers, and revelators are described as "plants of renown and watchmen upon her walls" (D&C 124:61). They are tried and true men of righteousness, planted in the midst of the people and positioned upon the walls where they can watch for, recognize, and warn the people of impending dangers. Elder Henry B. Eyring said, "Because the Lord is kind, He calls servants to warn people of danger. That call to warn is made harder and more important by the fact that the warnings of most worth are about dangers that people do not yet think are real."[10] There are many who argue there would be no *real* danger—to individuals or to society as a whole—if same-sex marriage were legalized. They cannot *see* the danger recognized by the Lord's *seers*.

President Ezra Taft Benson said: "If we are living the gospel, we will feel in our hearts that the First Presidency of the Church not only have the right, but are also duty bound under heaven to give counsel on any subject which affects the temporal or spiritual welfare of the Latter-day Saints, regardless of whether or not some men may think such counsel may have political implications."[11] *Our* duty, the Lord said, is to "give heed unto all [their] words and commandments . . . as if from mine own mouth, in all patience and faith" (D&C 21:4–5). It certainly can be a test of our faith and

---

10. Henry B. Eyring, "A Voice of Warning," *Ensign*, Nov. 1998, 32.
11. Ezra Taft Benson, *So Shall Ye Reap* (Salt Lake City: Deseret Book, 1960), 61.

a trial of our patience to be obedient to counsel we may not agree with or understand. But, "how we respond to the words of a living prophet when he tells us what we need to know, but would rather not hear, is [the real] test of our faithfulness [to our testimony of prophets]."[12]

Regarding the position of the Church on same-sex marriage, President Gordon B. Hinckley explained:

> We regard it not only as our right but as our duty to oppose those forces which we feel undermine the moral fiber of society. Much of our effort . . . is in association with others whose interests are similar. . . . Latter-day Saints are working as part of a coalition to safeguard traditional marriage from forces in our society which are attempting to redefine that sacred institution. God-sanctioned marriage between a man and a woman has been the basis of civilization for thousands of years. There is no justification to redefine what marriage is. Such is not our right, and those who try will find themselves answerable to God. Some portray legalization of so-called same-sex marriage as a civil right. This is not a matter of civil rights. It is a matter of morality. Others question our constitutional right as a church to raise our voice on an issue that is of critical importance to the future of the family. We believe that defending this sacred institution by working to preserve traditional marriage lies clearly within our religious and constitutional prerogatives. Indeed, we are compelled by our doctrine to speak out.[13]

The doctrine to which President Hinckley referred is the revealed doctrine of marriage and the family. Unless we understand that doctrine, we can never understand why the Church is so pro-family, why it is opposed to the legalization of same-sex marriage, and why as individual members it is especially important, on this matter, to be true to our covenant "to stand as witnesses of God at all times and in all things, and in all places." Indeed, the blessings of being "redeemed of God" and being "numbered with those of the first resurrection," (Mosiah 18:9) with those who will inherit eternal life, are predicated upon faithfulness to that, and other covenant responsibilities. Let me address a few important ideas relative to the doctrine of marriage and family that may help you better understand the position the Church has taken on same-sex marriage.

First, God's creation of both Adam and Eve, a *male* and a *female* was essential to the plan of happiness. The crowning achievement of the cre-

---

12. Ezra Taft Benson, "Fourteen Fundamentals of a Living Prophet," address given at Brigham Young University, February 26, 1980. Available at http://speeches.byu.edu/?act=viewitem&id=88 (accessed May 28, 2013).

13. Gordon B. Hinckley, "Why We Do Some of the Things We Do," *Ensign*, Nov. 1999, 54.

ation of this earth was the creation of Adam and Eve. "God created man in his own image, in the image of God created he him; *male* and *female* created he them" (Gen. 1:27). Thus, God's plan began with, and required, both a *man* and a *woman*. Why would both a man and a woman be essential in God's plan? And, why would an omniscient God define marriage uniquely and solely as a relationship between a *man* and a *woman*?

"All human beings," states the Proclamation on the Family, "are created in the image of God. Each is a beloved spirit son or daughter of heavenly parents, and, as such, each has a divine nature and destiny. Gender is an essential characteristic of individual premortal, mortal, and eternal identity and purpose."[14] In our day, "gender differences increasingly are dismissed as trivial, irrelevant, or transient, thus undermining God's purpose in creating both men and women."[15] Proponents of same-sex marriage argue that gender is irrelevant in marriage as long as two people love each other and are fully committed to the relationship. However, that argument fails to recognize the revealed truth that while both men and women possess a *divine* nature, their natures are different. Elder Boyd K. Packer said "there is a distinct *masculine* nature and a distinct *feminine* nature [and both are] essential to the foundation of the home and the family."[16] The full development of either the masculine or the feminine nature is dependent upon the presence of the other. Paul taught the Corinthians: "Neither is the *man* without the *woman*, neither the *woman* without the *man*, in the Lord" (1 Cor. 11:11; emphasis added). Stated another way: "It takes a *man* and a *woman* to make a *man* or a *woman*."[17] Further, for either a man or a woman to become like God, to become partakers of *His* divine nature, it requires the influence and complementing strengths of both a man and a woman.

Men and women are each endowed "with unique traits specifically fitted for their individual responsibilities [and roles].... Those roles are different.... In the Lord's plan, it takes two—a *man* and a *woman*—to form a whole. Indeed, a *husband* and *wife* are not two identical halves, but a wondrous, divinely determined combination of complementary capacities

---

14. "The Family," 102.

15. "The Divine Institution of Marriage," The Mormon Newsroom, August 13, 2008, http://www.mormonnewsroom.org/article/the-divine-institution-of-marriage (accessed May 28, 2013). This statement was released in 2008 and explains the Church's reasons for defending marriage between a man and a woman as an issue of moral imperative.

16. Boyd K. Packer, "The Relief Society," *Ensign*, May 1998, 73.

17. Russell M. Nelson, *The Power within Us* (Salt Lake City: Deseret Book, 1988), 109; emphasis added.

and characteristics."[18] "Those complementing differences are the very key to the plan of happiness."[19] "Whatever disturbs or weakens or tends to erase that difference erodes the family and reduces the probability of happiness for all concerned."[20]

"The first commandment that God gave to Adam and Eve [and symbolically to every married couple] pertained to their potential for parenthood as *husband* and *wife*."[21] They were commanded to "be fruitful, and multiply, and replenish the earth" (Gen. 1:28). Certainly one of the most basic and most important distinctions between a man and a woman is found in their physiological differences—differences which allow them to unite as one flesh and to employ the distinct powers of procreation found within each one for the purpose of bringing children into the world. Packer taught:

> The plan of happiness requires the righteous union of *male* and *female*, *man* and *woman*, *husband* and *wife*. . . . A body patterned after the image of God was created for Adam and he was introduced into the Garden. At first, Adam was alone. He held the priesthood, but alone he could not fulfill the purposes of his creation. No other *man* would do. Neither alone nor with other men could Adam progress. Nor could Eve with another *woman*. It was so then. It is so today.[22]

The Lord said, "Marriage is ordained of God unto man. Wherefore, it is lawful [i.e., in accordance with the law and pattern established by God in the very beginning] that *he* should have one *wife*, and they twain shall be *one flesh*, and all this that the earth might answer the end of its creation; And that it might be filled with the measure of man" (D&C 49:15–17). In our day, the First Presidency and the Council of Twelve Apostles have proclaimed "that marriage between a *man* and a *woman* is ordained of God and that the *family* is central to the Creator's plan for the eternal destiny of His children.[23] Same-sex marriage prevents the earth from "answering the end of its creation" because two people of the same gender cannot, by themselves, procreate. Years ago, the First Presidency explained:

> The Lord has told us that it is the duty of every *husband* and *wife* [in other words, every married couple] to obey the command given to Adam to multiply and replenish the earth, so that the legions of choice spirits waiting for

---

18. Richard G. Scott, "The Joy of Living the Great Plan of Happiness," *Ensign*, Nov. 1996, 73; emphasis added.
19. Boyd K. Packer, "For Time and All Eternity," *Ensign*, Nov. 1993, 21.
20. Packer, "The Relief Society," 73.
21. "The Family," 102.
22. Packer, "For Time and All Eternity," 21; emphasis added.
23. "The Family," 102; emphasis added.

their tabernacles of flesh may come here and move forward under God's great design to become perfect souls, for without these fleshly tabernacles they cannot progress to their God-planned destiny. . . . No loftier duty than this can be assumed by mortals.[24]

Too often, the emphasis in the world today is upon rights, instead of responsibilities. It is important to recognize, "the Church does not object to rights (already established in California) [for same-sex couples] regarding hospitalization and medical care, fair housing and employment rights, or probate rights, so long as these do not infringe on the integrity of the family or the constitutional rights of churches and their adherents to administer and practice their religion free from government interference."[25]

But, the Church opposes same-sex marriage because same-sex couples disregard one of the most important and most basic God-given responsibilities associated with marriage—the responsibility to procreate and bring children into the world. Further, same-sex marriage prevents children from receiving the birthright blessing extended by God to all of His beloved sons and daughters. All children, the Proclamation on the Family says, "are entitled to birth within the bonds of matrimony, and to be reared by a *father* and a *mother* who honor marital vows with complete fidelity. . . . We warn that individuals who violate covenants of chastity . . . or who fail to fulfill family responsibilities will one day stand accountable before God."[26] Though "some couples who marry will not have children, either by choice or because of infertility, the special status of marriage is nonetheless closely linked to the inherent powers and responsibilities of procreation, and to the inherent differences between the genders."[27] Privilege, such as the privilege of employing the powers of procreation or of parenthood, always brings responsibility and responsibility always brings accountability.

Second, marriage, which is of divine origin, was intended from the beginning to be an *eternal* union. Before the Fall, Adam and Eve were sealed in an *eternal* relationship as husband and wife *by God himself*.[28] Since death

---

24. "Message of the First Presidency," *Report of the Semi-Annual Conference of the Church of Jesus Christ of Latter-day Saints*, Oct. 6, 1942 (Salt Lake City: Church of Jesus Christ of Latter-day Saints, semi-annual), 12.
25. "The Divine Institution of Marriage."
26. "The Family," 102; emphasis added.
27. "The Divine Institution of Marriage."
28. See Joseph Smith, et al., *History of the Church of Jesus Christ of Latter-day Saints*, ed. B. H. Roberts, 7 vols. (Salt Lake City: Deseret Book, 1948 printing), 2:320; Spencer W. Kimball, "The Blessings and Responsibilities of Womanhood," *Ensign*, Mar. 1976, 72; Joseph Fielding Smith, *Answers to Gospel Questions*, 5 vols.

had not yet entered the world at the time of their marriage, their union was intended to be an eternal relationship. The Savior taught, "From the beginning of the creation God made them *male* and *female*. For this cause shall a *man* leave his father and his mother, and shall cleave to his *wife*.... What therefore God hath joined together, let not man put asunder" (Mark 10:7–9; emphasis added). He explained that Moses had permitted divorce (and thus, a temporary union) only "because of the hardness of your hearts" and because the people would not live the higher law of eternal marriage, "but from the beginning it was not so" (Matt. 19:8).

In a similar way, knowing that marriage is a divine institution and was defined by God as an eternal relationship between a *man* and a *woman* only, we could also say, "therefore, let not man put asunder" the very definition of marriage. As President Hinckley declared, "such is not *our* right, and those who try will find themselves answerable to God." To redefine marriage as any legal relationship between two consenting adults is to usurp a right that belongs only to the Creator. President Hinckley warned that "unless there is an underlying acknowledgement . . . a strong and fervent conviction . . . that the family is an instrument of the Almighty, [that] it is His creation,"[29] the world-wide disintegration of the family will continue and worsen in the future. The disintegration of the family, warned the First Presidency and Council of the Twelve Apostles, "will bring upon individuals, communities, and nations the calamities foretold by ancient and modern prophets."[30] Any who knowingly contribute to the disintegration of the family will bear responsibility for their actions and will be accountable to God.

When the law of marriage was restored to the Prophet Joseph Smith in our dispensation, the Lord made it clear that "all who will have a blessing at my hands shall abide the law which was appointed for that blessing [i.e., the same law that was established by God in the beginning], and the conditions thereof [e.g., between a man and a woman only] or he shall be damned" (D&C 132:5–6; emphasis added). "Behold, mine house is a house of order, saith the Lord God, and not a house of confusion." To emphasize His point, the Lord then posed three questions: "Will I accept of an offering . . . that is not made in my name? Or will I receive at your hands that which I have not appointed? And will I appoint unto you, saith the Lord, except it be by law, even as I and my Father ordained unto you, before the world was?" (D&C 132:9–11).

(Salt Lake City: Deseret Book, 1957–66), 5:65; emphasis added.
    29. Gordon B. Hinckley, "Look to the Future," *Ensign*, Nov. 1997, 69.
    30. "The Family," 102.

The Lord then answered his own questions, saying, "I am the Lord thy God; and I give unto you this commandment—that no man shall come unto the Father but by me or by my word, which is my law, saith the Lord. And everything that is in the world, whether it be ordained of men, by thrones, or principalities, or powers, or things of name, whatsoever they may be, that are not by me or by my word, saith the Lord, shall be thrown down, and shall not remain after men are dead, neither in nor after the resurrection, saith the Lord your God. For whatsoever things remain are by me; and whatsoever things are not by me shall be shaken and destroyed. . . . Their covenant and marriage are not of force [i.e., not valid] when they are dead and when they are out of the world" (D&C 132:12–15).

Even the vows made in a civil marriage include the commitment to, at least, remain together until death. One of the social blights of our day is the high rate of divorce. Within Heavenly Father's plan, marriage was always intended to be eternal. Nevertheless, the Church recognizes that, in some circumstances, divorce may be necessary. Proponents of gay rights often point to the high divorce rate of heterosexual couples and claim the longevity and stability of same-sex relationships is no worse. However, research does not support that contention. In a study conducted by the National Center for Health Statistics in 2001, it was found that 66 percent of first marriages (for heterosexual couples) lasted more than ten years while 50 percent of them remained intact for twenty years or longer.[31] Similar results were found in a study commissioned by the U.S. Census Bureau in 2002.[32] In comparison, the 2003–2004 Gay/Lesbian Consumer Online Census surveyed the lifestyles of 7,862 homosexuals. Of those who reported being in a "current relationship," only 15 percent had been in that relationship for more than twelve years. Only 5 percent had remained a couple for twenty years.[33] While the results of these studies certainly do not represent absolute predictors of the longevity of homosexual relationships,

---

31. Matthew D. Bramlett and William D. Mosher, "First Marriage Dissolution, Divorce and Remarriage: United States," *Advance Data, National Center for Health Statistics* (May 31, 2001): 1. Citations for notes 31–33 and much of the accompany text have been directly copied from Timothy J. Daily, "Comparing the Lifestyles of Homosexual Couples to Married Couples," Family Research Council website, April 4, 2004, http://www.frc.org/get.cfm?i=IS04C02 (accessed July 24, 2013).

32. Rose M. Kreider and Jason M. Fields, "Number, Timing, and Duration of Marriages and Divorces: 1996," *Current Population Reports, P70-80, U.S. Census Bureau, Washington, D.C.* (February 2002): 5.

33. "Largest Gay Study Examines 2004 Relationships," *GayWire Latest Breaking Releases*, www.glcensus.org.

they do show that few same-sex relationships achieve the longevity common in most heterosexual marriages.

Far more significant than how long a marriage may or may not last in mortality is the reality that without repentance, same-sex marriage prevents participants from returning to the presence of God as heirs of eternal life and make it impossible for a couple and/or family to be united eternally. But why is that the case? Eternal life, or exaltation ("eternal fatherhood and eternal motherhood"),[34] is not only predicated upon faithful obedience to the commandments of God. It also requires the sealing ordinance of *husband* and *wife* available only in the temples of God. The Lord said, "In the celestial glory there are three heavens of degrees; and in order to obtain the highest a man [and a woman] must enter into this order of the priesthood (meaning the new and everlasting covenant of marriage); and if [they] do not, [they] cannot obtain it" (see D&C 131:1–3).

The Proclamation on the Family declares, "Marriage between a *man* and a *woman* is *ordained* of God."[35] Elder Packer taught that to ordain is the "process of putting things in rows of proper relationship," and an ordinance is the "ceremony by which things are put in proper order."[36] For a marriage to be *ordained* of God—to be put in full and proper order within the eternal plan of God—it must include a *man* and a *woman* and it must involve the sealing ordinance available only in the temple. To be eligible to receive that ordinance, participants must be worthy, including living in strict accordance with the law of chastity. Temple ordinances and covenants "make it *possible* for individuals to return to the presence of God and for families to be united eternally."[37] The *possibility* of an eternal union offered by the sealing ordinance becomes a *reality* only when both husband and wife remain faithful to the covenants associated with that ordinance. Since a marriage between two men or two women is not, and never will be *ordained* of God, it can never be sealed in holy temples. Further, an unsealed marriage means an unsealed family since children can only be sealed to a *mother* and a *father* who have first been sealed to one another. Thus, the Church stands strongly opposed to same-sex marriage because exaltation and eternal family units are at stake.

The Lord declared: "For behold, this is my work and my glory—to bring to pass the immortality and eternal life of man" (Moses 1:39). Immortality,

---

34. Ezra Taft Benson, *Teachings of Ezra Taft Benson* (Salt Lake City: Bookcraft, 1988), 548.
35. "The Family," 102; emphasis added.
36. Boyd K. Packer, *The Holy Temple* (Salt Lake City: Bookcraft, 1980), 145.
37. "The Family," 102; emphasis added.

living forever and possessing a body that will never again be subject to physical pain, sickness, or death, was made possible by the Atonement and resurrection of the Savior. Immortality is a gift freely given to all who live on this earth, regardless of the kind of lives they live. Eternal life, the privilege of living in the presence of God as an exalted being, is available only upon conditions of repentance and subsequent obedience, including being worthy to receive and then remaining faithful to all ordinances of salvation. Eternal life was the supreme purpose of the creation of this earth, the Atonement of Jesus Christ, and the restoration of the fullness of the gospel.[38] All the Savior has done and is doing for mankind—as well as the ultimate purpose of all we teach in the Church—is to "unite parents and children in faith in the Lord Jesus Christ [so] that they are happy at home, sealed in an eternal marriage, linked to their generations, and assured of exaltation in the presence of our Heavenly Father."[39] Only when a *husband* and *wife* are sealed to each other and to their children in holy temples, and are then linked to their generations, can family relationships be placed in rows of proper relationship and become eternal. Were these things not to happen, "the whole earth would be utterly wasted at [the Savior's] coming" (D&C 2:3).

Unless participants fully repent, same-sex marriage negates the possibility of eternal life. Therefore, in an ultimate sense the practice is a mockery of the Atonement and the price paid by the Savior to redeem all mankind. Elder Jeffery R. Holland declared:

> When one mocks the Son of Righteousness, one steps into a realm of heat hotter and holier than the noonday sun. You cannot do so and not be burned. Please, never say: 'Who does it hurt? Why not a little freedom? . . . You cannot with impunity 'crucify Christ afresh' (Heb. 6:6). 'Flee fornication,' (1 Cor. 6:18) Paul cries, and flee 'anything like unto it,' (D&C 59:6) the Doctrine and Covenants adds. Why? Well, for one reason because of the incalculable suffering in both body and spirit endured by the Savior of the world so that we could flee. We owe Him something for that. Indeed, we owe Him everything for that. 'Ye are not your own,' Paul says. 'Ye [have been] bought with a price: therefore glorify God in your body, and in your spirit, which are God's' (1 Cor. 6:19–20).[40]

Eternal life is the divine destiny of every son and daughter of God! Each of us, said Elder Eyring "must have [that] goal not just in our minds but in our hearts. What we want is eternal life in families. We don't just want it if that is what works out, nor do we want something approach-

---

38. M. Russell Ballard, "Equality through Diversity," *Ensign*, Nov. 1993, 90.
39. Boyd K. Packer, "The Shield of Faith," *Ensign*, May 1995, 8.
40. Jeffery R. Holland, "Personal Purity," *Ensign*, Nov. 1998, 76.

ing eternal life. We want eternal life . . . whatever its cost in effort, pain, and sacrifice."[41] Eternal life must be more than our hope. It must be our determination! The Church and its members have a sacred responsibility to bring people to Christ by whom eternal life is then made possible. We must follow the example of Ezra, of old who "prepared his heart to seek the law of the Lord, and to do *it*, and [then] to teach" (Ezra 7:10) it to others.

Third, the Church takes a strong stand against same-sex marriage because it believes the practice will threaten the moral fiber of society as a whole and will undermine the foundation of civilization. "God-sanctioned marriage between a man and a woman," said President Hinckley, "has been the basis of civilization for thousands of years." The moral decline of society has, throughout history, led to the downfall of civilization. It was so with Sodom and Gomorrah, where among other things, homosexuality was rampant. The Old Testament records a disturbing account that illustrates the degree to which the moral underpinnings of these cities had eroded. Lot, Abraham's brother, was visited by several holy men who had been among the people. Knowing the holy men were staying with Lot, some of the townsmen, driven by their lustful desires, went to Lot's house and pounded on his door. Genesis 19:5 reads: "And they called unto Lot and said, where are the men which came in to thee this night? Bring them out unto us, that we may know (i.e., rape) them." It was shortly thereafter that Sodom and Gomorrah were destroyed by "brimstone and fire" (Gen. 19:24).

In Paul's day, homosexual relationships were also commonplace. Paul wrote: "Wherefore God also gave them up to uncleanness through the lusts of their own hearts, to dishonour their own bodies between themselves: Who changed the truth of God into a lie, and worshipped and served the creature more than the Creator. For this cause God gave them up unto vile affections: for even their women did change the natural use into that which is against nature: And likewise also the men, leaving the natural use of the woman, burned in their lust one toward another; men with men working that which is unseemly, and receiving in themselves that recompence of their error which was meet" (Rom. 1:24–27).

Since the beginning of this earth's history, same-sex relationships have been promoted by the adversary to undermine God's plan of happiness. In our day, Elder Packer has warned: "Like a ship without a compass, society drifts from the family values which anchored us in the past. We are caught in a current of moral pollution so strong that unless we correct our course,

---

41. Henry B. Eyring, *To Draw Closer to God: A Collection of Discourses* (Salt Lake City: Deseret Book, 2004), 161.

civilization, as we know it, will surely be wrecked to pieces. The standards of the world are constantly adjusted to what *is*. The standards of the Church are fixed on what *ought to be*."[42]

"The Church has a single, undeviating standard of sexual morality."[43] "God has commanded that the sacred powers of procreation are to be employed only between *man* and *woman*, lawfully wedded as *husband* and *wife*."[44] Sexual relations between two unmarried people of any gender are a sin. Sexual relations between two partners of the same gender, even if married, also represent a violation of divine mandate. Alma said sexual sins are "most abominable above all sins save it be the shedding of innocent blood or denying the Holy Ghost" (Alma 39:5). Sin of that magnitude affects more than the individuals involved; it weakens society as a whole.

Pitirim A. Sorokin, founder of the sociology department at Harvard University, conducted a sociological study of major civilizations of the world, their rise and their fall; he concluded that common threads in the decline and demise of each one were deviations in the sexual and marital practices of their people. Concerned for the future of our own civilization, he warned, "if more and more individuals are brought up in the sex-saturated atmosphere [that now exists], then without deep [internalization] of religious, moral, and legal norms of behavior, they will become rudderless boats controlled only by the winds of their environment."[45] He noted that "the most decisive factor in the survival and well-being" of a society is marriage and that "any change in marriage behavior, any increase in sexual promiscuity, and illicit sexual relations is pregnant with momentous consequences" that would "drastically affect the lives of millions, deeply disturb the community and decisively influence the future of society. . . . In the long run, such a society would be increasingly composed of self-centered egoists incapable of acting altruistically and of being true good neighbors."[46] Similarly, Elder Neal A. Maxwell said, "take away basic moral standards, and observe how quickly tolerance changes into permissiveness. . . . Take away regard for the seventh commandment, and behold the current celebration of sex, the secular religion with its

---

42. Quoted in "President Packer Addresses Diplomats," *Ensign*, June 1995, 74.
43. "The Divine Institution of Marriage."
44. "The Family," 102; emphasis added.
45. Pitirim A. Sorokin, *The American Sex Revolution* (Boston: Porter Sargent, 1956), 55. Citations for notes 45 and 46 and the accompanying text were directly copied from Michael Craven, "In Defense of Marriage – Part III," Battle for Truth, July 21, 2008, http://www.battlefortruth.org/ArticlesDetail.asp?id=298 (accessed Jul 24, 2013).
46. Ibid., 6–7, 12.

own liturgy of lust and supporting music. Its theology focuses on 'self.' Its hereafter is 'now.' Its chief ritual is 'sensation'—though, ironically, it finally desensitizes its obsessed adherents, who become 'past feeling.'"[47]

Numerous studies have shown the majority of married *husbands and wives* remain faithful to their marital vows. For example, a study published in 1997 found that 77 percent of married men and 88 percent of married women had remained faithful to their partners.[48] Similarly, in a national survey conducted and published by the University of Chicago, 75 percent of husbands and 85 percent of wives reported they had maintained complete fidelity to their spouses.[49]

In contrast, studies have shown significant patterns of promiscuity among *homosexual partners*. One study found that male homosexuals who reported being committed to a "steady" companion still had an average of eight sexual partners each year.[50] Another study found that 43 percent of white male homosexuals had sex with 500 or more partners in their lifetimes while 28 percent of those surveyed reported having one thousand or more sex partners.[51] The legalization of same-sex marriage would entitle homosexual couples to adopt children or to act as foster parents. Promiscuous patterns certainly can and do occur among heterosexual couples, and children experience the consequences of parental infidelity and the subsequent disharmony and divorce that often follow. However, the preceding studies suggest greater tendencies for infidelity and break-up among same-sex couples than among heterosexual couples. Consequently, children adopted by same-sex couples or children who live under the

---

47. Neal A. Maxwell, "Put Off the Natural Man, and Come Off Conqueror," *Ensign*, Nov. 1990, 15.

48. Michael W. Wiederman, "Extramarital Sex: Prevalence and Correlates in a National Survey," *Journal of Sex Research* 34 (1997): 170. Citations for notes 48–51 and much of the accompany text have been directly copied from Timothy J. Daily, "Comparing the Lifestyles of Homosexual Couples to Married Couples," Family Research Council website, April 4, 2004, http://www.frc.org/get.cfm?i=IS04C02 (accessed July 24, 2013).

49. E. O. Laumann, et al., *The Social Organization of Sexuality: Sexual Practices in the United States* (Chicago: University of Chicago Press, 1994), 216.

50. Maria Xiridou, et al, "The Contribution of Steady and Casual Partnerships to the Incidence of HIV Infection among Homosexual Men in Amsterdam," *AIDS* 17 (2003): 1031.

51. A. P. Bell and M. S. Weinberg, *Homosexualities: A Study of Diversity Among Men and Women* (New York: Simon and Schuster, 1978), 308, 309; see also A. P. Bell, M. S. Weinberg, and S. K. Hammersmith, *Sexual Preference* (Bloomington: Indiana University Press, 1981).

guardianship of same-sex foster parents might then be more likely to suffer the consequences of parental promiscuity or the dissolution of the marriage. But, even if same-sex marriage partners were faithful to each other and the marriage remained intact, the same lifestyle exemplified by same-sex parents would be more likely embraced by their adopted or foster children and promiscuity might become the pattern of the next generation. The results of a longitudinal study, reported in 1996, found children of homosexual parents were more likely to engage in a homosexual relationship or to at least consider doing so than children of heterosexual parents.[52]

Studies have repeatedly shown the most favorable environment in which to raise children is in a home with both a *mother* and a *father* who love and are committed to each other.[53] President James E. Faust warned:

> For us to have successful homes, values must be taught, and there must be rules, there must be standards, there must be absolutes.... A number of cultures are becoming essentially valueless, and many of the younger people in those societies are becoming moral cynics. As whole societies have decayed and lost their moral identity and so many homes are broken, the best hope is to turn greater attention and effort to the teaching of the next generation—our children. In order to do this, we must first reinforce the primary teachers of children ... the parents. The best environment should be in the home. Somehow, someway, we must try harder to make our homes stronger so that they will stand as sanctuaries against the unwholesome, pervasive moral dry rot around us.[54]

David Popenoe wrote: "The burden of social science evidence supports the idea that gender differentiated parenting is important for human devel-

---

52. S. Golombok and F. Tasker, "Do Parents Influence the Sexual Orientation of Their Children?" *Developmental Psychology*, 3–11, 32.

53. David Blankenhorn, *Fatherless America: Confronting Our Most Urgent Social Problem* (New York: Basic Books, 1995); Barbara Schneider, Allison Atteberry, and Ann Owens, *Family Matters: Family Structure and Child Outcomes* (Birmingham, Ala.: Alabama Policy Institute: June 2005); David Popenoe, *Life Without Father* (New York: Martin Kessler Books, 1996); David Popenoe and Barbara Defoe Whitehead, *The State of Our Unions 2007: The Social Health of Marriage in America* (Piscataway, N.J. (Rutgers University): The National Marriage Project, July 2007), 21–25; and Maggie Gallagher and Joshua K. Baker, "Do Moms and Dads Matter? Evidence from the Social Sciences on Family Structure and the Best Interests of the Child," *Margins Law Journal* 4:161 (2004). All references in notes 53, 54, and 55 were copied from "The Divine Institution of Marriage," LDS Newsroom, August 13, 2008, http://newsroom.lds.org/ldsnewsroom/eng/commentary/the-divine-institution-of-marriage (accessed October 20, 2009).

54. James E. Faust, "A Thousand Threads of Love," *Ensign*, Oct 2005, 2.

opment and that the contribution of fathers to childrearing is unique and irreplaceable."[55] Elaborating further, he noted, "the complementarity of *male* and *female* parenting styles is striking and of enormous importance to a child's overall development. It is sometimes said that fathers express more concern for the child's longer-term development, while mothers focus on the child's immediate well-being (which, of course, in its own way has everything to do with a child's long-term well-being). What is clear is that children have dual needs that must be met: one for independence and the other for relatedness, one for challenge and the other for support."[56] The Proclamation on the Family clearly differentiates, "By divine design, *fathers* are to preside over their families in love and righteousness and are responsible to provide the necessities of life and protection for their families. *Mothers* are primarily responsible for the nurture of their children. In these sacred responsibilities, *fathers* and *mothers* are obligated to help one another as equal partners."[57]

As the Church takes a strong and clear stance against same-sex marriage, it also opposes, as President Hinckley articulated, any "hatred, intolerance, or abuse of those who profess homosexual tendencies, either individually or as a group." "Our hearts reach out to those who refer to themselves as gays and lesbians," President Hinckley said. "We love and honor them as sons and daughters of God. They are welcome in the Church. It is expected, however, that they follow the same God-given rules of conduct that apply to everyone else, whether single or married."[58] Tolerance is a word we hear continually throughout the world. As a virtue, tolerance has replaced charity as the greatest of all in the minds of so many people. As President Hinckley stressed, we *are* to be tolerant. But, it is essential to understand the meaning of tolerance. In the Church we are often taught we must love the sinner without accepting the sin. The Savior said we are "required to forgive all men" (D&C 64:10). To belittle, to humiliate, or to be unforgiving of others whose views or practices differ from ours would be unbecoming a Latter-day Saint. A common definition of *tolerance* is "a fair, objective, and permissive attitude toward those whose opinions, practices, race, religion, nationality, etc., differ from one's own."[59] Without question, we must be tolerant of others. But, as Elder Nelson pointed out, "there is a difference

---

55. David Popenoe, *Life Without Father* (New York: The Free Press, 1996), 146.
56. Ibid., 145.
57. "The Family," 102; emphasis added.
58. Hinckley, "Why We Do Some of the Things We Do," 58.
59. See, for example, the definition of "tolerance" at Dictionary.com, http://dictionary.reference.com/browse/tolerance (accessed July 24, 2013).

between *tolerance* and *tolerate*. Your gracious *tolerance* for an individual does not grant him or her license to do wrong, nor does your tolerance obligate you to *tolerate* his or her misdeed. That distinction is fundamental to an understanding of this vital virtue."[60] To tolerate, popularly defined, is "to allow the existence, presence, practice or act without prohibition or hindrance."[61] We can love and forgive all men without condoning, advocating, endorsing or defending sin. "Tolerance," said Elder Oaks, "obviously requires a non-contentious manner of relating toward one another's differences. But tolerance does not require abandoning one's standards or one's opinions on political or public policy choices. Tolerance is a way of reacting to diversity, not a command to insulate it from examination."[62] Speaking at the World Congress of Families, Elder Bruce C. Hafen of the Seventy observed, "although society may *tolerate* homosexual behavior, the majority oppose same-sex marriage. Most people intuitively recognize that if the law endorses everything it tolerates, we will eventually tolerate everything and endorse nothing—except tolerance."[63]

Conclusion

The first and great commandment is to "love the Lord thy God with all thy heart, and with all thy soul, and with all thy mind.... And the second is like unto it, Thou shalt love thy neighbor as thyself" (Matt. 22:37–39). Exaltation will come to the valiant, those who have learned to put God first in their lives and to stand on the Lord's side of every issue. Pleasing him and doing his will should be our highest priority. But, we must also never forget the second commandment is to love all of his children and to help bring them to Christ. It is important that we strive to be courageous *defenders* of the faith without being *offensive* and to establish *boundary* lines without turning them into *battle* lines.

---

60. Russell M. Nelson, "Teach Us Tolerance and Love," *Ensign*, May 1994, 69.

61. See, for example, the definition of "tolerate" at Dictionary.com, http://dictionary.reference.com/browse/tolerate (accessed July 24, 2013).

62. Dallin H. Oaks, "Weightier Matters," Address given at Brigham Young University, February 9, 1999. Available at http://speeches.byu.edu/?act=viewitem&id=669 (accessed May 28, 2013).

63. Quoted in *LDS Church News*, March 29, 1997.

In "Toward a Post-Heterosexual Mormon Theology," Taylor Petrey explores how "Mormons might imagine different kinds of sealing relationships other than heterosexual marriage." He focuses on homosexual relationships, rather than either desires or practices, since ideal heterosexuality is also in terms of eternal relationships and not solely desires or practices. He concedes: "Some may feel that no reconciliation is possible, that LDS teachings cannot and should not accept homosexual relationships as intelligible" and that "position is certainly viable." But, he thinks, this position "requires defense rather than simply repetition and assertion." Since "much of the theological objection to homosexual relationships lies in current LDS understandings of the afterlife and the kinds of relationships that will exist there," Petrey focuses on three common understandings that seem to pose problems for the possibility of homosexual marriage in the eternities: first, that eternal relationships, at least among those who occupy the highest degree of the celestial kingdom, are reproductive relationships; second, that "the sealing ordinance binds these reproductive families together, sealing only those who can presumably reproduce either in this life or the next"; and third, that "the heterosexual pairs of men and women should possess the proper 'gender,' which is eternal. Homosexual relationships cannot be eternal because they are not able to reproduce by means of natural biological methods and confuse the natural gender they should possess." After taking examining these, Petrey suggests how "it may be possible to imagine sealed homosexual relationships as compatible with key doctrines of Mormonism."

Six

Toward a Post-Heterosexual Mormon Theology[1]

Taylor G. Petrey

> *Whatsoever you seal on earth shall be sealed in heaven; and whatsoever you bind on earth, in my name and by my word, saith the Lord, it shall be eternally bound in the heavens.* (D&C 132:46)

The issue of homosexual relationships is among the most public struggles facing religious groups in America today. The issue is not as simple as gay people versus religious groups, as rhetoric on either side often suggests, but it has become increasingly apparent that there is significant overlap of people who identify both as homosexual and religious. Mormon writing on homosexuality often has had a pastoral character, aimed either at easing the transition for those seeking to leave the Church or smoothing the way for those who desire to remain within it. Those who have thought to advocate change with the LDS Church and culture have focused primarily on "attitudes" toward homosexuality encouraging "understanding and tolerance for homosexual people."[2] Too often this discussion of homosexuality has focused on either its etiology, or its relationship to the will, though neither the appeal to nature nor nurture resolves the question of ethics and meaning. For Latter-day Saints, the question is a theological problem of soteriological significance.

What follows is a thought experiment on the question of how Mormons might imagine different kinds of sealing relationships other than heterosexual marriage. Such an experiment neither constitutes Church doctrine, nor intends to advocate itself as Church doctrine. Rather, this essay provides an occasion to think critically about the intellectual and theological problems posed by the reality of alternative relationships outside of heterosexual norms. This essay treats the theological resources that can account

---

1. This chapter was originally published in *Dialogue: A Journal of Mormon Thought* 44, no. 4 (Winter 2011): 106–41.

2. Lowell L. Bennion, "Foreword," in *Peculiar People: Mormons and Same-Sex Orientation*, ed. Ron Schow, Wayne Schow, and Marybeth Raynes (Salt Lake City: Signature Books, 1991), xi.

for and make legible particular kinds of homosexual relationships within Mormonism. I use the term "homosexual relationships" to describe the particular dilemma for Mormon thought. Though contemporary Mormon discourse distinguishes between homosexual desires and sexual practices, permitting the former but rejecting the latter, both desires and practices obscure relationships as a dimension of homosexual experiences. Given that Mormonism imagines ideal heterosexuality, not as desires or practices, but as eternal relationships, could this same framework help us to reimagine the permissibility of homosexual relationships within Mormonism? The LDS theological focus on marriage is not reducible to "sexuality" since there are many circumstances in which marriages may be entirely celibate, such as the case of physical incapacitation. Nor should we reduce homosexual relationships to "sexuality," since such an equation distorts not only the actual practice of such relationships but also is inconsistent with our own understanding of the salvific character of relationships per se—not the details of sexual practices performed within those relationships.

Any attempt to think creatively and theologically within Mormonism to reconcile the tension between the LDS Church and those who identify as homosexual must investigate the ideologies and theologies that inform the current tension. Some may feel that no reconciliation is possible, that LDS teachings cannot and should not accept homosexual relationships as intelligible. This position is certainly viable, though it requires defense rather than simply repetition and assertion. We are forced to diagnose either way what is problematic with homosexual relationships according to current LDS theology. As I understand it, much of the theological objection to homosexual relationships lies in current LDS understandings of the afterlife and the kinds of relationships that will exist there. First, these relationships are frequently understood to be reproductive relationships, at least among those who occupy the highest degree of the celestial kingdom.[3] Second, the sealing ordinance binds these reproductive families together, sealing only those who can presumably reproduce either in this life or the next. Finally, the heterosexual pairs of men and women should possess the proper "gender," which is eternal. Homosexual relationships cannot be eternal because they are not able to reproduce by means of natural biological methods and confuse the natural gender they should possess. I will address these claims

---

3. On the degrees of the celestial kingdom, see D&C 131:1–4. Though "celestial marriage" was a synonym for polygamous marriage in the early LDS Church, today it refers exclusively to any marriage sealed in a temple.

in order to suggest how it may be possible to imagine sealed homosexual relationships as compatible with key doctrines of Mormonism.

Celestial Reproduction

The belief in divine reproduction constitutes a central tenet for many Mormons, in spite of its rather thin canonical support. Even defining what exactly is meant by this belief in divine reproduction can be particularly unclear. At issue is determining exactly what is meant by the belief that human beings are a "spirit son or daughter of heavenly parents."[4] For instance, in a recent essay exploring "common ground" between womanist theology and LDS theology, professors of political science at Brigham Young University Valerie M. Hudson and Alma Don Sorenson asserted: "the primary work of God is to have children and nurture them into godhood." In a clarifying footnote, the authors backed away from this bold statement with the significant caveat: "Actually, *have* is not the right word here. In LDS theology, God does not create intelligence; rather, God *organizes* intelligences to the point that they can be called God's children, a process that is known as 'spirit birth.'"[5] The ambivalence on this point is a persistent tension in Mormon thought. That is, the doctrine of spiritual birth stands at odds with the doctrine of eternal intelligences, and to this day Mormonism has not resolved this tension. On the one hand, "spirit birth" is a divine reproduction that mirrors human reproduction, requiring a male and female partner; and on the other hand, "spirit birth" is a more metaphorical "organization" that bears little resemblance to reproduction as a result of sexual intercourse. The former model of spirit birth depends on a heterosexual pair (at least if divine bodies are biologically constrained without access to the kinds of technologies human bodies may benefit from) and is often used as the prototype for the heterosexual family, as the authors quoted above argue. The latter model of spirit birth, however, requires nothing in particular about the sexual or reproductive acts of God, whose organization of spirits likely has little to do with the reproductive organs he or she (or his or her partner) might have.

This doctrine of spirit birth faces a few significant challenges. In Doctrine and Covenants 93—and repeated in many other of Joseph Smith's

---

4. "The Family: A Proclamation to the World," *Ensign*, Nov. 1995, 102.

5. Valerie M. Hudson and Alma Don Sorenson, "Response to Professor [Linda E.] Thomas [on Womanist Theology]," in *Mormonism in Dialogue with Contemporary Christian Theologies*, ed. Donald W. Musser and David L. Paulsen (Macon, Ga.: Mercer University Press, 2007), 327.

speeches, translations, and revelations—individual human identity is thought of as eternal.[6] The doctrine of spirit birth seeks to reconcile itself with this doctrine of eternal intelligences by positing a four-fold progressive anthropology: from intelligence, to spirit, to mortal body, and finally to a glorified body. In this view, Heavenly Father and Heavenly Mother may not be the "parents" of intelligences, but are parents of spirits—in some sense having given "birth" to them. Advocates of "spirit birth" based on heterosexual reproduction generally insist that it is similar, if not identical, to the birth of mortal bodies. As it is frequently imagined, the process of male-female mutual divinization entails not only a sexual relationship, but also a reproductive one in order to populate future worlds. Such a notion may be tied to the promises of eternal increase, "a continuation of the seeds forever and ever" (D&C 132:19) in the revelation given on celestial marriage. In this view of the marital relationship, mixed-sex couples are eternally engaged in the reproduction of spirit children.

While articulating the spirit birth process as providing the intelligence with a spirit in a way analogous to how mortal birth provides the spirit with a physical body, the analogy is strained to the point of breaking. If reproduction as we know it now offers a model for heavenly reproduction so as to exclude homosexual relationships by definition, then must we imagine that male gods deposit sperm in the bodies of female gods (who menstruate monthly when they are not pregnant), that the pregnant female god gestates spirit embryos for nine months and then gives birth to spirit bodies? While some LDS thinkers imagine an eternally pregnant Heavenly Mother, I see no reason why we must commit to this kind of literal pregnancy as the only reason for divine female figures.[7] In mortal birth, parents

---

6. "Man was also in the beginning with God. Intelligence, or the light of truth, was not created or made, neither indeed can be. . . . For man is spirit. The elements are eternal, and spirit and element, inseparably connected, receive a fulness of joy" (D&C 93:29–33). There is significant scholarly debate about whether Joseph Smith taught spirit birth, and how it fit in his broader thinking about eternal kinship. Hale notes, "While it seems certain that Smith taught that gods procreate, he did not specify that their offspring are necessarily spirits. And it is equally unclear if the alternative possibility, that the offspring of the gods are physical children, would be any more plausible in the prophet's thinking." Van Hale, "The Origin of the Human Spirit," in *Line Upon Line: Essays on Mormon Doctrine*, ed. Gary James Bergera (Salt Lake City: Signature Books, 1989), 122.

7. Linda P. Wilcox, "The Mormon Concept of a Mother in Heaven," in *Women and Authority: Re-Emerging Mormon Feminism*, ed. Maxine Hanks (Salt Lake City: Signature Books, 1992), 3–21.

with bodies provide lower-stage spirits with bodies in order to bring them to the same level. However, in this view of spirit birth, divinized parents provide intelligences with spirits, two levels below their own stage of progression. Mortal bodies give birth to equal mortal bodies, yet in this understanding of spirit birth, glorified bodies give birth to inferior spirit bodies. There is no equivalency between the two understandings of birth because they accomplish very different things in very different circumstances.

What would it mean for homosexual relationships if we were to substitute the tentative doctrine of literal divine reproduction for other models of "birth"? For instance, the process of "birth" is not used to describe each of the series of progression from intelligence to spirit to mortal body to resurrection. Resurrected bodies need not be born from resurrected beings but could be organized from matter. We need not consider that spirit bodies must be literally born but may be "organized" in an analogous way to the resurrection. Even the model of baptism, which marks a spiritual rebirth, may be thought of as a model for how spirit children are born to divinized parents. In such models, biological reproduction is not needed to explain celestial parentage. Such ideas are certainly not the logical consequence of the notion of divine embodiment.

The issue of God's embodiment is not as clear-cut as it may initially appear. While we recognize continuity in appearance and even substance with the future exalted body, we also acknowledge that it is quite different. For instance, a divine body is not constrained by space and time in the ways that mortal bodies are. From scriptural accounts, divine bodies can appear, disappear, pass through walls, and resist entropy. While these scriptural accounts affirm that it is possible for divine bodies to perform functions such as eating and drinking, they also suggest that there is no requirement that they do so in order to sustain life. Why then, do we imagine that sexual union as we know it in mortality is a necessary function for the production of life in divine bodies if these bodies are so dissimilar in every other way from mortal bodies? Could not sexual union be a possibility for divine bodies but not be a necessity for creation, just as alimentary functions may be possible but not necessary?

Are there LDS models of creation and reproduction that can accommodate not only heterosexual pairs, but also male-male and female-female couples? In addition to the resurrection, the creation provides a better model for thinking about how this "spirit birth" might occur than the process of mortal parturition. To use one model, in both the canonical and ritual accounts of creation, heterosexual pairs of creators are entirely absent. Creation of the earth, organization of the elements, and even the creation of the living bodies of Adam and Eve all occur without the presence of female figures. The creation in LDS texts and ritual is performed with an all-male cast, putting a male-male relationship as the source of creativity, productivity, and the giving of life itself. The story of Adam and Eve in LDS scripture and ritual is often cited as the example of divinely authorized heterosexuality. Yet, the creation of both Adam and Eve does not in any way affirm heterosexual reproduction as the method of divine creation either spiritually or materially. Indeed, creation according to God's "word" is attested in all scriptural accounts available to Latter-day Saints (Gen 1–2, Moses 2–3, Abr. 4–5). Adam's body is formed "from the dust of the ground . . . but spiritually they were created and made according to my word" (Moses 3:7). Both spiritual and material formation takes place without any sexual union. Furthermore, males alone perform the creation of Adam's body in LDS text and ritual. Even Eve is "reproduced" from a male body with the help of other males. The Lord penetrates the body of Adam and creates Eve. The capacity for Adam's body to reproduce by means of another male provides scriptural precedent in the foundational story of humanity to the variety of possibilities available for Latter-day Saints to conceive of reproduction independent of heterosexual union.

Jesus's birth from Mary may also provide a way of thinking about the process of giving birth that does not involve heterosexual union. While male-male creation and male-female creation may be found in Mormon thought already, perhaps the model of the virgin birth—female pregnancy without male penetration—could serve as an example of how female-female relationships might reproduce with only minimal assistance of a male participant, like the sperm donor for the modern female-female reproductive relationship. Rather than seeing the conception of Jesus as a wholly exceptional event, James E. Talmage has suggested that this method of procreation was, "not in violation of natural law, but in accordance with a higher manifestation thereof."[8] While with Adam we have seen that male bodies may reproduce on their own, or with the help of another male, with Mary we may see that female bodies may also reproduce without sexual intercourse. Or, perhaps even the model of Adam reproducing Eve parthenogenically might also be a capacity of divine female bodies. Both scriptural accounts offer models of divine creation and reproduction not based on heterosexual union.

Although we have models of reproduction and creation that might suggest their possibility for same-sex partners, we Latter-day Saints face

---

8. James E. Talmage, *Jesus the Christ*, 6th ed. (Salt Lake City: Deseret Book, 1922), 81.

another theological question: Are creating and saving male-only priesthood activities? The possibility of reproduction in the female-female relationship does not address the centrality of the male-only priesthood in LDS thought. A male-only priesthood represents a significant limitation for female-female relationships, linking the exclusion of women from exercising priesthood power and authority to the exclusion of women's homosexual relationships. The fact that males can hold the priesthood allows the possibility for male-only creative relationships (like the male members of the Godhead) since priesthood may be held and exercised entirely independent of women in LDS practice. But if women do not have access to the priesthood—whatever we may mean by that term—would they be unable to create without men? The autonomy afforded to males to create in Mormon tradition comes at the expense of females. Historical precedents of women healing and blessing notwithstanding, most of the functions of the priesthood have not been exercised by women. Further, promises to women that they would be given the priesthood (or in some sense share it) were conditional on their relationship to their husband. Feminist concerns about the ability of men to act independently in the Church, while women are subject to male partnership as a prerequisite for their actions, are magnified in the consideration for female-female relationships. We may need to rethink women's dependent status with respect to the priesthood in tandem with rethinking the possibility of homosexual relationships. Parsing through what the priesthood means in an eternal context, which would presumably not include things like the authority to ordain offices, bless the sick, administer sacraments and other administrative or temporally bounded notions of priesthood authority, is an essential task for thinking about whether women might be excluded from the eternal priesthood activities of creating and saving.

If divine creation and reproduction cannot be used to exclude the possibility of non-heterosexual relationships in LDS theology, what about mortal reproduction? How can the command to "multiply and replenish" the earth be fulfilled (Gen. 1:27)? In practice, having children is neither a requirement for Latter-day Saint marriages after they have been sealed, nor is the ability to have children a prerequisite for sealing. Neither marriage nor sex is thought of in exclusively procreationist terms. While LDS teaching may consider procreation a religious *desideratum*, it cannot nor should not be a reason to exclude someone from receiving the blessings of sealing, especially if afterlife creation has nothing to do with mortal procreation. There is no requirement or expectation of natural fertility to qualify for marriages, even sealings, in Latter-day Saint practice.[9] There is no reason to exclude non-reproductive couples from the blessings of sealing on the basis of reproductive capacity alone. But this lack of capacity to reproduce in no way diminishes the responsibility to provide for and rear children. Indeed, this obligation to rear children is not connected to reproductive capacity at all, but rather the obligations that able couples have to provide children, by means of adoption or other forms of reproduction technologically available today, with the education and formation to become responsible adults. Further, it is certainly the case that it is, in fact, possible for non-heterosexual couples to take care of children, whether their own from previous relationships, through medical assistance, or by means of adoption. The authoritative teaching that families should care for and rear children into responsible adults suffers no harm if we continue to teach that all families, heterosexual or not, take this as a religious responsibility.

Sealings as Kinship

The LDS rite of sealing currently authorizes relationships between heterosexual couples and their children. Past and present practices of sealings also point to ways that we might reconceive of sealing as untethered from the heterosexual biological family. I suggest that the practice of sealing is about ritually producing kinship relations that are not reducible to reproductive couples and bloodlines. Kinship may be defined as the practices of ritually marking relationships of care, trust, and bonding that are greater than friendship or community. That is to say, there are no pre-determined relationships that count as kinship, but rather kinship emerges as a special kind of relationship within society. Sexual and reproductive relationships are one way that human societies practice kinship, but by no means the only way. Indeed, the biological basis for kinship is neither universal in human society nor the only way that Latter-day Saints think about kinship. Rather, kinship is a way of making the biological results of sexual reproduction meaningful. In this understanding, reproduction *acquires* the significance of kinship rather than being constitutive of it. The topic

---

9. Joseph Smith was sealed in celestial marriages to women who were well past childbearing years, like Patty Bartlett Sessions (age 47), Elizabeth Davis Durfee (age 50–51), Rhoda Richards (age 58), and Fanny Young (age 56). Todd Compton, *In Sacred Loneliness: The Plural Wives of Joseph Smith* (Salt Lake City: Signature Books, 1997), 4–6.

specifically at issue here is whether non-heterosexual kinship may qualify as a recognizable form of kinship. Certainly, there are numerous forms of kinship that do not conform to the reproductive heterosexual family organized by legal marriage. Contemporary kinship studies denaturalize the biological family as the basis of kinship and complement alternative ways of ordering society.

LDS sealings for non-heterosexual relationships could offer a set of regularizing terms under which such existing social relationships are ritually legitimized. For the Church to acknowledge non-heterosexual unions would be to acknowledge what already happens in practice—namely, that homosexual relationships of care and commitment, including the raising of children, exist. As it stands, the Church legitimizes heterosexual marriage as the only acknowledged way of marking kinship. To expand this definition is not to authorize any and all practices. Rather, same-sex marriage is really modeled on heterosexual practices of establishing legitimacy by means of long-term relationships of filiation. For the Church to accept gay marriage would be to continue to privilege certain kinds of kinship over others, excluding certain sexual and relational possibilities. The relevant questions for sealing non-heterosexual couples are not the legal issues that link health care, hospital visitation, and tax benefits to marital status. For Latter-day Saints, the sense of purpose and divine partnership, as well as spiritual safeguards and consolation in life and death that sealings endow, are blessings that might apply to kinship relationships beyond the heterosexual, reproductive family.

These broader understandings of kinship practices not only serve as a better anthropological model for the multiplicity of culture, including modern Western culture, but also better explain historical precedents of the LDS sealing ritual, which similarly created kinship in non-reproductive relationships. Though discontinued by President Wilford Woodruff in 1894, many men and women (most often married couples) were sealed to prominent nineteenth-century Church leaders through the "law of adoption" regardless of blood or reproductive relationships.[10] Prior to the Woodruff reform, the adoption sealing was intentionally a means of es-

---

10. Jonathan A. Stapley, "Adoptive Sealing Ritual in Mormonism," *Journal of Mormon History* 37, no. 2 (Summer 2011): 53–117. See also Gordon Irving, "The Law of Adoption: One Phase of the Development of the Mormon Concept of Salvation, 1830–1900," *BYU Studies* 14, no. 3 (Spring 1974): 291–314. Samuel M. Brown, "Early Mormon Adoption Theology and the Mechanics of Salvation," 3–52; and Jonathan A. Stapley, "Adoptive Sealing Ritual in Mormonism," *Journal of Mormon History* 37, no. 2 (Summer 2011): 53–118.

tablishing new kinds of kinships other than familial-reproductive, though utilizing the vocabulary of the family. As Samuel Brown explains, "The Mormon heaven was emphatically not the Victorian hearth of the increasingly popular domestic heaven.... Smith's heaven consisted of one boundless family of eternal intelligences."[11] The practice of "adoption," in which men and their families were sealed to other men and their families points to alternative ways of establishing kinship. Instead of sealing genealogical chains, this system of kinship connected new social units of non-biological families with the ultimate goal of uniting all of humanity into one sacred network.[12] In Orson Hyde's "Diagram of the Kingdom of God," he envisions the universal family tree made up of different branches with prophets at the head of each branch. To each prophet is sealed large kingdoms. From each of these branches extend still smaller branches, with even smaller branches stemming from them. Hyde describes how, in this patriarchal order, "every man will be given a kingdom and dominion, according to his merit, powers, and abilities.... There are kingdoms of all sizes, an infinite variety to suit all grades of merit and ability."[13] This sense of rulership is not meant to suggest that the prophets are the literal fathers of the greatest number of people, but rather that, because of righteousness (not fecundity), their kingdoms are the greatest. In Parley P. Pratt's terms, the "royal family" is one singular family that consists of "friends and kindred."[14] This bond is not forged by a genealogical link, but by the sealing itself. As Joseph Smith proclaimed in the King Follett Discourse, "use a little Craftiness & seal all you can & when you get to heaven tell your father that what you seal on earth should be sealed in heaven."[15]

It wasn't until after Woodruff's temple reforms that proxy temple sealings were administered for deceased ancestors, including those who had rejected the faith in mortality. In 1894, the Utah Genealogical Society was formed as a response to this new interest in proxy temple work made pos-

---

11. Samuel Brown, "The Early Mormon Chain of Belonging," *Dialogue: A Journal of Mormon Thought* 44, no. 1 (2011): 1–52.

12. Stapley and Wright, "Female Ritual Healing in Mormonism," *Journal of Mormon History* 37 (Winter 2011): 55.

13. Orson Hyde, "Diagram of the Kingdom of God," *Millennial Star* 9 no. 2 (January 15, 1847): 23.

14. Parley P. Pratt, "Celestial Family Organization," *Millennial Star* 5, no. 12 (May 1845): 193.

15. Scott G. Kenney, ed., *Wilford Woodruff's Journal, 1833–1898*, 9 vols. (Midvale, Utah: Signature Books, 1983–85), 2:364–65, as quoted in Brown, "The Early Mormon Chain of Belonging," 1.

sible by the new revelation and policy shift.[16] Woodruff explained the new practice which reversed the previous ban on sealing of children to deceased parents: "The Lord has told me that it is right for children to be sealed to their parents, and they to their parents just as far back as we can possibly obtain the records, and then have the last obtainable member sealed to the Prophet Joseph Smith."[17] This new practice centered on biological families, but also relied on the earlier notion of kingdoms, with Joseph Smith as the adoptive father of this dispensation. In time, the notion of dispensational kingdoms would recede ever more behind kingdoms based on individual lineage, thus paving the way for the contemporary emphasis on the nuclear family.[18] The new proxy sealings of married couples reduced the need for proxy adoption and also introduced greater flexibility in who could be sealed to whom, allowing for those who hadn't been members of the Church in mortality to be sealed posthumously to living spouses or for ancestors to be sealed to one another. Less emphasis was placed on getting the earthly sealings absolutely correct, shifting the ultimate decisions about validity of a sealing from earthly ordinances to justice in the afterlife, noting that there, "all will be made right."[19] More important than making sure that one was sealed to a righteous person was performing the sealing itself.

One need not return to this earlier notion of the sealing as kinship for examples of non-reproductive or biological relationships, but rather explore the misrecognition of how the ritual is practiced today to link non-reproductive or biological kin. The clearest example is the current understanding of the theology of LDS adoption after the reformation of the adoption practices in the late nineteenth century. The case of nineteenth-century adoptions as a practice of establishing kinship in ways that are not biologically based poses a challenge to the assumption that biology is the basis of kinship. Anthropologists have traditionally distinguished between "true" and "fictive" kinship, though this distinction rests on an assumption that privileges the biological relationship regardless of how families themselves treat such children. But the assumption that parents have a dif-

---

16. For the relevant events, see Stapley, "Adoptive Sealing Ritual in Mormonism," 106–12.

17. Abraham H. Cannon, Journal, April 5, 1895. Quoted in ibid., 108. Stapley notes that, over time, the quest to find one's dead proved an endless task and the idea of linking to Joseph Smith was eventually dismissed or forgotten: "In 1922, editors removed the instructions about sealing ultimate ancestors to Joseph Smith." Ibid., 114.

18. Ibid., 111.

19. Woodruff and Joseph F. Smith, Letter to John D.T. McAllister, April 26, 1894, quoted in ibid., 116.

ferent relationship to biological than to "fictive" kin fails to account for how kinship may be extended at all. It is, of course, often the case that families make no distinction between biological and adoptive children, and often reject the premises of the distinction. Indeed, in LDS practice, nonbiological children are ritually incorporated into a new kinship structure by means of the sealing following legal adoption.

Perhaps one might suggest in anthropological terms that the LDS sealings of legally adopted children do mark adoptive kin as separate from those "born in the covenant." The ritual itself certainly marks the crossing of a boundary, but the point is that, after the ritual, there is no meaningful distinction between biological and adoptive kin. In fact, though incredibly rare, it is possible that even those who were "born in the covenant" may be sealed anew to adoptive parents.[20] Rather than consider the biological child who has been born within a LDS kinship structure as already covered by the blessings of sealing a priori, it is possible for this child's sealing to take place in the adoptive family. Here, the sealing ritually marks how the kinship structure takes precedence over and replaces the biological family.[21] The case of divorce and the cancellation of sealings further reinforces the principle that biology is less important than the sealing itself. President Ezra Taft Benson explained that the children of parents whose sealing was cancelled "are entitled to birthright blessings, and if they remain worthy, are assured the right and privilege of eternal parentage regardless of what happens to their natural parents or the parents to whom they were sealed."[22] Benson's view here represents a continuation of the reforms un-

---

20. I am personally aware of one occurrence in the past decade where an adopted child who was "born in the covenant" was sealed to the adoptive parents. The adoptive parents were informed by letter how rare their situation was.

21. Other examples of kinship that are not based on reproduction or biological relation are prevalent in LDS practice. Many members of the Church are "adopted" into the House of Israel, even while others are considered to be direct descendants. Discourse on Israelite identity has variously been asserted in terms of lineage and in terms of adoption. Armaund Mauss, *All Abraham's Children: Changing Mormon Conceptions of Race and Lineage* (Champaign, Ill.: University of Illinois Press, 2003), 17–40. While some versions of this doctrine imagine a change in the "blood" of the adoptee as part of this process, the very possibility of adoption across bloodlines already points to a kinship structure that precedes the reproductive family. Further, the notion of transformation itself, here in terms of transracial identity, as the result of the adoption may offer a model for transsexuals, who might also be ritually "adopted" into a new sex, perhaps as a part of a patriarchal blessing.

22. Ezra Taft Benson, quoted in Elaine Walton, "Children of Divorce," *Ensign*, August 2002, 40–41. (http://lds.org/ensign/2002/08/children-of-divorce?lang=eng,

der Woodruff that emphasized the sealing itself as important, not necessarily to whom one is sealed. Further, it distinguishes biological kin from the blessings of kinship through sealing, promising kin on the basis of the sealing even if biological kin cannot fulfill that role.

When kinship replaces reproduction in the logic of the sealing, we may consider how alternative relationships of care, modeled on, but not identical to parent-child and husband-wife, as well as those not yet regularized or named, offer a better model for understanding both the purpose and possibilities of the sealed relationship, whether those sealings entail a sexual relationship between partners or not. Mormon models of kinship, both past and present, displace and replace the biological and the sexual relationship as markers of kinship, suggesting alternative modes and models for establishing such relationships. The heteronormative notion of family neither corresponds to a universal ideal nor reflects the actual practice of kinship among Latter-day Saints. Understanding sealings as ritually marking and normalizing relationships as kinship offers a more accurate understanding of how sealings have been practiced and are practiced today, as well as how they may be practiced at some future time.

Eternal Gender

The concept of "gender" remains an important term in LDS discourse about homosexuality and is a necessary site of critical inquiry. The question of homosexual relationships is intimately bound up in conceptualizations of gender differences. The semi-canonical 1995 document "The Family: A Proclamation to the World" (hereafter "Proclamation") announces: "Gender is an essential characteristic of individual premortal, mortal, and eternal identity and purpose."[23] The notion of an eternally persistent gender functions to regulate normative behavior that is believed to correspond to the attributes of an eternally "gendered" subject. In the context of the Church's endorsement of ballot initiatives in several states to define marriage as between a man and a woman in the 2008 elections, the Church explained its interest in the issue in a document called "The Divine Institution of Marriage" that appeared in the online LDS Newsroom on August 13, 2008. This document suggests that same-sex marriage causes "gender confusion," with the result that "the rising generation of children and youth will find it increasingly difficult to develop their natural identity as a man or a woman." It further as-

---

accessed July 20, 2011.)
23. "The Family," 102.

serts that there are "inherent differences between the genders."[24] The appeal to a "natural" and "inherent" sexual identity that is at risk of being "confused" presumes a certain kind of sexual difference rooted in heterosexuality. LDS concepts of gender difference are as much about rejecting homosexuality as they are about ordering the relationship between men and women. It is necessary to address the ideas of incommensurable "genders" as the basis of heterosexual priority in the Church.

What exactly is meant by the term "gender" in LDS discourse? Since second-wave feminism divided biological "sex" (meaning male and female bodies) from socially constructed "gender" (meaning culturally assigned social roles), the sex/gender distinction has had a great impact on how the term "gender" is understood in American society. Yet in my reading of LDS statements on the subject, this distinction is not operative, and significant attention to defining the term is absent. The term "gender" seems to be deployed without a single definition of what is meant, leaving the broadest possible semantic range. Gender as a category is variously applied to cover three separate aspects of human identity, though they are often conflated under this single term. As one example of this, an official LDS booklet, *A Parent's Guide*, published in 1985, explains: "Gender identity involves an understanding and accepting of one's own gender, with little reference to others; one's gender roles usually focus upon the social interaction associated with being male or female."[25] Parsing this definition reveals that, first, gender refers to the morphological bodies of males and females—what is taken to be self-evidently "one's own gender." Second, gender refers to an "identity" that males and females are supposed to possess that corresponds with their bodies, including heterosexual desires. Third, gender refers to the differing "roles," purposes, and responsibilities that some Church leaders understand to be assigned to males and females. These three definitions refer to quite different things, which makes it difficult to know how exactly the term is used in different contexts. When one adds the idea of gender as an eternal characteristic, these three definitions become even more complicated. I will examine each of these three notions of "gender" as they might serve as an objection to homosexual relationships.

---

24. "The Divine Institution of Marriage," The Mormon Newsroom, August 13, 2008, http://www.mormonnewsroom.org/article/the-divine-institution-of-marriage (accessed May 28, 2013).

25. *A Parent's Guide* (Salt Lake City: The Church of Jesus Christ of Latter-day Saints, 1985), "Chapter 4: Teaching Children: from Four to Eleven Years," http://lds.org/manual/a-parents-guide/chapter-4-teaching-children-from-four-to-eleven-years?lang=eng (accessed June 23, 2011).

First, "gender" is understood to refer exclusively to the morphological differences between bodies labeled "male" and "female." In this sense, "gender" is simply a synonym for "sex," the identifiable bodily characteristics of maleness and femaleness. If we restrict the understanding of "gender" to mean simply bodily difference, it is not clear that homosexual relationships would be impacted at all. Homosexual relationships do not interfere with this minimal definition of "gender" since male and female bodies persist as such in these relationships. Non-heterosexual relationships, it would seem, do not require a changed belief in an eternal "gender" at all, as long as "gender" is understood to refer exclusively to bodily morphology. In the same way that the sex/gender distinction was deployed by second-wave feminists to argue for a fixed notion of different sexes, while suggesting that the way that those differences were given meaning in culture were changeable, one could argue that homosexual relationships also affirm a fixed, eternal notion of sex, while seeing the particular configurations of relationships as variable.

The notion of an eternal gender, referring to physical differences alone, faces significant theological problems. If gender is "an essential individual characteristic of premortal, mortal, and eternal identity and purpose," then presumably the premortal spirit of each individual necessarily corresponds in appearance to the body it inhabits as a kind of facsimile. The challenge with such a view is in saying what kinds of bodily characteristics correspond to one's preexistent spirit. What is the relationship between one's eternal identity and one's contingent genetic makeup, including "sex"? What are the characteristics that make up a morphological sex? Is it just the genitals, or are premortal bodies also capable of reproduction? Do things like performed gender differences, relative height and weight, chemistry, hormones, and muscle build also factor into what makes the "genders" eternally different? Do premortal spirits have chromosomes? What defines physical "gender" that it can persist eternally?

The whole question of the relationship of the premortal spirit to the mortal body is at stake in the claim that "gender" belongs to both equally. If any of the particularities of one's genetic and environmental circumstances may be said to not preexist with a particular spirit in a deterministic way, why then is sexual difference the exception? To assert that "gender" is more fundamental to one's identity than these other contingent features requires us to ask: Of the many different features of human identity, why does sexual difference—whatever that may refer to—occupy a privileged place in the account of the eternal nature of the human being?

In the second understanding of "gender," the term refers not only to particular bodies, but also to an "identity" that is supposed to match to those bodies. Gender identity is the relationship between sex, gender, and desire, and it is done correctly when all three align according to heterosexual norms. Early twentieth-century discourse about homosexuality thought of it in terms of pathological gendered "inversion," suggesting that men and women who engaged in homosexual activity mistook their proper sexual identity as a result of confused social roles. Current LDS discourse sometimes uses the term "gender confusion" to speak about homosexuality.[26] Here, the stereotypical notion of male homosexuals as effeminate and female homosexuals as masculine functions to explain homosexuality. A correct gender identity can only be thought of in terms of heterosexuality. In this discourse, the transsexual and homosexual are indistinct since both have identified with a "sex" or "desire" that does not correspond correctly to their body. Such "identities" are rendered failures—or even impossible—in a framework that recognizes only some identities and is the impetus behind the pathologization of nonconforming gender identities.

Church teachings assert two ideas about gender identity that are in significant tension: first, that gender is an eternal, immutable aspect of one's existence; and second, that notions of gender identity and roles are so contingent that they must be constantly enforced and taught, especially to young children.[27] To say that one "is" a particular gender by virtue of that indi-

---

26. This view appears in many recent descriptions of homosexuality in LDS discourse. For instance, "If governments were to alter the moral climate by legitimizing same-sex marriages, gender confusion would increase, particularly among children." No author, "Strengthening the Family: Within the Bonds of Matrimony," *Ensign*, August 2005, 17. (http://lds.org/ensign/2005/08/strengthening-the-family-within-the-bonds-of-matrimony?lang=eng, accessed July 19, 2011.) See also Boyd K. Packer, "I Will Remember Your Sins No More," *Ensign*, May 2006 (http://lds.org/ensign/2006/05/i-will-remember-your-sins-no-more?lang=eng, accessed July 19, 2011); "The Divine Institution of Marriage."

27. "But members of the Church must not be deceived about one immutable truth: there is eternal significance in being a man or a woman. The history of the gospel from Adam to this final dispensation documents equal respect for the roles of men and women and the need for all men and women to develop their gifts to the utmost through living the commandments of God. But within that same gospel framework are some realities about differences between the two genders. This means that there are some exclusive things men are to do and some that women are to do. A most appropriate time for this development is the interlude between early childhood and adolescence." *A Parent's Guide*, "Chapter 4: Teaching Children: from Four to Eleven Years."

vidual's body, and also that one's disposition or identity is of that gender, suggests that, in the latter case, gender is not a question of ontology but of achievement. "The Divine Institution of Marriage" manifests this tension by appealing to an "inherent . . . natural identity" with respect to gender, but also positing that nature is so unstable as to require heterosexual marriage to make sure that it can "develop."[28] In this understanding, male and female "identity" is not secured by the possession of a male or female body alone but must be enforced and made legible as "male" or "female" through practices like heterosexuality. As Douglas A. Abbot and A. Dean Byrd put it, heterosexuality must be "encouraged" in children in order for it to take.[29] But gender "identity" cannot be both inherent and taught. The contingency of "gender identity" here reveals that it is not, in fact, "natural" at all but rather must be maintained and enforced juridically. Gender is constantly at risk of failing to correspond to the sexed body. As Judith Butler explains, "there is no gender identity behind the expressions of gender; that identity is performatively constituted by the very 'expressions' that are said to be its results."[30] The idea that gender is performed, not possessed, reveals just how unstable it is as a category for defining people. Such a view that gender is something that develops, or is achieved, suggests that there is no true or false gender, nor one that coheres with a precultural "nature."

The use of the category of "gender" to describe one's desires and sexual practices has been heavily discredited over the last several decades. Rather, given the vast variability of gender "identities" of culturally recognized "masculine" or "feminine" traits among those who identify as either heterosexual or homosexual, the assumption that any given gender performance corresponds to a particular object of desire is entirely contingent. The old

---

As recently as 2009, Elder Bruce Hafen of the Seventy defended the idea that homosexuality is the result of a prepubescent "block" on "normal emotional-sexual development." He continues, "Adult men who have had such childhood experiences can often resume their normal development by identifying and addressing the sources of their emotional blockage, which usually includes restoring healthy, appropriate male relationships." "Elder Bruce C. Hafen Speaks on Same-Sex Attraction" Evergreen International nineteenth Annual Conference September 19, 2009. (The address is posted in full at http://newsroom.lds.org/article/elder-bruce-c-hafen-speaks-on-same-sex-attraction, accessed July 19, 2011.)

28. "The Divine Institution of Marriage."

29. Douglas A. Abbot and A. Dean Byrd, *Encouraging Heterosexuality: Helping Children Develop a Traditional Sexual Orientation* (Orem, Utah: Millennial Press, 2009).

30. Judith Butler, *Gender Trouble: Feminism and the Subversion of Identity* (New York: Routledge, 1999), 33.

binary categories of heterosexuals and homosexuals—with the caveat of bisexuals—does little to capture the wide variety of gender performance and sexual preference. The experiences of transsexuals, transgender, drag, intersexuality, and the variety of gender performances in gay, lesbian, and straight cultures are not adequately understood through the category of gender as a system that matches "masculine" and "feminine" sexual desires to "male" and "female" bodies. The history of this categorization of sexual preferences in connection with gender relies on the same heterosexual matrix that it attempts to explain. Gender simply fails as a category for thinking about sexuality, and LDS discourse should move beyond such an infelicitous conflation.

The third understanding of "gender" in LDS discourse sees it as more than bodies and identity, but also as comprising roles—or as the Proclamation on the Family puts it, "eternal identity and purpose." Gendered "purposes" or roles are laid out in the document: "By divine design, fathers are to preside over their families in love and righteousness and are responsible to provide the necessities of life and protection for their families. Mothers are primarily responsible for the nurture of their children." Earlier teachings of Church leaders suggested an even more expansive notion of gender roles that included prescribed ways of dressing and acting so as to appear properly male or female.[31] Like gender identity, gender roles must also be taught to children in order for them to be carried on.[32] This notion of "gender" as roles operates as a critique of homosexual relationships because at least one "confused" partner fails to conform to his

---

31. President Spencer W. Kimball stated: "Some people are ignorant or vicious and apparently attempting to destroy the concept of masculinity and femininity. More and more girls dress, groom, and act like men. More and more men dress, groom, and act like women. The high purposes of life are damaged and destroyed by the growing unisex theory. God made man in his own image, male and female made he them. With relatively few accidents of nature, we are born male or female. The Lord knew best. Certainly, men and women who would change their sex status will answer to their Maker." "God will Not Be Mocked," *Ensign*, November 1974, 8.

32. One official manual teaches that proper gender roles are communicated through positive feelings that parents have about gender roles: "We should also help children understand gender roles. This will help a child have a good feeling about being a girl or boy. Parents who feel good about their roles as men and women pass this feeling along to their children," in "Lesson 9: Chastity and Modesty," *The Latter-day Saint Woman: Basic Manual for Women, Part A* (Salt Lake City: The Church of Jesus Christ of Latter-day Saints, 2000). (http://lds.org/manual/the-latter-day-saint-woman-basic-manual-for-women-part-a/lesson-9-chastity-and-modesty?lang=eng, accessed July 19, 2011.)

or her "proper" gendered identity as masculine or feminine. Such a view of gendered roles may not include any assumed correspondence to capacity, but rather responsibilities which each gender is meant to assume.[33]

This view may be used to object to homosexual relationships because such relationships may include one or both same-sex parents as subverting the role assigned to their "gender." In this sense, "gender confusion" is the result not of the presence of both "masculine" and "feminine" parents, but the failure of these traits to be possessed by men and women respectively. The notion that women are more innately caring and nurturing reinforces the instruction for women to reproduce and be the primary caregivers of their children. In recent LDS discourse, the title "mother" does not refer to a period in a woman's life, one particular aspect of how a woman's identity may be performed, or a particular category of women who have children.

In spite of the emphasis that parents must act as both masculine and feminine (ideally by males and females, respectively), LDS discourse has increasingly emphasized "equality" in the marital relationship. The Proclamation teaches that "fathers are to preside over their families" and that "fathers and mothers are obligated to help one another as equal partners." The tension between these two positions—fathers presiding but both parents as "equal partners"—remains largely unresolved. Yet, while the rhetoric of equal partnership could and would apply to parents of the same sex, when it comes to the issue of "gender confusion" in homosexual relationships, the question of who presides is much more important than the fact that there is an equal partnership. The retention of earlier language about "presiding" alongside more modern emphasis on "equal partnership" reveals the necessity of hierarchical views of males and females in marriage as an aspect of marking same-sex relationships as illegitimate.

The problem with an interpretation in which "gender" refers to roles is that it cannot explain what these roles might be in premortal and postmortal life. If we accept a definition of "gender" that suggests that men's role is being a "breadwinner" and women's role is caring for children, cooking, cleaning, and other hallmarks of the twentieth-century American family division of labor, this understanding of gender is meaningless in an eternal realm. Further, the problem with dehistoricizing modern American divi-

---

33. Current official statements on eternal gender suggest a kind of role complementarity, "The nature of male and female spirits is such that they complete each other." The Church of Jesus Christ of Latter-day Saints, *Handbook 2: Administering the Church*, Section 1.3.1 (Salt Lake City: The Church of Jesus Christ of Latter-day Saints, 2010). Available at https://lds.org/handbook/handbook-2-administering-the-church/families-and-the-church-in-gods-plan?lang=eng#1.3.1 (accessed July 20, 2011).

sions of labor is that such divisions fail to describe "gender" historically and cross-culturally. Anthropologists and theorists have shown the variability of "sex roles," showing not only the cultural, but also the historical contingency of what is considered to be masculine and feminine, which is what precipitated the theoretical division between sex and gender in the first place. Even if one restricts gender roles to reproductive function, stripping away the divisions of household labor or access to public power as contingent features of mortal life, it is not clear that such roles could be construed as applying equally to the three phases of one's eternal life—premortal, mortal, and postmortal. The main problem for any theology that begins with a fixed notion of roles, gender binarism, or innate characteristics of what constitute masculine and feminine characteristics is that it is rooted in a fantasmatic idealization of such differences rather than any universal instantiation.

Finally, I would like to address the frequent charge that homosexual relationships constitute gender "separatism." The assertion faces a number of problems. In this understanding of same-sex relationships, the only meaningful and politically valuable mixed-sex interactions happen in marriages and procreation. But this assumption that non-heterosexuals cannot or will not engage in meaningful interactions with members of the opposite sex, including parents, siblings, children, co-workers, neighbors, and friends has no basis. The kinds of "separatist" feminist and gay and lesbian movements from earlier eras were more of a response to the injustice of patriarchal, heterosexual culture than a desire to cease all interaction with members of the opposite sex. If learning to interact with members of the opposite sex (or gender) really does hold a privileged position as a means to salvation over learning to master other kinds of relationships—such as those of different social, economic, racial, linguistic, national, or even religious backgrounds—there is no reason to suppose that same-sex companions cannot or would not develop those relationships. But the question of why mixed-sex relationships should be privileged above others must be seriously asked and explored.

Conclusion

At the turn of the twentieth century as the Church began to embrace the new post-polygamy conception of families and formally ended the "law of adoption" as it had been practiced between adults, Wilford Woodruff prophetically suggested that there were more changes to come: "I have not felt satisfied, neither did President Taylor, neither has any man since the

Prophet Joseph who has attended to the ordinance of adoption in the temples of our God. . . . [W]e still have more changes to make, in order to satisfy our Heavenly Father, satisfy our dead and ourselves. . . . [W]e have got to have more revelation concerning sealing under the law of adoption."[34] The possibility of creating theological space within Mormonism for homosexual relationships rests not on the abandonment of any central doctrine of the Church, but rather on the revival of past concepts, the recovery of embedded theological resources, and the rearticulation of existing ideas in more expansive terms in order to rethink the possibilities of celestial relationships. At the heart of this recovery is a displacement of biological reproduction as the sole way of imagining kinship as well as the model for celestial (pro)creation based on heterosexuality. In both cases, reproduction fails to offer a universal foundation for meaningful kinship relationships as well as being a doctrinally suspect account of divine relationships. Such a recovery project has the benefit not only of including homosexual relationships, but also of laying a more solid ground for non-reproductive heterosexual relationships and other forms of kinship.

The numerous critiques of the category of gender in recent years cannot be ignored, even if Latter-day Saints opt for a continued emphasis on binary sexual difference. Whether from the critique of gender roles, gender essentialist notions of innate characteristics, or even the notion of biological difference itself, LDS theology faces serious credibility issues by continuing to hold to precritical assumptions about sexual difference. At the same time, however, there is nothing preventing Latter-day Saints from moving past these assumptions in order to more clearly focus on Mormonism's distinctive teachings about kinship and salvation. There are two options we may take. First, we might note that the unimportance of gender as a category for salvation is repeatedly affirmed in scripture: "There is neither 'male' nor 'female' in Christ Jesus" (Gal. 3:28) and "he denieth none that come unto him, black and white, bond and free, male and female; and he remembereth the heathen; and all are alike unto God" (2 Ne. 26:33).

Second, perhaps by appealing to the social basis of gender, rather than a supposed eternal standard, we may better make sense of its place and significance in our theological thinking. To admit the social basis of gender does not entail the elimination of gender, nor does it require a leveling of difference toward some androgynous ideal. Quite the opposite. Instead, we may see more of a proliferation of "genders," released from the constraints of fantasies about a neat gender binary. Just as we do not imagine that only

---

34. Quoted in Stapley, "Adoptive Sealing Ritual in Mormonism," 109.

one (or two) races, body types, and hair colors are represented in the resurrection, we may also see a variety of "genders," understood as either different kinds of bodies, different kinds of identities, and even different roles. We need not abandon the idea of "eternal gender," but rather we can embrace the possibilities that it opens for us once freed from its artificial constraints. As one LDS manual puts it, backing away from its earlier claims about the fixed nature of gender: "There is nearly as much variation within each gender as there is between the genders. Each human being is unique. There is no one model except the Redeemer of all mankind. Development of a person's gifts or interests is one of life's most enjoyable experiences. No one should be denied such growth."[35] Perhaps LDS ritual and rhetoric may embrace this variation, including homosexual relationships in the blessings of growth offered by sealing.

---

35. *A Parent's Guide*, "Chapter 4: Teaching Children: from Four to Eleven Years."

Richard Williams discusses the assumptions underlying arguments being made for same-gender marriage and the assumptions that "shape a thoughtful response to those arguments." Against a naturalistic line of thought in which human actions lack intrinsic moral meanings, he suggests that we "must begin [with] a view of human nature that understands us to be fundamentally and irreducibly moral agents." Even though "self-expression has become the hallmark of freedom," he thinks we should "hope that freedom is nobler than mere self-expression, and that sexual self-expression is not the primary aspect of freedom."

Williams argues that "there is unique [moral] meaning in dual-gender conjugal sexual intimacy . . . because it creates relationships and binds us to others across generations in unique ways. It allows us to participate in the meaning of what it is to be the kind of beings we are, bound to each other in ways that can only be expressed through uniting males and females by covenant, thus bodily affirming our sexual complementarity and participating in fruitfulness and creativity affirmed in the bearing and rearing of children, and through the perfecting of love in fidelity and sacrifice in conjugal family life."

He gives three reasons Latter-day Saints should enter the discourse regarding same-gender marriage and the traditional family: First, gospel understandings about our nature, sexuality, and marriage and family have much to contribute to the reasoned defense of dual-gender marriage and family. Second, our society's decision "about the legal status of same-gender marriage will have a major effect on the moral climate; the meaning of sexuality, marriage, and family; and the stability and success of marriages and families." It will also impact what rational and legal arguments can be made in defense of traditional sexual integrity, marriage, and family. Third, "the discourse on same-gender marriage has profound implications for religious liberty and freedom of conscience."

Seven

Making Meaning and Making Families: Evaluating the Assumptive Grounds for Advocacy For or Against Same-Gender Marriage

Richard N. Williams

My introduction to American politics, and to what passes too often for political debate and discourse in our culture, came from my eighth grade social studies teacher. That year I was a "Goldwater Republican" in a predominantly Democratic area. I am not sure how the question arose, but I was asked about my views on the election and why I supported Senator Goldwater. I think I mentioned as an example Goldwater's opposition to massive grain sales to the Soviet Union, which seemed to me to be unwise propping up an antagonistic and dangerous enemy. My teacher's response was something very close to, "Well, so you want to see millions of Russian people starve to death."

I knew even in my fourteen-year-old mind that there was more to the issue than preventing starvation of innocent people. I could also sense that my teacher had rhetorically shifted the grounds of the discussion from whether selling wheat to people (who, then quite recently, had promised to "bury us") was sound public policy, to whether I was a compassionate and generous person. I knew somehow, albeit vaguely, that there were more issues in play than my teacher was allowing. I felt neither the capacity nor the desire to continue the discussion, especially in front of the whole class. So I took my lumps and shut up, but the experience has stayed with me and has been instructive. I learned that almost always there are more issues in play, more assumptions being made, and more at stake than public discourse immediately reveals.

The current discussion regarding the legalization of same-gender marriage[1] is the sort of discussion that requires careful engagement at the most

---

1. There are significant terminology problems quickly encountered in any discussion of issues related to homosexuality (including the term "homosexuality"). I am aware of most of these terminology problems. I am also aware of the distinctions made in the

basic levels where assumptions, assertions, and starting points are clearly understood, and where implications are fully articulated. In my experience, current discourse on same-gender marriage is too often like my discussion with my eighth grade teacher. People on both sides of the issue can move too quickly to the "show stopper." For example, "So you are intolerant and think it's alright to deny some people basic rights," or "So you don't really believe in the importance of the family." This strategy is a species of logical fallacy known as *ad hominem*—refuting a position by attacking the proponent.

This essay will critique some ideas that are commonly found as part of the assumptive base for support of same-gender marriage. It will, in the process, outline alternative assumptions which support dual-gender marriage or refute the common assumptions underlying arguments for the legalization of same-gender marriage. While there are a variety of positions from which same-gender marriage is advocated, it is always important to understand and uncover the grounding assumptions from which the arguments are made.[2] Many of the most important assumptions are found woven through much of our contemporary culture. The purpose of this essay is to identify grounding assumptions and their logical implications so that the consequences of the ideas and arguments can be made clear. This is done in a spirit of compassion that acknowledges that while people always deserve respect, ideas do not. It is important to be able to untangle ideas from the people who are often wrapped up in them, so that intellectual or moral opposition to ideas is not interpreted as denigration of persons.

I start by opening several topics relevant to the discussion of same-gender marriage. These topics, in turn, reflect what I understand to be the ethos that has, in large part, fueled the advocacy for same-gender marriage. These topics are (a) a false understanding of our human nature that considers us to be only smart natural organisms; (b) the problematic sexual ethos that misunderstands sexuality by, among other things, privatizing morality

---

literature between "sex" and "gender." I have chosen the term "same-gender marriage" over "same-sex marriage" because of some work I have recently done in which the terms "same-gender" and "dual-gender" were the primary terms of choice. I also prefer the use of "gender" because the Church's Proclamation on the Family uses the term "gender" in an important way. I also use these terms because I am speaking at a level and in an area where I anticipate that nothing crucial will be clarified by a distinction between "sex" and "gender." See "The Family: A Proclamation to the World," *Ensign*, Nov. 1995, 102.

2. See, for example, the discussion of assumptions and implications in Brent D. Slife and Richard N. Williams, *What's Behind the Research?: Discovering Hidden Assumptions in Social Science Research* (Thousand Oaks, Calif.: Sage Publications, 1995).

and politicizing sex; (c) the question of what sexuality, marriage, and family can and should *mean* in our culture and how those *meanings* can be lost or destroyed; (d) the fact that human agency plays a crucial role in all of these issues, and finally; (e) the ways understandings available to us as Latter-day Saints about these same issues can contribute fundamentally important perspectives to the discourse on marriage, family, and sexuality.

In short, this essay does not present a specific argument against same-gender marriage or for dual-gender marriage. The arguments in play are too diffuse and varied to present a full argument in the space available. Rather, the essay lays out the assumptions that underlie the arguments being made for same-gender marriage, and also some assumptions that shape a thoughtful response to those arguments. My final analysis is that arguments for same-gender marriage are unpersuasive because their grounding assumptions do not affirm our true human nature or faithfully capture our human experience, and are, therefore, inadequate and wrong. The wrongness carries over into arguments and exacerbates the negative consequences that would accrue if these arguments were to triumph. The essay lays out some alternative assumptions from which to launch an adequate refutation of the call for same-gender marriage and from which dual-gender marriage can be defended. While dual-gender marriage exhibits problems arising from all of the frailties and failings of humanity, its grounding assumptions are right, and so it is remediable, and even perfectible with the help of Christ.

When the Wrong Understanding of Human Nature Hooks up with the Wrong Understanding of Sexuality

When I was in my doctoral program in psychological sciences in the mid-seventies, research on human sexuality was just finding its way into mainstream social psychology. Both in the laboratory and out in the "field" researchers were unbridled in their optimism that the most important questions—as well as the most intimate questions—of our social behavior and our human nature would be successfully answered by the traditional scientific methods and models that were in vogue in the social sciences at that time. Of course, this would mean that the essence of our human social and moral world would be translated into a language of mere biological impulses, invisible social forces, and simple habits formed by cultural forces. Since many of these impulses and forces also govern the behavior of non-human species, that brand of science made us just one of a continuum of species—albeit obviously the most intelligent species due to the size and complexity of our brains. In other words, this brand of science takes us to be merely "monkeys with large brains."[3] Unfortunately, this view of our human nature has found its way into our culture through textbooks, curricula, arts, and opinion leaders, and is accepted with little argument, particularly in many academic, intellectual circles. If we accept this naturalistic, deterministic explanation of ourselves, then all the genuinely human aspects of our own nature, such as love, altruism, and moral agency, have to be given up along with our commonly felt and understood sense of what it is—what it means—to be a human being, as opposed to some other sort of lesser organism. Our previous, more humane view of ourselves is now judged to be illusory, and we now feel obliged to adopt a view of ourselves as a type of natural organism with natural impulses, subject to pushes and pulls from environmental forces, but otherwise not exceptional (except for being smarter, and having language and a few other natural advantages).

Only a moment's reflection shows us that if we really are just one type of natural organism, lacking agency, whose nature and behaviors are caused by the same environmental and biological conditions that produce behaviors in other species, then our actions do not really mean anything more than the actions of other critters. Because we are smarter we can "make our actions mean something," as in the case of an act of love, but the meaning we give it is cooked up by ourselves and is thus only meaningful *to us*. There is no independent self-transcending meaning to what we do. The conclusion of this line of thought is that there are no intrinsic moral meanings or content to human actions—just the meanings we make for ourselves to achieve our biologically or environmentally driven ends.[4] Thus, what we do does not really *mean* anything. It just is what it is, and it can mean only what we make it mean. This idea has been applied even to human sexuality. As Edwin E. Gantt and Emily Reynolds point out, "Insofar as social scientific theories of sexual attraction deny the possibility of human agency in their accounts of sexual relationships and desires, they cannot help but embrace a dangerous and virulent form of intellectual and cultural nihilism. Once the conceptual

---

3. See "The Personal Philosophy of Richard Posner," Big Think, November 21, 2009, http://bigthink.com/ideas/1384 (accessed January 5, 2013).

4. There are now suggestions that the chemicals that make up our genes cause everything from religious experience through sexual orientation, to television viewing with political liberalism and conservatism included for good measure—but don't provide a single adeqaute explanatory model of *how* genes could actually cause such things.

door is shut on the possibility of agency in our social science accounts of human relationships, the door to nihilism is the only one left open."[5]

It was probably an inevitable consequence and implication of the sexual revolution of the late 1960s and 1970s that sexuality also came to be understood as simply rooted in biological processes and environmental factors. It was assumed that the meaning of sexuality is just a product of history and culture without any innate moral importance. The morality traditionally attached to sexuality came to be understood as a cultural artifact (arbitrarily) perpetuated by historical institutions, chiefly religion, in order to control people. Thus the meaning of sexuality and sexual activity came to be regarded as intensely private and centered around fulfillment. With that understanding, the only relevant answer to the question of what sexuality or sexual activity "means" is "what it means to me." Anyone or any organization that tries to moralize and advocate or dictate a general morality of sexuality is either out of touch with the modern world, holding to an old tradition, or trying to control people by controlling the meanings they give to sexual behavior, and thereby stifling self-expression.

Though seldom voiced or even recognized, the problematic views of human nature and of sexuality that I have described here hang together and make sense—and might be legitimately compelling to people—if and only if it is true that we really are, by our very nature, just natural organisms, more like than different from other natural organisms. Seldom do we think about that assumption or its implications. But the key assumption of this claim that makes everything seem reasonable is that we are not agents—we really make no meaningful contribution to our own behaviors. Instead they just happen to us. When we do seem to choose, the choice itself is produced by something happening to us. This is to claim that we are not self-governing, self-determining beings in any meaningful sense, and, therefore, that what we usually refer to as agency is an illusion or, at best, a useful myth.[6] In addition to the tenet that says there is no real hu-

---

5. Edwin E. Gantt and Emily Reynolds, "Meaning, Morality and Sexual Attraction: Questioning the Assumptions of Biologism and Social Constructionism," in *What's the Harm?: Does Legalizing Same-sex Marriage Really Harm Individuals, Families or Society?* ed. Lynn D. Wardle (Lanham, Md.: University Press of America, 2008), 174.

6. While I am concentrating on the damage such assumptions do to our conception of the human person, it is useful to point out that those who deny human agency are also logically inconsistent. As Robert P. George and others point out, "the denial of free choice is rationally untenable, because it is a self-referentially contradictory claim, a self-defeating proposition. No one can rationally deny free choice, or claim as illusory our ordinary experience of freely choosing, without

man agency, this contemporary problematic view of human nature and sexuality also pre-supposes that there are no foundational truths or moral principles that transcend environmental conditions or biological realities. "Against the backdrop of deterministic explanatory strategies our understanding of the nature and meaning of marital and family relationships become morally relativised and nihilistic. . . . marriage in and of itself does not mean anything and no form of marriage is in any way morally superior to any other."[7] The resulting position is that morality is always relative, and that there are no foundational moral truths. Though it may not be immediately obvious, the denial of the reality of human agency, and the rejection of the existence of foundational truths and principles are at the conceptual heart of the contemporary portrayal of human nature and sexuality.

In what ways does this non-agentic account of our human nature and the rejection of non-local moralities play a role in the current discussions of same-gender marriage? In most cases, the argument for same-gender marriage seeks to neutralize the moral stigma that has traditionally been associated with homosexual behavior. One way to accomplish this is to disassociate morality and sexuality altogether. Adopting a view of human nature devoid of any real agency implies that nothing about sexuality can be considered agentic in any important sense. That sexual preferences and attractions are not agentic is an important part of most arguments to legitimate same-gender marriage and to establish sexual orientation as worthy of legal protection.[8] Finally, arguments for same-gender marriage will generally

---

presupposing the possibility of free choice. To deny free choice is to claim that it is more rational to believe that there is no free choice than to believe that there is. But this, in turn, presupposes that one can identify norms of rationality and freely choose to conform one's beliefs to those norms. It presupposes that we are free to affirm the truth or falsity of a proposition, our desires or emotions or preferences to the contrary notwithstanding. Otherwise, the assertion of no free choice is pointless. The person who says people can't freely choose presupposes that there are reasons for accepting his claim; otherwise his act of asserting it would be pointless. But our ability to understand and act upon such reasons is incompatible with the idea that one is caused by his desires or by outside forces to accept or not accept such claims. So someone who denies free choice implicitly contradicts his own claim." Robert P. George, "A Clash of Orthodoxies," *First Things*, Aug–Sept. 1999, at http://www.firstthings.com/article/2008/12/a-clash-of-orthodoxies-25, visited January 5, 2013.

7. Gantt and Reynolds, 175.

8. Some advocates of same-gender marriage consider the question of whether sexual orientation is agentic to be irrelevant to the questions of legal status. See Edward Stein, "Sexual Orientations, Rights, and the Body: Immutability, Essentialism, and Nativism," *Social Research: An International Quarterly*, Vol. 78, No. 2, 633–58,

promote it based on the fact that marriage and families have no transcendent moral status. And the special status that marriage and family have enjoyed is a mere social convention, generally imposed by the preferences of the politically and religiously powerful. As such, the special status of dual-gender marriage reflects the arbitrary socio-cultural forces at work in the world. The only legitimate purposes of marriage and family, therefore, are to enhance the genuine personal fulfillment, and growth and the development of individuals and couples who find these relationships meaningful.

From my experience, the current popular, but wrong, understanding of our human nature as being that of non-agentic natural organisms, coupled with an understanding of human sexuality as being a biological phenomenon providing primarily personal fulfillment but having no special moral import, provides the intellectual foundation for many arguments in favor of same-gender marriage. And their broad acceptance in the larger culture is routinely mistaken for validity of the arguments. Clearly, therefore, any cogent and coherent arguments for maintaining the privileged status of dual-gender marriage, which thus refute the legitimation of same-gender marriage, must begin by positing and defending a view of human nature that understands us to be fundamentally and irreducibly moral agents. It is crucial to establish the reality—both theoretical and empirical—of an agentic component infused through all human phenomena, including sexuality. While this is not the venue to explicate them, there are many arguments, models, and philosophical approaches within which the nature and importance of moral agency and a non-reductive model of human actions are established and defended.[9] In fact throughout our Western intellectual history, this has been the dominant view. It has only been in recent decades that the non-agentic, natural causal model of human beings has enjoyed such popularity.

Morality and Sexuality as Self-Expression

The perspective on sexuality, meaning, and morality described above that has emerged in our contemporary culture first became real to me by way of an example one of my professors used at the end of his textbook on human sexuality. He used a hypothetical example to summarize his under-

---

Summer 2011, http://cardozo.yu.edu/uploadedFiles/Cardozo/Profiles/estein-472/SexualOrientations,Rights,and%20the%20Body.pdf (accessed January 5, 2013).

9. For an example within the LDS tradition see Richard N. Williams, "Agency: Philosophical and spiritual foundations for applied psychology," in *Turning Freud Upside Down: Gospel Perspectives on Psychotherapy's Fundamental Problems*, ed. A. P. Jackson, L. Fischer, and D. Dan (Provo, Utah: BYU Press, 2005), 116–42.

standing of sexuality—what it is and what it means. The example involves a race of aliens from another planet who are very much like us except that while we eat in public and engage in sexual behavior in private, on their planet, they engage in sexual behavior in public but eat in private. When they visit Earth, they find the idea of eating in public to be repugnant and immoral. The hypothetical is intended to illustrate that all our human social acts, and the meaning and morality of those acts, derive from social rules and traditions that have developed in cultures over years but which were at some point arbitrary, reflecting, perhaps, the preferences of a particular powerful group. Social behaviors, including sexual ones, have no intrinsic or transcendent meaning deeper than cultural "accident." There is no human or moral truth above, behind, or beyond the simple evolution of social practices from arbitrary origins. My professor's conclusion was that we will never be truly free (from arbitrary cultural constraints on our freedom) until there is no more stigma or sanction attached to sexual activity than there is to eating.

This example and conclusion are problematic on so many levels that it is hard to know where to begin. First, it is odd for a person convinced that all our behaviors are caused by biological and environmental forces we can neither resist nor control to argue that we could be free at all. Clearly, this is not an argument for freedom as self-determination, but rather merely freedom from a particular restraint. The strategy of invoking a popular, high-sounding universal principle like "freedom" to a defend what, in the end, is only a desire for an individual privilege of self-expression, is common in public discourse surrounding same-gender marriage and other causes, but it is merely another example of the "show-stopper" strategy employed by my 8th grade teacher in the example I described above. Invoking freedom as a universal good, and arguing that sexuality is simply biologically and environmentally caused allows one to argue that being allowed to do what one's nature impels one to do is good. Whatever is natural is good—and, conveniently, sexuality is always natural.

What my professor's claim illustrates is that, in contemporary culture, self-expression has become the hallmark of freedom. We are natural organisms, and it is good to express that nature. Lamentably, this freedom of self-expression is perhaps the most common, and commonly defended, form or aspect of freedom. We have the right to hope that freedom is nobler than mere self-expression. Certainly it is easy to see that no society can survive and no viable culture can form with the principle of self-expression as a cardinal virtue. Cultures need broadly held and affirmed ideas, virtues, and meanings—ideas and meanings bigger than persons—to which persons contribute by acceptance and commitment, and from which they derive meaning and purpose for their lives. Freedom is thus not about self-expression in any but a relatively trivial sense.

From an LDS perspective this point should be clear. Life has a fundamentally moral and fundamentally eternal purpose, including the freely giving of oneself to the truth and goodness manifest in the will of God. Morality that is greater than self, and is not mere self-expression, is not meant to suppress the self or the self's nature, but to enhance it, sustain it, and eternalize it.

When we see sexuality in this light, we begin to understand the intimate relationship between sexuality and morality. Sexuality in the modern world has become increasingly disconnected from all other aspects of life, including the moral. It seems to have taken on a life of its own, running in parallel to all other life concerns, independent and self-sustaining. This is a very problematic understanding of sexuality. It simultaneously makes too much and too little of sexuality. It makes too much of sexuality by assuming it is an autonomous reality in our nature that establishes our very identity, infiltrates all other human concerns, and provides the most powerful but temporary pleasures of life. This understanding makes too little of sexuality, by assuming that there is no transcendent meaning, and no moral core or moral purpose in sexuality that unfolds for us and in us what it means to be a human being at our very best, and intimately bound to others in profoundly moral ways.

Arguments for same-gender marriage that invoke a right to freedom as self-expression are unpersuasive because self-expression is not the essence of human freedom or human sexuality—rather than one possible manifestation of them. Self-expression is certainly not the kind of freedom on which cultures, legal systems, and moral ideals can be erected or sustained. And these have never had as a central purpose the sustenance and preservation of self-expression. Sexual self-expression is not fundamental to any important understanding of freedom or of sexuality per se. The enhancement of self-expression (sexual or otherwise) is not a foundational principle on which families or enlightened societies have ever, or could ever, be built or maintained.

The Destruction of the Meaning of Sexuality, Marriage, and Family

Referring once more to the comment from my professor's book on human sexuality—that we will never be truly free until there is no more stigma or sanctions attached to sexual activity than there is to eating—I remember when it struck me what the effect on our humanity would be if his recommendation ever became reality. Simply put, the effect would be that sexual activity would have no more meaning in our lives than eating does now. Sexual intimacy would have about as much meaning for us as a cheeseburger and a Diet Coke. Perhaps this image makes my point too harshly, but the point holds. Even if we were to use the comparison of a much better meal, it would still be the case that no meal, nothing we eat, touches the essence of our nature and our existence in the way sexual intimacy within a dual-gender marriage does. There is no higher, grander, revelatory meaning toward which eating points us, unless it is a sacramental meal (which, rather than consumption can be a sort of consummation), though obviously my professor didn't have a sacrament in mind.[10]

In short there is unique meaning in dual-gender conjugal sexual intimacy by virtue of its very nature and ours. There is something transcendent about it.[11] It points beyond itself, and in so doing it has meaning and power of a moral nature because it creates unique relationships and binds us to others across generations in unique ways. It allows us to participate in the meaning of what it is to be the kind of beings we are, bound to each other in ways that can only be expressed through uniting males and females by covenant, thus affirming in and with out bodies our sexual complementarity and participating in fruitfulness and creativity affirmed through the bearing and rearing of children, and through the perfecting of love in fidelity and sacrifice in conjugal family life.

This meaning and transcendence is at the core of our human nature. To negate these rich meanings, and reduce the meaning of sexuality to bodily satisfaction, self-expression, or even personal emotional fulfillment—perhaps even the fulfillment of relation to a partner and rearing children—is to seriously diminish the meaning of sexuality, and to lose a profoundly important part of what it means to be us. To anchor the importance of the bearing and rearing of children in self-enrichment is to negate the meaning that inheres by nature in sexuality, marriage, and family. Even if not recognized—and I assume that most people do not explicitly recognize this—the view that marriage is about self-fulfillment, self-enrichment, or even freely chosen companionship makes the meaning of family a function of personal fulfillment rather than of something beyond the self.

---

10. Jeffrey R. Holland, "Of Souls, Symbols, and Sacraments," Address at Brigham Young University on January 12, 1988. Available at http://www.familylifeeducation.org/gilliland/procgroup/Souls.htm (accessed January 5, 2013).

11. See Truman G. Madsen, *Eternal Man* (Deseret Book: Salt Lake City, 1966); Truman G. Madsen, *Four Essays on Love* (Deseret Book: Salt Lake City, 1971).

Some advocating same-gender marriage might argue for its legitimacy precisely to allow same-gender couples to participate more fully in the richer and fuller meanings of sexuality, marriage, and family that have just been expressed here. As counterexamples such arguments sometimes refer to the case of infertile couples who cannot participate fully in all the meaningful aspects of family life, or to the case of fertile couples who choose not to have children. At first glance it appears that there is no essential difference between those cases and the case of those in a same-sex marriage.

However, all the meaningful aspects of conjugal marriage articulated here have their origin in the intimate interdependence of male and female, in sexual complementarity, and both the literal and symbolic meaningfulness of the procreative act. To seek to affirm some of the meaningful fruits of the fullness of covenanted, conjugal sexuality (fidelity, commitment, emotional intimacy, etc.) while actively dis-affirming, and refusing to participate in its fundamental meaningful manifestation (the union of male and female in symbol, spirit, and sexual complementarity) substantially alters the meaning of the integral and fecund whole that is sexuality, marriage, and family.

Beyond the fact that same-gender couples can presumably be as committed to and loving toward one another and their adopted children as those in traditional marriages, to affirm the fruit of a covenanted conjugal marriage and reject the root covenanted conjugal intimacy itself is a fatal inconsistency. To reject participation in the expressions of meaning that transcend the couple which lie at the heart of the meaning of sexuality, marriage, and family (sexually complementary union) while at the same time trying to appropriate full participation in all other facets of sexuality, marriage, and family will unavoidably alter the meaning of the whole for all who participate in marriage of any type. Infertile couples affirm all that they can of the fullness of sexuality, marriage, and family, and would do all if they could. Dual gender married couples who choose not to have children affirm the root of conjugal marriage and family by affirming sexual complementarity, and its association to fecundity but choose not to participate in all its fruits as a family. Same gender couples affirm all that they want of the fruits common to conjugal marriage, but refuse to affirm or participate in the essential core, hoping that the fruits can be severed without consequence from the root. If the core of meaning of sexuality, marriage, and family is not intact and honored, the meaning of the whole is lost from the experience of all other aspects of sexuality, marriage, and family.

My professor's flawed understanding and narrow vision of human sexuality was lamentable, but understandable. It came directly from the ethos of the sexual revolution. What got lost in the wake of the sexual revolution is the meaning and purpose of sexuality itself. This had consequences for the meaning we attach to marriage and family as well. History, culture, institutions, and, for Latter-day Saints and other religious people, revelation, establish the meaning of life itself and all aspects of life, including marriage, family, and sexuality. When these sources of meaning are rejected or unraveled, the very meaning of our lives and our understanding of what matters are unraveled as well. No amount of personal expression or self-fulfillment can re-create or constitute these meanings and mattering that anchor our sense of ourselves and provide us a sustainable understanding of *what matters* and *why* it matters. Unfortunately, when meaning is lost collectively and individually, there is a substantial cost that must be borne by individuals, often across generations. The cost is measured in terms of meaning and purpose that informs our sense and experience of love, intimacy, sensitivity, relatedness, and our understanding of the good and worthwhile, making it difficult for people to sense whether they are becoming better in ways that matter.

Articulating the Defense of Dual-Gender Marriage

In one sense it seems strange that sexual responsibility and integrity, dual-gender marriage, and traditional families should need careful conceptual, philosophical, and legal defense. But for many reasons, some of which were articulated above, this is the position in which we find ourselves. Unfortunately, many families and marriages in our culture are in trouble. It would be easier to defend traditional dual-gender marriage against the legalization of same-gender marriage if numbers of intact marriages and families were higher and if rates of out-of-wedlock births were lower. However, it must be kept in mind that the same cultural ideas and forces that currently press for legalization of same-gender marriage are the ideas and forces that are at the heart of many of the problems in traditional families. In other words, false understandings of our human nature, rejection of notions of agency and responsibility, the wrong view of sexuality as a self-existent biological urgency, confusion of morality with self-expression, and the legacy of the sexual revolution over the past half-century are at the core of the decline in the stability and strength of traditional marriage and family as well as the support for dual-gender marriage.

It is certainly clear that marriage and family will not be strengthened and improved by accepting, embracing, and codifying into law the very perspectives that have weakened families and marriages over fifty years. We will not solve a problem of drifting from the prudent and humanity affirming course by accelerating the speed of the drift. If the underlying assumptions, understandings, and ideas that have led to the problems marriages and families now face are socially validated, legally legitimated, and incorporated into the mainstream of our culture, the arguments and perspectives that can correct the problem will be marginalized, alternative discourse will be weakened, and the possibility of course correction—or even the perceived need for course correction—is likely to just fade away. If the cultural world-view is currently wrong, legalizing same-gender marriage can only serve to reinforce the wrongness. This is the answer to the frequently asked question, "What's the harm in allowing same-gender marriage to have equal status with dual-gender marriage?"[12] An often cited bit of wisdom tells us that "the law is a teacher." What it permits, it validates and legitimates; and affirming intellectual and cultural discourse grows up around the newly legitimate practices.

The defense of traditional marriage and family, and the concomitant refutation of arguments for same-gender marriage, really revolve around a few clusters of key issues. Arguments for same-gender marriage reflect an unclear—even false, though perhaps not obviously so—understanding of our human nature. Defending traditional understandings of marriage, family, and sexual integrity requires getting right about our nature, teaching the proper understanding of our nature broadly across the culture, and deriving views of sexuality, marriage, and family based on the right views.

In this regard, the current body of work (philosophical, legal, theological, and social scientific) coming from a number of faith traditions is growing. For example, work carried out within the Natural Law perspective has contributed extremely important insights, arguments, and resource materials. Work in the area of Natural Law comes largely from a Catholic tradition and may not be well known among LDS Church members. There are, within this tradition, very strong arguments against same-gender marriage. Latter-day Saints who are unaware of or not confident about good arguments and reasons (other than our religious views) for opposing same-gender marriage might profitably look at the body of work in the Natural Law perspective.[13] The arguments I have outlined here reflect, in some ways, the spirit of Natural Law arguments.

---

12. See the essays in Lynn D. Wardle, ed., *What's the Harm?* (Lanham, Md.: University Press of America, 2008).

13. See, as a good introduction, Sherif Girgis, Robert P. George, and Ryan T. Anderson, *What is Marriage?: Man and Woman: A Defense* (New York: Encounter Books, 2012). See also, Sherif Gergis, Robert T. George, and Ryan T. Anderson, "What is Marriage?" *Journal of Law and Public Policy* 34, no. 1 (Winter 2010): 245–87.

A second important cluster of arguments relevant to the refutation of arguments for same-gender marriage revolve around getting right about our understanding of human sexuality and our nature as beings inherently endowed with moral agency—so that we are not just natural organisms subject to purely natural forces. If we are fundamentally moral agents (not subject to any causes in the moral/intellectual/cultural sphere to which we do not contribute or yield ourselves), then sexuality is not a powerful natural force but a natural, morally relevant context in which we are privileged to exercise our eternal agency. Accepting the fundamental status of moral agency and our nature as moral agents alters how we understand sexuality, marriage, and family.

There is much more to say on this topic, though not space enough here to say it. Again, Natural Law theorists have done good work in this area and scholars from other faith traditions have made important contributions. In my conclusion, I will deal with the issue briefly in the context of discussing what our LDS perspective can provide us in our defense of sexual integrity,[14] dual-gender marriage, and the importance of the conjugal family.

A third cluster of arguments regarding opposition to same-gender marriage revolves around legal issues. The issues focus on matters of rights and distinctions between unalienable rights and rights granted by the state, along with questions regarding the rights of society to prefer and foster particular family structures, private relationships, and even private behaviors. There are also issues related to justice, fairness, equal protection, free expression, the best interests of children, and religious liberty to name a few. I have virtually nothing to say about these issues because they are highly technical and I am not trained in the law. However, it is important to note that, here again, legal scholars within the Natural Law perspective have been focused and active in creating a body of quality scholarship. However, scholars from other faith traditions have also been active nationally in the courts, in the political process, and in academia. I have found these arguments to be sophisticated and, often, persuasive.

Discourse about opposition to the legalization of same-gender marriage and the defense of sexual integrity, dual-gender marriage, and the traditional family has been done from a Natural Law perspective. While some Latter-day Saints have been active in all of these areas, much more remains to be done to educate, persuade, and energize our culture by the

---

14. The term "sexual integrity" is borrowed from the Love and Fidelity Network (www.loveandfidelity.org).

force of good and compelling ideas. I believe it is time for more Latter-day Saints to contribute in defense of conjugal marriage and family.

There are several forms our contribution might take. First, understandings of our nature, of sexuality, and of marriage and family available to us from the restored gospel have much to contribute to the reasoned defense of dual-gender marriage and family. We can make some sophisticated and strong arguments, because of our doctrines, that might be compelling even to those who do not share our doctrinal commitments. Second, what our society finally decides about the legal status of same-gender marriage will have a major effect on the moral climate; the meaning of sexuality, marriage, and family; and on the stability and success of marriages and families, as well as an effect on what rational and legal arguments can be made in defense of and for the protection of sexual integrity, marriage, and family. It would be unfortunate if proponents of same-gender marriage were to capture the discourse and establish the content and the underlying philosophy that will inform all future discussions. That, simply put, would entail living out the intellectual and cultural effects of the sexual revolution of fifty years ago for another fifty years into the future. Third, the discourse on same-gender marriage has profound implications for religious liberty and freedom of conscience. Some of these are already findng their way through in the legal system. It seems clear that the position our society ultimately takes on the legalization of same-gender marriage will have substantial impact on the free exercise of conscience and religious liberty.

Perspective Provided by the Restored Gospel

Finally let me present a brief treatment of a number of understandings about ourselves and the nature of sexuality, marriage, and family that offer us insights and perspectives that can support clear and cogent arguments in favor of sexual integrity, dual-gender marriage, and the traditional family. The fact that these understandings can be derived from our religion (some can also be derived from other intellectual sources) does not mean that they should appeal only to Latter-day Saints, or that our arguments reflect only religious faith. Our opportunity and, I believe, our duty is to take these insights and do the hard work of rendering the insights and implications in reputable and compelling scholarly language, and introduce that language into the public discourse. Revealed truths are true for all people, not just for Latter-day Saints. I think we do not want to assert that revealed truths are either irrational or impossible to defend. Our job is to work out the defense so it can be useful to our brothers and sisters on both sides of the same-gender marriage issue. The potential insights offered here reflect my own thinking and not official declarations from the Church. I trust these interpretations are orthodox; I hope they are helpful. The insights that I take to be implicit in a reasonable reading of the gospel are presented as a list, in no particular order, that is intended to foment thought and, if they are useful, inform further thought and discourse.

1. There is a fundamentally moral purpose to creation, and a fundamentally moral purpose to the life of every human being (Moses 1:39, Abraham 3:24–26). In addition to whatever moral tests may arise in the context of social justice and the protection of human rights and dignity, there is also a profoundly personal moral purpose to life. Personal morality is not just the product of ultimately arbitrary socio-cultural processes. It is at the heart of the life of every person by virtue of his or her being a human being and a moral agent, and by virtue of the Light of Christ. Personal morality matters, and it matters that we be clear about what we morally can be and should be. There is work to be done in helping people know there is moral purpose to human life and in revitalizing and re-emphasizing the place and importance of personal morality in society. We need to work out an effective and persuasive public discourse about personal morality.

2. We are eternal uncreated pre-existent intelligent beings (Abr. 3:18, 22–25; D&C 93:29). This gives rise to two relevant implications. First, since the intelligence that constitutes us is eternal, it was not made out of nothing (creation ex nihilo). Thus, it is much harder for me to claim that God "made me the way I am," or that "I have specific morally relevant proclivities that God gave me." The good news is that our challenges are built into what we *do*, not what we *are*; we are not locked into doing what we do, being what we are, or wanting what we want. Our current nature, inherited from the fall can be changed, with the help of others and of Christ. We are perfectible. The second possibility is that, because we are eternal, our actions and moral commitments have eternal implications.

3. "Gender is an essential characteristic of individual pre-mortal, mortal, and eternal identity and purpose."[15] This statement from the proclamation suggests that gender, and all that it implies, is not rooted simply in biology nor is it the mere product of socio-cultural forces. This statement also suggests some permanence to gender.

---

15. "The Family," 102.

4. We believe "the means by which mortal life is created to be divinely appointed."[16] Sexuality is associated with the divine aspects of our nature. Sexuality is also a fundamentally moral activity—neither simply biological nor simply personal. That proclamation states further: "We further declare that God has commanded that the sacred powers of procreation are to be employed only between man and woman, lawfully wedded as husband and wife."[17]

5. The proclamation also teaches, "Children are entitled to birth within the bonds of matrimony, and to be reared by a father and a mother who honor marital vows with complete fidelity."[18] This implies that both mothers and fathers (each possessed of gender as part of his or her eternal identity) are important for optimal rearing and nurturing of children. This statement comes close to expressing an argument for the rights of children—that they have a right to the influence of parents of both genders in their lives. It also implies that men and women make unique contributions to the family and to children.

6. Dual-gender marriages and the relationships created by the families they produce are intended to persist eternally. "The divine plan of happiness enables family relationships to be perpetuated beyond the grave. Sacred ordinances and covenants available in holy temples make it possible for individuals to return to the presence of God and for families to be united eternally."[19] Apparently some of the defining purposes of life are achievable only as dual-gender married couples. This possibility sounds reasonable in the face of what appear to be promises of eternal progress related to increase and fecundity. It would appear that fecundity, even if not fully possible in this life, is an inherent part of our nature and, therefore, should be an inherent part of both the meaning and the actuality of sexuality, marriage, and family.

7. Families are not temporary single-generation institutions. They are meant to connect people in familial bonds across many generations (D&C 128). One of the problems with same-gender marriages is that they purposefully place constraints on the "'welding' link" that constitutes families in the eternal sense. Couples in same-gender marriages deliberately place themselves in a position of needing to borrow future

---

16. Ibid..
17. Ibid..
18. Ibid..
19. Ibid..

inter-generational bonds as well as fecundity from other people. This presents not just a technical problem (which can perhaps be only partially resolved technologically) but it suggests a repudiation and refusal to participate in the important principle of eternal familial sealing bonds.

8. Human agency is at the heart of our nature and at the foundation of our doctrine. The Book of Mormon speaks of a fundamental division between types of created things—those that act, and those that are acted upon (2 Nephi 2:13). Agency can be considered in some sense the most fundamental doctrine of the gospel, without which nothing else would make sense. Illustrations of the importance of agency are replete in scripture, so I will not take the space to build a case here. The most important summary point is that our doctrine of agency implies that, because agency is fundamental to our being, everything we do, including what we want, what and how we desire, what we give ourselves to, and what we thus are, fully manifest the presence and the workings of agency. To be sure, our agency is deeper and richer than the capacity for making deliberative choices—though this capacity is important. Choice is necessary to agency, but agency goes beyond deliberative choice. A more robust understanding of agency leads to the conclusion that even desires, attractions, and our identity itself, are, in a deep and profound way, agentic. The most wonderful implication of this, in turn, is that, since virtually everything about us is produced by subtle and yet profoundly agentic actions in which we meaningfully participate, all of these things can also change by the same subtle and profoundly agentic actions made efficacious by the active participation of a powerful, loving, atoning personal Savior.

Summary

I have not given here an argument specifically aimed at defending dual-gender marriage against claims made for the legitimacy of same-gender marriage. Rather, I have attempted to show that this whole controversy is not the result of a suddenly enlightened discovery of a long-lived injustice that calls for a straightforward modification of social practice and attitude. Instead, our current situation is simply the result—the latest avatar—of a set of ideas that had their greatest social and intellectual currency during the sexual revolution and the accompanying social movements of the 1960s and 1970s. It has taken some time for these ideas to move through cultures and institutions, but we are now living out the results of ideas based on thin and inconsistent rationality, a faulty understanding of our nature, self-indulgence and self-assertion—which ideas have, unfortunately, choked out, or attempted to choke out, better ideas. Sometimes the connections between those underlying ideas and their contemporary expressions have been so lost as to go unnoticed.

No adequate response can be made to the challenge of same-gender marriage unless we are clear about the real and often forgotten underlying issues, assumptions, and errors that undergird the entire issue and the public discourse it generates. Very bad ideas and assumptions are being promoted. Good ideas must be marshaled to meet the challenge. The wrong view of our human nature; the reduction of human sexuality to merely biological impulse, environmental conditioning, or a means of self-expression; and the negation of our moral agency have come together in a "perfect storm" to challenge the values and understandings that have sustained our families, our culture, and our religion.

I hope that we as a people will respond with charity. But we must also respond with ideas, analyses, and arguments that go to the heart of the crucial issues and positions on which advocacy for same-gender marriage is based. No other responses will be adequate. The restored gospel is a great blessing, in part because it offers the understandings from which an adequate response and defense of sexual integrity, dual-gender marriage, and the conjugal family can be constructed. The gospel also provides compelling motivation to defend the status of dual-gender marriage, preserve our religious freedom,[20] and insure that our children and our brothers and sisters can achieve the moral purposes that dual-gender marriages and families are uniquely able to provide.

---

20. See William McGurn, "The Cult of Anti-Mormonism," *Wall Street Journal*, October 27, 2011, available at http://www.becketfund.org/the-cult-of-anti-mormonism-2 (accessed January 5, 2013).

In this essay, Camille Williams recounts her experiences in attempting to reconcile the doctrine and practices of the Church of Jesus Christ of Latter-day Saints with feminist theories of equality—and to make sense of both in her everyday life. She was uncomfortable with sex role division in the home, church, and society, and found the transition to motherhood particularly difficult. Her accepting counsel for mothers to care for their own children where possible tested her ability to understand scriptures, feminist theory, and the moral practice of mothering. Through her study and experiences, she came to recognize "that Christ's work was done in the flesh. . . . [and that because] he has graven us on the palms of his hands, he knows us in his flesh, just as a mother knows in her flesh the child she has carried within her own body, the child she nursed, changed and bathed." This insight helped her better understand the calling of mothers and the importance of the work of women in the family, home, and church.

While a significant part of her experience was based on study and analysis, she clearly had to rely on the Spirit to discern the value and priority of competing views of women's roles. She refused to allow what she did not understand take precedence over what she knew by the Spirit to be good. She acknowledges validity in some aspects of a feminist critique of social, political, and religious practice, but concludes that no –ism has the power to solve the problem of evil in this world. She asserts that because LDS doctrine better explains mortality, it is the only doctrine which sufficiently understands and values women. Finally, she now understands why her mother sang in the kitchen as she made breakfast for the family.

Eight

In Your Patience Possess Ye Your Souls[1]

Camille S. Williams

You remember the story of Esau, how he sold his birthright for a mess of pottage (Gen. 25:29–34)? That was almost my story, too, although I can blame no brother for my inability to distinguish between the fleeting and the fundamental—only myself. Nor can I claim that my experience parallels that of any other Latter-day Saint interested in women's issues, although I expect that some of our concerns may be similar. I will tell you of the wrestle I had with God over the status of women in the Church and in the world—over my status.[2]

The equality of women with men was axiomatic to me as a young adult. Axiomatic, but also a matter of faith, for while I knew that "he inviteth [all the children of men] to come unto him and partake of his goodness; and he denieth none"—not black nor white, not bond nor free, not male nor female (2 Ne. 26:33)—it did appear that males were given preeminence in the home and in the Church because of their priesthood office. During the first three years of our marriage while both my husband and I were in college and working part-time, our first two children were born. I was struck by the disproportionate division of labor in reproduction and childrearing,[3] and in priesthood leadership in the home and the Church. While there are probably a thousand discrete offenses that I took over the years, they can be grouped generally under the following: priesthood, patriarchal order, polygamy, and priorities.[4]

---

1. Luke 21:19; D&C 101:38.

2. I acknowledge that searching for the self as I did can often result in entirely too much focus on self at the expense of weightier matters.

3. Although when home or with the children, my husband Richard has always done whatever needed to be done without regard to whose role or turn it was.

4. Some of those concerns do not seem to bother my daughters' generation, although I have seen among my students a kind of uneasiness among the males with how they are to function in the home as a priesthood leader without encroaching upon the autonomy and dignity of their wives. Among some of the female students, there is a concern over the "opportunity costs" of being at home

While these complaints might be considered the presenting "symptoms," the malady itself was my uneasiness about being a woman, especially being a mother. Some of the difficulties I experienced no doubt arose from my own immaturity, selfishness, and pride, but at some level I did not recognize the value of mothering my own children myself. As Victoria Wynn Leonard expresses it, "In our contemporary culture we are so imbued with the importance of productivity that it is hard to 'just be' with an infant. The endless job of cleaning, feeding, changing and playing with an infant often feels unproductive, empty of meaning and importance, especially since mothers aren't paid for it: the cardinal measure of productivity in our culture."[5] I had much to learn about mothering.

"Hast Thou but One Blessing, My Father? Bless Me, Even Me Also, O My Father" (Gen. 27:38)

We married the year *Roe v. Wade* struck down abortion restrictions; during the first few years of our marriage, the Equal Rights Amendment ratification procedure was being debated in various state legislatures, and the status of women was a topic of concern not only to me but to the nation. Some of the women in our neighborhood met to discuss women's issues, and I met with them to discuss the issues of the day. We also read and discussed some of the feminist books popular at the time and considered what we might do to improve women's status in society. While I had always been interested in politics, current events, and women's issues, it was shortly after the birth of our first child that the status of women—my status—became of overriding importance to me.

I was not very good with babies and children but thought I might be good in academics or administration. The advice that mothers be at home with their children seemed misplaced as applied to me: I had no intrinsic gifts for the job and almost no experience. My husband had to teach me how to diaper a baby and how to talk baby talk. I was quite sure that he could do a better job than I was doing at mothering, and it seemed to me that if all married men were not required to till the earth as was Adam, it was unreasonable to require that all married women devote themselves full-time to homemaking and child care. Surely God would not consign

---

with children for any significant length of time.

5. Victoria Wynn Leonard, "Mothering as Practice," in *Caregiving: Readings in Knowledge, Practice, Ethics, and Politics*, ed. Suzanne Gordon, Patricia Benner, and Nel Noddings (Philadelphia: University of Pennsylvania Press, 1996), 138.

me to spend my life doing something for which I was ill-suited, rather than something at which I might prove apt.

I studied all of the scriptures I could think of that dealt with women, marriage, or family; I read the commentaries on the scriptures; I read feminist critiques of religion, society, and gender roles. I tried to figure out my place in the world, in the temple, in church, sometimes feeling comfort, sometimes great distress.

Our beautiful son slept no more than 45 minutes at a time those first six weeks of his life; I was sleep-deprived and anxious as I prepared for finals that first semester in graduate school. I tried to nurse him as I studied my Old English text, but he would stop nursing to look at the page above him and resumed only when the book did not catch his eye. Pregnancy, labor, and delivery had already disabused me of the notion that I was in control of my body and my life; now it seemed that my life/our lives, were completely rearranged, again and again, to meet the needs of the child.

I had deliberately avoided courses in family sciences and child development because I thought I knew enough. I had also supposed that women who took those courses were at college just to look for husbands and were not particularly serious students.[6] I was surprised at my own ineptitude as a mother. I began to make some progress when I tried to imagine what it would be like not to be able to speak words or even not be able to grasp an object in front of my face. I developed some empathy for children by viewing them as "handicapped adults," as it were.

Part of this time was joyous, as we came to know this new person who challenged our creativity, patience, humor, and stamina; but it was very hard for me to accept the notion that the traditional roles of women as homemakers, childbearers, and childrearers, was in fact the equal of the roles of men as priesthood holders and providers. It was even harder to see my path separating from my husband's, as he continued on a professional track, and as I became more involved in childcare and less in study. After reading what seemed to be yet another pamphlet advising women to stay at home with their children, I concluded that I would try it but would not be happy with it.

Sex-role division had been an abstract concept; it was now a visceral reality, and I didn't much like the role assigned me despite the assurances made in church meetings and conferences about the importance of women and mothers. This seemed to me to be a kind of benign male dominance, which

---

6. Obviously I was wrong on both counts. I had to do those "courses" the hard way—by experience and my own study.

still resulted in female subordination. I did not like to think of myself as worthy of subordination, benign or otherwise. I concluded that the Church was a bit behind the times but might catch up soon to notions of equality.

Then the Church announced its opposition to the Equal Rights Amendment. I was deeply shocked by the news. When our Relief Society President announced that the Church opposed the ERA, I told her—politely and publicly—that she must surely be wrong; she referred me to the *Church News* editorial, and I told her—there in Relief Society, as she stood before us in opening exercises—that the *Church News* must have it wrong. I felt that the Church's opposition to the ERA undercut all of the assurances about the importance of women, and I felt betrayed. Over the course of the following weeks, I pendulated between anger and despair, rationality and emotion, over this opposition to the ERA. One day, I saw the two-page spread of general authorities of the Church. As I looked at the pictures of the First Presidency, the Council of the Twelve, and the other general authorities, all male, I thought to myself: What do you know about being a woman? Almost before that question was completed, another came into my mind, this one aimed at me: What do you know about being a prophet?

This question was disconcerting. I had been praying to know why God had allowed male dominance to reign, why priesthood was restricted to males, and why polygamy was instituted. I was angry much of the time and unhappy about my inferior lot in life. But I had to admit that I knew little or nothing about being a prophet. As I thought about it, it occurred to me that God could tell his prophet to oppose the ERA, or to ordain males, or to practice polygamy without necessarily telling the prophet *why* those things should be done. My prayers changed from the accusatory why-are-women-subordinated kind, to queries more akin to "Is it Thy will that men hold the priesthood? Didst Thou direct Joseph Smith to reinstitute polygamy? How can I understand it?" I cannot say that my concerns were resolved quickly; I did, however, experience a greater sense of peace about women's issues once I quit trying to pick a fight with God over the things I did not understand. I also tried to be open to other ways of interpreting those aspects of the Church over which I was distressed.

"I Know that He Loveth His Children; Nevertheless, I Do Not Know the Meaning of All Things" (1 Ne. 11:17)

I read Rex Lee's *A Lawyer Looks at the Equal Rights Amendment*, which demonstrated that there were good reasons for opposing the ERA and was reconciled to the position of the Church on that matter. I found feminism's support of elective abortion repugnant and contradictory to notions of equality. Even if women are disadvantaged, taking the lives of children as a means to "equality" cannot be justified.[7] It was also apparent, even then, that feminist support for the acceptance of homosexuality would undercut family relationships as well as gender identities.

Becoming reconciled about other matters happened piecemeal over years. Early on I was almost persuaded by the argument of some Mormon feminists that the sisters in the early part of the restoration seem to have functioned as though they had priesthood office; the retrenchment seemed to come later, apparently, because of what might be interpreted as a bit of competition between the women and the men over the power to bless the sick. The role division on the basis of biological sex, so the argument went, made little sense because both mothers and fathers are expected to be active parents, kind, gentle, meek, and self-sacrificing. There was also the current argument that if men are less sensitive to the spirit, less spiritual, and less willing to sacrifice than are women,[8] then why ordain men at all—why not just ordain women? Or, at the very least, why restrict the priesthood office to only men when both could be ordained and bless the family? Besides, if we are to earnestly seek the best gifts (D&C 46:8), surely women ought to seek ordination and thereby obtain the best gifts to use in God's service.

I tried this argument out on one of my mentors, a philosophy professor and bishop at BYU. He thought about it for a minute and then said to me: "That is a species of envy." "Easy for you to say, Bishop," I responded. He seemed unperturbed: "That may be so. Nevertheless, what you describe is a type of envy." When the gender roles seemed so lopsided in terms of respect and burden, I wondered whether calling it envy was a matter of blaming the oppressed, the dominated, and the secondary for simply wanting to be equal and to equally share the tasks at home and at Church.

Never one to suffer in silence, I voiced my concerns and my complaints to my husband. He answered mildly, as a general rule, and it was during one of our conversations that some aspects of priesthood authority became clearer to me. It is that the priesthood office in the home, to be efficacious, must be recognized by the wife and by the family. There is no real "enforcement clause" to an ordination. A priest, teacher, deacon, elder, my husband, or the President of the Church has no power "over me," and in a real sense, he can-

---

7. See my "Thoughts of a Pro-Life Feminist," *The World & I*, October 1991, available at http://www.worldandischool.com/public/1991/october/school-resource19638.asp (accessed May 30, 2013).

8. These corollaries apparently arise from statements by Church authorities and members about the superior spiritual sensitivities of women and mothers.

not "do anything" to me or for me that God would not have done. If he were to try to use priesthood power against the will of the Lord, it would no longer be a priesthood function. I am not subordinate to any priesthood holder. I can either follow priesthood counsel or not. I can seek the blessings of priesthood ordinances or choose not to. A priesthood holder is not autonomous in his priesthood activity. He works in concert with his brethren and recognizes a presiding officer. Significant portions of feminist theory are imbued with notions of power relations, and such a view of the world leaves little room for self-sacrifice, altruism, or mutuality except as negotiated settlement. While it is clear that authority and position can be misused, I concluded that each of us can misuse whatever gifts, resources, and relationships available to us. Men have no corner on sin or stupidity.

I had been toying with the idea of writing a book that would help Latter-day Saints make sense of women's issues in ways that might advance women's status. It would also open up Church members to the notion that action was needed to solve the problems women face, particularly if we wanted to encourage women to convert. One of my friends from the women's issues discussion group was also interested in the project. For reasons I don't recall, we were allowed to interview some members of the general Relief Society presidency. I remember in particular, the non-defensive way in which Janeth Cannon answered our questions, pointing out that too frequently the comparison of gender roles was skewed—the worst jobs mothers and homemakers performed were being compared to the best aspects of a profession. Any job, any profession, has its downside, she pointed out. She offered the view that the reason motherhood and priesthood were "equivalent" in value is that each teaches deeper ways of loving and serving. Additionally, men need the experience of priesthood service because they cannot experience the bearing and rearing of children in the same ways that women can. The idea that priesthood ordination was a compensation for men's less-intensive parenthood experiences initially seemed a stretch to me, but her straightforward manner was encouraging and her warmth was engaging.

We were surprised when we were told that we could meet President Kimball and talk with him for a few minutes. He was also gracious and interested in what we were doing. I was nervous and did not want to be insulting; we wanted to keep the tape recorder going as we tried to ask the list of questions we had drafted, including asking him whether he thought women would be ordained to the priesthood at some time in the future. "No," he said. For some reason, his response did not sound harsh to me. As we talked with him, I felt that I was filled from head to toe with the knowledge that he was a prophet of God, just as though the top of my head had opened and spirit had flowed into my whole body. My impulse was to testify to those in the room and tell them: "This man is a prophet of God." I looked at those in the room: his secretary, the Relief Society presidency, and my friend. Surely they all knew this as well as I did and felt that same testimony. My questions seemed suddenly much less important than my testimony. It was as though I had an answer but needed to find the right questions.

This was not a matter of telling myself that "when the Lord speaks through his prophet, the conversation stops." Rather it was an extension of earlier experiences in which the Holy Spirit has witnessed truth and comforted me. Many of those experiences occurred while accepting the ministrations of the priesthood. If the practice of priesthood were infirm, it seemed to me that infirmity would be manifested in failed ministration; and that rather than peace, comfort, and enlightenment, I would have felt darkness. I was unwilling then and am unwilling now to let what I do not know take on greater importance than what I do know by the Spirit.[9] I have learned by my own experience why it was important for me to be the primary caregiver—the mother—to my own children.

As a young mother I was very focused on my own ineptitude at mothering, my paltry skills of household organization, and my repeated failures of patience, kindness, and charity. The only thing I really had to offer my children was my love for them. It is that loving bond that invited me to keep trying to mother them and to keep seeking forgiveness. I learned to accept their love and the love of God—not as rewards based on merit but as gifts. The strength and immediacy of that desire for the welfare of my children initially surprised me and frustrated my attempts to order my life. At the same time, that desire has become an overriding cause for gratitude and joy. I do not suppose that LDS women in general are as ill-prepared spiritually as I was for mothering, but I know of no mother who finds the experience easy, and few who consider themselves adequate.

I found some comfort and encouragement in some of the conference talks, such as Elder Neal A. Maxwell's "The Women of God," in which he acknowledged that we "know so little . . . about the reasons for the division of duties between womanhood and manhood as well as between motherhood and priesthood."[10] Less comforting, perhaps, was Elder Packer's ques-

---

9. How we know and what constitutes knowledge are topics for a whole branch of philosophy. I subscribe to Moroni 10:5: "And by the power of the Holy Ghost ye may know the truth of all things."
10. Neal A. Maxwell, "The Women of God," *Ensign*, May 1978, 10.

tion to sisters: "If you are absenting yourself from Relief Society because 'you don't get anything out of it,' tell me, dear sister, what is it that you are putting into it?"[11] While I wasn't exactly absenting myself from Relief Society, I had a strong preference for the cognitive, the spiritual, and skills basic to homemaking—and I admit that I had something akin to disdain for crafts and what seemed to me to be the frivolous arts. I was pierced by Elder Packer's charge: I had not given my best to the Church's organization for women. I thought it time to repent and show myself a worker. In effect, I had been focused on understanding the role of men before I had understood the role of women. It seemed time to give that some thought.

It was probably when I was pregnant with our third child and chasing two toddlers that I began to better appreciate the work of mothers. I was exhausted, always exhausted. When I had morning sickness and was sitting on the bathroom floor feeling that my breakfast was not going to stay down, I could hear the footfall of the two-year-old and the babble of the baby in the other room. I was sick and afraid that I already did not have the stamina or even enough arms to handle three young children, much less the charity needed to love them and treat them kindly in all the circumstances of their neediness. It occurred to me that this is why some women abort: they are afraid they cannot care for the child, that they will be a bad mother, or that they will have no help. I knew I could call my own mother—who was thrilled about any possibility of another grandchild—call my husband home, or even call my visiting teachers if need be. I only needed to ask for help. Relative to the difficulties other women endure, my pregnancies were easy. It was hard enough for me at the time, but I was still strong and healthy.

Admittedly, there were times when I felt that God cared little for women and how it feels to be pregnant, labor, and deliver. Trying to keep up with small children while pregnant or recovering from childbirth, I sometimes felt that women were merely conduits, the means to the end of bringing others into this world. I found that a most unhappy thought.

I am not sure when it dawned on me that Christ's work was done in the flesh. His sacrifice was not a cognitive exercise. He has graven us on the palms of his hands; he knows us in his flesh, just as a mother knows in her flesh the child she has carried within her own body—the child she nursed, changed, and bathed. Certainly the Church requires ordinances, but much of the day-to-day living testimony of members male and female is expressed in the actions of embodied beings serving each other. Much

---

11. Boyd K. Packer, "The Relief Society," *Ensign*, Nov. 1978, 7.

of that service can be and is performed by women. Conversely, if women were to stop bearing children or to decide not to recognize priesthood authority, the work of the Lord could not continue.[12] This seemed to me to be evidence for the need of male-female cooperation, though not necessarily a brief for why role division is recommended.

A common response is to dismiss sexual difference as relatively little importance, but that would be a mistake. Carrying and bearing a child is a life-changing experience, as is the never-ceasing service required to rear a child. Since sexual dimorphism is an eternal aspect of our being, it is not unreasonable to suppose that there may be endowments or gifts that come with that sexual difference.[13] I am no fan of biological or "spiritual" determinism, nor would I want to encourage "a sentimental view of mothering that obligates women to motherhood because of their biology." Rather, I recognize mothering as a "moral practice"[14] with profound consequences in this life and in the next.[15] Truly much of what we learn about who we are and the meaning of our relationship to God and to other people arises from our relationship with our mothers, whatever their virtues or vices. That foundational relationship will color and shape other relationships throughout our lives. I have also learned that the relationship a mother has with her children will teach her about who she is and the meaning of her relationship to God and to other people; this relationship will be profoundly important to her happiness and well-being.

We sometimes mistakenly view mothering as the list of tasks performed by a mother, and so we generally recognize the only physical tasks uniquely performed by females as gestation and lactation. On the basis of that assumption, it is argued that at least the responsibilities of childrearing and

---

12. I've developed these in Camille S. Williams, "A Dialogue on Feminist Theology, A Response to Professor Ruether," in *Mormonism in Dialogue with Contemporary Christian Theologies*, ed. David L. Paulsen and Donald W. Musser (Macon, Ga.: Mercer University Press, 2007).

13. See Camille S. Williams, "To What Purpose Is this Waste? Rehabilitating Female Roles in the Family," in *Virtue and the Abundant Life*, ed. Lloyd D. Newell, et al. (Salt Lake City: Deseret Book, 2012), 136–50.

14. Leonard, "Mothering as Practice," 126.

15. I elaborated this concept in Camille S. Williams, "More Freedom from Earth-Stains, More Longing for Home," *The Religious Educator* 10, no. 1 (2009): 101–12. The moral practice of mothering is not restricted to women who themselves bear children. My children have been "mothered" by a variety of good and generous women—some of whom are the mothers of many children, and others who have never married or never borne children.

providing economically for the family could be equally shared. I do not have special insight as to why the Church recommends that fathers are to be the primary providers and mothers the primary nurturers. I do know that each is a difficult and important task, and my own experience has convinced me that dividing up the tasks equally between the spouses would not necessarily be an improvement. I've argued elsewhere that "the [Church's] recommended division of labor within the family recognizes that children are worthy of our best care. Pregnancy, birth, lactation, and child care are both important and taxing so women should, where possible, be relieved of the necessity of wage-earning during childbearing and child-rearing years."[16] It is one thing to construct a reasonable argument for role division within the family, and that can be done. It is quite another to feel right about it as a choice in one's own life. For me, the bond with the children came first, and I recognized possible reasons for role division over time and trial. However, if the LDS First Presidency had not counseled mothers to care for their own children where possible, I would have focused much more on career and much less on rearing my children. I would have missed out on being with my own children. I regret that I did not recognize earlier that being a mother is a calling, not simply a cultural practice defined by the larger tradition. It makes some sense for us to accept that calling, despite our lack of confidence and its many challenges, and to anticipate that by accepting the calling we are entitled to God's help in understanding and fulfilling that calling.[17]

There are practical reasons for why so many couples do not each work part-time and care for children part-time. With few exceptions, part-time work has lower pay, lacks seniority, will not qualify a worker for insurance, and has less job security. Two part-time workers are unlikely to earn as much over time in wages and benefits as one full-time male worker with a good job. In addition, a part-time position will usually have the same impact as a full-time job in terms of costs of commuting and is inefficient in terms of continuity either at work or at home. At home, there is also some evidence that women and men respond differently to children and that children respond differently to men and women. These responses in adults might be attributed to acculturation, but it is harder to understand why infants would respond differently to an adult on the basis of the sex of the child and the sex of the adult—unless one is willing to hold open the

---

16. Williams, "A Dialogue on Feminist Theology, A Response to Professor Ruether," 287.

17. The Catholic notion of marriage and motherhood as a vocation seems to recognize this important task as God-given.

idea that there really are some inherent, nonbiological differences between men and women, and that those differences matter.[18]

It seems to me that too often when the question of sex-role division in the family is broached, the real question is something like "why do women get stuck with the kids?" There is often the unspoken assumption that childrearing and homemaking get in the way of the real work of the world—work in family and home is a poor second. If we were genuinely convinced that it is important for children to be born into this world and reared well, we might ask what needs to be done to encourage the birth of children into an atmosphere where they could thrive? One possible answer would be sex-role division of responsibility in the family.

Pregnancy and lactation are stressors on the body, emotions, and mind.[19] If women are committed to the workforce for whatever reason, they may be more likely to curtail the number children born in order to minimize the physical and emotional toll, as well as the amount of time lost from paid employment. If work takes women out of the home, they are less likely to breastfeed their children, and their children then do not have the benefits of breast over bottle-feeding. It may be that the recommendation that husbands and fathers provide for the family could give mothers the opportunity to experience pregnancy, lactation, and caring for children with less physical stress if she is not required to simultaneously work at a paid job. There have been proposals to restructure the workplace to accommodate part-time work for parents, but that is not yet a reality. There are some indicators that men and women approach work differently—just as they tend to approach child care differently—and that children respond differently to a female parent than to a male parent.[20] For example, one study of university faculty who took leave after the birth of a child indicated that the women actually used the time to recuperate and be with the

---

18. See Steven E. Rhoads, *Taking Sex Differences Seriously* (New York: Encounter Books, 2004).

19. I am not alleging that cognitive function dwindles with motherhood, merely that a child or children become an additional major focal point apart from whatever else is occupying the mother's mind, such as work.

20. I briefly discuss this issue in "Family Norms in Adoption Law: Safeguarding the Best Interests of the Adopted Child," *St. Thomas Law Review* 18 (Winter 2005): 686–88. For a more in-depth treatment, see A. Dean Byrd, "Gender Complentarity and Child-rearing: Where Tradition and Science Agree," *Journal of Law & Family Studies* 6 (2004): 213.

child, while the men tended to use the time as an opportunity to complete some work that would advance their careers.[21]

Over the years I have begun to better understand the strengths of women and to see more clearly, I think, some of the strengths and vulnerabilities of men. I had little understanding of the difficulties my father and brothers may have experienced as I was growing up. They seemed pretty self-assured to me. It wasn't until I saw a bit of what my own sons went through as they negotiated their way from childhood to adolescence to adulthood that I had a sense of how difficult life can be for a male. (There's a sentence I never thought I'd write.)

I can mark some of the milestones of maturing as a mother, sometimes small, such as the day I realized that the idealized mother described in sermon and on greeting cards was not the actual expectation of the Church or anyone else. I did not have to try to be that kind of mother. I only needed to be the mother I could be to my children: maybe more inclined to read to them than to do crafts with them, or to play ball with them—though I could not play piano for them.[22] It was a great relief to feel that although I lacked many of the gifts stereotypically attributed to women, the children and I could make do with developing our gifts and interests together. I have also come to appreciate that I needed these experiences of femaleness to better understand what it is to be human. Each day's cooking and washing—the looking after the physical—and doing it all again is part of living after the manner of happiness in the flesh. I finally understood why my mother sang in the kitchen in the mornings as she made breakfast for our family.

"I Will Refuse To Be Comforted" (Moses 7:44)

It seemed that even as I thought myself making progress toward "figuring out" the "woman question,"[23] I sometimes felt overwhelmed by grief or anger over the miserable conditions in which so many women have lived and in which so many now live. Women's history on this earth includes sexual exploitation, assault, slavery, domestic violence, loss of life

---

21. Rhoads, *Taking Sex Differences Seriously*, 10–13.

22. See Lili Anderson and Camille S. Williams, "Faithful Mothering," in *Helping and Healing Our Families: Principles and Practices Inspired by The Family: A Proclamation to the World*, ed. Craig H. Hart, Lloyd D. Newell, Elaine Walton, and David C. Dollahite (Salt Lake City: Deseret Book Co., 2005), 172–77.

23. Discussed in Camille S. Williams, "Women in the Book of Mormon: Inclusion, Exclusion, and Juxtaposition," *Journal of Book of Mormon Studies* 11, no. 1 (Spring 2002): 66–79.

in childbirth, and an inferior status in society and is therefore harrowing to read. Some scriptural texts from the Old Testament to the Doctrine and Covenants seem to contain harshness toward women in various narratives, sermons, or doctrines. So, for me this was not just history. I deeply felt the sorrows of my sex. Maybe other women saw themselves as Esther or as Rachel, but I felt something of Leah's desperate longing for love and respect and some of Emma's puzzled frustration. I, like Deborah, was relieved to not be part of the spoils of war at this time, but I felt quite aware that other women still are.

Readings of history, literature, newspapers, and case law suggested that raw and widespread evil against women seemed to undercut all that is good. This, of course, is merely one subset of what might be called the problem of evil, as applied to women.[24] While I have faced that in the abstract, unlike many women, I have not been victimized by men or anyone else. I have been well-treated. I had to admit that men, too, have suffered in a variety of ways; children have suffered most. For a time I tried to think of what kind of system would be invulnerable to corruption, a system that would confer equality on all and prevent exploitation. I could not invent or identify such a system. There is no lasting human solution to these human problems. Ultimately, it is the preaching of the Gospel of Jesus Christ, the power of the word, which will change hearts and behaviors—despite what we may achieve politically or socially. Only Christ can heal us—those directly harmed and those indirectly harmed. I still have a responsibility to work toward solutions, but the presence of evil in the world—or the presence of evil against women—does not mean that there is no good or no God in the world. Both are here, and we know that good is more powerful than evil, ultimately and on a daily basis.

Many feminists have indicted patriarchy as the root cause of the evils against women. The problem with that analysis is that as patriarchies in Western nations have weakened, the evils have arguably merely shifted without decreasing: we still have sexual exploitation and assault, abortion, pornography, and other serious problems which seem to disproportionately victimize women, whether instigated by males or females.[25] Other cultures have their own sins against women. I understand the emotive as-

---

24. I discuss the problem of evil and women in ideas elsewhere. See Camille S. Williams, "Redeeming Religion: A Feminist Testament," *The World and I*, June 1999, available at http://worldandi.misto.cz/_MAIL_/article/mtjun99.html (accessed May 31, 2013).

25. The actions of the daughter of Jared caused harm to both men and women of her nation (see Ether 8).

pect of feminism, but we should not be surprised that feminist theory and practice—like all mortal systems—lack solutions to the problem of evil and to many of the problems women face generally. It seems to me that rather than judging the Church by the standards of the world, it is necessary to use the restored gospel as the measure against which the philosophies of men (or women) may be judged. Feminist theories remain standpoint theories. As such, they may reveal weaknesses in our culture, but they may also hide or distort aspects of our cultural practices.[26] It might be argued, in fact, that feminism is sometimes part of the problem (for example, in its heavy support for elective abortion and same-sex relationships).[27] Certainly feminist theology, even Mormon feminist theology, creates more problems than it answers about roles for men and women.[28]

The feminist critique of social, political, and religious life has some validity, but it is less than rigorous in its self-critique. Certainly any theology that does not understand or value mortality does not sufficiently value women. LDS doctrine accounts for our mortal state better than other belief systems—even feminist ones. While feminists have condemned patriarchy as serving the needs of men, both ancient and modern scripture link the fathers, the patriarchs, with blessings. Our holiest ordinances make reference to the patriarchal order of the priesthood. We must not confuse that order with male dominance or male-dominated institutions. Perhaps the patriarchal blessing is a prototype for the patriarchal order: one ordained of God pronounces blessings and promises upon the heads of those, like Abraham, who "having been . . . a follower of righteousness, desiring also to be one who possessed great knowledge, and to be a greater follower of righteousness, and to possess a greater knowledge, and . . . desiring to receive instructions, and to keep the commandments of God" sought the blessings of the fathers (Abr. 1:2). Those blessings are the endowment of all who seek righteousness, both male and female.

---

26. For a brief review of feminism and standpoint theories, see "Feminist Epistemology and Philosophy of Science," Stanford Encyclopedia of Philosophy, http://plato.stanford.edu/entries/feminism-epistemology/#supercede (accessed July 28, 2007).

27. I have argued elsewhere that the recognition of same-sex marriage will ultimately disadvantage women. See "Women, Equality and the Federal Marriage amendment," 20 *B.Y.U. Journal of Public Law* 487 (2006).

28. Mormon Feminist theology suffers some of the same difficulties as feminist theologies generally. See my discussion in Ruether and Williams, "A Dialogue on Feminist Theology: A Response to Professor Ruether," 275–95.

These views may be dismissed by some as politically naïve or an unwillingness to recognize structural and systemic oppression. They may be viewed as an endorsement of the counsel given to Emma Smith to "murmur not because of the things which thou hast not seen, for they are withheld from thee and from the world, which is wisdom in [the Lord] in a time to come" (D&C 25:4). I acknowledge that accepting a calling as a mother frequently seems to mean eschewing money, power, and status—even though those things come in mighty handy in this life.

I cannot say that every question I have ever had about women's issues has been answered by scripture, personal revelation, or official Church statement. I can say, however, that the feminist alternatives, by comparison, are wholly inadequate. Whatever else I do not know or understand, I will not separate myself from the multitude of blessings poured out upon us by the restoration of the Gospel of Jesus Christ. When I have considered turning away from Church teachings, I have, instead, felt to echo Peter when Jesus asked the Twelve, "Will ye also go away?" Down to my bones, I have known the only answer for this member of Christ's church is, "Lord, to whom shall we go? thou hast the words of eternal life" (John 6:68).

In "For Louisa," Kristine Haglund begins with her hope that her daughter will be both a feminist and a Mormon. Blending personal narrative with historical and theological reflection, she explores feminism, Mormonism, and particularly the heritage of Mormon feminism. Building on Louisa Greene Richard's belief that "every reflecting mother, and every true philanthropist can see the happy medium between being selfishly home bound and foolishly public spirited," Haglund suggests three areas in which she hopes the women of her daughter's generation will be able to find the "happy medium": the balance between the public and private spheres, the development of a broader understanding of female identity apart from motherhood, and the establishment of an equilibrium in the governance of the Church that will enable both men and women to fully and freely offer all of their gifts in the collective project of building Zion. She thinks that Mormon theology—including the (not-always-fully-worked-out) principle of vocation, divine embodiment, and the ideal of working together to build God's kingdom—offers unique resources to respond to challenges that face Mormon culture and feminism generally. Referring to early Mormon women, she writes, "they use Mormon scriptures and precepts as warrant for their feminism, and there is a certain theological boldness that I think is possible, in part, because their identity as Mormons was unquestioned." So while she wants her daughter to "be a feisty, spunky feminist, to accept the gifts that feminism has given her and so many other girls," she also hopes she will be a "Mormon feminist, that she will help articulate a feminism in the service of Zion, because that is the best hope of creating a sisterhood that is not merely metaphorical or aspirational."

Nine

For Louisa

Kristine Haglund

I am the outrageously blessed mother of a 12-year-old girl. Like all 12-year-old girls, she is an exquisitely beautiful creature, growing into the clever idealism of the young woman she will soon be, but still full of the wisdom of her little-girl self.

We are almost nothing alike, she and I—when I was twelve, I was melancholy and bookish, already angsty about the Church's historical practice of polygamy and the obvious unfairness of ordaining those irresponsible, obnoxious, *smelly* boys to wield the very power of God, while we girls worked to earn a dumb necklace. My first sacrament meeting talk opened with the borrowed bumper-sticker slogan of a feminism I could not yet articulate for myself: "a woman without a man is like a fish without a bicycle."

My daughter has a bicycle, but no apparent interest in fish or bumper stickers. Except for one glorious outburst at age 4, when she stood up on the pew during a baby blessing and demanded, "Hey! Where are the mommies?" she has cheerfully accepted the discrepancies between boys' and girls' opportunities in the Church that were so galling to me. I've worked hard to answer her questions and not push her to ask mine. And I recognize the folly of overspecified parental expectations, the terrible tightrope dance of conveying hopes without ever implying that a child's different choice will make her a disappointment. Still, I hope she will be a feminist. And a Mormon. If she is not, if she chooses a path that leads away from one or the other of these identities, I hope I will handle it as gracefully as I managed her plea for the Easter dress with a rhinestone belt and fur cape, her preference for talking on the phone instead of reading books, and her choice to quit violin to take acting classes (perhaps a bit more gracefully than that last!). But I don't want it to be because she didn't know that there is such a thing as a Mormon feminist. I want her to understand that this heritage is irrevocably hers—it has been in her from the very beginning, starting in the moment she was named.

Her name is Louisa. I did not choose the name so much as recognize it, the moment her father first tentatively said it aloud, and I knew, instantly and joyously, that Louisa was the being who was coming to live with us. We had declined the ultrasonic revelation of our expected baby's sex, and I had studiously avoided (I thought) hoping for a daughter. But driving along the New Jersey Turnpike (past the city of Elizabeth, which had prompted our renewed discussion of girls' names), I was certain that a daughter would come, and that she already had a name to fit her soul. It took only a few minutes to think of all the reasons to love the name, to place her in the long line of Louisas who might bestow their blessings on her.

First, there is Lois, in the New Testament. 2 Timothy 1:7 had sustained me for many years, rescued me often from the restless anxiousness that I so easily fell into: "For God hath not given us the spirit of fear; but of power, and of love, and of a sound mind." I had brushed by the prologue to that verse many times, and had only recently been reminded by a friend that Timothy's spiritual strength is credited not to the "faith of his fathers" but to his maternal ancestors:

> To Timothy, my dearly beloved son: Grace, mercy, and peace, from God the Father and Christ Jesus our Lord. I thank God, whom I serve from my forefathers with pure conscience, that without ceasing I have remembrance of thee in my prayers night and day; greatly desiring to see thee, being mindful of thy tears, that I may be filled with joy;
>
> When I call to remembrance the unfeigned faith that is in thee, which dwelt first in thy grandmother Lois, and thy mother Eunice; and I am persuaded that in thee also. (vv. 2–5)

My Louisa, too, has maternal ancestors who left a heritage of lively devotion, a faith which was not only "unfeigned," but considered and intelligent and searching. They were women who asked hard questions and then bravely lived the answers. (They also did things like earning a pilot's license. In Utah. In the 1930s.)

Another Louisa who flashed through my mind in that moment was Louisa Swain, the first woman to vote in an American election (Wyoming, 1870). She was, by all accounts, not an activist or a woman with political ambitions, but a housewife who rose early to run errands and decided to vote when she passed by the polling place on her way to buy yeast. I love the story of her accidental feminism, the matter-of-factness of her certainty that a plain working woman had a contribution to make to the life of the polis, that she *mattered*.

And of course there was Louisa May Alcott, whose feisty, prickly heroines had made me feel less alone in the world in the years when I was prickly, but not yet feisty enough to know how to make my way.

Most importantly, the Louisa who came and stayed in my mind, the one I most hope will be a spiritual guide for my daughter, is Louisa (sometimes "Lula") Greene Richards. Louisa Greene was born in 1849 in Kanesville, Iowa. Her family moved to Salt Lake City in 1852 and was just getting settled there when her father was asked to help lead the settlement of Provo. In 1859 they moved again, to Grantsville, and then again to Smithfield in 1864. Louisa's education was disrupted with each move, and she lamented the difficulty of getting what she thought to be a "proper" education:

> I want to be a very good teacher, and do not know how. I feel that I am not competent yet to do justice in this respect and so am not satisfied with what I do.
>
> I do so wish I could attend a good school. . . . And oh, how I would study! And how much I could learn, and what lots of things I'd write about.[1]

She, however, never let these insecurities get in the way of doing what needed to be done. She plunged in, trusting in God's help and in her own capacity and determination. Among the things that needed to be done were the expression of her thoughts and the development of her talent for words. The earliest surviving poetry of Lula Greene's is from when she was fourteen. Before she was twenty, she had editorial and publishing experience to her credit with the "Smithfield Sunday School Gazette." I love the story of her first paid publication: she had gone to Salt Lake to begin working and was called home to Smithfield because of an illness in the family. She needed money to pay her way back home, and so she stayed up all night writing poetry which she sold the next day to *The Salt Lake City Herald*.[2]

Most of her career unfolded following this pattern—she simply and confidently set about doing the work at hand. She seems not to have been ambitious for fame or personal recognition, and her poetry and other writing moves seamlessly from the mundane to the lofty. *The Woman's Exponent*, the Utah women's newspaper of which she was the founding editor, is a wondrous hodgepodge of editorials about the large political issues of the day, exhortations to diligent Sainthood, and explorations of Mormon theology, right alongside explanations of how to inexpensively make vinegar for pickling and the importance of daily baths for children.

---

1. Carol Cornwall Madsen, in *Sister Saints*, ed. Vickie Burgess Olson (Provo, Utah: Brigham Young University Press, 1978), 439.
2. Sherilyn Cox Bennion, "Lula Greene Richards: Utah's First Woman Editor," *BYU Studies* 21, no. 2 (Spring 1981): 158–59.

Louisa (and her newspaper) took women's homemaking work seriously but didn't believe it was the only work women could or should do:

> If there be some women in whom the love of learning extinguishes all other love, then the heaven-appointed sphere of that woman is not the nursery. It may be the library, the laboratory, the observatory. . . . Does such a woman prove that perfect liberty of education unspheres woman? On the contrary it has enabled that woman to perceive exactly what God meant her to do . . . God lead us to find the true woman in the free American home.[3]

And she also wrote, a few years later, when she resigned the editorship of the *Exponent* to care for her small children,

> I have decided that during the years of my life which may be properly devoted to the rearing of a family, I will give my special attention to that most important branch of "Home Industry." Not that my interest in the public weal is diminishing, or that I think the best season of a woman's life should be completely absorbed in her domestic duties. But every reflecting mother, and every true philanthropist can see the happy medium between being selfishly home bound, and foolishly public spirited.[4]

This practical, flexible approach to structuring her life seems very contemporary, and her concern to find the "happy medium" is, I think, worthy of imitation. There is a host of questions to which this pragmatic, moderate approach might prove helpful, but I want to describe a few that I think may be particularly salient for my daughter's generation of Mormon women: 1) the balance between the public and private spheres that Louisa Richards seeks in the paragraph above; 2) the development of a broader understanding of female identity apart from motherhood, including a discourse about sexuality that recognizes women as sexual subjects and situates that subjectivity in a moral context that requires more than the consent of mature participants; and 3) the establishment of an equilibrium in the governance of the Church that will enable both men and women to fully and freely offer *all* of their gifts in the collective project of building Zion.

Sometime in the decades following the shuttering of Louisa Greene Richards's and Emmeline B. Wells's *Woman's Exponent*, we seem to have lost sight of that moderate stance about women's varied talents and the roles to which they were well-suited. We have become unfortunately com-

---

3. *Woman's Exponent* 1 (1 April 1873): 3, cited in ibid., 7.
4. *Woman's Exponent* 6 (August 1, 1877): 4, cited in ibid., 9.

mitted to some calcified and brittle ideologies about gender that have prevented us from paying close or rational attention to what families really look like, what family forms offer the best chance of health, longevity, and happiness to *all* of their members—we have mythologized women's sacrifices, rather than thinking about which of them are truly necessary and helpful. The Church is by nature a conservative institution, and the institutional response to the tectonic shifts in family life in the second half of the twentieth century was to simply cling to the older forms. Now that the dust of the 1960s and 70s has finally settled, it is time for a new generation of young women to help us find new ways of thinking about family and work life, about the contours of women's lives now that most of us are likely to live two or three decades before and after our active years of childrearing. There is beginning to be some softening of the injunction for women to eschew careers—conference addresses have admonished women not to judge each other for choices about work and childcare, although we have still not come as far as the 1873 editorial acknowledging that some women might *want* to work. Economic necessity is still cited as the only reason a woman—or at least a mother—might legitimately choose to work for pay.

Unfortunately, our discourse on women's roles—particularly homemaking and motherhood—has borrowed too heavily from American ideologies that have as much (or more) to do with creating a consumption-based economy as with raising healthy, happy children. The Church has been entirely too successful in making one particular *form* of family life the central commitment of Mormons. We have focused on the external markers of what we understood to be happy families a couple of generations ago—professional fathers and mothers at home with (relatively) large numbers of children. But unlike, for instance, conservative evangelical Christians who understand their commitment to particular gender roles as a mode of overt resistance to modern American life and economies, Mormon women are unlikely to articulate a doctrinal rationale for their choices. Mormon prescriptions about family form have more to do with the centrality and timelessness of the family as a whole than a robust notion of male headship. Pressed to explain their commitment to "traditional" gender roles, most Mormons would cite the warrant of a few sentences in "The Family: A Proclamation to the World": "By divine design, fathers are to preside over their families in love and righteousness, and are responsible to provide the necessities of life and protection for their families. Mothers are primarily responsible for the nurture of their children." This patriarchal language, however, is immediately followed by two caveats that allow at least an ambiguous reconciliation with more egalitarian contemporary modes of family life: "In these sacred responsibilities, fathers and mothers are obligated to help each other as equal partners," and "circumstances may necessitate individual adaptation."

Moreover, up until the moment they are married, LDS women are encouraged to take advantage of the opportunities afforded them by the gains of the women's movement. They are admonished to become educated to the highest level they have opportunity for and to prepare for careers. Even general Relief Society president Julie Beck, often a staunch proponent of full-time at-home motherhood, told young students:

> Whatever your dreams are, go for it. . . . Sometimes you don't have control over the Lord's time and plan. . . . Go for broke, but don't lose sight of the gospel. When the time comes to marry and have children, re-evaluate.[5]

This advice, to "go for" dreams is in contrast to a Young Women's curriculum that has become ever more focused on marriage and family in the last few decades; thus, mild support for individual aspiration and achievement is countered by very strong cultural imperatives to abandon those dreams as soon as the primary goals of marriage and motherhood are attained. Examples of single women in general auxiliary presidencies are rare enough to be counted on the fingers of one hand, as are women who have maintained careers while they had school-aged children. It is easy for girls to conclude that Mormon identity for women is coextensive with a model of mothering and housewifery recognizable from old sitcoms. There's nothing wrong with this model, of course, and it works very well for many families—the problem arises when young women are given confusing messages about what is gospel truth and what is a lifestyle choice. Young women just older than my daughter seem to be adopting Mormonism as a part of their personal brand if stay-at-home motherhood is appealing to them (and possible); and they seem to be leaving the Church if the rigid gender roles prescribed in the Young Women's program do not appeal to them.

More attention to the spiritual content of family life—the real needs of children and the varied parenting styles and childcare arrangements, the patterns of education and work life that contribute to marital longevity and satisfaction—is likely to yield a much broader (and truer) ideal of Mormon family life. This extra attention would allow more women to comfortably maintain their identity and affiliation with the Church. If women are assigned the primary duties of housewifery and childcare, it is comforting

---

5. Cited in Armand Mauss, "Rethinking Retrenchment," *Dialogue: A Journal of Mormon Thought* 44, no. 4 (Winter 2011): 10.

to believe that this division of labor is "natural," that somehow being biologically female makes women enjoy the often tedious tasks involved with homemaking. Unfortunately, this is no truer of contemporary women than it was of LDS women in early Utah. Like men, many women enjoy working—in fact, several studies suggest that women with jobs (even jobs they don't especially like) are happier than women who are full-time homemakers and parents.[6] LDS rhetoric suggesting that motherhood is the most fulfilling possible activity for women—a relatively recent innovation in our rhetorical tradition, and delivered mostly by men—is at odds with both the data and with the reported experience of many women. It also strongly contrasts with the writing of Latter-day Saint women like Lula Greene Richards, which suggested that devoting oneself primarily to children for a time could be the best course, while still recognizing that doing so would require the sacrifice of other righteous aims and ambitions. That acknowledgment leaves room for women to be whole creatures, while the absolute equation of "woman" and "mother" constricts the acceptable range of emotions and experiences that can be expressed in contemporary LDS discourse. Such constriction cuts us off from the abundance of Mormonism's spiritual resources—we understand the profundity of Christian transformation only if we acknowledge as fully as we can who we are both before and after we submit our will and our understanding to God's.

In a way, even the emphasis on *choosing* full-time motherhood misses what a genuinely Mormon feminism might teach us. The "mommy wars" among American liberals and conservatives are, in a way, evidence of liberal feminism's success; they are contested on the grounds of either a rational evaluation of what "works" best for children (and sometimes, for mothers) by various sociological measures, or of an elusive but universally accepted concept of personal fulfillment. Feminists prioritize personal fulfillment; women who do not identify themselves as feminists pride themselves on eschewing fulfillment for the sake of their children or their religious commitments. What Louisa Greene Richards and her sisters seem to have understood is that choice and fulfillment are too slippery and too frequently self-contradictory (note Greene's matter-of-fact observation that her "interest in the public weal" is not diminished by her desire to devote more

---

6. For example, a recent Gallup poll found that "Stay-at-home moms at all income levels are worse off than employed moms in terms of sadness, anger, and depression." Elizabeth Mendes, Lydia Saad, and Kyley McGeeney, "Stay-at-Home Moms Report More Depression, Sadness, Anger," Gallup Wellbeing, May 18, 2012, http://www.gallup.com/poll/154685/Stay-Home-Moms-Report-Depression-Sadness-Anger.aspx (accessed June 12, 2013).

time to her children) to serve as scaffolding for the complicated balancing act of motherhood and family life. What is needed is the principle of vocation—the freedom for each "woman to perceive exactly what God meant her to do" and then have the support of her religious community in making the sacrifices required to do it. It is not enough for Mormon women not to judge each other for their choices—we must find a way to recognize all women's contributions to God's work. We should do so not to make peace with some new-fangled feminism, but in the name of Mormonism, by an insistence on the fundamental Mormon idea that each person partakes of intelligence that is co-eternal and co-equal with God, and entitled to personal revelation about the purpose and destiny ordained for that intelligence. Mormon women's commitment to families and to a practical religion which insists both that individuals ought to be willing to sacrifice all things *and* that those sacrifices must be made in the service of finding the joy which is the very purpose of human existence can add a necessary richness and unabashed aspiration toward nobility that is often missing from feminist discourse about balancing work and family life. I hope that my daughter will be part of a generation of Mormon women who reclaim the pragmatic wisdom and broad vision of their foremothers to translate the ideals of Zion into a modern global economy.

Current cultural prescriptions about gender roles are buttressed by entrenched essentialist ideas of gendered human nature. And if the discourse about how to balance one's interest in one's children with one's other interests and obligations is in need of wise Mormon feminism, our notions about the sexuality that gets us into those predicaments in the first place is *desperately* in need of that wisdom! It's a topic that nineteenth-century Mormon women would have written about in only the most oblique of terms, of course, but I think their moderate approach and their vision of Zion are absolutely essential patterns for thinking about it. Contemporary Mormon difficulties with thinking about women's bodies are entangled, of course, with our conflation of "woman" and "mother." It is uncomfortable to acknowledge that mothers have other desires, too, that self-abnegation isn't any more "natural" for women than it would be for men. If we speak of women as though they had no sexual desires of their own, and are always only the objects of male desire, we deny them their full humanity—which *requires* that they be subject to temptations and have opportunity to fully exercise their agency. Although the intention behind speaking as though women are more righteous than men by nature is benevolent, it ultimately distorts the gospel. Making women incapable of sin denies them full humanity just as much as blaming Eve for original sin.

Fully admitting the range of women's wants and desires would open avenues for necessary doctrinal and theological explorations. To sketch just one of myriad possibilities: if we stopped insisting that women are essentially good—spiritual and nurturing and pure and sweet—and men are essentially bad—craven, lustful, ambitious—we would gain more nuanced understanding of sin and atonement. We mostly think of sin as a linear response to "temptation," and we think and speak of sin mostly in terms coded "masculine"—violence, sexual exploitation, stealing, swearing. It follows that we understand repentance as a straightforward exercise of will to make righteous choices instead of wicked ones, and grace as transactional forgiveness—the canceling of the debt incurred by sin. Contemporary neuroscience, though, suggests the need for much more nuanced understandings of how agency operates and how it is constrained by genetics, neurochemistry, and socialization. Taking the sins women are prone to seriously—anger and aggressions that are manifest in less physical ways, unkindness bound up in hormonally-driven irritability or depression, sexual competition and envy, the kind of estrangement from God that is the result of mood disorders rather than transgression—might give us a more nuanced understanding of repentance and grace that could help us answer questions raised by our increased understanding of the mind.

Of course these are neither exclusively contemporary nor exclusively Mormon problems. Bodies, and particularly female bodies, have been troublesome to Christians since before they were Christians. Among the most vexing problems for would-be Christian feminists, and, indeed for Christianity itself, is the conflict between being an incarnational religion—insisting that God willingly took on flesh and was resurrected as an embodied personage—and the doctrine of original sin, with its attendant distrust of the physical, mortal, fallen body. Sallie McFague lays out the problem eloquently:

> [Christianity's] earliest and most persistent doctrines focus on embodiment: from the incarnation (the Word made flesh) and Christology (Christ was fully human) to the eucharist (this is my body, this is my blood), the resurrection of the body, and the church (the body of Christ who is its head), Christianity has been a religion of the body. . . . And yet, the earliest Christian texts and doctrines contain the seeds that, throughout history, have germinated into full-blown distrust of the body as well as deprecation of nature and abhorrence and loathing of female bodies.[7]

---

7. Sallie McFague, *The Body of God* (Minneapolis: Augsburg Fortress, 1993), 14.

Women trying to make sense of these competing strains of doctrine have found themselves battling each other as well as grappling with the tradition that blessed them *and* wronged them.

> Feminism has a different but also contentious relationship to embodiment and nature. Western culture and religion have a long and painful history of demeaning the female by identifying her with the body and with nature, while elevating the male by identifying him with reason and spirit. As a result, feminists are of two minds about aligning themselves with embodiment of any sort. Some insist that to do so is to reinforce the stereotypes that have oppressed women for centuries, while others feel that the liberation and salvation of women rest upon such an identification.[8]

Current Mormon discourse on women, and especially women's bodies, seems, unfortunately, to have absorbed some of this tension. As with the response to changes in family structure during the last half of the twentieth century, the Mormon cultural response to the sexual revolution has been one of simple denial and reiteration of older ideals. Among the pernicious effects of this wholesale rejection of feminist thinking on the topic of women's and girls' embodiment is that we have ended up importing worldly ideas that are in conflict with Mormon doctrine's unambiguous valorization of the body and of human desire as potentially sacralizing.

This is most evident in our discussions of modesty and pornography. Girls are told constantly that they should cover up, lest they tempt the young men, or even, in the unfortunate formulation of one recent General Conference talk, "become pornography." At the same time, they are clearly receiving the message that their status in the Church and their faithfulness to their own divine nature is largely dependent on attracting a mate and becoming mothers. Not only are women relentlessly constructed as objects of the male gaze by our talk about women, we teach girls to think of *themselves* this way, at younger and younger ages. We are now teaching little girls in Primary that there is something "immodest" about their bare shoulders or legs in the summertime. Moreover, in warning them to be careful not to tempt men, we offer them (and their brothers) a terribly damaging conception of male sexuality as a rabid and all-but-uncontrollable greed. It is only too easy to elaborate the damage that the stark binary between "naturally spiritual" women, who are always either righteously unwilling or wickedly provocative objects of male desire, never subjects of their own desire, and "carnal" men who lack the spiritual capacity to govern themselves, can in-

---

8. Ibid., 14–15.

flict on marriages and on working relationships between men and women in the Church. I wish that I could feel more certain that Church activity would help my daughter remain chaste *and* grow up with a healthy sense of herself as a whole being, with all the righteous and wicked desires common to human beings, as well as the spiritual intuition and strength that will help her master them.

Contemporary secular feminisms don't have satisfying solutions to these problems either. While feminists have done a great deal to counter the ideas and practices that reduce women to sexual objects, the resulting "rehabilitation" of women as sexual subjects has been unable to situate that subjectivity in a moral universe that makes it meaningful. A recent blogosphere kerfuffle among feminists about "hookup culture" highlighted the confusion that results when maximizing individual choice and self-expression is the only agreed-upon notion of "the good."[9] Almost everyone recognizes that sexual and emotional maturity are not often manifest simultaneously, but when being "prescriptive" or "judgmental" are the biggest sins, it becomes impossible to impart the wisdom of experience to youth. A generation of women who were encouraged by their second-wave feminist mothers to valorize their individual sensibilities over the prescriptions of sexist traditions still can't arrive at a shared understanding of what would be healthy for their daughters. Mothers are encouraged to cut their daughters' apron strings earlier and earlier, so that Delia's, PBTeen, and (God help us) Abercrombie and Fitch can initiate them as righteous consumers, with varieties of sexual pleasure available among the many elements of branded lifestyles. As in the case of decisions about balancing motherhood and work, one's own desires are an imperfect guide, at best—we all want too much, and an information age driven by a ferociously consumerist economy normalizes a restless insatiability that impedes the development of the moral context that makes personal choice meaningful. Becoming aware of one's own desires and working to fulfill them as completely as possible is no better preparation for the complicated dance of tender reciprocal submission that should characterize intimate relationships between men and women than complete denial of those desires.

---

9. See Rachel Simmons, "Is Hooking Up Good for Girls?" Rachel Simmons, February 25, 2010, www.rachelsimmons.com/2010/02/why-the-hook-up-culture-is-hurting-girls/ (accessed June 12, 2013); Kate Harding, "Hook-up Culture's Bad Rap," Salon, February 26, 2010, http://www.salon.com/2010/02/26/hook_up_culture/ (accessed June 12, 2013); and Amanda Marcotte, "It's not the Sex, It's the Sexism," The Raw Story, February 28, 2010, http://www.rawstory.com/rs/2010/02/28/pandagon-its_not_the_sex_its_the_sexism/ (accessed June 12, 2013).

What is desperately needed is reconciliation—atonement—between men and women, between women's bodies and women's capacity for moral reasoning, between desire and holiness. Mormon theology offers, at least, the hope of such reconciliations. By insisting that God is embodied, Mormonism denies the enmity between spirit and matter. Indeed, it denies *any* division: "all spirit is matter" (D&C 131:7). This understanding makes possible an inspired feminism that celebrates women's connection to the earth, and to their bodies' rhythms and intuitions, without thereby dividing them from God, or from spirit or reason. On this view, as well, Eve's decision to partake of the forbidden fruit in Eden becomes not original sin, but the very means of atonement—only by experiencing the paradoxical life of an embodied and mortal spirit can human beings become consubstantial with God. All of this complicated theology is captured beautifully in Louisa Greene Richards's suffrage song "Woman, Arise":

> Freedom's daughter, rouse from slumber,
> See the curtains are withdrawn,
> Which so long thy mind have shrouded.
> Lo! thy day begins to dawn.
>
> Chorus: Woman, 'rise, thy penance o'er,
> Sit thou in the dust no more,
> Seize the scepter, hold the van,
> Equal with thy brother, man.
>
> First to fall 'mid Eden's bowers,
> Through long suff'ring worthy proved,
> With the foremost claim thy pardon,
> When earth's curse shall be removed.
>
> Truth and virtue be thy motto,
> Temp'rance, liberty and peace.
> Light shall shine and darkness vanish.
> Love shall reign, oppression cease.[10]

The truest Mormonism overcomes the profound (if always only imagined) estrangement of reason and emotion, body and spirit, embodiment and exaltation. It also offers the possibility of overcoming the estrangement between women who answer these questions in myriad and particolored ways, and women whose minds and hearts are animated by different questions altogether. Feminism has been a fractious movement, always—an in-

---

10. Louisa Greene Richards, "Woman, Arise," in *Utah Woman Suffrage Songbook* (Salt Lake City: Office of the Woman's Exponent, 1890), 5–6.

evitability, probably, for a liberal project inspired by works with titles like "A Vindication of the Rights of Women," "A Room of One's Own," and "The Sex Which is Not One." Modern Western feminism was built on the foundation of a liberalism which privileges individual liberty, choice, and self-expression as alternatives to older moral orders grounded in religious dogma, tradition, and obedience to authority. This philosophical framework has been tremendously productive—establishing a concept of legal and moral personhood that is not abridged by gender or race and has moved the world appreciably toward the ideal of "liberty and justice for all."

But Western liberalism has its limits, as does the feminism that grows out of it. Ensuring individual liberty is noble, but it leaves open the question of what that liberty is for. Self-expression is a hollow goal unless there are opportunities and methods for developing the self—a cursory jaunt around the blogosphere amply illustrates the tendency of unfettered expressiveness to degenerate into an expansive cacophony punctuated by unpredictable flashes of brilliance. Charles Taylor describes this dilemma of modern identity:

> We are in an age in which a publicly accessible cosmic order of meanings is an impossibility. . . . [And] the basic moral standards of modernity, concerning rights, justice, benevolence, depend on . . . goods to which we don't have access through personal sensibility. But there are other important issues of life which we can only resolve through this kind of insight. . . . As our public traditions of family, ecology, even polis are undermined or swept away, we need new languages of personal resonance to make crucial human goods.[11]

The relativism required by liberal feminism can also have this atomizing effect: if the goal of feminist activism is to maximize individual choice, it's almost inevitable that the movement will fracture along the fault lines of those choices—pro-choice feminists will feel that pro-life feminists are betraying the cause, mothers who stay home with their children will condemn mothers who maintain careers for being inadequately devoted to their children, while mothers who choose to remain employed will condemn mothers who don't for making insufficient use of their education and talents, women of color and white women may misunderstand and mistrust each other, women in industrialized countries will be reluctant to make moral judgments about abusive practices in the global South, youth and elders will be unable to find a common language in which to speak meaningfully.

---

11. Charles Taylor, *Sources of the Self* (Cambridge, Mass.: Harvard University Press, 1989), 512–13.

And if feminism potentially alienates women from each other, of course it can even more readily alienate them from men who might be their allies and partners. There is always tension between self-expression or self-actualization and the need to belong. My sense of early Mormon feminism is that it is rooted in a deep and abiding conviction of belonging—they never seem to have worried that their feminist convictions made them less Mormon. Indeed, they use Mormon scriptures and precepts as warrant for their feminism, and there is a certain theological boldness that I think is possible, in part, because their identity as Mormons was unquestioned. They write boldly, confident that their call to widening women's spheres is part of the project of building Zion. Eliza R. Snow, hardly a radical, wrote:

> We are to be progressing, and growing better.... We believe in eternal progression.... [The] works and duties of the women of Zion are constantly increasing. No where on the earth has woman so broad a sphere of labor and duty, of responsibility and action, as in Utah.... Do we let Zion take full possession of our desire, our ambition?
>
> We have self all absorbed in the interest of the work of God. We are here to perform duties, and to do our part towards establishing God's Kingdom. We, my sisters, have as much to do as our brethren have. We are to work in union with them.[12]

What it looks like to "work in union" with our brethren is something that Mormon women are still working out. In Eliza's and Louisa's day, women had more to do than they do now. The formalizing of priesthood rituals that began in the first part of the twentieth century and the drive to streamline and centralize church governance and curriculum that became known as "Correlation" in the mid-twentieth century, had the unintended effect of narrowing opportunities for women to serve in the Church. Even leaving aside the thorny question of women's ordination, there is a great deal of education and work to do to make sure that "the duties of the women of Zion are constantly increasing," that they are invited to contribute in meaningful ways, and that their voices are heard in the governing councils of the Church as well as in General Conference and all of our meetings.

My Louisa knows I don't always manage to do this work with equanimity and patience—while I haven't quoted Gloria Steinem over the pulpit in some time, I'm not especially shy about calling out sexist practice or language when I see it. There have been many Sundays when I have thought I simply could not bear one more week of listening to men talk

---

12. Eliza R. Snow, Address delivered in the Ogden Tabernacle, August 14, 1873, in *Woman's Exponent* 2, no. 8 (September 15, 1873).

about how wonderful women are and then not batting an eye as they sing about Christ coming "to rule among the sons of men" or bumbling through the presentation of the Young Womanhood Recognition award after announcing the dinner and Court of Honor for her brother, the Eagle Scout. Well-intentioned or unconscious sexism can be as damaging as outright misogyny, and it is all the more insidious for its benevolent mien. I worry, often and deeply, about the morality of raising a daughter in a culture in which she will, along with the many, many beautiful truths she is taught, inevitably absorb the pernicious ideas that women are not leaders or decision-makers (except in the limited spheres men give them permission to act in), that women are "naturally" more spiritual than men, that ambition and assertiveness are not "feminine," that woman is synonymous with mother, and on and on. I know why women leave and I don't blame them; but I wish they would stay, and I hope my daughter will stay, because I think God is to be found in the thicket of relationships that include disagreement, anger, puzzlement, conflict, *and* love. The "patriarchy" is made up not of abstract oppressors, but of human beings, of good and flawed men trying to find out what God wants of them. In her essay "Border Crossings," Laurel Ulrich quotes Margaret Fuller, a nineteenth-century feminist:

> Were thought and feeling once so far elevated that Man should esteem himself the brother and friend, but nowise the lord and tutor, of Woman—were he really bound with her in equal worship—arrangements as to function and employment would be of no consequence.[13]

I'm convinced this is so, that feminism works when women and men are working together toward a common goal. It is this sense of shared higher purpose that has been so elusive for contemporary feminisms—that final 's' can make a lonely virtue of authentic selfhood. I want my daughter to be a feisty, spunky feminist, to accept the gifts that feminism has given her and so many other girls. I am profoundly grateful that she will have so many choices about her education, her reproductive health, her family, her career—so many opportunities to discover and express her authentic, wondrous self. But I hope she will also be a *Mormon* feminist, that she will help articulate a feminism in the service of Zion, because I believe that is the best hope of creating a sisterhood that is not merely metaphorical or aspirational. It turns out that human beings can't theorize themselves into compassion; the ties that bind are not ideological. The daily, bodily practice of religion—kneeling in prayer to acknowledge my smallness before God,

---

13. Laurel Thatcher Ulrich, "Border Crossings," *Dialogue: A Journal of Mormon Thought* 27, no. 2 (Summer 1994): 5.

cleaning houses, tending the sick, paying offerings, singing, having earnest conversations, offering a shoulder to cry on, crying myself, breaking bread together, and living in community with people who are not like me are (I hope) making me a better feminist. I hope to learn, and bequeath to my daughter, a feminism grounded not in grievance, but in generosity, and humility, and kinship that transcends political and philosophical differences.

******

One summer afternoon when I was 9 years old, I was reading a book my aunt had given my father, which he in turn had given to me. It was titled *Mormon Sisters: Women in Early Utah*, edited by Claudia Bushman. I knew it had been written by some friends of my aunt, and I vaguely sensed that it was a brave book, though I couldn't have understood the contours of its courage, and didn't yet have any inkling of the second wave of Mormon feminism it represented. But I loved it, fell into it in the glorious way that 9-year-olds can fall into books (as my daughter, at 12, still can—just barely), moved into that dusty nineteenth-century world so completely that I could feel the parching Utah sun, taste the bitter herbs of the midwives' medicines, and almost hear the rustle of those black silk skirts. And then, suddenly, I really did hear them. I felt the real and immediate presence of a dozen or so of these pioneer women, and heard, in some deep inward part of myself, "these are your mothers." I am the child of an experimental physicist, a thoroughgoing empiricist in most ways, a university-trained skeptic. But I have never doubted the truth of that childhood intuition. I am as sure of my connection to those women as I am of the warm, sweet heaviness of my Louisa's head on my shoulder when we read together. These are my mothers, and hers. I see their gifts to her in her happy faith, her deep, strong sense of herself as loved and worthy. She is a partaker of the grace bestowed by her still unconscious belonging to a covenant of sisterhood that has known and claimed her since before she was born, since before I knew her name.

Drawing from her experiences, Marleen Williams examines the first two waves of feminism and explains how she came to see both the great value and the limitations in many popular philosophies and politically correct agendas. Williams also examines how her spiritual beliefs provided a touchstone by which she could evaluate these movements. The first wave of feminism, which occurred in the late 1800s and was rooted in enlightenment philosophies, sought to secure equal rights—primarily political rights—for women. Williams found that the Church's teachings harmonized with and even surpassed the principles of equality espoused by first wave feminism. Friedan's *Feminine Mystique* (1963) signaled a second wave of feminism, one focused on the systemic oppression of women through institutions like marriage and motherhood and the consequent need for liberation. Williams feared, however, that this radical feminism recreated the inequality of the sexes since it found men "incapable of moral behavior and righteous use of power." By contrast, she writes, "the Church spoke forcefully concerning the worth of women, their eternal destiny and the importance of ending any form of abuse. The focus, however, differed from the militant feminist agenda." Rather than trying to free women from men, marriage, and motherhood, they hoped to "secure safety and support in pursuing these goals." She concludes, after poignantly drawing from her own experiences and those of others: "My spiritual beliefs have helped me to channel the great wave of feminist thought [that] . . . brought spiritual casualties as well as opportunities for women to develop their divine potentials. . . . The discipline provided by my spiritual beliefs gave me the freedom to channel, direct, and express the God-given power of being a woman."

Ten

A Journey through Feminism: Reflections of an LDS Woman

Marleen S. Williams

I was a child of the 60s, a decade of social, political, and civil upheaval that challenged our thinking about war, gender, race, sexuality, and work. As I ended my adolescent years and entered young adult life, I was surrounded by a cacophony of theories and political views. They all promised me the correct path to a fulfilling adult identity and life mission. The Vietnam War, the civil rights movement, protests, marches, and sit-ins were daily news stories. The Beatles and the subsequent Cultural Revolution that introduced white middle-class society to marijuana, cocaine, and LSD had thrown American culture out of the predictable, bucolic world of the 50s. In the midst of this great war of words came the second wave of feminism. As a young adult Latter-day Saint woman, I had a strong desire to make sense of these competing philosophies within the framework of my spiritual beliefs. I wanted not only knowledge but also the wisdom to use it for a good purpose.

I am now in the seventh decade of my life, and I am still on that journey. Feminism has appeared frequently along the path. Although I still have much of the journey yet ahead, the path looks clearer and lighter than it did as a young woman. The purpose of this essay is to share with the reader some of that journey and the lessons I learned.

The First Wave of Feminism

Can a woman be a Latter-day Saint and accept any of the tenets of feminism? Others, outside of my faith, frequently ask me this question. Feminism has many faces. It is a construct that can describe very different sets of beliefs. The first wave of Feminism, as it came to be distinguished from more recent feminist movement, occurred in the late 1800s. This movement had its roots in eighteenth- and nineteenth-century philosophies related to enlightenment, natural rights, and rational thought.

Feminist thinkers such as Elizabeth Cady Stanton, Susan B. Anthony, and Sarah Grimke believed that women as well as men were endowed with the capacity for rational thought and judgment. Women were capable of thinking critically and exercising agency. They were therefore entitled (along with men) to exercise the natural or inherent rights acknowledged in the Declaration of Independence and the United States Constitution. Feminist writer Mary Wollstonecraft observed that many women were being taught that they had no need to cultivate their minds. They need only cultivate physical beauty, using that beauty to secure a marriage proposal and thus supposedly lifelong protection and satisfaction. Elizabeth Cady Stanton used her knowledge of the Bible to conclude that the Godhead possessed all positive attributes and qualities described by the culture of her day as either only masculine or only feminine. She believed that God possessed a perfection of all that was good.

Equality and the use of power became strong concerns for the feminist movement. Feminists asserted that without power, women were easily subjugated by men. Inequality and male dominance resulted in the sexual, physical, and political abuse of women. What constitutes power and equality continues to be debated among feminists today. This first wave, however, focused on political power. Suffragists such as Alice Paul and Lucy Burns experienced imprisonment, beatings, and confinement to a mental asylum for picketing the White House in support of women's enfranchisement. In 1920, American women were secured the right to vote. Enfranchising women opened the door to political power and thereby opened other opportunities for women.

I first read of feminist history as a high school student. I recognized that my religion had incorporated these principles concerning women long before the first wave of feminism. Prior to these events, the restoration of Christ's Church through the Prophet Joseph Smith had already challenged American culture by giving rights back to women that were divinely instituted. In Joseph Smith's day, women could not enroll in most colleges. Most professions and trades were closed to women. Legally, women, like African-Americans and criminals, did not have independent rights as citizens. Women could not vote and were legal possessions of their husbands. A husband was entitled to his wife's earnings and the use and custody of her person, and he could seize these rights by force. G. Stanley Hall, one of the early founders of psychology, taught that women were unfit for education. He concluded that an excessive mental effort would cause the physical degeneration of women's reproductive capacity and thereby bring about the destruction of the human race. Paradoxically, medical science taught that most personality disturbances or symptoms of mental illness in women could be cured by surgical removal of their reproductive system. Their reproductive capacity made them different from men and therefore inferior. Theologically, churches taught that Eve had thwarted God's plan for men's happiness by causing his fall through seduction. Women were believed to be beneath men biologically and spiritually and were therefore incapable of agency and self-determination. They could not act for themselves but must be acted upon by men.

I could still see vestiges of these beliefs in American culture, but they were in stark contrast with what I learned from the scriptures. During the Savior's earthly ministry, he showed great respect and a concern for women that was uncharacteristic of his culture. Christ taught women the gospel directly and personally. He declared his identity as the Messiah to the Samaritan woman at the well (John 4:25–26). He taught parables using both male and female examples, showing that his Gospel was equally applicable to women and men. He healed women and raised a woman from the dead (Matt. 15:28, Mark 5:41). He was in close association with women both as friends and as disciples (Luke 10:38–41, Matt. 27:56). It was a woman who anointed him with oil prior to his crucifixion (Mark 14:3–9, John 12:3–8). While experiencing the pain of his own crucifixion, he tenderly showed concern for his mother (John 19:25–27). Christ chose to appear first to a woman following his resurrection and appointed to her the assignment of telling his apostles (John 20:11–17). In the early Christian church, women initiated good works and showed faith and personal spirituality (Acts 9:36, 17:4; Heb. 11:35, 1 Pet. 3:5).

From the beginning of the Restoration, the Church responded to women very differently than the prevailing beliefs of their day. The more I learned of LDS history, the more convinced I became that feminism, as I knew it, was consistent with the practices and beliefs of my church. Women voted along with men in sustaining church leaders and supporting the building of Zion. Women participated in temple ordinances. The gift of the Holy Ghost was conferred on women as well as men. Women were admonished to seek personal knowledge and their own testimonies of the principles of salvation. Joseph Smith organized the first Relief Society, remarking that the Church could not be fully organized without the women's organization. When the Saints reached Utah, women were also given the right to vote in government affairs as well. Under Brigham Young, married women had the same legal rights as single women, including the right to own property and represent themselves in court. Women controlled their own property, taught at universities, were active in politics, and ran hospitals and businesses. Brigham Young spoke for women's rights to pursue vocations traditionally seen as "the domain of men":

> We believe that women are useful, not only to sweep houses, wash dishes, make beds and raise babies, but that they should stand behind the counter, study law or physics, medicine, or become good bookkeepers and be able to do the business in any counting house, and all this to enlarge their sphere of usefulness for the benefit of society at large. In following these things, they but answer the design of their creation.[1]

The first elected female Senator in the United States was Dr. Martha Hughes Cannon from Utah. She ran against her husband Angus Cannon and won by more than 3,000 votes. The Church supported women's involvement in education and public affairs. LDS women were actively involved in the National Women's Suffrage Movement and representatives from the Relief Society and Young Women's Mutual Improvement Association were charter members of the National Council of Women of the United States.

Revelations given by God through Joseph Smith also addressed many of the false teachings and practices of the times. The revelation given to the Prophet while in Liberty Jail speaks against the evils of the abuse and misuse of power. This revelation, now recorded as Section 121 of the Doctrine and Covenants, is particularly directed at men who are ordained priesthood holders. Tyranny and coercion are labeled "unrighteous dominion." This revelation gives the directive that power or influence must be maintained, "only by persuasion, by long-suffering, by gentleness and meekness, and by love unfeigned; by kindness, and pure knowledge, which shall greatly enlarge the soul without hypocrisy and without guile" (D&C 121:41). This revelation also teaches that relationships can only be everlasting when they are held together by righteous behavior rather than by "compulsory means" (v. 46).

The coming forth of the Book of Mormon taught that "all are alike unto God" and that women have an equal invitation to "come unto Him and receive of his goodness" (2 Ne. 26:33). It preaches powerfully against the abuse and mistreatment of women. Men such as Jacob and Captain Moroni showed deep concern for the welfare of women. They worked hard to eliminate injustices (Jacob 2:7–11; Alma 46:12, 13, 54:11). Mormon and Moroni both warn of the horror of abuse to women when civilization degenerates into chaos (Morm. 4:12–15, Moro. 9:8–10).

---

1. Brigham Young, as quoted by Leonard Arrington in *American Moses* (Champaign: University of Illinois Press, 1986), 339.

The scriptures of the restoration clarified the purpose for the fall of Adam (2 Ne. 2:25; Moses 1:39, 5:9–12; Abr. 3:22–28). These latter-day scriptures help us understand that Eve was not an evil force who sought to defy God's plan but was rather a noble woman who was part of God's plan that existed from the beginning. They show her to be a full partner with Adam (Moses 5:1–5, 11–12, 16; 6:6, 9).

Revelations concerning marriage also restored knowledge of God's divine purposes for women. Doctrine and Covenants 132:4 makes it clear that men cannot progress to their highest potential without women. Section 132 teaches that both men and women must be willing to enter into the "new and everlasting covenant of marriage" in order to receive exaltation. In speaking of the blessings of this covenant, the Lord uses the pronoun "they," conveying that the blessings and promises apply to both men and women equally. Verse 20 tells us: "Then shall *they* be gods, because *they* have no end; therefore shall *they* be from everlasting to everlasting, because *they* continue; then shall *they* be above all, because all things are subject unto them. Then shall *they* be gods, because *they* have all power, and the angels are subject unto *them*" (emphasis added). These doctrines, teaching that in God's kingdom women share power with men and can receive equal blessings with men, were rare in the religious teachings of churches of the time.

These doctrines were not new but were a restoration of truths concerning the eternal nature of relationships between men and women. These truths had been lost. The world's understanding of women had reduced them from daughters of a Divine Being with a divine destiny to having fallen even lower than their male counterparts. The restoration of Christ's church restored woman to her rightful place as a companion and *equal* partner with her husband. The first wave of feminism seemed to me to be part of the spirit of enlightenment that came with the restoration.

I was raised in a LDS home. My parents taught me the doctrines of the restored gospel. I watched my father treat my mother with the respect that should be given to a daughter of God. She loved being a wife and mother. My mother also treated my father as a son of God. She was proud of his activity in the Church and grateful that he had a strong testimony. I knew that when I grew up, I wanted the kind of love that they shared. Although my mother had little interest in academic pursuits, my father recognized that I loved to study and learn. He saw this attribute as part of my pre-mortal disposition and as a gift from God—given to me for a purpose. He encouraged me to study and read all that I could. He promised me that this love of learning was part of my divine nature and would have a holy purpose in my life. My father and I shared wonderful discussions about astronomy and Abraham, geography and God's love for all of his children, geology and the creation and destiny of the earth. Scriptural and academic studies were not separate disciplines but both were parts of a larger truth. He taught me that both academic and spiritual knowledge could bless my life if I sought to understand them through the lens of the Gospel.

My father died shortly before I graduated from high school, and my mother was left to raise eight young children alone. She had only a high school education and few employable skills. She supported us by working for minimum wage at a retail sales job. I knew then that I wanted an education.

The Second Wave of Feminism

In 1963, Betty Friedan published *The Feminine Mystique*. This book signaled the beginning of the second wave of feminism. Friedan argued that oppression of women had created a nation of stifled, repressed, dehumanized housewives. She claimed that women had been "coaxed into selling out their intellect and their ambitions for the paltry price of a new washing machine." Release from the drudgery of housework was the path to freedom. Return to the work force was the answer to women's oppression. The book opened the floodgates from which a wave of angry women poured. Gloria Steinem proclaimed, "A woman without a man is like a fish without a bicycle." She advocated freedom from traditional roles and admonished women to "do whatever they [expletive] well please." Radical feminist groups such as the Redstockings and the New York Radical Feminists criticized traditional beliefs and practices such as love, family, marriage, and normative heterosexuality.

Many feminists preached that all men oppressed women and were innately incapable of benevolent treatment of women. Therefore, all traditional gender roles and institutions should be eliminated. Many of their doctrines reenacted the historical mistreatment of women, but this time men were the victims. The politics of radical feminism recreated the inequality of the sexes by implying that men were *inherently* incapable of moral behavior and righteous use of power. Men could not be trusted to use power benevolently and were beneath women morally and spiritually. Some preached that God could not possibly be male because men were incapable of "Godly" behavior. The tools of inequality, aggression, and domination were now turned against men. This deeply troubled me. Although I could see inequities and injustices, I could also see many benevolent men who made personal sacrifices for the welfare of others and used the power they held for righteous purposes. I also saw women who were abusive toward men. Turning the anger against all that was male seemed to me a form of abuse in itself. I could not accept that responding to inequity by reversing that inequity was an appropriate solution. This was not my idea of equality. Still in my late teens, my dualistic brain struggled with reconciling how both good and evil can exist in political causes.

Militant feminism advocated rejection of men, marriage, and motherhood as solutions to inequities and injustices. The anger in the rhetoric shouted so loudly that many real concerns for women often were not heard. For example, millions of women were already in the work force—most of them single mothers or women of color who lived in poverty—working in oppressive conditions for low pay. Release from men and marriage had not brought them happiness. Many in this situation, like my mother, deeply loved their children despite the hardships they experienced.

Women's rights groups spread throughout university campuses, and feminism became integrated into college curriculums. Like others of my generation, I wondered what this meant for me. The Women's Liberation Movement, as it was named by the press, offered women unlimited freedom. Yet they promised liberation from many of the things I wanted most.

While in college I chose to marry. My husband was kind, shared in doing the housework, and enjoyed my enthusiasm for learning. When his career assigned him to the Middle East, it meant that I must choose either to be separated from him or to discontinue my own university education. I chose to stay with my companion whom I loved. My husband promised me that if I wanted, when the time was right, he would support me in finishing my education. I embarked on a path that eventually included four children. Like my mother and my grandmothers before me, I loved being a mother.

While I was busily involved in traditional women's roles, the feminist movement gained momentum. My world broadened as I lived among cultures different from my own childhood background. I saw many women who were not as fortunate as I had been. I saw women coerced into marriages not of their own choosing. They were not companions and "helpmeets" to their husbands but were treated as property. They had to submit to survive. My community service involvement and callings in stake and ward Relief Society positions made me more aware of the deep pain experienced by many women. I visited frequently with a woman who had made several attempts to take her life. She had experienced painful sexual and physical abuse as a child. This had left her with little awareness of her own divine nature and few skills for self-protection. I wept, with another woman, as she shared a story of coercion into an abortion as a teenager.

She was told that the penalty for bearing the child would be worse than the repercussions of the abortion. She described the unbearable feelings of loss that came from annihilating the growing life within her. She was later taught of the atonement and baptized into the Church. She described the joy and healing that came from her temple marriage and the birth of her children. I felt overwhelmed and appalled as women confided in me their stories of abuse, uncharitable treatment, and lack of power to make critical decisions on their own behalf. I began to realize many women did not enjoy the love and respect that I had received from both my father and my husband. The Spirit within me shouted that this was wrong and not God's plan for His daughters.

The wave of feminism swelled as more women became aware of injustices against women. Latter-day Saint women also began to think more deeply about these issues. Depression in the Church became a focus of that inquiry. In 1979, KSL television aired a program focusing on the experiences of LDS women with clinical depression. Sonia Johnson, a member of the Church, subsequently spoke before the American Psychological Association concerning the plight of LDS women whom she described as subjugated by a "male patriarchy." She claimed that we were manipulated into obedience and were "immature, politically naïve, obedient, subordinate, submissive and somnambulant." She also quoted an article that had appeared in the *Salt Lake Tribune* reporting that several Salt Lake City therapists claimed that three-fourths of their LDS patients were women who experienced depression related to low self-esteem and lack of fulfillment. This report, however, ignored the fact that more women than men seek counseling and psychotherapy nationally, regardless of religious affiliation. Women in the United States experience double the rate of depression as men. Depression is one of the most frequent concerns in mental health care. In an area with a high-density population of any group, it is expectable that a similar proportion of that group will seek mental health care. Ms. Johnson claimed a rising epidemic of female depression in the Church. She could not substantiate her claims with empirical research and held no credentials as a researcher or a mental health professional. However, she received a standing ovation from an audience whose professional standards place a high value on these requirements. Eventually she founded a women's commune that advocated fulfillment through freedom from committed sexual relationships as well as freedom from enforced housework. The commune eventually dissolved. Her version of freedom did not result in fulfillment of the things I sought.

Sonia Johnson's conceptualization of women in the Church did not match my own observations. Although I saw injustices, they did not come from living the counsel of Church leaders but rather from misinterpretations of doctrine or rationalizations of mistreatment by distorting doctrine. More often, when abuses occurred, it was because of failure to follow the teachings of the Church concerning the treatment of women. I also knew that I had made my choices, not blindly, but after serious study, prayer, and faith. My choices were not a consequence of subservience or lesser intelligence, as Ms. Johnson had implied. They were consequences of deep thought and use of my agency to choose. My religious beliefs and choices frequently came under scrutiny and even attack by other women who were not of my faith. The insinuation that LDS women were duped or brainwashed was insulting to the many intelligent, educated, competent, strong-spirited women who were deeply committed to living their LDS faith. Choosing differently than militant feminists was not evidence that we were lesser beings. We had freely used our intelligence and agency to choose our path.

Empirical research followed the uproar. No published empirical study has ever found LDS women to experience higher rates of depression than non-LDS women. Empirical evidence also shows no relationship between endorsement of traditional gender roles and depression in LDS women.[2] No differences in depression rates have been found between LDS women who work outside the home and those who are full-time homemakers.[3] A more recent study using a national sample found that LDS women reported higher satisfaction in their marriages and that stronger church affiliation was associated with a lower prevalence of depression when compared with the non-LDS national sample.[4] Although empirical evidence and published professional articles speak against the stereotype, I still professionally encounter many who hold the belief that LDS women experience higher rates of depression and subjugation.

---

2. D.C. Spendlove, D.W. West, and W.M. Stanish, "Risk Factors and the Prevalence of Depression in Mormon Women," *Social Science & Medicine* 18, no. 6 (March 1984): 491–95.

3. M. Williams, "Family Attitudes and Perfectionism as Related to Depression in Latter-day Saint and Protestant Women," in *Religion, Mental Health and the Latter-day Saints*, ed. Daniel K. Judd (Salt Lake City: Bookcraft, Inc., 1999).

4. Sherrie Mills Johnson, "Religiosity and Life Satisfaction Among LDS Women," *Journal of the Association of Mormon Counselors and Psychotherapists* 28 & 29 (Spring 2004): 29.

Latter-day Saint priesthood leaders were not silent observers as the focus on women's welfare increased. They reinforced eternal principles that govern relationships between men and women. Elder Boyd K. Packer spoke of the equal responsibility of *both* men and women to care for each other. He also clarified the concept that housework and childcare were the responsibility of both parents. They were not divinely assigned solely to women:

> It is not meant that the woman alone accommodate to the priesthood duties of her husband and sons. She is of course to sustain them and support and encourage them. Holders of the priesthood, in turn, must accommodate themselves to the needs and responsibilities of the wife and mother. Her physical and emotional and intellectual and cultural well-being and her spiritual development must stand first among their priesthood duties. There is no task, however menial, connected with the care of babies, the nurturing of children, or with the maintenance of the home that is not a husband's equal obligation.[5]

Elder Richard G. Scott reminded men of the Lord's plan for power and agency within the family:

> Occasionally a man attempts to control the destiny of each family member. He makes all the decisions. His wife is subjected to his personal whims. Whether this is the custom or not is immaterial. It is not the way of the Lord. It is not the way a Latter-day Saint husband treats his wife and family.[6]

Men and women who represented the Church spoke forcefully concerning the worth of women, their eternal destiny, and the importance of ending *any* form of abuse. The focus, however, differed from the militant feminist agenda. They spoke not to free women from men, marriage and motherhood, but to secure safety and support in pursuing these goals. They did not preach that men were incapable of Godly behavior but taught them to be accountable so that they could also learn to act as sons of God.

I also observed that the Church did not ignore the escalating "feminization of poverty." This occurred as divorce in the United States increased and more mothers were compelled into the workforce. Single mothers headed the majority of households living in poverty. The changing social values concerning marriage and the "sexual revolution," demanded by many women as an attempt to be "equal" to men in sexual freedom, contributed to national trends toward later marriages and increasing numbers of women who never married. Many women who wanted to choose marriage and motherhood did not have the opportunity to do so. Many men

---

5. Boyd K. Packer, "A Tribute to Women," *Ensign*, July 1989, 75.
6. Richard G. Scott, "Receive the Temple Blessings," *Ensign*, May 1999, 26.

chose to enjoy the sexual benefits that had previously been confined to marriage without committing to the responsibilities of marriage. Meanwhile, the Church continued to endorse the same standard of sexual purity before marriage and fidelity after marriage for *both* men and women. The establishment of payment of court-ordered child support as a condition of temple attendance also protected women from unfair treatment.

The Church had always recognized the value of education for women. As more women entered the workforce, however, there was a stronger call for women to be prepared for "any eventuality." Elder Dallin H. Oaks, while serving as President of Brigham Young University, admonished the students:

> A young woman's education should prepare her for more than the responsibilities of motherhood. It should prepare her for the entire period of her life. ... [W]e make no distinction between young men and young women in our conviction about the importance of an education and in our commitment to providing that education.[7]

I began to feel strongly that it was time to continue my own education. My husband had experienced some health problems and I painfully remembered my mother's experiences. I shared my concerns with my husband, who listened with respect and concern. We both fasted and prayed to know the Lord's will concerning our family. We made the decision together that it was time for me to return to school and finish my education. I returned to finish my bachelor's degree. Within a year, my beloved husband was diagnosed with terminal cancer. I have been very grateful for the promptings and spiritual confirmations that lead to the decision we made. It was the right decision for our family.

My husband lived long enough to see me graduate with an undergraduate degree in psychology, be accepted into a clinical psychology PhD program, and begin my graduate studies. It was difficult and painful to become a widow and finish my education as a single mother. However, there was always the peace that I was following God's plan for my life. My father had been right; my innate love of learning had a holy purpose in my life. The lessons he taught me as a child concerning what it means to be a daughter of God have been a strength to me all of my life.

My professional work has focused on women's mental health. I have found purpose and joy in helping others recover from abuse, secure safety, and find meaning in their lives. The opportunity for an education made my transition into the workplace easier than it had been for my mother. I enjoy freedoms and opportunities that were unavailable to many women

---

7. Dallin H. Oaks, "Women and Education," *Ensign*, March 1975, 57–58.

throughout history. I am grateful for the blessings of being a Latter-day Saint woman. The gift of the Holy Ghost has helped me to make many difficult decisions and to find peace in those decisions. Righteous men, marriage, and motherhood have blessed my life. My children and grandchildren have given me a glimpse of the joys of eternity. Because I long to eradicate abuse, poverty, and the loss of the right to use one's agency, and I work to secure dignity and safety for women, I am labeled by some as a feminist. If this is the definition of being a feminist, then I am proud of being a Latter-day Saint feminist. I rejoice in being a Latter-day Saint woman. My spiritual beliefs have helped me to channel the great wave of feminist thought that flooded my generation. That wave brought spiritual casualties as well as opportunities for women to develop their divine potentials. I have learned that I cannot endorse all popular philosophies and politically correct agendas without personally and prayerfully sorting out which strengthen my eternal goals. Martha Graham, the great, innovative choreographer of modern dance, concluded that real freedom of expression requires submission to discipline. The discipline provided by my spiritual beliefs gave me the freedom to channel, direct, and express the God-given power of being a woman.

In "All God's Children Got a Place in the Choir," Margaret Blair Young examines racial misunderstandings among members of the Church, focusing on the priesthood restriction. The common temptation to reduce people into commodities blinds us to their divinity. Although clear in slavery and racism generally, Young suggests that we can also view individuals guilty of these prejudices and practices as mere compositions of their "dwarfish ideas," rather than in the fullness of their divine possibilities. Even though historical evidence suggests the priesthood restriction began with Brigham Young and was not a continuation of Joseph Smith's position, Margaret Young cautions, "let us not yield to the temptation to view Brigham Young as nothing but a racist." Joseph Smith's position on the issue is complicated: as a presidential candidate, he spoke in favor of abolition, and as a prophet, he ordained several men to the priesthood, but some claimed he said that blacks were restricted from the priesthood. She concludes that the Church's position seems to be that we simply don't know why there was a restriction. But the fact that prominent church leaders made statements perhaps based primarily upon inherited traditions ought not to challenge our faith. As Young writes, we do not believe in the infallibility of our prophets—like each of us, they were "works in progress." She concludes by discussing how the works of God can be made manifest through those who face challenges in this life, whether as a result of physical ailment or racial prejudice. Young believes our differences can help us learn the highest lessons of love: "As we embrace our differences and begin to realize what contributions each culture brings to humanity, what insights each individual carries, and what gifts each presents from their individual endowment, we form a sort of marriage, fertile with possibility" in which we all partake of the grace of Christ, liberated by love.

Eleven

All God's Children Got a Place in the Choir: Race and the Restored Gospel

Margaret Blair Young

My husband, children, and I stood in a long, sweaty line to enter Florence's Galleria della'Accademia, where Michelangelo's David was on display. We had seen at least forty art museums during our European tour, and I was doubtful that the David could be worth this muggy wait.

At last we were inside the doors. Following the slow swarm of tourists ahead of us, we passed by Michelangelo's statues called (according to various translations) "The Captives" or "Prisoners" or "Slaves." These half-finished pieces were once intended to become the pillars of a tomb for Pope Julius II. Now they line the path to the David, depicting men who appear to be emerging from stone in an excruciating, incomplete birth.

Because of the crowds, I could not see the David until we were nearly to its pedestal. Then I gasped. It was more magnificent than anything I had imagined. I walked slowly around the statue. I gazed at the veins in the marble legs, the perfect muscles, and the noble face. This was a vision of man in all his glory, naked and ready for victory over Goliath but also, eventually, for the forbidden embrace of Bathsheba, and finally for the passion which would create the psalms.

The statue is nearly fourteen feet high—larger than life. But those very words remind me of Toni Morrison's defense after being accused of making her characters larger than life. "I think I make them AS LARGE as life," she said. "Life really is that large."[1]

For fifteen minutes, I walked around the David. I found my eyes tearing as I followed the marble from David's feet to his hair and to his slingshot.

Of course, I had seen little replicas of the statue. Italy abounds in them. You can get lampshades crowning a ceramic copy of David, keychains exploiting Michelangelo's work, little sterling silver imitations, and neckties focusing on particular parts of David's anatomy. I imagine you could even

---

1. Toni Morrison, *Profile of a Writer* series (VHS), Home Vision Entertainment, 1987.

buy a David action figure. All of these kitschy copies are made obscene by the real thing. The idea that you could reduce the David to an indistinct imitation so small you could put it in your pocket is somehow heretical, and recalls the very words slave owners once used to euphemize the human trade: "Massa goin' put you in his pocket." In other words, Massa is about to exchange you for coins. And those words evoke yet another, that of Judas holding thirty pieces of silver.

The temptation to reduce a person to a commodity, or to something fully manageable and predictable, is chronicled throughout history and throughout the scriptures. We see Cain killing Abel to get gain, the earth dwellers whom God weeps over because they are "without affection and they hate their own blood" (Moses 7:33), Miriam and Aaron reducing Moses' wife to her nationality of "Ethiopian" (more accurately translated as "Cushite," meaning descending from Ham's eldest son, Cush)—for which Miriam is taught that if she really wants white skin, God can certainly provide it (Num. 12:10)—though the whiteness will come from leprosy. And we see Joseph's own brothers selling him to a band of Ishmaelites. In recent history, we recall the Jews and gypsies murdered en masse under Hitler's order, and thousands of Japanese—not even visible from the bombers—killed in a supremely ironic burst of light. We remember that slavery, murder, and genocide are hardly new to our planet.

Certainly in the LDS perspective, where God has proclaimed that we, who may feel we are nothing, are in fact His "work and [His] glory" (Moses 1:39); human potential is "larger than life." Philosopher Emmanuel Levinas puts it this way in *Totality and Infinity*: "The strangeness of the Other, his irreducibility to the I, to my thoughts and my possessions, is precisely accomplished as a calling into question of my impulses."[2] For Levinas, whose own family perished at the hands of Nazis, the "Other" refers to any other person, and the "I" to oneself. As we attempt to reduce the Other to the I—that which we can fully comprehend and even possess—we ignore what is irreplaceable, unique, unknowable, and divine in that other person.

The reduction of the Other to something pocketable and easily labeled has been attempted throughout history with whole races of people. Indeed, racism, often cloaked in euphemisms and sometimes mingling the philosophies of men with the scriptures, continues to tempt all nations and people, including the Latter-day Saints.

---

2. Emmanuel Levinas, *Totality and Infinity* (Pittsburgh: Duquesne University Press, 1969), 43.

I was introduced to this temptation early in my life. As a young woman in my first year of seminary, I was quickly aware that my seminary teacher was a proud scriptorian, a fiercely loyal Mormon, and a racist. His prejudice was not hard to identify, since he casually used the "N" word during several class periods. Toward the end of the year, he asked us students to write evaluations of his teaching. From my precocious, fourteen-year-old heart, I wrote, "I think you say things sometimes which could incite racism."

The next time our class met, this teacher addressed my comment publicly. He read my words out loud and announced that he knew who had written them. He then proceeded to testify—using the same, deep, authoritative voice he used to witness that Jesus was the Christ—that blacks really were inferior, which was why they did not have any right to the priesthood. He said that we as Utah-grown children couldn't possibly know what he, having lived in the larger world, knew: the black race was cursed by God and the priesthood restriction was divinely instituted.

This was a man I had admired, but that day I knew he was wrong. I knew he was bearing false testimony, and that knowledge made me ask myself what other false things he had testified of in his resonant, defiantly certain voice.

I have often wondered what June 8, 1978, was like for my seminary teacher—the day the lifting of the priesthood restriction was announced. Interestingly, I later worked in the temple with him. I wondered how much of his thinking he had had to undo when the ban was undone. Was he successful? Had his heart been purified of the prejudice that he hadn't even recognized as a sin? Of course, such are questions for the Lord, not me, to ask. I am required to view my seminary teacher—who is now a very old man—in the fulness of his possibilities, and not composed merely of his past dwarfish ideas. In other words, I cannot reduce him to his racism and put him in my pocket. I must not shrink a David.

In the subject of charity, my seminary teacher, like Michelangelo's unborn statues, was a slave when I first knew him, not yet emancipated from the weighty stone of his own tradition and blindness. He was partially reborn in Christ, but the process was incomplete.

Tragically, his views represented those of many Latter-day Saints during my lifetime. Racial prejudice was woven into United States culture, symbolized by segregation, and consummated by unthinkable acts of violence against men, women, and children who were descended from enslaved Africans. And we Mormons were hardly immune from the national plague. There is no getting around the fact that our Church literature was liberally peppered with statements about race that should make us cringe, and that leaders who otherwise stood as special witnesses of Christ were nonetheless "captives" to tradition and fear in issues of civil rights and human equality. It would be easy to write a terribly demeaning picture of Latter-day Saints by focusing only on those statements—and indeed, several groups have done just that, posting their findings on the internet and printing them in pamphlets. Missionaries inevitably encounter the "race question," and some are caught by surprise when confronted with these offensive declarations. Black investigators or converts are soon challenged by the literature, and we find that the very group who best responds to the gospel message—African Americans—is the group most likely to quit the discussions or abandon the Church after baptism. Many leave because they feel deceived once they read statements made from the time of Brigham Young until well into the 1970s. And some become persuaded that the Book of Mormon supports racism.

So let's talk openly about this issue.

Pigment and the Book of Mormon

One evening when I was teaching Spanish Institute, my Mexican assistant said, "I was looking at all of you white people in the temple last week, and I thought how beautiful you are. We, on the other hand, are Lamanites, and we are ugly. But that is the way God intended it, isn't that so? We are ugly so we won't be enticing to you. You are the Nephites, aren't you?"

I dropped my lesson plan at once. I carefully addressed her misunderstanding of the scriptures, and we talked about the implications of believing in a God who is "no respecter of persons," and that beauty has many faces. During that same class, a Peruvian student offered a story from her own life. She had served a mission in Chile and encountered some misguided Caucasian missionaries. One had displayed the whiteness of his forearm and declared that her dark skin indicated her lower status in the pre-existence, and he implied a divine mandate that she marry someone with similarly dark skin and of the same economic station. Deeply troubled by his words, she prayed for understanding. Soon afterward she dreamed that she was being invited to a partially open portal where a great light shone between two doors. As she approached, the doors opened to even greater light and she saw the Savior smiling brilliantly, children of all skin tones surrounding him. He hugged the children and kissed them. All were equally and infinitely precious to him. That witness lingered with her long after the dream ended. She was no longer troubled by that missionary's words, only by the state of his heart.

In all honesty, we do have to deal with some troublesome scriptures. For example, how do we explain 2 Nephi 5:21?

> And he had caused the cursing to come upon them, yea, even a sore cursing, because of their iniquity. For behold, they had hardened their hearts against him, that they had become like unto a flint; wherefore, as they were white and exceedingly fair and delightsome, that they might not be enticing unto my people the Lord God did cause a skin of blackness to come upon them.

Some have suggested that if we follow the footnote on "skin" leading to 2 Nephi 30:6, then we see that "skin of blackness" is not a literal reference to pigment but refers to spiritual blindness. Surely there is some truth in that, since Joseph Smith himself made an editorial revision to 2 Nephi 30:6 changing "white and delightsome" to "pure and delightsome."[3]

However, I am not satisfied with that explanation as a final answer. I personally believe that many references to "darkness" in the Book of Mormon do refer to a spiritual state rather than a physical one. However, I also believe that Nephi brought his own culturally inculcated ideas to the New World, and that there was likely a change of pigment in his brethren—not a curse, referring to a separation from God because of wickedness—resulting rather from lifestyle. LDS scholar and apologist Hugh Nibley suggests this:

> A way of life produces this darkening of the skin, and it's the same way all over the world. . . . The people that live in the stone houses have white complexions, and the people that live in the tents (the houses of goat's hair) have dark complexions. Among the Arabs they always distinguished between these people. They are the same people, the same blood, but there is a great deal of difference between them. One is much lighter than the other. It's the same thing in Greek vase paintings. The women were always painted with white faces because they were in the house all the time.[4]

The important thing is not so much the difference in skin color but the perception of the Lamanites and the Nephites themselves—sustained through generations—that they were distinct peoples, separate "races."

We know that God is no respecter of persons, and we know that men and women are tempted to view themselves as superior to others based on

---

3. John Tvednes, "The Charge of Racism in the Book of Mormon," FARMS Review 15, no. 2 (Fall 2003): 183–97.
4. Hugh Nibley, *Teachings of the Book of Mormon* (Provo, Utah: FARMS, 1993), 244.

gender, pigment, education, money, and so forth. Certainly we would not say that Samuel the Lamanite was cursed or that the people of Ammon were cursed. Indeed, the whole Book of Mormon could be read as a treatise against racism, for its culminating chapters show how the Savior's love unites all of his people regardless of their appearance, and that as they live the gospel fully there are no "ites" among them (4 Ne. 1:17). In fact, the re-introduction of Lamanites after the Savior's visit comes only as a "small part of the people" (v. 20) leaves the church, calling themselves Lamanites. Thus divided, these groups easily resurrect old grudges and traditions, and a society which had known no war is soon fully engaged in bloodshed.

Taken as a whole, the Book of Mormon addresses racism in great detail and provides the remedy—the Atonement, where all who accept the invitation become one in Christ. Nonetheless, individual verses in the Book of Mormon have certainly been interpreted as racist. Because of these verses, some Latter-day Saints have even believed that God color-codes His children—an idea which flies in the face of the most fundamental gospel teachings.

History of the Priesthood Restriction

The history of the priesthood restriction itself is tangled. There is no written revelation putting the restriction into place, and it's very hard to link it to Joseph Smith—especially since he ordained at least one black man (Elijah Abel) to the Melchizedek priesthood,[5] and the Prophet's brother, William, ordained another (Q. Walker Lewis). Though some argue that Brigham Young's fidelity to Joseph is evidence that the policy originated with Joseph Smith, there is no solid support for this origin. From all the written material available, I personally conclude that it was Brigham Young who put the policy into place in 1852—even though five years earlier he had referred to Q. Walker Lewis as "a fine elder—an African."[6] Just two years after that description of Lewis, Young made a statement which seems a precursor to the canonization of the policy:

---

5. Eunice Kinney's "My Testimony of the Latter-day Work," an unpublished letter circa 1885, states specifically that Joseph Smith Jr. ordained Elijah Abel. A copy of the first part of the letter may be found at http://www.blacklds.org/kinney (accessed June 12, 2013). Elijah Abel was probably bi-racial, but census records consistently identify him to be of African lineage, two labeling him as "mulatto" and another as "black."

6. Minutes, March 26, 1847, Brigham Young Papers, LDS Church History Library.

> [T]he Lord cursed Cain's seed with blackness and prohibited them the priesthood, that Abel and his progeny might yet come forward, and have their dominion, place, and blessings in their proper relationship with Cain and his race in the world to come.[7]

The official LDS view of racial issues and slavery in particular underwent drastic changes from the time Joseph Smith died in 1844 to the time Brigham Young gave his famous speech as territorial governor in 1852. During the latter, Utah prepared to enter the union as a slave-holding territory.

Joseph Smith was quite a radical in his racial views, especially given the era in which he lived. Though he believed in the Curse of Cain and Canaan, we see considerable evolution in his thought from the Missouri years to the last years of his life, such as when he invited African American convert Jane Manning James to be adopted into his family as a child,[8] and when he suggested that Blacks were disadvantaged by their circumstance. "Change their situation with the whites," he stated in 1843, "and they would be like them. They have souls, and are subjects of salvation. Go into Cincinnati or any city, and find an educated negro, who rides in his carriage, and you will see a man who has risen by the powers of his own mind to his exalted state of respectability."[9]

Six years before the Fugitive Slave Act would give slave holders the right to reclaim their human "property" even in northern states, Joseph Smith was unabashedly calling for the end of slavery. In his presidential campaign he stated:

> [T]he Declaration of Independence holds "these truths to be self-evident, that all men are created equal; that they are endowed by their Creator with certain unalienable rights; that among these are life, liberty, and the pursuit of happiness," but at the same time some two or three millions of people are held as slaves for life, because the spirit of them is covered with a darker skin than ours.... Break off the shackles from the poor black man.[10]

Given the passion of Joseph's words, it is rather surprising that slave holders brought their slaves on the pioneer trek (three hand-chosen "col-

---

7. Quoted in Lester Bush and Armand Mauss, *Neither White Nor Black* (Midvale, Utah: Signature Press, 1984), 70.

8. Jane Elizabeth Manning James, "Life Story," transcribed by Elizabeth J.D. Roundy, Wilford Woodruff Papers, LDS Church History Library.

9. Joseph Smith et al., *History of the Church of Jesus Christ of Latter-day Saints*, ed. B. H. Roberts, 7 vols. (Salt Lake City: Deseret Book, 1948 printing), 5:217–18.

10. Ibid., 6:205.

ored servants" served in the Vanguard Company), continued buying and selling them in Utah, and even offered them or their labor as tithing. Even more surprising, given Smith's platform, is the fact that Utah chose to be a slave-holding territory after the California Compromise. Such a policy change reflects the views of the new leadership, which was not focused nearly so much on the rights of black men and women as it was on the daunting details of the Mormon migration, the establishment of functioning cities in the Rocky Mountains, the seeking of financial means to support new settlements, and the gathering of Latter-day Saints from all over the world. Clearly, Brigham Young had notions about race which reflected his day and were hardly unique. They likely did not consume much of his time, however, since the black population in Utah was so small and Young's sense of purpose was focused on the white pioneers. He was convinced that the slavery issue would be resolved outside of Utah. How could he have foreseen that his time-bound words would be quoted a century after his death, that new technology would resurrect his ideas and disseminate them to any who plugged his name into a Google search, and that pamphlets highlighting his words would actually interfere with the missionary work he loved so much?

But let us not yield to the temptation to view Brigham Young as nothing but a racist. As was my seminary teacher, Brigham Young was a "captive" in this issue. Although fairly mainstream in his racial attitudes for his day, in other areas he was prescient and even remarkable. Some have labeled him the most brilliant mind of his century. Certainly all must recognize him as a leader of leaders and an extraordinary planner. He was doggedly stubborn in his views and stated them with no apologies, yet he acknowledged contrary positions, respecting the candor of those who disagreed with him.

There were several who questioned his views on the priesthood issue, asking bold questions about it after his death in 1877. Had Brigham Young's words on blacks and the priesthood been accepted as the "voice and will of God," leaders after Young would have considered the matter settled, but that was not the case. In 1879, John Taylor summoned a private council to learn what exactly Joseph Smith had said about the issue. The council was called because Elijah Abel, who had been washed and anointed in the Kirtland Temple but had been living in Cincinnati when the endowment was presented in Nauvoo, had petitioned to be sealed to his wife—a petition he had already raised without success to Brigham Young. The question President Taylor asked was not what the policy was according to Brigham Young, but what Joseph Smith had said about it. Thus was convened the most important meeting prior to 1978 to address the issue. Attending were

President John Taylor and his personal secretary, L. John Nuttall, along with Abraham O. Smoot, who had once held slaves and had been a missionary in the South, and Zebedee Coltrin, who claimed to have heard Joseph Smith's declaration on the matter.

Smoot said that he was told not to ordain slaves to the priesthood—which was almost certainly true, since the policy of the early Church was to never baptize a slave without the master's consent and to not ordain any slaves to the priesthood. But could the policy regarding slaves be globalized to embrace all blacks?

Coltrin's claims were more specific. He said he had been arguing with a Brother Green on the subject of blacks and priesthood and had finally turned the question over to Joseph Smith. In L. John Nuttall's Journal we find:

> Saturday, May 31st, 1879, at the house of President Abraham O. Smoot, Provo City, Utah, Utah County, at 5 O'Clock p.m. President John Taylor, Elders Abraham O. Smoot, Zebedee Coltrin and L. John Nuttall met. Coltrin: "I have heard him [Joseph Smith] say in public that no person having the least particle of Negro blood can hold the Priesthood." Coltrin recounted his argument with Brother Green and said that the two drove directly to the Mansion House to ask the prophet in person. According to Coltrin, "Brother Joseph kind of dropped his head and rested it on his hand for a minute, and then said, 'Brother Zebedee is right, for the spirit of the Lord saith the Negro has no right nor cannot hold the Priesthood.'" Coltrin went on to say: "Brother (Elijah) Abel was ordained a Seventy because he had labored on the Temple, and when the Prophet Joseph learned of his lineage he was dropped from the Quorum, and another was put in his place. I was one of the 1st Seven Presidents of the Quorum of Seventy at the time he was dropped."[11]

Coltrin's assertions were soon contested by his contemporary, Joseph F. Smith, who was certain that Abel's priesthood had never been withdrawn, since he had personally seen two certificates verifying Abel's status—one issued in 1841 and another after Abel's arrival to the Salt Lake Valley. These certificates were provided by Abel himself, and the suggestion that he had been dropped from the quorum was tabled.[12] Thus, Coltrin's story was brought into doubt. On the question of whether or not Joseph Smith had

---

11. L. John Nuttall, Journal, May 31, 1979, LDS Church History Library, 290–93.

12. Newell K. Bringhurst, "Elijah Abel and the Changing Status of Blacks within Mormonism," in Lester Bush and Armand Mauss, *Neither White Nor Black* (Midvale, Utah: Signature Press, 1984), 138.

said that blacks were restricted from the priesthood, we have only Coltrin's words—and they are contradicted by the known ordinations of a few black men, at least one by Joseph Smith himself.[13]

How, then, do we deal with the fact that the Church of Jesus Christ, though never practicing official segregation, had a policy restricting blacks from its greatest blessings? I will list some prominent beliefs about the policy—most of which I do not fully accept. (My own belief is that the policy was *allowed* but *not imposed* by God, that it was a reflection of the times and influenced by predominant thought of the time.)

When the LDS Church was first organized, blacks were commonly viewed as the descendants of Cain brought through the flood via Ham and cursed to be "servants of servants" (Gen. 9:25)—an idea touted for centuries by many religions to justify enslaving Africans. These concepts seem contrary to fundamental Church doctrine (such as the second Article of Faith, which indicates that men are responsible for their own sins and not for their forefathers' transgressions), so it is not surprising that some early Church leaders speculated that those born into African families on earth were being judged for poor performance in the pre-existence.[14] Perhaps those born into African lineages were fence-sitters during the War in Heaven, or maybe they simply did not want the priesthood.

---

13. According to Connell O'Donovan's yet unpublished research, these men were Black Pete, Elijah Abel, Isaac Van Meter, Joseph T. Ball, Q. Walker Lewis, William McCary, and Enoch Lovejoy Lewis. Van Meter's ordination is alluded to in a letter from Wilford Woodruff, in which he mentions that Van Meter, an elder, had left the Church. In "Woodruff's journal, January 15, 1838 (From His Own Pen)," *Millennial Star* 27, no. 19 (May 13, 1865), the ordination of Joseph T. Ball is referred to. There is no solid documentation on Black Pete or Enoch Lovejoy Lewis.

14. Orson Hyde, for example, speculated in a speech before the High Priests' Quorum (Nauvoo, April 27, 1845—after Joseph Smith's death) that blacks were in fact "those spirits in heaven that rather lent an influence to the devil, thinking he had a little the best right to govern, but did not take a very active part." Orson Hyde, *Speech of Elder Orson Hyde* (Liverpool: James and Woodburn, 1845), 30. Orson Pratt supported this idea, though Brigham Young did not. Young believed in the Curse of Cain, as did most Americans of his day and many clergymen, but thought the War in Heaven was of such a decisive nature that it was not possible to refuse "to take a very active part." Hyde's idea fits into the category which Elder Dallin Oaks has called "spectacularly wrong" in his interview with the Associated Press: "Some people put reasons to revelation," said Elder Oaks, "and they turned out to be spectacularly wrong." Dallin H. Oaks Interview with Associated Press, in *Provo Daily Herald*, June 5, 1988.

Many state that the policy originated by revelation and could be removed only by revelation. Such was certainly the belief of many Church leaders. It is significant that in 1978, while President Kimball was preparing to ask the Lord for further light and knowledge on this subject, he requested that the Quorum of the Twelve investigate the history of the restriction. Each looked into what past Church leaders had said and tried to separate folklore from inspiration. It mattered to President Kimball that his associates search out the issue in their own minds before approaching God for an answer to this important question.

Many are certain that the policy—whether of God or of man—served ultimately as a test of faith, "the Mormon Cross," as Eugene England put it—not only for black members but for white as well.[15] Others suggest that white Mormons were not ready to accept blacks into full fellowship, and so the Lord allowed them to live a "lesser law" in the same way he allowed the Israelites to live only what they were prepared for after they showed themselves to yet be slaves of Egypt even after their deliverance. Still others believe that because of slavery and third-world politics, blacks were not prepared for the onerous burden of the priesthood.

Many look to the scriptural precedent of an exclusive priesthood, pointing out that at one time only the tribe of Levi could administer priesthood ordinances and conclude that God has always restricted priesthood and continues to do so, since those who have no opportunity to hear the Gospel (such as those in mainland China or in Muslim states) also have no opportunity to receive the priesthood.[16]

A few still hold with the "Missouri Thesis"—which avers that because of the fiery debate over slavery that threatened the stability of the Saints, the policy had to be introduced to preserve Mormon lives—but of course, this idea does not account for those of African descent who were, in fact, ordained to the priesthood during Joseph Smith's lifetime.

One of the most popular speculations today is that the priesthood is given according to God's scheduling as the Gospel spreads across the earth nation by nation. This idea seems to be what Jane Manning James was

---

15. G. Eugene England, "The Mormon Cross," *Dialogue* 8, no. 1 (Spring 1973): 78–86.

16. This particular idea, as well as the concept that God has always required a waiting period before giving the priesthood, always struck me as odd, since we are the restored Church of Jesus Christ—not of Moses. Paul is very clear about who is entitled to the blessings of the gospel in Galatians 3: "There is neither Jew nor Greek, there is neither bond nor free, there is neither male nor female: for ye are all one in Christ Jesus. And if ye be Christ's, then are ye Abraham's seed, and heirs according to the promise" (vv. 28–29).

challenging when she wrote to President John Taylor: "And God promised Abraham that in his seed all the nations of the earth should be blessed. As this is the fullness of all dispensations—is there no blessing for me?"[17]

The Church's position now appears to be that we don't know why there was a restriction. The Church no longer cites the Curse of Cain, or any other curses, but simply says, "We don't know." Elder Jeffrey R. Holland reiterates that position in these words: "[T]he folklore must never be perpetuated. . . . [H]owever well intended the explanations were, I think almost all of them were inadequate and/or wrong. It would have been advantageous to say nothing, to say we just don't know."[18]

The most direct response to the change in policy was given by Bruce R. McConkie at a CES symposium in August 1978:

> I would like to say something about the new revelation relative to our taking the priesthood to those of all nations and races. . . . All I can say to that is that it is time disbelieving people repented and got in line and believed in a living, modern prophet. Forget everything that I have said, or what President Brigham Young or President George Q. Cannon or whosoever has said in days past that is contrary to the present revelation. We spoke with a limited understanding and without the light and knowledge that now has come into the world. We get our truth and our light line upon line and precept upon precept. We have now had added a new flood of intelligence and light on this particular subject and it erases all the darkness and all the views and all the thoughts of the past.[19]

The words are typically forthright and unapologetic, and those of us who remember Elder McConkie can recall his strong, certain voice. However, we as a Church are still moving into the light and truth McConkie refers to and have not fully arrived. Many of us are yet captives of tradition. Many allow the "pocketing" of blacks under labels the Church itself has abandoned. Sadly, there are still books on the shelves that reflect the captivity of the past and lump all of the races of men into easy categories. These books and false teachings must be dealt with. Elder Holland stated boldly in 2007: "We don't pretend that something wasn't taught. . . . But I

---

17. Jane's words are from her letter to John Taylor, December 27, 1884—the day of Elijah Abel's funeral.

18. "Interview: Jeffrey Holland," PBS - The Mormons, http://www.pbs.org/mormons/interviews/holland.html (accessed June 13, 2013).

19. Bruce R. McConkie, "The New Revelation on Priesthood," in *Priesthood* (Salt Lake City: Deseret Book, 1981), 132.

think we can be unequivocal . . . in our current literature, in books that we reproduce, in teachings that go forward. . . . [W]e need to. . . . put [a] careful eye of scrutiny on anything from earlier writings and teachings [so] that [the folklore] is not perpetuated in the present."[20]

There are still teachers in Sunday Schools, Seminaries, and Institutes who have not fully walked into the light and truth implied by the revelation of 1978. President Hinckley addressed any still clinging to such falsehoods with this reproach:

> How can any man holding the Melchizedek Priesthood arrogantly assume that he is eligible for the priesthood whereas another who lives a righteous life but whose skin is of a different color is ineligible? . . . Let us all recognize that each of us is a son or daughter of our Father in Heaven, who loves all of His children. Brethren, there is no basis for racial hatred among the priesthood of this Church. If any within the sound of my voice is inclined to indulge in this, then let him go before the Lord and ask for forgiveness and be no more involved in such.[21]

Some feel their faith challenged by the suggestion that past teachings on this subject should be abandoned or by the idea that Brigham Young might have made statements based more on the traditions he grew up with and on political expediency than on revelation. How could Brigham Young be a prophet and say what he said?

Joseph Smith provides one good answer for this in the King Follett discourse:

> When you climb a ladder, you must begin at the bottom, and ascend step by step until you arrive at the top; and so it is with the principles of the Gospel: you must begin with the first, and go on until you learn all the principles of exaltation.[22]

Lorenzo Snow's statement from April 1900 Conference is also helpful:

> Seventy years ago this Church was organized with six members. We commenced, so to speak, as an infant. We had our prejudices to combat. . . . We advanced to boyhood, and still we undoubtedly made some mistakes, which . . . generally arise from a . . . lack of experience. We understand very well, when we reflect back upon our own lives, that we did many foolish things when we were boys. . . . Our errors have generally arisen from a lack of comprehending what the Lord

---

20. "Interview: Jeffrey Holland."
21. Gordon B. Hinckley, "The Need for Greater Kindness," *Ensign*, May 2006, 58.
22. *History of the Church*, 5:306.

required of us to do. But now we are pretty well along to manhood. . . . While we congratulate ourselves in this direction, we certainly ought to feel that we have not yet arrived at perfection. There are many things for us to do yet.[23]

As a Church, we do not believe in the infallibility of our prophets. Events during the "Mormon Moment," when Romney was running for President of the United States, gave the Church motivation and urgency to address this reality—thanks particularly to a BYU religion professor who was certain his speculations were endorsed by the Church. He blithely agreed to an interview with *Washington Post* reporter Jason Horowitz and stated something to which a Mormon audience might have given a glib nod, while others would be astounded. The professor explained that the LDS priesthood restriction was not only necessary because the curse of Cain/Canaan affected all of African lineage, but also because blacks hadn't been ready for the responsibility and power of that priesthood. Jason Horowitz's article quotes him saying, "God has always been discriminatory" when it comes to whom he grants the authority of the priesthood. The professor, according to Horowitz, compared blacks to a young child prematurely asking for the keys to her father's car: "Until 1978 . . . the Lord determined that blacks were not yet ready for the priesthood."[24] Two strongly worded Church statements almost immediately rebuked the professor's statements and claimed that he did not represent the teachings and doctrines of the Church of Jesus Christ of Latter-day Saints.

The Church's first statement channeled the language of Bruce R. McConkie's previously quoted talk to CES employees:

> For a time in the Church there was a restriction on the priesthood for male members of African descent. It is not known precisely why, how, or when this restriction began in the Church. . . . The Church is not bound by speculation or opinions given with limited understanding. We condemn racism, including any and all past racism by individuals both inside and outside the Church.[25]

---

23. Lorenzo Snow, *Report of the Semi-annual Conference of the Church of Jesus Christ of Latter-day Saints*, April 6, 1900 (Salt Lake City: Church of Jesus Christ of Latter-day Saints, semi-annual), 1–2.

24. Randy Bott, as quoted in Jason Horowitz, "The Genesis of a church's stand on race," WashingtonPost.com, February 28, 2012, http://articles.washingtonpost.com/2012-02-28/politics/35443157_1_george-romney-first-mormon-presidential-nominee-michigan-governor (accessed June 26, 2013).

25. "Church Statement Regarding 'Washington Post' Article on Race and the

The second statement continued in the same vein:

> The origins of priesthood availability are not entirely clear. Some explanations with respect to this matter were made in the absence of direct revelation and references to these explanations are sometimes cited in publications. These previous personal statements do not represent Church doctrine.[26]

Those already sensitized to the issue considered this a repudiation of the Curse of Cain, pre-mortal performance, and any other speculation stated by any Mormon. However, without the specific naming of which teachings were "racist," many Mormons (including the professor) continued to teach and believe in the "curse of Cain" and other common ideas.

In April 2012 General Conference, just a month after the *Washington Post* article, Elder D. Todd Christofferson gave a capstone sermon highlighting the problem of accepting everything a Church leader has said as official Church teachings. After citing Acts 10:34 ("God hath shewed me that I should not call any man common or unclean. Of a truth I perceive that God is no respecter of persons"), he said, "[I]t should be remembered that not every statement made by a Church leader, past or present, necessarily constitutes doctrine. It is commonly understood in the Church that a statement made by one leader on a single occasion often represents a personal, though well-considered, opinion, not meant to be official or binding for the whole Church."[27]

Many Mormons following the series of Church statements saw this sermon as a direct response to the professors's unfortunately racist speculations. A talk by Elder Jeffrey R. Holland on Church leaders' fallibility in General Conference a year later reiterated what Elder Christofferson had said: "[B]e kind regarding human frailty—your own as well as that of those who serve with you in a Church led by volunteer, mortal men and women. Except in the case of His only perfect Begotten Son, imperfect people are all God has ever had to work with."[28]

Church," MormonNewsroom.org, February 29, 2012, available at http://www.mormonnewsroom.org/article/racial-remarks-in-washington-post-article (accessed June 26, 2013).

26. "Race and the Church: All Are Alike Unto God," MormonNewsroom.org, available at http://www.mormonnewsroom.org/article/race-church (accessed June 26, 2013).

27. D. Todd Christofferson, "The Doctrine of Christ," LDS General Conference, April 2012.

28. Jeffrey R. Holland, "Lord I Believe," LDS General Conference, April 2013.

Almost a year to the day after this professor claimed that blacks were cursed because of Cain and unprepared for the priesthood until 1978, the Church released a new preamble to "Official Declaration II" (the end of the priesthood restriction):

> The Book of Mormon teaches that "all are alike unto God," including "black and white, bond and free, male and female" (2 Nephi 26:33). Throughout the history of the Church, people of every race and ethnicity in many countries have been baptized and have lived as faithful members of the Church. During Joseph Smith's lifetime, a few black male members of the Church were ordained to the priesthood. Early in its history, Church leaders stopped conferring the priesthood on black males of African descent. Church records offer no clear insights into the origins of this practice. Church leaders believed that a revelation from God was needed to alter this practice and prayerfully sought guidance. The revelation came to Church President Spencer W. Kimball and was affirmed to other Church leaders in the Salt Lake Temple on June 1, 1978. The revelation removed all restrictions with regard to race that once applied to the priesthood.

Are we Mormons now ready to invest ourselves fully in the journey toward equality? Certainly, this new addition to the scriptures indicates that we are moving toward a different framework than we had previously, and that we must look at past statements with discernment and even forgiveness. Just as we seek forgiveness for our own weighty sins, so we must show mercy to those who have gone before. Even Jesus's disciples had much to learn during their time with him. When they encountered a man who had been born blind, they immediately made assumptions about why he had been afflicted. Had he committed some sin in the pre-existence? Or was his affliction due to his parentage? Note that these disciples used the same speculations often given for the priesthood restriction before 1978: pre-mortal sin and lineage. "Who hath sinned?" they asked, "this man or his parents, that he should be born blind?" The Savior answered, "Neither hath this man sinned nor his parents, but that the works of God should be made manifest" (John 9:1–4). The Savior's rejection of his disciples' ideas harmonizes with other scriptural declarations—that children are not responsible for the sins of their parents, and that all are born innocent.

We would not regard race as a handicap, but many from particular lineages and even with particular pigment have indeed been afflicted with hard burdens. How should the works of God be made manifest through them?

The answer is clear: God's works are made manifest through charity. In Levinas's terms, the face of the Other calls us to responsibility. If we allow ourselves to ignore the divine in the Other through the sins of prejudice and reduction, we likewise ignore the Savior. We become pillars of a whited sepulcher rather than liberated manifestations of the love, the work, and the glory of God. And what of the poor and afflicted? How might they manifest the works of God? Surely they too are called to grow in love and unity in the midst of their trials. (And we might well debate who has the harder burden—the rich man or the poor.)

I believe that race, as we perceive it, is a gift and a test.[29] We are intended to be different from each other in order to learn the highest lessons of love. As we embrace our differences and begin to realize what contributions each culture brings to humanity, what insights each individual carries, and what gifts each presents from their individual endowment, we form a sort of marriage, fertile with possibility. In an exalted world, the Other reveals himself or herself as a magnificent David or a redeemed Bathsheba, not a captive, and certainly not a pocketable imitation mass-produced by eager stereotypists. Joseph sits on a resplendent throne, surrounded by his brothers. He is the deliverer of those who enslaved him. Elijah Abel stands beside Brigham Young as co-heirs with Christ. Zebedee Coltrin and Green Flake, a former slave once paid as tithing, become radiant beings capable of receiving all the gifts God offers. Jane Manning James, a black Mormon pioneer who gave half of her flour to a starving white pioneer, takes her place as an image of the Divine Feminine. My seminary teacher, dressed in his priesthood robes, becomes a man of good will and full charity, no longer bound to the curses of custom but liberated by love. And all of us partake of the grace of Christ, who once was sold for thirty pieces of silver by a man who had no idea whose inextinguishable life he held in his hands.

---

29. I am indebted to Darius Gray for his insights on John 9. He influenced much of my thought about diversity being a test. His unpublished paper, "Not a Curse but a Calling," written in August 1998, has provided me with great insights.

Bruce Young reminds us that the Church is led by the "Prince of Peace" and that the Gospel "requires of us charity, forbearance, respect for and appreciation of all of God's children, and a desire for peace. The gospel does not and should not encourage anger, hatred, enmity, or pride. All of us should be troubled by war." Although Latter-day Saints have a duty to their countries in times of war—even when fighting on opposing sides—the Church consistently takes a position of peace, encouraging peaceful resolution of conflicts. Quoting President Hinckley, Young writes: "Along with our obligation as citizens and our desire to defend liberty, we should be among those 'who long for peace, who teach peace, who work for peace.'" Above all, "the gospel teaches that our efforts to rid the world of evil must begin with our own repentance and be followed by teaching the gospel through example and precept."

Twelve

Following Christ in Times of War: Latter-day Saints as Peacemakers

Bruce W. Young

The official position of the Church on war is reasonably clear. War itself is evil, but members are encouraged to fulfill their duties as citizens, including the duty of military service when required. In fulfilling that duty—as long as they do it in the right spirit—Church members who are required to take lives are not guilty of murder. The guilt for such actions, if any, lies with those ultimately responsible for the conflict.[1]

The moral and spiritual complexities of war and peace make applying the Church's position to specific situations a challenging task. Scriptures and statements by Church leaders seem to lead in a variety of directions, sometimes denouncing war, sometimes seeming to justify it. Among faithful, believing Church members a wide range of attitudes may be found, from strict pacifism to enthusiastic militarism, with most members located somewhere in the middle, troubled by the evil of war but wanting to be good citizens who honor the sacrifice of those who perform military service.

In this essay, I explore war and peace from a gospel perspective with the aim of helping those who have experienced pain or confusion trying to make sense of these issues. I especially want to help any who, like me, have sometimes felt judged or excluded because their views do not match those of many of their neighbors or ward members. I believe that no one who favors peace should feel like an outsider in the Church headed by the Prince of Peace. Though there is great room for individual understanding

---

1. In addition to First Presidency statements cited below, the Church position may be found in the article "War" in *True to the Faith: A Gospel Reference* (Salt Lake City: The Church of Jesus Christ of Latter-day Saints, 2004), 183. Edward Kimball has summarized the Church position as follows: "The Church position appears to be that war is evil, that defending one's country is excusable and even laudable, and that conscientious objection to military service is permissible but not encouraged." Edward L. Kimball, *Lengthen Your Stride: The Presidency of Spencer W. Kimball* (Salt Lake City: Deseret Book, 2005), 284.

and application, the gospel—above all, the gospel as it has been restored in the latter days—requires of us charity, forbearance, respect for and appreciation of all of God's children, and a desire for peace. The gospel does not and should not encourage anger, hatred, enmity, or pride. All of us should be troubled by war.

One of the great challenges in dealing with these issues is to avoid anger and harsh judgment toward those we disagree with. Those who favor peace during times of war often have a hard time truly being peacemakers in private and public conversations on the subject. And so while making a gospel case for peace on a global scale, I want to be a peacemaker in how I make that case. I believe the scriptures and teachings of Church leaders support efforts for peace and justify war only as a rare exception. But I acknowledge that others can look at the same evidence and come to different conclusions. The Lord has commanded us to "renounce war and proclaim peace" (D&C 98:16). At the same time there is scriptural support for the idea that war is sometimes a tragic necessity. Taken as a whole, however, the scriptures and statements of Church leaders—and especially the words and example of the Savior—consistently encourage us to seek peace, to exercise charity, and in every way possible to avoid violence, hatred, and revenge in our interaction with others.

Lessons of the Book of Mormon

On questions of war and peace, the scriptures offer a wide range of examples and attitudes, from the complete self-sacrifice of the people of Ammon to the Israelites' wars of annihilation, in which entire peoples, including women and children, were killed—an example used tragically centuries later to justify exterminating Native Americans. Obviously, scriptural examples must be used with care and considered in the light of modern revelation.

With so many chapters describing armed conflict, the Book of Mormon has much to say about war. The war chapters have troubled many readers and to some have seemed to support war as a preferred option for solving problems. This last view, I believe, is seriously mistaken. Carefully read, the Book of Mormon shows the horrors of war, the dangers of war-fever and the lust for bloodshed and revenge it leads to, and the need for repentance and a change of heart brought about by the Atonement before evil can be overcome on either an individual or a national scale. Among the many lessons of the Book of Mormon on war are these:

1. The Lord will preserve his people, but they must do their part. That part includes practical preparation (for instance, the defenses overseen by Captain Moroni) but most importantly sincere faith, humility, and obedience. For example, when the Nephites ceased to be righteous and relied on their own strength, they lost the Lord's protection.
2. The Lord can preserve his people in many ways. The Book of Mormon reports the Lord at times commanding military strategy and combat and at times commanding other options, including escape from enemies, patient endurance through years of bondage, and missionary work to change enemies' hearts.
3. The word of God is a stronger weapon than the sword: "the preaching of the word had a great tendency to lead the people to do that which was just—yea, it had had more powerful effect upon the minds of the people than the sword, or anything else, which had happened unto them" (Alma 31:5). Even with the terrible threat posed by secret combinations, the righteous Lamanites used missionary work along with other methods and succeeded in "destroying" the robbers by converting them (Hel. 6:37).
4. Even enemies in war are in reality our brothers and sisters. Once it is noticed, the constant reference to the Lamanites as "our brethren" sends a powerful message: through the centuries of conflict, the record keepers did not forget their familial relationship with those who were at times their enemies and who caused so much grief and destruction.[2]
5. Enmity and the desire for revenge bring destruction. Even when it is necessary or justified, war is essentially evil—in Nephi's vision of the Tree of Life it is associated with "the depths of hell" (1 Ne. 12:15–16). The Book of Mormon is unflinching in its grim portrait of the horrors of war. Battle is called "the work of death" (Alma 43:37–38, 44:20; Hel. 4:5); the books of Mormon and Ether especially depict "horrible" scenes of "blood and carnage" (Morm. 2:8, 4:11, 5:8; Ether

---

2. Contrast King Noah and his followers who delight in killing Lamanites: "And it came to pass that king Noah sent his armies against them, and they were driven back, or they drove them back for a time; therefore, they returned rejoicing in their spoil. And now, because of this great victory they were lifted up in the pride of their hearts; they did boast in their own strength, saying that their fifty could stand against thousands of the Lamanites; and thus they did boast, and did delight in blood, and the shedding of the blood of their brethren, and this because of the wickedness of their king and priests" (Mosiah 11:18–19).

14:21); and the atrocities on both sides are appalling (see Moro. 9). Besides these general evils, the Book of Mormon emphasizes the terrible effects of war on people's hearts. Especially as the Jaredite and Nephite civilizations collapse, the people "boast in their own strength" and swear to "avenge themselves of the blood of their brethren who had been slain by their enemies" (Morm. 3:9); "every heart was hardened, so that they delighted in the shedding of blood continually" (Morm. 4:11); they "march forth from the shedding of blood to the shedding of blood," "drunken with anger" (Ether 14:22, 15:22). Stunned by the depravity of his people, Mormon laments their lack of "order" and "mercy," describes how "they have lost their love, one toward another," and says: "if they perish it will be like unto the Jaredites, because of the wilfulness of their hearts, seeking for blood and revenge" (Moro. 9:18, 5, 23).

6. The horrors of war may bring either humility and repentance or hardness and despair: "But behold, because of the exceedingly great length of the war between the Nephites and the Lamanites many had become hardened . . . and many were softened because of their afflictions, insomuch that they did humble themselves before God, even in the depth of humility" (Alma 62:41). At another point, the people see their sufferings in war as a judgment sent by God "because of their wickedness" and are "awakened to a remembrance of their duty" (Alma 4:3). For us as well, hope of salvation in times of war lies in our responding with humility, repentance, and faith.

7. The gospel brings peace. The only true and permanent source of peace is the change of heart brought about by repentance and faith in Christ. Besides the examples of converted Lamanites and of Nephites whose hearts are softened so they "could not bear that any human soul should perish" (Mosiah 28:3), the Book of Mormon tells in Fourth Nephi of an entire era when enmity ceased "because of the love of God which did dwell in the hearts of the people" (4 Ne. 1:13–18).

Given the obvious evils of war, it is no wonder that the Book of Mormon describes the righteous as often being reluctant to wage it. Helaman says that he and his stripling warriors "would not slay our brethren if they would let us alone" (Alma 56:46). The Nephites are at times "compelled reluctantly to contend with their brethren"; "they were sorry to take up arms against the Lamanites, because they did not delight in the shedding of blood; yea, and this was not all—they were sorry to be the means of sending so many of their brethren out of this world into an eternal world, unprepared to meet their God" (Alma 48:21–23). War was at best a grim necessity in which the righteous engaged as an act of compassion to rescue those who would otherwise be subjected to "barbarous cruelty" (Alma 48:24). The Lord sometimes justified war with the aim of self-defense, but never—in the Book of Mormon at least—as an act of aggression.

Happily, righteous figures in the Book of Mormon found—or under divine inspiration were prompted to take—alternatives to the sword. Alma and his people prayed that the Lord would soften their enemies' hearts (Mosiah 23:28–29). Through missionary work, the sons of Mosiah sought to "cure [the Lamanites] of their hatred toward the Nephites, that they might become friendly to one another" (Mosiah 28:2). Many of their fellow Nephites mocked their efforts, claiming the Lamanites were completely evil and urging, "Let us take up arms against them, that we destroy them and their iniquity out of the land, lest they overrun us and destroy us" (Alma 26:23–25). In contrast, the sons of Mosiah went "not with the intent to destroy our brethren, but with the intent that perhaps we might save some few of their souls" (v. 26). Of course, their success far exceeded their expectations.

The people of Ammon present one of the most powerful examples in all of scripture of an alternative to warfare. By willingly allowing themselves to be killed, they inspired compassion and repentance on the part of many of their enemies, so that "the people of God were joined that day by more than the number who had been slain" (Alma 24:26). Some have felt this is a special case that we should not feel obligated to follow—that the people of Ammon were justified in not taking up arms *only* because they needed to keep the covenant they had made as part of their repentance for their previous murders.

But the admiration recorded in the Book of Mormon toward the people of Ammon suggests that their refusal to fight was more than simply an exceptional condition for repentance. Ammon praises their willingness to "rather sacrifice their lives than even to take the life of their enemy" as an expression of "love" and then asks, "has there been so great love in all the land? Behold, I say unto you, Nay, there has not, even among the Nephites." Then he contrasts the Nephite practice of military self-defense with the loving self-sacrifice of the people of Ammon (Alma 26:31–34). Ammon perhaps implies that these converted Lamanites were living a *higher* law, a law of perfect love that the Nephite people as a whole were unable to live at the time. Yet the record also praises the Nephites for risking their lives to protect the people of Ammon, suggesting not only that the Lord justified them in doing the best they could in the circumstances but that they too were demonstrating Christ-like love, though in a different way.

The main message of this episode may be the one stated in Alma 24:27: "the Lord worketh in many ways to the salvation of his people." A wholesale decision to follow the example of the people of Ammon might have preserved the Nephites as thousands more of their enemies were converted; or perhaps their enemies would have resisted conversion, requiring the Lord to justify the Nephites in taking up arms not only because of their own imperfections but also because of those of their enemies. In any case, the Book of Mormon offers the people of Ammon as a powerful example of goodness—demonstrating faith, love, and integrity—to which we can aspire, prompting us to examine our own hearts as we face difficult circumstances comparable to those of the people of Ammon and their Nephite protectors.

The Savior's Teachings and Example

The Savior's teachings and example are, of course, the most authoritative guide for Latter-day Saints. The Savior pronounced a blessing upon "the peacemakers." He taught that we must "love our enemies" and respond with a desire for their welfare even when they mistreat us. Many have pointed out that, however difficult, that must be our attitude even if we are required to defend ourselves.[3] Though bold in his opposition to evil, the Savior forgave those who took his life. He advised his followers not to return evil for evil but to "turn the other cheek."[4] For strict pacifists, the Savior's counsel—which he himself demonstrated in action—has been a literal guide. Others have taught that, while we should aspire not to retaliate in our personal lives, we cannot follow those teachings literally on an international scale. To me the challenge of following the Savior's teachings internationally is not that they are not literally true—I believe that if followed by an entire nation they would have miraculous power—but that nations are such complex entities that coming to true unity on this matter would require a conversion that would itself be a miracle. In the meantime the Savior's teachings should guide our attitudes and efforts and inspire us toward a truer and deeper change of heart.

---

3. For example, see *True to the Faith*, 183: Those in military service "should go with love in their hearts for all God's children, including those on the opposing side."

4. See Matt. 5:9, 39, 44; Luke 6:27, 35; 3 Ne. 12:9, 39, 44.

The Savior also announced that he brought "not peace but the sword," apparently referring to the conflict that would come, especially within families, as some accepted his teachings and others did not (see Matt. 10:34–36). But I do not believe the Savior rejoices in the conflict he knew would come. He also taught that "they that take the sword shall perish with the sword" and that "it is by the wicked that the wicked are punished" (Matt. 26:52; Morm. 4:5; see also D&C 63:33).

Christ's teachings on contention and anger are potently clear:

> [H]e that hath the spirit of contention is not of me, but is of the devil, who is the father of contention, and he stirreth up the hearts of men to contend with anger, one with another. Behold, this is not my doctrine, to stir up the hearts of men with anger, one against another; but this is my doctrine, that such things should be done away. (3 Ne. 11:29–30)

In place of contention and anger, the Lord invites us to exercise charity, a pure love not limited to friends or those we account as "good," but universal in its scope.[5]

Statements of Church Leaders

Official statements by Church leaders over the past hundred years have focused on three issues: the need to avoid hatred during times of war; the comfort extended to Church members called to military service, especially to relieve them of feelings of guilt for the destruction and bloodshed in which they may be involved; and the power of the gospel of Christ to bring peace. Individual Church leaders have sometimes expressed personal views on war and peace, favoring or opposing specific military actions or discussing the dangers of and possible justifications for war.

During World War II, the First Presidency presented two messages responding to that conflict. In April 1942, they reminded members of the scriptural command, "Therefore, renounce war and proclaim peace" (D&C 98:16), explaining that "the Church is and must be against war. The Church itself cannot wage war, unless and until the Lord shall issue new commands. It cannot regard war as a righteous means of settling international disputes; these should and could be settled—the nations agreeing—by peaceful negotiation and adjustment."[6]

---

5. See 1 Ne. 11:17; 2 Ne. 26:24; Ether 12:33–34; Mor. 7:46–48; and many other references.

6. "First Presidency Message," *Report of the Semi-annual Conference of the Church of Jesus Christ of Latter-day Saints*, April 1942 (Salt Lake City: Church of Jesus Christ of Latter-day Saints, semi-annual), 94 (hereafter cited as *Conference*

Nevertheless, the First Presidency acknowledged that Church members "have always felt under obligation to come to the defense of their country when a call to arms was made" and that, in both World Wars, Saints had "served loyally their respective governments, on both sides of the conflict," and should be honored for their heroism and sacrifice. Such men are not personally guilty of violating God's commands when they take life in war. When responding to the "civic duty" that requires them to enter military service and when, "obeying those in command over them, they shall take the lives of those who fight against them, that will not make of them murderers, nor subject them to the penalty that God has prescribed for those who kill." In such cases, soldiers are "the innocent instrumentalities" of governmental authority; they are "powerless to resist." God will hold responsible—and judge in his own time and way—"those rulers in the world who in a frenzy of hate and lust for unrighteous power and dominion over their fellow men, have put into motion eternal forces they do not comprehend and cannot control."[7]

Knowing of the challenges of military life, the First Presidency encouraged those in the armed forces to keep the commandments and draw close to the Lord, promising them that if they would do so, the Lord would comfort them: "you will feel His presence in the hour of your greatest tribulation."[8] Yet while promising the Lord's blessings, they also acknowledged that the righteous suffer along with the wicked and that not all faithful Latter-day Saints would survive the conflict.

The following October, the First Presidency renewed their "declaration that international disputes can and should be settled by peaceful means," called "upon the leaders of nations to abandon the fiendishly inspired slaughter of the manhood of the world now carrying on and further planned," and stated that peace "will never be imposed by armed force," for such a peace will be merely "the beginning of another war." Reminding members that "this Church is the Church of Christ, who taught peace and righteousness and brotherhood of man," the First Presidency stated that "war is of Satan" and that followers of Christ will seek peace.[9]

Among the First Presidency's greatest concerns was that members of the Church, in or out of the military, should not be caught up in a spirit

---

Report). For similar teachings during World War I, see Joseph F. Smith, *Teachings of Presidents of the Church: Joseph F. Smith* (Salt Lake City: The Church of Jesus Christ of Latter-day Saints, 1998), 399–406.

7. "First Presidency Message," *Conference Report*, April 1942, 93–95.
8. Ibid., 96.
9. "First Presidency Message," *Conference Report*, October 1942, 15–16.

of hatred and revenge: "Hate can have no place in the souls of the righteous. We must follow the commands of Christ Himself," including the command, "'Love your enemies'. . . . These principles must be instilled into the hearts of our children. . . . Woe will be the part of those who plant hate in the hearts of the youth, and of the people, for God will not hold them guiltless; they are sowing the wind, their victims will reap the whirlwinds. Hate is born of Satan; love is the offspring of God. We must drive out hate from our hearts, every one of us, and permit it not again to enter."[10]

Early in World War II the Allies had condemned the bombing of civilians. Even before the United States entered the war, President Franklin Roosevelt called the practice a "form of inhuman barbarism" and said: "The ruthless bombing from the air of civilians in unfortified centers of population . . . has sickened the hearts of every civilized man and woman, and has profoundly shocked the conscience of humanity."[11] Yet as the war progressed, the Allies themselves resorted to the practice, firebombing many cities in Germany and Japan and finally dropping atomic bombs on Hiroshima and Nagasaki. Though the LDS Church never announced a position on the subject, J. Reuben Clark, a counselor in the First Presidency, spoke against the bombing of civilians. In a General Conference address after the war ended, President Clark argued that we had declined into "barbarism" by departing from internationally agreed upon standards for the treatment of civilians, as well as of prisoners of war and the wounded. He pointed specifically to the bombing of Dresden, "where it is said we killed in two nights more than two hundred fifty thousand people, men, women and children," and to the killing of "hundreds of thousands" in Japan by the atomic bomb, which he called "the crowning savagery of the war" and "a world tragedy." He lamented that Americans not only were not shocked but generally approved "of this fiendish butchery" and went on to condemn ongoing efforts in the United States to devise new ways of "exterminating peoples." In response to experimentation with this aim, he said: "I protest with all of the energy I possess against this fiendish activity, and . . . call upon our government and its agencies to see that these unholy experimentations are stopped." He warned, "God will not forgive us for this," and called for God to help "put hate out of our hearts, a hate that is consuming us."[12]

---

10. "First Presidency Message," *Conference Report*, April 1942, 90–91.

11. Franklin D. Roosevelt, "Appeal of President Franklin D. Roosevelt on Aerial Bombardment of Civilian Populations, September 1, 1939," available at http://www.dannen.com/decision/int-law.html#E (accessed June 13, 2013).

12. J. Reuben Clark, *Conference Report*, October 1946, 88–89.

My memories of living in a time of war date to the Vietnam conflict, which divided Latter-day Saints as it did Americans generally. The Church repeated earlier statements about the general evils of war and the duty of military service. Elder Gordon B. Hinckley, then a member of the Quorum of the Twelve Apostles, gave a memorable address in 1968 "call[ing] [our] attention to that silver thread, small but radiant with hope, shining through the dark tapestry of war—namely, the establishment of a bridgehead, small and frail now; but which somehow, under the mysterious ways of God, will be strengthened, and from which someday shall spring forth a great work affecting for good the lives of large numbers of our Father's children who live in that part of the world." Noting that he would "make no defense of the war from this pulpit," he nevertheless bore testimony that God would turn the misery of war to good ends in his own time and way.[13]

Though some General Authorities disagreed (for the most part privately) about the war in Vietnam, officially the Church said, "We make no statement on how this country can or should try to disengage itself from the present regrettable war in Vietnam."[14] As a junior high and high school student during the conflict, I went from vague approval to pained opposition. The turning point for me was in 1966 when I began noticing and was soon revolted by news reports of what were called "kill ratios"—supposedly positive news that mathematically compared the proportion of our enemies' deaths to our own in combat. Growing up in Utah, where most people supported the war, I found myself for the first time feeling like an outsider. I was somewhat comforted when I heard Church leaders speak occasionally of the evils of war.[15] I was surprised but thrilled to hear President Harold B. Lee, in his prayer at the inauguration of Utah's governor in 1973, ask that the engines of war might cease to wreak destruction on the earth—what I took to be a reference to the bombing of Cambodia, which was taking place at that time.

In speaking of war and peace, Church leaders have usually discussed general principles, but occasionally the Church has taken an official position on a controversial issue. For instance, in 1981 President Kimball and his counselors announced their opposition to a plan to base the MX missile

---

13. Gordon B. Hinckley, "A Silver Thread in the Dark Tapestry of War," *Conference Report*, April 1968, 24.

14. "First Presidency Takes Stand on Vietnam War," *The Church News*, May 24, 1969, 12.

15. See Harold B. Lee, "From the Valley of Despair to the Mountain Peaks of Hope," *New Era*, August 1971, 4–9, and "Teach the Gospel of Salvation," *Ensign*, January 1973, 60–63.

system in Utah and Nevada. Noting that "our fathers came to this western area to establish a base from which to carry the gospel of peace to the peoples of the earth," they saw placing a massive weapons system there as "a denial of the very essence of that gospel." The statement also warned against "the terrifying arms race" in which nations were then engaged and "deplore[d] in particular the building of vast arsenals of nuclear weaponry."[16]

In December 1990, with war approaching in the Persian Gulf, the First Presidency stated, "At a Christmas season in which we witness turmoil in the world, we pause to remember that His gospel is our only hope for peace on earth and goodwill toward men"; and then, four months later, they expressed gratitude for the end of the Gulf War along with a "fervent hope and prayer that all nations involved will work in concert for a lasting peace. The collective prayers of the nation and the world should focus not only on a lasting peace, but on the needs of the many on both sides who lost loved ones and endured suffering in the conflict."[17]

As war began again in 2003 with the American invasion of Iraq, President Hinckley gave an address in General Conference titled "War and Peace." He repeated the Church position that, though war is evil, we are under obligation to our respective governments to respond to the duties of military service and added his view that "there are times and circumstances when nations are justified, in fact have an obligation, to fight for family, for liberty, and against tyranny, threat, and oppression."[18] He expressed sympathy for a mother who had sent her son to the war, but also for "other mothers, innocent civilians, who cling to their children with fear and look heavenward with desperate pleadings as the earth shakes beneath their feet and deadly rockets scream through the dark sky."[19] President Hinckley acknowledged differences of views among nations and among members of the Church on the rightness and wisdom of the current war and cautioned members to avoid contention as they expressed their views: "We can give our opinions on the merits of the situation as we see it, but never let us become a party to words or works of evil concerning our brothers and sisters in various nations on one side or the other. Political differences never justify hatred or ill will. I hope that the Lord's people may be at peace one

---

16. "Statement of The First Presidency on Basing of the MX Missile," *Church News*, May 9, 1981, 2; Kimball, *Lengthen Your Stride*, 156–58.

17. "The First Presidency Christmas Message," *The Church News*, December 8, 1990, 3; "First Presidency Endorses Presidential Proclamation," *The Church News*, March 23, 1991, 5.

18. Gordon B. Hinckley, "War and Peace," *Ensign*, May 2003, 80.

19. Ibid., 79.

with another during times of trouble, regardless of what loyalties they may have to different governments or parties."[20]

Given differences of opinion among Church members, President Hinckley focused on what all of us should do: pray for those in harm's way; comfort those who lose loved ones; and "hope and pray for that glorious day foretold by the prophet Isaiah when men 'shall beat their swords into plowshares, and their spears into pruninghooks: nation shall not lift up sword against nation, neither shall they learn war any more' (Isa. 2:4)."[21] God "must have wept," President Hinckley said, "as He has looked down upon His children through the centuries as they have squandered their divine birthright in ruthlessly destroying one another."[22] Though we may find this war justified, "we of this Church are people of peace. We are followers of our Redeemer, the Lord Jesus Christ, who was the Prince of Peace." Along with our obligation as citizens and our desire to defend liberty, we should be among those "who long for peace, who teach peace, who work for peace."[23]

I found President Hinckley's talk both moving and challenging—challenging because he called my attention to things that, in my revulsion at war, I had neglected. President Hinckley's words have heightened my concern with those suffering from oppression and other evils around the world. Still, I believe that in responding to such problems, there is much we can and should do short of war—that war, in fact, generally causes greater problems than it solves and, if ever deliberately chosen, should be a last resort. As President Hinckley said, reflecting three years after his General Conference address "on the terrible cost of war": "What a fruitless thing it so often is, and what a terrible price it exacts."[24]

Conditions that Might Justify War

Though all that I know of war repels and grieves me, I acknowledge that there may be rare circumstances when war is necessary. If it is at best a response of last resort, we must do much more to practice patience and forbearance and seek understanding and mutually acceptable solutions, even

---

20. Ibid., 80.
21. Ibid., 81.
22. Ibid., 79.
23. Ibid., 80.
24. Gordon B. Hinckley, "Experiences Worth Remembering," Devotional address given at Brigham Young University, Oct. 31, 2006, available at http://speeches.byu.edu/?act=viewitem&id=1646 (accessed June 13, 2013).

if they are unpopular. Merely being passive is not an adequate response to injustice and oppression. But many kinds of efforts short of violence are possible: bearing bold witness against evil, promoting goodness and goodwill, engaging in non-violent resistance to injustice, and exercising faith in God's power to resolve problems that appear beyond human solution. War and other violent actions bring short-term results; but the long-term effects, including bitterness and a desire for revenge, often take generations to overcome. As the First Presidency stated in 1942, "force always begets force."[25] In counseling Latter-day Saints in South America, President Kimball encouraged them to avoid violence in seeking to deal with evil and injustice: "Wouldn't [those seeking change] be far better off to align themselves with the constructive forces and attempt a slower, more peaceful way to reach the same ends?"[26]

If injustice, oppression, and evil do not justify war as the preferred response, what then might justify war?

The Book of Mormon teaches that we should "defend [our] families even unto bloodshed," though it also suggests that the Lord may offer alternative ways of dealing with attack or oppression (Alma 43:47, 48:15–16). The Doctrine and Covenants outlines a "law" for Latter-day Saints indicating that, if they are attacked once or even twice or three times, they should not retaliate but should "bear it patiently and revile not against them, neither seek revenge" (D&C 98:33, 23). But if they are attacked a fourth time after having given their enemy warning, the Lord may "justify them in going out to battle." Even in that case, however, "if thou wilt spare him, thou shalt be rewarded for thy righteousness" (vv. 36, 30–31). The main principle here seems to be that, though defense is justifiable, every effort should be made to make peace even when we are threatened with attack. In no case should Latter-day Saints give the first offense. Like the ancient Nephites, we are taught "never to give an offense, yea, and never to raise the sword . . . except it were to preserve their lives" (Alma 48:14).

President David O. McKay expanded upon these ideas by listing cases when, in his view, war might or might not be justified. After asserting that war "produces hate" and "is incompatible with Christ's teachings," he notes that nations may, nevertheless, be justified in taking up arms on two or perhaps three conditions: "There are . . . two conditions which may justify a truly Christian man to enter—mind you, I say enter, not begin—a war: (1) An attempt to dominate and deprive another of his free agency, and,

---

25. "First Presidency Message," *Conference Report*, April 1942, 95.
26. Kimball, *Lengthen Your Stride*, 333.

(2) Loyalty to his country. Possibly there is a third, viz., Defense of a weak nation that is being unjustly crushed by a strong, ruthless one." According to President McKay, the conditions that do *not* justify war include "a real or fancied insult given by one nation to another," "a desire or even a need for territorial expansion," or "an attempt to enforce a new order of government, or even to impel others to a particular form of worship, however better the government or eternally true the principles of the enforced religion may be."[27] In President McKay's view (which does not represent an official Church position but which I believe is in harmony with gospel principles), war is not justified as a means of overthrowing an evil regime or bringing greater light or civilization to benighted peoples.

Perhaps another condition that might justify intervention is a breakdown of civil order that threatens innocent lives. As thousands have been slaughtered in Rwanda, Darfur, and elsewhere in recent years, I have wondered whether nations working together could have done more, including the use of armed force, to prevent bloodshed.

What of responding to an attack *before* it happens—in other words, what of preemptive warfare? Recent events have shown that such an approach is hazardous, that in response to an imagined threat a nation may itself become the aggressor and create turmoil rather than containing it. The Book of Mormon suggests that preemptive warfare also brings moral and spiritual hazards. Gidgiddoni counseled the people to not attack the Gadianton robbers and instead to "wait till they shall come against us," "for if we should go up against them the Lord would deliver us into their hands" (3 Ne. 3:20–21). When military campaigns are undertaken by the Nephites to revenge previous offenses or to prevent future ones, the results are always disastrous. At one point the Nephites' success in battle leads them to "boast in their own strength" and swear that "they would go up to battle against their enemies, and would cut them off from the face of the land." Describing the destruction that results, Mormon says that "it was because the armies of the Nephites went up unto the Lamanites that they began to be smitten; for were it not for that, the Lamanites could have had no power over them" (Morm. 3:9–11, 4:4).

I do not pretend that these Book of Mormon examples exactly parallel modern conditions. Yet as a book written for us, the Book of Mormon ought to guide our approach in significant ways, especially in reminding us that righteousness will be our greatest protection and that taking an aggressive posture in order to protect ourselves may lead to our destruction.

---

27. David O. McKay, *Conference Report*, April 1942, 71–72.

In recent years, some have presented yet another possible justification for war, arguing that we must rid the world of evil and that we must do so by destroying the perpetrators of evil. To me, this seems a particularly dangerous notion, based on a profound and unscriptural misunderstanding of evil and its role in our world. Indeed, some of the greatest evils the world has seen have been committed by those who thought they were destroying evil. The pagans of the ancient world easily identified their enemies as evil and sought to destroy them; too many in the modern world have followed their example. The gospel of Christ provides a profoundly different understanding.

First, the gospel teaches us that God is in charge of punishing evil: "Vengeance is mine," the Lord says (Morm. 3:14–15). Second, Christ teaches that the world is not divided into good people and evil people, but that all of us are in varying degrees subject to sin. We have all "gone astray" and, even at our best, are "evil" compared to a perfect Heavenly Father (see Matt. 7:11).[28] Some of God's children are, in fact, deeply caught in the web of evil, and we must make necessary efforts to protect ourselves and our loved ones. But the solution to evil will not come by identifying the most hardened or enslaved sinners and destroying them. For one thing, we "cannot always tell the wicked from the righteous" (D&C 10:37). "[T]he whole world groaneth under sin and darkness" and will never come fully out of that bondage through violence, but only through repenting and accepting God's will (D&C 84:53–58; see also D&C 123:7).

Another way the gospel of Christ provides a profoundly different understanding is by teaching that evil is a necessary condition of our mortal experience, a natural consequence of the principle of agency. To seek to destroy evil by force is to succumb to Satan's plan. If successful, such efforts would frustrate one of the purposes of our lives, which is to encounter evil yet choose good instead. An ancient apocryphal source quotes the apostle Peter as saying, "We must bear wicked men with patience, . . . knowing that God who could easily wipe them out, suffers them to carry on to the appointed day in which the deeds of all shall be judged. Wherefore should we not then suffer whom God suffers?" God knew his children would do

---

28. Compare the truth expressed by the great Russian writer Aleksandr Solzhenitsyn: "the line separating good and evil passes not through states, nor between classes, nor between political parties either—but right through every human heart." Aleksandr I. Solzhenitsyn, *The Gulag Archipelago 1918–1956: An Experiment in Literary Investigation, III–IV*, trans. Thomas P. Whitney (New York: Harper & Row, 1975), 615.

much evil, "but as one who knew there was no other way to achieve the purpose for which they were created, he went ahead."[29]

Finally, the gospel teaches that our efforts to rid the world of evil must begin with our own repentance and be followed by teaching the gospel through example and precept. President Joseph F. Smith taught,

> Let us conquer ourselves, and then go to and conquer all the evil that we see around us, as far as we possibly can. And we will do it without using violence; we will do it without interfering with the agency of men or of women. We will do it by persuasion, by long-suffering, by patience, and by forgiveness and love unfeigned, by which we will win the hearts, the affections and the souls of the children of men to the truth as God has revealed it to us.[30]

Patriotism in a Worldwide Church

Our efforts to come to a gospel understanding of war and peace and to purify our own hearts are complicated by our being members of larger communities, to which we owe loyalty. The Church has long taught that we should be good citizens wherever we live and that our citizenship may include the obligation of military service.

True patriotism, as I understand it, involves gratitude for the blessings that come with living in a particular nation and positive efforts to improve and protect that nation. At the same time, the gospel requires us to take a global view: "Know ye not that there are more nations than one? Know ye not that I, the Lord your God, have created all men?" (2 Ne. 29:7). Loyalty to our own nation may tempt us to denigrate those of other nations, even to consider their lives expendable while we hold those of our compatriots precious. Joseph Smith opposed such partiality: "[W]hile one portion of the human race is judging and condemning the other without mercy, the Great Parent of the universe looks upon the whole human family with a fatherly care and paternal regard; He views them as His offspring, and without any of those contracted feelings that influence the children of men."[31] Consequently, "A man filled with the love of God, is not content with bless-

---

29. Quoted in Hugh Nibley, *The World and the Prophets* (Salt Lake City: Deseret Book, 1954), 167–68.

30. Joseph F. Smith, *Teachings of Presidents of the Church: Joseph F. Smith* (Salt Lake City: The Church of Jesus Christ of Latter-day Saints, 1998), 250.

31. Joseph Smith, *Teachings of the Prophet Joseph Smith*, ed. Joseph Fielding Smith (Salt Lake City: Deseret Book, 1977), 218.

ing his family"—or his own nation—"alone, but ranges through the whole world, anxious to bless the whole human race."[32]

True patriotism does not mean believing God is on our nation's side, simply because it is our nation. Wiser souls have suggested that God may not be pleased with either side in an armed conflict and that, rather than assuming God is on our side, we should seek to be on *His* side. Near the end of the American Civil War, Abraham Lincoln submitted that "The Almighty [had] His own purposes" in that conflict and that neither side could rightly claim complete divine approval.[33] Lincoln's words were echoed by the LDS First Presidency during World War II when they said, "On each side they believe they are fighting for home, and country, and freedom. On each side, our brethren pray to the same God, in the same name, for victory. Both sides cannot be wholly right; perhaps neither is without wrong. God will work out in His own due time and in His own sovereign way the justice and right of the conflict."[34]

Perhaps the greatest danger of what many take to be patriotism is its association with pride. While the word "pride" sometimes means nothing more than affection and gratitude, national pride often involves the enmity and egotism President Benson associated with the word.[35] Can pride be a national sin? That is yet another lesson of the Book of Mormon. Latter-day Saints are advised to "beware of pride, lest ye become as the Nephites of old" (D&C 38:39). Mormon tells us that "the pride of this nation . . . hath proven their destruction except they should repent" (Moro. 8:27).

In our own day, President Kimball has warned Latter-day Saints of a false patriotism based on enmity and pride:

> We are a warlike people, easily distracted from our assignment of preparing for the coming of the Lord. When enemies rise up, we commit vast resources to the fabrication of gods of stone and steel—ships, planes, missiles, fortifications—and depend on them for protection and deliverance. When threatened, we become antienemy instead of

---

32. Ibid., 174.

33. Abraham Lincoln, "Second Inaugural Address of Abraham Lincoln," The Avalon Project, http://avalon.law.yale.edu/19th_century/lincoln2.asp (accessed June 14, 2013).

34. "First Presidency Message," *Conference Report*, April 1942, 95.

35. In the address "Beware of Pride," President Benson said, among other things: "In the scriptures there is no such thing as righteous pride—it is always considered a sin. . . . The central feature of pride is enmity—enmity toward God and enmity toward our fellowmen. . . . Pride is essentially competitive in nature." Ezra Taft Benson, "Beware of Pride," *Ensign*, May 1989, 4.

pro-kingdom of God; we train a man in the art of war and call him a patriot, thus, in the manner of Satan's counterfeit of true patriotism, perverting the Savior's teaching: "Love your enemies, bless them that curse you, do good to them that hate you."[36]

Despite President Kimball's strong language, the Church has not condemned its members who have chosen military service or had it required of them. In fact, it has honored them for their courage and faithful service. Among the General Authorities have been many who have served in time of war and even a few professional military men. Several great figures in the Book of Mormon, including Mormon and Moroni, were soldiers as well as prophets. However, they often performed their duties with sadness. Mormon even refused to lead his people into battle as they became increasingly wicked, and when he returned to his work as a military leader he did so with no hope that his people would avoid spiritual and physical destruction.

Since Latter-day Saints live in many nations, they owe their loyalty to various kinds of governments and sometimes have found themselves on opposing sides of international conflicts. It must have been difficult for Germans to understand what true patriotism meant during Hitler's reign, especially since the Church still expected the German Saints to be loyal to their country. Under oppressive regimes, disagreement with a country's leaders can be deadly, as it proved to be to at least one young Latter-day Saint in Hitler's Germany, a young man named Helmuth Hübner.[37] Such regimes have regularly used "lack of patriotism" as an excuse to persecute those who disagree.[38]

President Hinckley has emphasized that, when we disagree with our political leaders, we should do so respectfully and legally. But he has reminded us that, in democracies at least, we *can* disagree, even on matters of war and peace.[39] I believe that true patriotism not only allows but at times requires disagreement with the decisions of national leaders and with the

---

36. Spencer W. Kimball, "The False Gods We Worship," *Ensign*, June 1976, 6.

37. Blair R. Holmes and Alan F. Keele, eds., *When Truth Was Treason* (Urbana: University of Illinois Press, 1995), 257–58.

38. While imprisoned for trial after World War II, Hermann Goering was quoted as saying: "Why, of course, the people don't want war.... [Yet,] voice or no voice, the people can always be brought to the bidding of the leaders. That is easy. All you have to do is tell them they are being attacked and denounce the pacifists for lack of patriotism and exposing the country to danger. It works the same way in any country." G. M. Gilbert, *Nuremberg Diary* (New York: Farrar, Straus and Company, 1947), 278–79.

39. Hinckley, "War and Peace," 80.

views of one's fellow citizens. If I believe my nation's leaders are mistaken, I should present my views as clearly and persuasively as I can. But I should do so respectfully, not demonizing other people because I disagree with their views.

For me, it has been challenging and sometimes painful to find myself surrounded by neighbors and family members—most of them members of the Church—who disagree with me. At times I have felt my Church calling prevented me from speaking openly lest I offend others or seem to be presenting my personal views as Church doctrine. At all times, I have wanted to preserve charity and fellowship. As I have tried to listen carefully and sympathetically to others who disagree with me, I've found far more common ground than I might have thought: I've discovered that we share the same fundamental values but view their application differently. I have generally come away respecting those I disagree with, finding elements of their views that have helpfully tempered my own, and especially recognizing that, despite their views, which I have sometimes found abhorrent, I should be grateful for the goodness of their lives and their hearts. Again and again, I have been reminded of my own imperfections and the limitations of my understanding. To me, it would be tragic if I allowed the bond of charity to be sundered by differences in political views, and it would be tragically ironic if I allowed my appeals for peace to become an occasion of enmity and conflict.

The Condition of Our Hearts

As I have done my best to understand the teachings of the Church on war and peace, I have been impressed that these teachings, though often challenging, form a consistent whole in harmony with the spirit and teachings of Christ. War is evil, yet we must remain faithful and seek to be righteous even in the midst of its horrors. God is at the helm and will turn all things to His purposes. We must be good citizens, yet our vision should be attuned to God's will rather than to narrow national self-interest; and we must broaden our hearts and seek to love and serve all of God's children.

As the world grows more dangerous, I am afraid we may be tempted to think we are exempt from these teachings as we focus on mere survival. Depicting the Nephites and Jaredites descending into barbarity as they approached destruction, the Book of Mormon may be warning us precisely against such an attitude. Self-protection at all costs may lead to actions that will make us unworthy of being protected. If, in order to protect ourselves, we engage in torture, oppression, and the slaughter of innocent civilians, why should we be preserved rather than the enemies who are guilty of similar offenses? Perhaps the final lesson of the Book of Mormon is that those who become like their enemies in wickedness will be destroyed because the Lord will remove his protection. Desperate efforts at self-preservation may have the effect of self-destruction—first, moral self-destruction, then physical.

The Book of Mormon teaches that we must be willing to protect our families, even unto the shedding of blood—which I assume means our own blood as well as (possibly and unfortunately) the blood of our enemies. Yet this teaching is tempered by other gospel principles: that we should seek solutions short of bloodshed, that we should trust in God and follow His commands even when they seem contrary to our self-interest, and that we must love all of God's children. Ultimately, the reason we should seek to protect ourselves is so that we can be of service, like Alma, who prayed for protection so that he could "be an instrument in [God's] hands to save and preserve this people" (Alma 2:30). Yet, as the Savior taught, we should fear the destruction of our souls more than that of our bodies (see Matt. 10:28). I believe that, likewise, we should worry more about inflicting harm than about suffering it.

Why is war so evil? It produces hatred, cruelty, suffering, and despair—and these are bad enough. But perhaps worst of all, it leads us to view other people—our brothers and sisters, precious children of our Heavenly Father—as threats or obstacles or objects to be destroyed. One of the worst things about warfare, as Elder Robert Oaks has pointed out, is that it leads us to forget that the people against whom we are directing deadly force are individual human beings, with faces.[40]

The Savior taught that, as conflicts and calamities increased in the last days, "men's hearts" would fail them "for fear," and "the love of many [would] wax cold" (Luke 21:26; D&C 88:91; Matt. 24:12; D&C 45:27). The most terrible effect of such turmoil is clearly the hardening of hearts it can produce, a hardening I see in such familiar phrases as "Let's go kill some bad guys." I have been deeply troubled to see many, including some Latter-day Saints, taking joy in the destruction of war. A few years ago, a patriotic program was organized in my community for school children and their parents. I was horrified to learn that the audience had been encouraged to cheer as they watched slides showing planes unleashing their bombs. I imagine the Savior responding as he did to his disciples when they wanted fire to descend on their enemies: "Ye know not what manner of spirit ye

---

40. *Let Not Your Heart Be Troubled—a Message of Peace for Latter-day Saints in Military Service*, DVD (The Church of Jesus Christ of Latter-day Saints, 2005).

are of. For the Son of man is not come to destroy men's lives, but to save them" (Luke 9:55–56). Elder Lance Wickman has taught that we should be repelled by the evils of war, not rejoice in them. To soldiers in the battlefield, he says: "Be grateful if you are repelled by what you have seen in the combat zone. Revulsion is how righteous and spiritually sensitive people react to the horrors of warfare."[41]

In his dedicatory prayer for the Kirtland Temple, Joseph Smith said, "O Lord, we delight not in the destruction of our fellow men; their souls are precious before thee; but thy word must be fulfilled. Help thy servants to say, with thy grace assisting them: Thy will be done, O Lord, and not ours" (D&C 109:43–44). That seems to me precisely the attitude we must have toward the destruction of war. Evil will bring evil consequences, and "the wicked shall slay the wicked" (D&C 63:33). Yet we must never imagine that the Lord delights in the destruction of his children: "neither doth he will that man should shed blood, but in all things hath forbidden it, from the beginning of man" (Ether 8:19; see also D&C 63:31).

Living in such times as ours is a test of what we really believe. We can anxiously focus on physical survival, or we can have faith that God will protect us—especially protect us in the most important, eternal ways—if we trust in him. We can put our trust in "gods of stone and steel—ships, planes, missiles, fortifications," or we can believe that the word of God really is more powerful than the sword.[42] We can view our enemies as monsters who must be destroyed, or we can grieve for the evils they do and seek to return good for evil, even as we do what we can and must to protect ourselves.

Even if battle seems the only alternative, we must never delight in bloodshed or cease to pray for the gift of charity. Shortly after World War II, an apostle taught that we should feel compassion and brotherly love even for someone as appallingly evil as Hitler.[43]

We must also extend respect and kindness toward those we disagree with on issues of war and peace. And—another lesson that many including myself need to learn better—we must seek to understand in some measure

---

41. Ibid.

42. Kimball, "The False Gods," 6.

43. The apostle—George F. Richards—had a dream in which he embraced Hitler as a brother. After describing the dream, he said: "I think the Lord gave me that dream. Why should I dream of this man, one of the greatest enemies of mankind, and one of the wickedest, but that the Lord should teach me that I must love my enemies, and I must love the wicked as well as the good?" George F. Richard, *Conference Report*, October 1946, 140.

the challenges and horrors soldiers in battle undergo, feel compassion for their suffering, and honor their courage and devotion to duty.

Meanwhile, I believe the troubles of our times should not distract us from our positive mission as Latter-day Saints. I have always loved Joseph Smith's description of the essence of the restored gospel: "Friendship is one of the grand fundamental principles of 'Mormonism'; [it is designed] to revolutionize and civilize the world, and cause wars and contentions to cease and men to become friends and brothers."[44] As President Kimball put it, "Our assignment is affirmative: to forsake the things of the world as ends in themselves; to leave off idolatry and press forward in faith; to carry the gospel to our enemies, that they might no longer be our enemies."[45]

We must pray for peace and for the softening of our own and others' hearts. We must "renounce war and proclaim peace" in our personal lives as well as in nations and the world at large. We must do so not only by seeking peaceful solutions to world problems but by being peaceable in all our relationships and our communications. I believe we may reasonably differ on specific applications of gospel principles on war and peace. But we can agree that "the greatest of these is charity." And we can all experience the peace Christ brings to our hearts as we turn to him in faith and seek to follow his example and teachings.

---

44. Smith, *Teachings of the Prophet Joseph Smith*, 316.
45. Kimball, "The False Gods," 6.

Adapting a talk he gave at an LDS service member conference in Afghanistan in 2004, Eric Eliason makes a case for "A Moral and Spiritual Basis for Latter-day Saint Military Service Today." Drawing from personal experience and scriptural precedent, Eliason emphasizes the importance of motivation and purpose when judging the morality of a certain action. The question of the essay, posed originally to those serving in Afghanistan, was "how can we train to kill and at the same time follow a God who says, 'Thou shalt not kill'?" This dilemma, loaded with all too real implications for its initial audience, leads Eliason to treat a variety of issues related to war, including a defense of liberating countries under oppressive regimes to an exploration of the possibility of military spending as a very real, and perhaps more fundamental, element of actual US foreign aid. By creating a safe place for people to live and pursue their lives, Eliason argues that wars can enable us to establish "the principles on which lasting peace can be founded."

Thirteen

Why We Fight: A Moral and Spiritual Basis for Latter-day Saint Military Service Today

Eric A. Eliason

"That all war is physically frightful is obvious; but if that were a moral verdict there would be no difference between a torturer and a surgeon." C. K. Chesterton

Introduction

I am sure it is because I am a recent combat veteran as a chaplain with the 19th Special Forces and also a BYU humanities professor that I have been asked to contribute to this volume. I can think of no better way to share my convictions on the morality of just war in general—and impart whatever insights my unusual combination of professions may give on current conflicts in particular—than to revisit some thoughts I gave on April 25, 2004, at an LDS service member conference at Bagram Airbase, Afghanistan, attended by Mormon military people and civilian contractors from all branches of the service and from several different countries. All of the congregation was armed and in battle dress; many had seen combat. I drew many themes from ideas LDS military people have expressed to me over the years, so I believe this sermon represents some fairly common understandings. Since coming home, I have adapted and considerably expanded these thoughts for purposes beyond a church meeting setting. Hopefully it will give you a sense of why we fight. Not being sure when this essay will come to print and what might happen next in our current war, my thoughts here necessarily reflect the situation of early 2004; however, I hope that the ideas and principles discussed here reflect universals that underlie any particularities of time and place.[1]

---

1. In mid-2004, no one would have imagined that in late 2008, the Iraq War would be seen as, in essence, over, with the Americans and the soldiers of Iraq's democratic government as victors or that the Taliban and terrorist violence would

If some of the thrust and lingo seems peculiar to military types in a war zone, I hope you enjoy this texture and feel invited to peer through the window it provides into their world. Remember they are people just like you, and in our citizen-soldier military you can be one too. Our country is at war and the effort needs people willing to develop all kinds of skills. If, after reading the case below, this cause is not for you, then I hope my thoughts will at least give you some sense of how Latter-day Saints service members understand our roles in the light of the Gospel.

Even if you don't get in the fight yourself, you may be asked whether you support it. I hope this essay shows how the liberation of places like Afghanistan and Iraq can be justified very clearly on gospel grounds widely understood by LDS service members fighting in your name on the behalf of not just Americans but, more importantly, of Afghans and Iraqis. So, even if it sounds like I am speaking just to soldiers, I am really speaking to everyone.

When I was a student at the Chaplain Officer Basic Course, one of the instructors gave us some good advice. He said, "Now, not every sermon you give has to have some kind of military tie in. It doesn't always have to be about Moses and the children of Israel's great ruck march through wilderness" or, for you Marines, Noah's amphibious landing on Mt. Ararat. I have generally followed this advice and most of my sermons have tried to focus on general principles of life and salvation. In a sense, a chaplain's sermon can and sometimes ought to be an escape from military life.

However, occasionally it is good to pause and reflect on the moral and spiritual implications of our work. If we think our job is just like any other job, we are kidding ourselves. From a moral and spiritual point of view, the stakes are very high. The risks are great, but if we do our job right, the rewards can be even greater.

So, today I'd like to talk about how we can be soldiers at war, yet serve a God of peace. A story from my Dad's life illustrates this dilemma. My dad was a career fighter pilot in the Air Force. When he was a kid growing up on a farm in South Dakota, he made model airplanes and dreamed of flying. He also enjoyed farming and might have kept doing that were it not for his severe hay fever. (Now, hay fever is supposed to prevent you from being a pilot too, but that is another story.) When my dad served in Vietnam, he

---

be on the upswing in the south and west of Afghanistan. At the time Iraq seemed headed toward debacle and Afghanistan seemed to be progressing well. This is illustrative of the importance of staying with a good cause, even in its darkest days when fair weather patriots look for exit strategies.

carried an Air Force survival knife with him. I carry the same knife with me here in Afghanistan to remind me of my Dad's example.

Some of you may have seen the movie or read the book, *The Great Santini*, by Pat Conroy. In the movie, Robert Duvall plays a Marine fighter pilot who verbally and physically abuses his family. He demeans and humiliates them on a regular basis. He really is one of the great evil father-figures of American literature and has unfortunately become a military stereotype. At the end of the story, however, the Great Santini makes the ultimate heroic sacrifice by dying with his crippled F-4 Phantom rather than ejecting and letting his plane crash into a populated area. The Great Santini was not a unified personality. He was a hero as a soldier but a villain as a father.

My father was not like the Great Santini at all. He was as kind and encouraging a father as a boy could hope for. He suspected that some of the culture and values of the military might be in conflict with being a family man committed to Christ and tried to keep them separate.

You can see how he might get this idea from the Bible. Jesus at the Sermon on the Mount speaks of turning the other cheek and says that if a soldier of an occupying army compels you to carry his sword for a mile, you do not resist but "go with him twain"—hence the origin of the saying "to go the extra mile." When they came to get Jesus from the Garden of Gethsemane before his crucifixion and his chief apostle Peter struck off the ear of an arresting soldier, Jesus rebuked him saying, "He who lives by the sword, dies by the sword."

These scriptures came to my dad's mind when he had a disturbing dream one night of a loving Jesus Christ standing in a cloud holding out his arms and beckoning my father to come to him. Now this seems like a pretty pleasant dream actually, except that Jesus was wearing the flight jacket and g-suit of a fighter pilot. This perplexed my dad, who had tried hard to not confuse military with Christian values. The scriptures attest in many instances that dreams from God can seem strange and disturbing until properly interpreted. In time, my dad began to realize that the Lord was trying to tell him that He loves and understands us how we are and is the God of all of us regardless of our chosen profession. Moreover, the Lord empathizes with the needs and trials of everyone—even fighter pilots.

But I think there is even more to this dream. I believe Jesus loves and understands warriors especially, because he *is* one. The Lord makes this clear in several places in the Bible. Jeremiah 20:11 says, "The Lord is a dread Warrior." Zephaniah describes the Lord as "a warrior who gives victory." In the Psalms, David says the Lord is "strong and mighty in battle," he "trains my hands for war."

The same God of the Old Testament is the God of the New Testament as well, for he changeth not. In a recent conference address about our current war, President Hinckley quoted Jesus in Matthew 10:34, "Think not that I am come to send peace on earth: I came not to send peace but a sword."[2]

However, a righteous warrior does not fight for vengeance or for the spoils of war but to protect the weak, free the captive, and liberate the oppressed, or "*De Oppresso Liber*" in Latin. This motto of the US Army Special Forces means a lot to me and is one of the reasons why I sought out the 19th Special Forces when considering becoming a chaplain.

One of the most famous things Jesus said is "Greater love hath no man than this, but he that layeth down his life for his friends" (John 15:13). These words mean more to a soldier than they do to anyone in any other profession. To a soldier this is not some hypothetical platitude, but it is what he or she stands ready to do every day.

Politicians and generals may decide to send you to war. They may have their own reasons that you may or may not agree with. But either way, you can chose why you fight. And why you fight makes all the difference. You may think you are here to pay for school, for adventure, for family tradition, to test your manhood. But there are other ways to do these things. If you search your soul—and you don't even have to admit it to anyone—you know you are here because you love freedom and want to help secure that freedom for others.

If you've been watching the news the last few years, you know that not everyone sees current military action in this light. A lot of people have taken to the streets waving signs. "War is wrong." "Violence does not solve problems," they say. They say we should not be in this war. You have seen them; you know what I am talking about. I saw a sign once that said, "God says thou shalt not kill." Well, he does, doesn't he?

When reporters interview soldiers, the soldiers often say, "It is not my job to make policy or comment on it; my job is to do my duty when my country asks me to." These kinds of responses are good for some situations, but they are not enough for us as we discuss how we can best serve Christ. We need some tools to put what we do on strong moral ground and if we cannot find them, then we should not be here.

When our family members, wives, or children ask us why we have to leave and be gone for months or even over a year—"What could possibly

---

2. Gordon B. Hinckley, "War and Peace," *Ensign*, May 2003, 78

be more important than being here with us?"—what do we say? When we die and face the judgment bar of God and the Lord asks us, "Why did you fight?" what will we say? This is an all-volunteer military. No one forced us to be here. We are much more morally responsible for what we have chosen than are draftees. We need to take seriously the morality of our profession as soldiers and our involvement in this particular conflict.

So, how can we train to kill and at the same time follow a God who says "Thou shalt not kill"? The simple answer is that, understood properly, we can and we must, but it is all a matter of motivation, purpose, and the nature of the enemy we face. Brethren and sisters our motivation and purpose and the outcomes likely to result from our actions mean everything. If we lose sight of this we can lose our souls. Let me offer a few stories to illustrate.

- A man walks into a room. Another man is strapped on a table. The first grabs a knife, cuts the man on the table open, pulls out a chunk of innards and throws it away. This could be a torture chamber where an unspeakable crime is being committed. But it is not. It is an operating room; a surgeon just saved a man's life by taking out a ruptured appendix. Again, motivation, purpose, and likely results make all the difference.
- An old lady is crossing the street; imagine she's your own grandmother. A big hulking guy runs at her full tilt, slams into her, shoves her onto the sidewalk, breaking her arm and cutting her horribly. Later she has to stay in the hospital for a long time and endure painful physical therapy for months. An awful crime? The guy should be locked up right?
    - What if two seconds after the guy slams into her a truck rushes right by the spot where the old woman stood?
    - What if the big guy was still there when the truck came and was run over and killed in her place?
    - What if he didn't know the truck was coming and pushed her just for pleasure? (Motivation makes all the difference.)
    - What if he only thought the speeding truck was going to hit her but actually it would have missed her by a few inches? Is he is still a hero? (What if everyone thought there were weapons of mass destruction in Iraq but there turn out to be none?) Again motivation and purpose make all the difference.
    - What if the big fellow thought to himself, "I want to save that woman's life even if that means she might fall and I might get killed?" That makes all the difference.

I hope these stories—both of which involve terrible violence and collateral damage incidental to the noble main goal—show how good and evil situations can look almost the same without deeper understanding. If we go to war, it is understandable that some people without a clear vision will watch us and think we are doing wrong.

I want to take a moment to look at our particular war from the point of view of the additional light and knowledge we have as Latter-day Saints, because I feel very strongly that there is a clear vision to be had of what this war is all about.

Before doing so, I want to make clear that nothing I say should be taken as an indictment of Islam. We have more to gain than to lose in supporting the free exercise of Islam and we may be unique among Christian denominations in officially and specifically affirming in a 1978 First Presidency declaration that Mohammed (p.b.u.h.) was at least partly inspired by God.[3] Neither should what I say be taken as a criticism of traditional Afghan culture, which is enterprising, ingenious, and creative. I have had the opportunity to witness tribal councils and the traditional Afghan legal system, or *Pashtunwali*, in action on several occasions. Their ability to bring about justice, reconciliation, and forgiveness is something from which our confrontational winner-takes-all legal system could learn a lot. I also hope that nothing I say will be misconstrued as the Church's official position on this or other conflicts. There are many noble pursuits that Latter-day Saints as private individuals may undertake of their own volition that the Church is not officially involved in. We are encouraged to be anxiously engaged in good causes. There are lots of them out there. My only hope is to suggest that our work as soldiers in this war is among them.

We know that the very beginnings of our existence as children of God have to do with war—the great war in heaven about the proposed conditions of our mortal probation. In Moses 4:1–4 Lucifer says, "Behold, here I am, send me, I will be thy son, and I will redeem all mankind, that one soul shall not be lost . . . wherefore give me thine honor." The Lord responded,

---

3. The 1978 First Presidency declaration "God's Love for All Mankind" reads in part: "The great religious leaders of the world such as Mohammed, Confucius, and the Reformers, as well as philosophers including Socrates, Plato, and others, received a portion of God's light. Moral truths were given to them by God to enlighten whole nations and to bring a higher level of understanding to individuals. . . . Our message therefore is one of special love and concern for the eternal welfare of all men and women, regardless of religious belief, race, or nationality, knowing that we are truly brothers and sisters because we are sons and daughters of the same Eternal Father."

"Because Satan had sought to destroy the agency of man . . . I [the Lord] caused that he should be cast down."

Satan's goal to save everyone sounds good, right? But his *means* to this end by destroying agency was not only wrong but also impossible under the conditions necessary for our salvation. This Satanic tactic of promising that a seemingly good end could be achieved by means that restrict human agency was a lie from the beginning and is a theme that has popped up in Satan's counterfeits to God's plan many times in the history of the world.

When the Lord reveals a new program to his prophets, the adversary is often right on their heels with a counterfeit. In the 1830s the Lord began revealing a series of revelations to Joseph Smith about how we might live in a society of economic cooperation and justice. We have come to know these revelations collectively as the Law of Consecration and United Order. As this was happening, Karl Marx and Friedrich Engels issued their masterworks, *The Communist Manifesto* and *Das Kapital*, proposing how an inevitable utopia of economic equality would be achieved by the irresistible predetermined workings of history and pushed forward—as later elaborated by Lenin—by a small vanguard group imposing their "enlightened" will on others.

Despite Marxism's appeal to many, its results crushed freedom and creativity, destroyed economies, displayed horrible brutality, and allowed massacres of millions. the likes of which the world has never seen before or since—all in the name of human progress and betterment. Marxism rested on that original Satanic promise of salvation through coercion, and Lucifer reveled in its every bloody advance. Again, Satan's trick is making tyranny and destruction of agency seem necessary to achieving something good.

Recently, we have seen again this pattern of a Satanic counterfeit coming on the heels of divine revelation. In 1995 the First Presidency issued "The Family: A Proclamation to the World" which includes the teaching, "By divine design, fathers are to preside over their families in love and righteousness and are responsible to provide the necessities of life and protection for their families. Mothers are primarily responsible for the nurture of their children."[4]

One year later, in a strange parallel, the Taliban, rulers of Afghanistan, issued the official document "Decrees Relating to Women and Other Cultural Issues after the Capture of Kabul, 1996,"[5] which includes the line, and this is an exact quote from their own translation into English:

---

4. "The Family: A Proclamation to the World," *Ensign*, Nov. 1995, 102.
5. A publication of this document can be found in Ahmed Rashid's *Taliban: Militant Islam, Oil & Fundamentalism in Central Asia* (New Haven and London:

"Husband, brother, father have the responsibility for providing the family with the necessary life requirements (food, clothes, etc.). Women have the responsibility as a teacher or coordinator for her family."

While these ideas of our enemies may seem surprisingly similar, compare how the gospel says they should be implemented to how the Taliban says they should be. The Taliban says, and again these are all direct quotes from their proclamation and are sentiments widely shared by militants responsible for terrorism and repression around the world:

- "We request family elders to keep tight control over their families ... otherwise [they] will be severely punished ... by the forces of the religious Police" (Munkrat).
- "The religious police are allowed to go for control at any time and nobody can prevent them."
- "If a cassette is found in a vehicle, the driver will be imprisoned."
- "To prevent beard shaving ... they should be arrested and imprisoned until their beard gets bushy."
- "To prevent idolatry ... the monitors should tear up all pictures."
- "To prevent interest on loans ... criminals will be imprisoned for a long time."
- [In case of] "music and dancing at wedding parties ... the head of the family will be arrested and punished."
- "To prevent not praying ... if young people are seen in the shops [during prayer time] they will be immediately imprisoned."

Are you beginning to see the pattern here? We may or may not agree with some of the goals expressed, but that is not really the issue. What is really the issue is that the Taliban offered coercion and agency restrictions as the primary means to promoting righteousness. The Pearl of Great Price clearly shows who the author of this method is.

Compare The Taliban's methods to what the restored gospel teaches:

- "Successful marriages and families are established and maintained on principles of faith, prayer, repentance, forgiveness, respect, love and compassion."[6]
- Rather than urging patriarchs to exercise "tight control," mothers and fathers are called "equal partners" and "individual adaptation" is allowed in their respective roles.[7]

Yale University Press, 2000), 215–219.
  6. "The Family," 102.
  7. Ibid.

- "I teach them correct principles and let them govern themselves."[8]
- "If I esteem a man to be in error, shall I bear them down? No, I will lift them up and in their own way too."[9]
- "No power or influence can or ought to be maintained by virtue of the priesthood, only by persuasion, by longsuffering, by gentleness and meekness, and by love unfeigned" (D&C 121:41).

Our fight here in Afghanistan looks like nothing less than the continuation of the War in Heaven by other means in another place. In Iraq, also, our enemies of both the secular and religious stripe are clear enough about their goals and motivations. With this clarity they reveal the source of their inspiration. Compare what the scriptures say in Article of Faith 11, "We claim the privilege of worshipping Almighty God according to the dictates of our own conscience, and allow all men the same privilege, let them worship how, where, or what they may," to the views Abu Musab al-Zarqawi—the terrorist commander behind much of Iraq's violence—spelled out in his declaration in January 2004. He said, "We have declared a fierce war on this evil principle of democracy and those who follow this wrong ideology," because it is based "on the right to choose your religion," and that is "against the rule of God."[10]

If This Is His Doctrine, Who Exactly Is His God?

Compared to this conflict of ideas, our enemy's actions in the physical world conflict of bullets and bombs have been even grimmer than their statements. They purposely target women and children, looking for ways to kill more of them and glamorize those who blow themselves up to bring this about. This is far different than women and children tragically and inadvertently being killed after taking great measures to ensure that only combatants are targeted.

Some have said that revelations about our treatment of prisoners at Iraq's Abu Ghraib prison have undercut our moral high ground. They have indeed and are tragic. But it is important to put this in perspective and remember that in an open society we can come to know what happened at Abu Ghraib,

---

8. Joseph Smith, as quoted by John Taylor, "The Organization of the Church," *The Latter-day Saints' Millennial Star* 13, no. 22 (November 15, 1851): 339.

9. Joseph Smith, *Teachings of the Prophet Joseph Smith*, ed. Joseph Fielding Smith (Salt Lake City: Deseret Book, 1977), 314.

10. "Purported al-Zarqawi tape: Democracy a lie," CNN.com, http://www.cnn.com/2005/WORLD/meast/01/23/iraq.main/ (accessed June 17, 2013).

argue about it openly, and hold accountable those responsible. Back when Saddam ran the place no one dared talk about it; the government paid and protected the perpetrators, and prisoners had their fingernails pulled out, their genitals electrocuted, and were hung live from meat hooks on the ceiling. Even worse, prisoners were taken home to their families to watch experts torture their wives and rape their children until they divulged the information the secret police wanted. Sometimes the secret police did not want any particular information but just did such things to show who was boss. I apologize for these graphic descriptions, but it is important not to forget what we are up against in deciding which side of this conflict is in the right. We should never expect to see the totally accurate headline "Iraqi Prison Conditions Dramatically Improve under Americans." And while we should, of course, be held to a higher standard because of our ideals, to condemn American actions at Abu Ghraib over Saddam's or to compare the unfortunate accidental civilian deaths we have caused with the estimated one million Iraqis killed by Saddam's system of terror (400,000 of whose mass graves have been found) shows a profound lack of moral clarity.

Considering Saddam's track record of war-mongering and internal repression, it is very likely that even with the violence necessary to topple Saddam's regime and fight the unexpected subsequent insurgency, less people have been killed in Iraq over the past few years than if we had left his murderous warmongering regime in power.

While some want to turn the Iraq war issue on its head by making American liberators the bad guys, the moral issues of this war are really not that muddy. Magazine editor Jamie Glaze says it well in a recent online discussion on the morality of the Iraq War:

> We are at a war with an evil ideology. Our enemy is bad. We are good. Yes, I know it makes a lot of people cringe to hear language like this and I am sure there are many people who will roll their eyes and scoff when they hear these words. But I really don't see the complexity in this paradigm. Was there complexity in who was bad and good at Auschwitz, Dachau, and Buchenwald?
>
> There is no occupation of Iraq. There is a liberation of Iraq. And the liberation is headed by forces of liberty and democracy that seek to bring peace, prosperity, self-determination and freedom to the Iraqi people. There are also forces that want to enslave Iraqis to a monstrosity of totalitarianism and terror—under forms of Sharia law. These forces engage in acts like suicide bombing—killing innocent people—to destroy any possibility of freedom coming to Iraq. These people are *terrorists*.[11]

---

11. Jamie Glazov, "Symposium Iraq: A Report Card," FrontPageMag.com, http://www.frontpagemag.com/Articles/ReadArticle.asp?ID=19031 (accessed June 17, 2013).

If you are soldier in the US Army, Marines, or Air Force, or a contractor for KBR, you are a soldier of love. (I am not talking about some cheesy old Donny Osmond song here.) You are a soldier of love because your service is benefiting the people here in Afghanistan and keeping Americans at home safe. Sometimes, as in your service here, or with a surgeon in an operating room, violence is an act of love—a necessary act of love. And yes indeed, despite what you may have learned in kindergarten, violence properly applied very often *does* solve problems. The US military has solved a lot of problems through violence. It has been the greatest force of human liberation in history and it has accomplished this through violence.

- The US military threw off the yoke of British rule and allowed our constitutional government to become the model for good government around the world.
- The US military marched to war singing the Battle Hymn of the Republic's immortal lines "as He died to make men holy let us die to make men free" and liberated hundreds of thousands of American slaves from cruel bondage in the most wrenching war our nation has ever known.
- The US military liberated millions in Europe and Asia from the crushing boot of fascism and helped even Germany and Japan, the very countries who launched WWII, become relative models of peace and freedom.
- In the last half of the twentieth century, the United States military held at bay the greatest threat ever to human freedom, the Soviet Union, in both hot and cold wars until State socialism collapsed under the weight of its own preposterous and unsustainable evil and under the moral witness of universal values as championed by the United States' powerful military.

In each of these examples was every act committed by every soldier moral? Of course not. Was every policy or effect that came from war positive? Of course not. But the overall morality of our collective action has been clear. Frankly, the threat of religious-inspired tyranny and terrorism we face today is probably not as great as Nazism or communism. Our enemy someday may acquire a few atomic weapons, but no massive arsenal of nuclear tipped missiles and no industrial base to produce their own mighty military. Our current enemies are parasites on the economic life of the world—more Gadianton robber than Lamanite. They do not create or contribute anything, not even their own weapons of war. They only destroy. And to do so, they have to lift our technology (airplanes for September 11, radio control equipment for roadside bombs, etc.). However, as Afghans tell me, our common enemy is a threat to civilization and freedom, as the Taliban decree makes clear. The threat is still dire and we are right to counter it.

This noble tradition of liberation continues here in Afghanistan and in Iraq. As I have traveled all around this country visiting soldiers at firebases on the front lines I have had a particularly good vantage point to witness with my own eyes the fruits of your labors. All of you in the roles that you play, though you may not see it, are part of a great miracle that is taking place in this country. It is sometimes hard to see, in the limited world of the supply room, the finance office, or the motor pool, how what you are doing makes that much difference. But I guarantee you that it does. Without every piece of the military machine doing its part, the whole system achieves less than it could. You all can take satisfaction that your labors have made the following remarkable developments possible.

In Kabul I have seen block after block of city once leveled by the Russians and civil war and left to rot for years now swarming with construction equipment and sprouting new high-rise buildings. This is not just the result of foreign aid, US military reconstruction, or opium poppy cultivation; it springs more significantly from the newly-freed ingenuity and enterprise of the Afghan people. This liberated human energy has led to a six-fold increase in average yearly salary in two years for Afghan workers since shrugging off the yoke of oppression.

Our efforts have helped unleash not only economic but also cultural and political freedom. In several towns I listened to people excitedly preparing for elections for the first time in their lives and openly discussing their different opinions about candidates without fear.

In the city of Asadabad I sat in on the first ever US meeting with the local council (or *shura*) of leading women in the community. Before the meeting—the brothers of the women helped coordinate in keeping with local custom—we did not even know there was a women's shura! The women sought us out to discuss ways of improving women's rights and rebuilding and resupplying girls' schools. They told us that they would not have dared meet as a shura before we came. Their friends who had tried to organize for women's issues under the Taliban had been raped, shot, or both. They thanked us profusely for our efforts in creating a space for Afghan women to express their freedom.

In the Pesch Valley, one of the most conservative parts of the country, the teachers at a school that had been teaching only half days decided they wanted to teach full days so they could teach girls in the afternoon. Since the American firebase was right across the street from the school, the teachers asked us to come visit the new girl students. We happily obliged and brought supplies to donate and photos of our own daughters to show the students. Had the Taliban not been driven from the Pesch Valley, this free choice to start school for girls could never have happened. Forcing girls out of school was one of the most infamous Taliban policies and few things have been more satisfying for me than to see girls going to school in classrooms all over the country.

Also in Pesch I helped train Maseullah, a *mullah* (a Muslim religious leader), to be a chaplain for the local Afghan Security Forces. In Maseullah's previous religious training, he had been taught that Americans were the Great Satan and that minority forms of Islam should be suppressed. After seeing how Americans and Afghans were cooperating to bring peace and prosperity to his valley—including helping reconstruct battle-damaged mosques—he was eager to hear about the chaplain's role of safeguarding his soldiers' religious freedom. As we chatted, he talked eagerly about the day when, as a chaplain in the Afghan National Army, he would ensure that minority Shiite Muslim soldiers would have just as much right to practice their religion as the majority Sunnis. This was 180 degrees different from what he learned in his *madrassa* (religious school) in Pakistan and 180 degrees different from what the Taliban did in Shiite provinces in 1998—when they massacred Shiites by the thousands. In fact, at great personal risk, Maseullah went back to visit his instructors in Pakistan to tell them about the great friendships being formed and great work being accomplished by Christians and Muslims working together in the Pesch Valley. An enemy propaganda push at the time had tried to claim that the Americans were crusaders come to destroy Islam. This propaganda push could not get much traction when the valley's own *mullahs* were heading to Pakistan to praise what good friends Americans were being.

Perhaps the greatest measure of whether we have achieved something good or not is the millions of refugees streaming back to Afghanistan from Pakistan, Iran, and around the world since the fall of the Taliban. Think about this for a second, refugees streaming *into* a war zone. This is fairly astounding considering the general pattern of world history. Free people voting with their feet and going where they want to be when they have a choice is perhaps the greatest measure of whether any enterprise is really benefiting the people it seeks to serve. Imagine what it would be like to be forced away from your home country for years by chaos and oppression and then be able to return with hope to your own place, your own home, in a new climate of liberty and stability. Millions of Afghans are now experiencing this thanks to your efforts.

But what about efforts to liberate the oppressed that don't go as well? Watching ethnic groups fight each other and settle old scores now that they are freed from tyranny, one might wonder if all those who have been liberated much appreciate our efforts. (The complaints the children of Israel made to Moses after he liberated them from Pharaoh come to mind.) If efforts at liberation are not appreciated, if rebels resist their freedom and fight to reimpose tyranny, has liberation been in vain? If our efforts to liberate are spurned, well then, we are in very good company. Who has sacrificed to liberate us from death and sin, but Jesus Christ? Is not his ultimate liberating gift often met with rebellion or ingratitude by us—those very souls he died to free? As we emulate Jesus' example in liberating the oppressed to what may sometimes seem like little thanks or outright rejection, let us remember we are in good company. Was Jesus a fool or an imperialist for trying to liberate us when so many of us choose not to be saved? Neither are we.

Are there still deep problems in this country of Afghanistan? Sure. Are women's rights still beyond grim in most parts of the country? Certainly. Will they ever have the degree and kind of freedom we enjoy in the West? Maybe not. Are they moving in the right direction? Yes they are. Even in such little things as kites flying again over the streets of Kabul, songs from Indian movie soundtracks wafting through the bazaar, and children wearing homemade *tarwis* charms (that the Taliban suppressed as pagan) we see the people here beginning to take deep breaths of the fresh air of freedom because of our presence. If our goal has been to liberate (and not dominate) this country and allow it to grow into practicing universal ideals of freedom following its own path, then, by the grace of God, we are succeeding in a most spectacular fashion. And again, you have the privilege of contributing to this noble effort in the work you do every day.

If I have learned anything from my interaction with Afghans in this war it is that freedom is not just some abstract principle for discussing in a political science class. It is a real condition of human lives that makes all the difference to people in terms of their happiness, fulfillment, and prosperity in life. It is worth fighting for.

The Doctrine and Covenants is clear that the benefits of freedom are not just political and economic but religious as well, and that the Lord not only allows bloodshed to bring about the conditions of freedom but calls it "redeeming" in the case of the American Revolution. In words that seem written for our day, the Lord says that the principles enumerated in the US Constitution (and by extension in the new constitutions of Iraq and Afghanistan),

> should be maintained for the rights and protection of all flesh, according to just and holy principles; That every man may act in doctrine and principle

pertaining to futurity, according to the moral agency which I have given unto him, *that man may be accountable for his own sins in the day of judgment.* Therefore it is not right that any man should be in bondage one to another.

And for this purpose have I established the Constitution of this land . . . and *redeemed the land by the shedding of blood.* (D&C 101:78–80; emphasis added)

The great Nephite general, Captain Moroni, led men into battle for "their homes, their liberties, their children, and their all, yea, for their rites of worship and their church" (Alma 43:45). And if this is noble to do for your own home and family, wherein you have a personal interest, how much more noble is it to do it for the benefit of people you don't know in a country far away for a people whose religion is not your own? Is this not the kind of love the Samaritan showed the injured traveler on the road to Jericho in Jesus' parable—namely the desire to aid an oppressed stranger from a different country of a different religion at great personal risk?

Early American philosopher Lysander Spooner explained the morality of violence against oppressors as follows:

> When a human being is set upon by a robber, ravisher, murderer, or tyrant of any kind, it is the duty of the bystanders to go to his or her rescue, by force if need be. . . . This duty being naturally inherent in human relations and necessities, governments and laws are of no authority in opposition to it. If they interpose themselves, they must be trampled underfoot without ceremony, as we would trample under foot laws that should forbid us to rescue men from wild beasts, or burning buildings.[12]

With all this in mind from past wars and our war here, we can rightly see the morality of our military service in quite a different light than our critics. At the beginning of these remarks, I asked, "How can we serve a God of Peace while practicing the art of war?" We can do so by only fighting on the right side for the right motives for the right ends by the right means. We do so by winning wars decisively and being victorious over tyrants and establishing the principles on which lasting peace can founded. While tyrants lead their nations to war frequently, democracies going to war against each other is virtually unheard of.[13] So when we fight to

---

12. Lysander Spooner, *A Plan for the Abolition of Slavery* (and) *To the Non-Slaveholders of the South* (n.p., 858).

13. I do not use the term "democracy" in the limited sense of countries who qualify for the designation only by having officials in place by popular election, but rather I use it in the broader sense of a civil society with limited government, respect for rule of law and private property, freedom of press and assembly, protections for the rights of unpopular ethnic and religious minorities. Hamas led Palestine vs. Israel or the Confederacy vs. the United States of America do not

help others secure democracy and overthrow oppressors, we "increase the peace" as the saying goes, in the same way a surgeon can increase a person's health by cutting them open. When we appease and allow tyrants to thrive, we increase the chance that they will continue to oppress, destroy, and foment war against us and each other. A God of Peace is best served by practicing the most effective means to bring peace about. This is not by undermining the liberating actions of the armies of democracy but by supporting them in their efforts to be victorious over Satan's plans on earth.

Some may read this and think, "yes I agree but if the same ends can be brought about through means such as diplomacy, Ghandi-style non-violence, development aid, or conflict resolution shouldn't they be preferred over violence?"[14] Of course they should! In both Afghanistan and the Philippines, I myself have been witness to the power of cultural sensitivity, reconstruction work, patient negotiation, and conflict resolution skills. But it takes wisdom to know when these strategies will work and when they will not. And they always work better when adversaries know that we will not flinch from effective force if these strategies fail.

I once listened to an excited presentation by a Bible scholar who reviewed the history of schools of thought that oppose and try to prevent war and proposed a synthesis program he seemed to hope held the key to bringing peace on earth. In the Q&A period I asked him what he thought of the following parable which came to me on the spot:

The Parable of the Five Samaritans

> Five Samaritans walked along the road to Jericho. Each in turn met a different traveler about to be attacked by bandits.
>
> The first Samaritan said, "I am a pacifist and I refuse to add to this cycle of violence." So he stood by and watched as the bandits beat and robbed the traveler.
>
> The second Samaritan said, "I believe non-violent direct action will serve as a moral witness against this injustice." So he stepped between the bandits and the traveler. The bandits beat and robbed the Samaritan and then beat and robbed the traveler.
>
> The third Samaritan said, "I believe in just war theory, so will do nothing until the bandits attack first." So he waited until the bandits started beating the traveler, then stepped in to fight off the bandits. The traveler was badly injured but not robbed.

---

serve as counter examples of democracies at war by this definition.

14. *See extended note at end of chapter.

The fourth Samaritan said, "I believe in conflict resolution. We can get beyond this dispute by listening to each other." So he sat down with the chief bandit and talked while the other bandits beat and robbed the traveler. They also beat and robbed another traveler who had happened by during the talking. When the bandits were done, they motioned to their chief. He got up, thanked the Samaritan for his willingness to listen, then left with his accomplices.

The fifth Samaritan could tell what the bandits planned to do, so he immediately jumped in, violently hitting them with his walking staff until they ran away. But one bandit had stabbed the Samaritan in the fighting and he fell to the ground and died. The traveler continued on his way unbeaten and with all his belongings.

Who of these five do you think was a neighbor to the traveler attacked by bandits?

Being wise, the scholar did not answer the parable directly but mentioned that General Petraeus in Iraq was using some of his techniques. I was pleased to hear this since I did like his ideas and was only concerned that anyone might think they would apply in every situation.

In sum, then, military service, and even violence to liberate others, does not have to be in conflict with Christian commitment. In fact, properly understood and properly done, soldiering is among the noblest paths of Christian living one can choose to follow. When Paul urges us in Ephesians 6:11–18 to "put on the whole armor of God" writing of breastplates, shields, and swords, is he doing more than giving great advice on how to stay faithful? Is he perhaps also validating our profession with his choice of metaphor?

I am honored to be associated with you and humbled to be in your presence, knowing what a great work you are doing. I hope that an understanding of the spiritual and moral roots of our current conflict illustrate why the following thought and popular poem speak such profound truths:

> War is an ugly thing, but not the ugliest of things. The decayed and degraded state of moral and patriotic feeling which thinks that nothing is worth war is much worse. The person who has nothing for which he is willing to fight, nothing which is more important than his own personal safety, is a miserable creature and has no chance of being free unless made and kept so by the exertions of better men than himself.[15]

> It is the Soldier, not the minister
> Who has given us freedom of religion.
>
> It is the Soldier, not the reporter
> Who has given us freedom of the press.

---

15. John Stuart Mill, *The Contest in America* (Boston: Little, Brown and Co., 1862), 31.

> It is the Soldier, not the poet
> Who has given us freedom of speech.
>
> It is the Soldier, not the campus organizer
> Who has given us freedom to protest.
>
> It is the Soldier, not the lawyer
> Who has given us the right to a fair trial.
>
> It is the Soldier, not the politician
> Who has given us the right to vote.
>
> It is the Soldier who salutes the flag,
> Who serves beneath the flag,
> And whose coffin is draped by the flag,
> Who allows the protester to burn the flag.[16]

And I would add:

> It is the veteran, not the war protestor,
> Who has given us peace.

. . . and not just us but, God willing, Afghans and Iraqis too. And all this, however, but by the grace of God. And let us pray that we will be victorious in our efforts, not to sate our own pride but so that we may liberate the oppressed.

Works Consulted

In addition to LDS service members and the scriptures, several books have been instrumental in formulating the ideas presented here. I recommend the following for further reading:

Darrell Cole, *When God Says War is Right: The Christian's Perspective on When and How to Fight* (New York: Waterbrook Press, 2002).

Stephane Cortois, et al., *The Black Book of Communism: Crimes, Terror, Repression* (Cambridge: Harvard University Press, 1999).

Victor Davis Hansen, *Between War and Peace: Lessons from Afghanistan to Iraq* (New York: Random House, 2004).

Christopher Hitchens, "A War to Be Proud of," *Weekly Standard*, September 5, 2005, http://www.weeklystandard.com/Content/Public/Articles/000/000/005/995phqjw.asp (accessed June 17, 2013).

---

16. Charles M. Province, "It Is the Soldier," available at http://www.pattonhq.com/koreamemorial.html (accessed June 17, 2013).

Michael Novak, *The Universal Hunger For Liberty: Why the Clash of Civilizations Is Not Inevitable* (New York: Basic Books, 2004).

R. J. Rummel, *Death by Government* (Somerset, NJ: Transaction Publishers, 1997).

Natan Sharansky, *The Case for Democracy: The Power of Freedom to Overcome Tyranny and Terror* (New York: Public Affairs, 2004).

---

* Some who would even concede the point that military service can be a good cause might argue that there are worthier causes that better utilize our time and resources, such as foreign aid to fight hunger, poverty, and disease. Some would argue that every dollar spent on the military detracts from these other important priorities presumed to benefit mankind so much more. The United States is often characterized as a country more interested in war-mongering than the welfare of the world's most vulnerable people. The dual facts that we have the largest military budget in the world and a relatively low government foreign aid budget for our gross national product per capita compared to other developed countries are often cited, in and of themselves, as evidence of the immorality of our national priorities.

However, looking more closely at such charges reveals several serious problems of analysis. One is that because our economy is so vibrant, US military spending is actually very small as a percentage of our GNP (especially compared to places like North Korea, China, Iran, Syria, and Pakistan). Also, the total we give in humanitarian foreign aid looks much better comparatively when we count it per person, not per GNP per person. The fact we are wealthier per capita than countries such as France and Spain means we can give more per person than they do and we do. The total amount received means more to the recipient than what percentage it is of the per capita GNP of the donor.

We should also remember that the true measure of a country's generosity is not how heavy an involuntary tax burden its rulers place on its citizens to fund its foreign aid budget, but rather the true measure is how much its citizens voluntarily give to charities. There has long been a recognized, and understandable, correlation between high taxes and low rates of charitable giving. So by keeping taxes low (and hence government foreign aid budgets low) Americans are free to give more voluntarily to private aid groups—which are much more efficient than governments in making sure aid gets directly to the needy in forms they can use rather than going to high bureaucratic overhead and bloated programs inappropriate to the primary needs of recipients. This is not just a theory of how it might work; this is what Americans have long done and are doing right now. By the measure of voluntary giving per capita we are among the most generous people in the world. ("U.S. Giving Routinely Underestimated," Forbes, http://www.forbes.com/business/2005/11/11/government-private-aid-cx_1114oxford_aid.html).

But these clarifications of misleading accusations still miss the central false premise of the charge against America's priorities, which is this: American military spending and humanitarian aid are different and opposing things and the former steals from the latter. Actually, American military spending *is* humanitarian aid and it has a historical track record of being perhaps the most effective kind there is. For people to be free of violence, poverty, hunger, and disease, they need many things: food, water shelter, medical care, a clean environment, etc. Whereas other countries focus almost exclusively on these things in their giving, Americans do all this but also spend much more than others in providing the thing people need most—the thing that if it is not present makes all other kinds of contributions meaningless or impossible—that is security from tyranny and oppression.

Providing security is *the* fundamental form of humanitarian aid and security is provided by soldiers with guns. People with guns cost money. When a nation is secured from threats of violence and market economies are allowed to develop, nations begin to provide for themselves and no longer need humanitarian aid but rather attain a position to supply it to others. Is this not the best kind of aid program, the kind that ends the need for aid?

Again this is not just some nice theory; it is what has happened in history and continues to happen today. Consider the case of what was once one of the biggest threats to human well being—famine. Famine still exists in the world, but thanks to robust economies, free trade, and the green agricultural revolution (and possibly longer growing seasons and higher crop yields due to global warming) it is no more an act of nature as it was in the past. Within the last seventy years, famine has been wiped out in places where it was once common, notably India, China, and South Korea. Places where the threat of it lingers are a virtual who's who of the world's worst regimes, North Korea, Sudan, Zimbabwe, and Iraq before Saddam's removal (but notably not Iraq now). Famine has become, not an unavoidable natural calamity but a policy option tyrants impose on their subjects. The best form of famine relief now would be the removal of dictators.

Those countries liberated from tyranny or protected from it under the umbrella of American military foreign deployments have enjoyed peace, prosperity, and health in abundance when compared to nearby and culturally similar countries that have not enjoyed American military protection but suffered under the kind of oppressors the US military has worked to stave off. For example, compare Western Europe to Eastern Europe from 1945 to 1989—and especially East Germany to West Germany—by any measure of human happiness one might wish to devise and Western Europe has excelled while the East endured miseries of all kinds. What is the difference? Culture? Climate? Natural resources? No. The difference is simple, the East had the jackboot of Communism at its neck for sixty years and the west was shielded from Soviet aggression by the US military.

The money that European budgets spend so freely on foreign aid has only been made possible by America shouldering the lions' share of the defense budget for their liberation from fascism and their protection from communism. Americans have done Europeans' military spending for them, freeing them to imagine that they live in a world where they don't need to and are thus more moral for not doing so. Had Western Europeans been Soviet vassals for the last sixty years, which they assuredly would have been without American military spending, their economies would be in no shape to spend the kind of money they do now on foreign aid. In a very real sense, European foreign aid is *America's* gift to the world.

Look up any reference work of international social and economic data and pick any two places—one where American military coupled with market economic policies have succeeded and another nearby place that America has not chosen to, or has been unable to, protect—and then pick any statistic indicative of well being that you wish (GNP per capita, infant mortality rates, rates of state-sponsored homicide, environmental degradation, etc.) and compare the two places. Try Austria vs. Hungary, Thailand vs. Laos, Taiwan vs. Mainland China, or Havana vs. Miami and the results will be dramatic and the same.

Also look at the net movement of refugees. Say what you want about Cuba's "enlightened" social policies and glorious system of socialized medicine, but are people fleeing Florida to get there? How many people ever tried to escape eastward across the Berlin wall compared to those who tried to go the other direction? How many camps for Thai refugees were there in Vietnam or Cambodia in the 1970s and 1980s?

Perhaps the most illustrative example of the benefits of American military spending vs. other forms of aid is South Korea. As recently as 1960, South Korea and Ghana in West Africa had about the same GNP per capita and both were poor undeveloped societies with histories of colonial occupation (Korea's much more brutal than Ghana's). Billions of humanitarian and development aid has poured in into Ghana over the years with little effect other than to line the pockets of kleptocrats. It is still a poor society with a host of social ills. Billions have poured into South Korea in military aid, and it has developed first into a prosperous first world country and then into a democracy more quickly than any other country on Earth. South Korea is now a net donor of foreign aid. (See Frank Agyekum, "South Korea: A Success Story Worth Emulating," GhanaWeb, http://www.ghanaweb.com/GhanaHomePage/features/artikel.php?ID=92213 [accessed June 17, 2013]).

Ghana is culturally a very different place than Korea and, one might argue, perhaps an inappropriate comparison. Okay then, let's compare Korea to its closest cultural relative and nearest neighbor, North Korea. In recent years the DPRK (Democratic People's Republic of Korea) has been wracked by famines that hit children especially hard, and its people suffer under a tyranny and oppression unlike any other in the world. What is the difference between the North and the South? The North has endured decades of Marxist centrally-planned economy that the South would also have had to endure, for it surely would have been overrun and dominated by the North were it not for American military spending.

Reliable figures are difficult to come by for North Korea, but few doubt that it spends more on military spending as a percentage of its GNP than any other country. Doesn't this contradict the argument that military spending is a good thing? It does only if all military spending is regarded as morally equal. It is not. Military spending for armies that liberate the oppressed and protect against aggressors and defend free market economies is one thing; spending for armies that oppress their own people, threaten their neighbors, and enforce unfree economies are a different matter entirely. To conflate the two shows a distinct lack of moral clarity.

Perhaps a better way to measure generosity is to *add* military spending to the total amount a country spends on charitable assistance. But only for militaries that establish and protect civil liberties and free enterprise as does ours. By this measure, America's generosity is unparalleled.

Is our military spending a measure of our morality then? Perhaps no more than European foreign aid budgets are when they come from expropriated taxes. Perhaps the day when we are truly moral will come only when, as the old saying goes, "the Air Force has to hold a bake sale to buy a bomber" and millions fully understanding the moral importance of their choice buy cookies to fund the purchase of new B-52s.

In "Why I Am a Republican," Bob Bennett discusses his reasons for becoming and remaining a Republican. He claims, "Democrats are the party of government. Republicans are the party of free markets." In a narrative part autobiographical and part historical, Senator Bennett traces some of the key differences between the parties, explaining the points that each party gets right as well as the reasons for his political affiliation. He admits, "sometimes the Democrats are right—governmental action can be the best way to solve a problem." But he thinks that "in most matters in our society—particularly economic ones—free markets do a better job of solving problems, which is why I am still a Republican."

Citing The Book of Mormon's injunction against seeking after wealth for its own sake and its extensive discussion of our responsibility to care for the poor, Bennett writes, "Democrats believe that redistribution of wealth through government action is the best way to do that. However, there can be no redistribution of something that doesn't exist in the first place, which brings us back, again, to the creation of wealth. . . . By supporting public policies that focus on creating wealth, which benefits everyone, very much including the poor, I believe I can face King Benjamin with as clear a conscience as any Democrat." He thinks "Republicans are right more often than the Democrats are," but he identifies as "an American first . . . Like my historic fellow Republicans—Lincoln, Dirksen, Eisenhower, and Reagan—when faced with a political decision, I have an obligation to do my best to do the right thing, even if it means leaving my ideological comfort zone, listening to and maybe even voting with the other side. I have very firm political convictions, but, as the prophets have instructed, I am committed to embracing truth wherever it may be found."

Fourteen

Why I Am a Republican

Bob Bennett

My Background

My being a Republican started at a very early age, when I was born into an orthodox Republican home. One of my early memories is of the reaction created there when, as a very innocent and naïve young boy, I said something nice about President Franklin Roosevelt. My siblings were thunderstruck; you would have thought I had uttered an obscenity.

They hastened to set me straight, to make it clear that Roosevelt was the enemy, a monster, whatever. I don't remember crying, but I was certainly as upset as a little kid can be in the face of such an onslaught. My mother told the others to back off and came to my defense, assuring me that if I wanted to be a Roosevelt supporter she would still love me.

I was grateful to her, but, as I'm sure she expected, peer pressure did its work. At the age of six, when Republican Presidential Candidate Wendell Wilkie came to Salt Lake, I thrilled at the sight of him as he drove down Main Street seated on the back of an open convertible. I proudly announced to my family that I was now a fully committed Republican. The fact that I can remember these details shows how big of a deal it was.

To be a Republican in Utah during my youth was to experience perpetual disappointment. We were a solidly Democratic state. Roosevelt carried Utah every time he ran since all of the members of the Utah delegation were Democrats, as were the Governors; and election night was spent huddled around the radio, listening to the returns, cursing the returns, and then going to bed mad.

Then came 1946. The election was a national revolt against incumbents, much like the 2010 election that delivered the House of Representatives to the Republicans. Arthur Watkins became Utah's first Republican Senator since Reed Smoot. (No one was more surprised than he.) In 1948, even though Truman carried the state, J. Bracken Lee became the first Republican governor in decades. Two in a row.

In 1950, Republican leaders went for three. Hoping to defeat Senator Elbert Thomas, they talked to my father about running and he agreed to do it. As a consequence, I went to my first Republican State Convention, did my first campaigning, and, when Dad beat the odds and won, had my first real taste of political triumph. I was a Republican because I was raised in a Republican home, but direct participation in a Republican campaign cemented the deal. In 1956, as an adult, I proudly cast my first vote for Dwight David Eisenhower.

In the years that followed, I continued laboring in the Republican vineyards, working not only in my father's subsequent campaigns but also helping out in others' campaigns. That thrust me into situations where I had to defend my positions, which meant that I had to think them through. This was particularly true in gatherings of Church members—not formal meetings, of course—where questions would be raised about which party was most identified with the Gospel. Democrats would defend social spending and government regulations by citing scripture emphasizing our responsibility to the poor, accusing us Republicans of ignoring King Benjamin's entreaties to serve our fellow beings and thus be in the service of our God. We would respond by talking about the doctrine of free agency and chastising them for their support of the tyranny of governmental interference in individual lives. Things often got quite heated.

In one such confrontation, I was particularly struck by the wisdom of a comment made by Neal Maxwell, then a young bishop of a student ward at the University of Utah: "I don't think the Lord really cares whether the minimum wage is $1.10 or $1.25." (The low numbers show how long ago that was.) He was making the point that this was less of a discussion of gospel principles and their application to politics and more of an attempt by the discussants to give metaphysical significance to their own prejudices.

That sort of thing still goes on today. My father described the attractiveness of this process very well. He said, "Some people would rather be certain than right."

Things I Have Learned

If we are going to be true to the repeated admonitions of the modern prophets, starting with Joseph Smith and coming straight through to Thomas Monson, and be willing to seek truth wherever it can be found, we are going to have to be open-minded while seeking it in the political realm. I am still very much a Republican, for reasons which I shall outline, but I have learned from a lifetime of observance and active participation in politics that all truth, virtue, and wisdom do not solely reside in the Republican Party, nor are foolishness, corruption and chicanery solely confined to the Democratic Party. There are plenty of dedicated, solid, smart, patriotic Americans in both, just as there are plenty of selfish, corrupt, clueless, pseudo-patriots in both.

To explain why I still choose to be a Republican, let me start by outlining what I see as the basic difference between the two parties.

Democrats are the party of government.
Republicans are the party of free markets.

This philosophical divide in modern American politics became dominant during the most traumatic economic event the nation has ever experienced: the Great Depression. In those terribly troubled times, Franklin Roosevelt preached the gospel of governmental action as the way to solve the nation's problems. Whatever their previous views about the role of government may have been, a large majority of Americans were converted to that gospel, which is why Roosevelt won every election.

Belief in government as the first and best institution for solving our problems became so much a part of the Democratic DNA that even now, over three-quarters of a century later, it is still the guiding principle on which the party operates. It holds such disparate groups as labor unions, who want drilling in Alaska so they can get jobs; and environmentalists, who think first and foremost about the caribou, within the Democratic coalition. Whatever else divides them, both groups believe they can get what they want through governmental action, and that is what makes them Democrats.

Republicans were driven into retreat by the Great Depression. Their message of the liberating power of free markets did not play well in that time, and the party was reduced to a permanent party of opposition, always in the minority and only snatching victories when Democrats made a mess of things.

To be sure, many things the Democrats proposed deserved to be opposed, and it was good to have a party that could do that. But most Republicans forgot that to be a majority party and hold power for any significant period of time, you must also be *for* things. We never really offered a coherent governing philosophy of our own. Even with Eisenhower, we won national elections primarily because we were seen as being more reliable than Democrats on the issue of standing up to the Soviet Union.

It is ironic that the one who brought the Republicans out of that intellectual funk was a Roosevelt Democrat whose formative political years were spent unhaunted by the sense of futility that plagued too many Republicans. When Ronald Reagan cast his first Republican vote—like mine, it was for Eisenhower—he did so not just to say "no" to something he opposed; he was also instinctively saying "yes" to things in which he believed; namely, a less intrusive government and more freedom in the marketplace.

My Senate colleague, Senator Pat Moynihan, an Irish Democrat from New York who served in both the Kennedy and Johnson Administrations (as well as a few years with Nixon, who was fascinated by Monynihan's brain) noted the coming of Reagan by saying, "The Republicans are now the party of ideas." We had had ideas before, of course, but framed them primarily in terms of opposition to Roosevelt's principles, which meant that even when Republicans won elections, Democrats set the agenda.

Under Reagan, the Republicans started to set the agenda. It was the Democratic Party's turn to be captured by the strategy of simply saying "no" to everything Reagan proposed. When I pointed this out to a senior Democratic senator, suggesting that the half-century historic roles of the two parties had been reversed, he said, "You are exactly right."

But who is right in the overall debate? The party of government, or the party of free markets?

The answer, of course, is that they both are. Start with the Democrats.

The most glaring example of their being right is our national struggle to give all Americans equal civil rights. A quick history of the issue, going back a century and a half, makes that clear.

It began after the Civil War, when the Constitution was amended in fundamental and necessary ways. The Thirteenth Amendment abolished slavery, rendering void the euphemistic "3/5ths clause" that had valued slaves as less than whole people. The Fourteenth Amendment made them full citizens, both of the country itself and of the states in which they resided. The Fifteenth Amendment denied the states the power to deny them the vote.

On paper.

In practice, particularly in the South, these Constitutional guarantees were a dead letter. Through a combination of traditional private practices and discriminatory state laws, former slaves and their descendants were denied their rights. It took action by the federal government to change that and deliver on the unkept Constitutional promises. Many Republicans came to understand this.

The earliest fighters for civil rights were Democrats, but the President who ordered US troops into a state to guarantee those rights was a Republican—Eisenhower. When Southern Democrats threatened to block passage of the Civil Rights Bill, the Senate Leader who lined up the swing votes needed to break the filibuster and pass the bill was a Republican—Everett Dirksen.

Even so, many Republicans, including that year's presidential nominee, Barry Goldwater, believed so strongly that the bill would violate an individual's right to choose those with whom he would associate or do business that they fought its passage. (A kneejerk reaction to anything Democrats were for?) The national debate about civil rights was as contentious as any we are having now.

My father was in the Senate at the time. He was a deeply conservative Republican who supported Goldwater as the nominee and was considered a pillar of conservatives within the Senate. However, he was also a deeply honest man who looked at the facts of the case.

He noted that many of the businesses that were denying service to African-Americans were publicly-held corporations; anyone could buy their stock. He said to me, "So, it's OK for a black man to be an owner of a restaurant but not one of its customers? That doesn't make sense." On this and other grounds, he deserted Goldwater and sided with Dirksen, voting to break the filibuster and for the bill. As a consequence of that action, he was opposed by a John Birch Society official in his next primary, who criticized his vote as having violated his oath to uphold and defend the Constitution.

Looking back, it is clear that my Dad's position was the correct one, from every standpoint, very much including the Constitution. (Goldwater was no bigot, and later changed his mind or possibly flip-flopped on the matter.) Since the passage of the Civil Rights Act, two of our Secretaries of State have been African Americans, as has one of our presidents. We would not be as far along in solving our race problems as we are had the federal government not acted.

So, sometimes the Democrats are right—governmental action can be the best way to solve a problem.

But not always.

In most matters in our society—particularly economic ones—free markets do a better job of solving problems, which is why I am still a Republican.

No one has summarized the beneficial impact of free markets on the world better that Tom Friedman in his book, *The Lexus and the Olive Tree*. Accordingly, I quote him here at some length. Like Adam Smith, he focuses on the process by which a nation gets wealthy, and says it happens when it puts on what he calls the "Golden Straitjacket":

> The Golden Straitjacket first began to be stitched together and popularized by Margaret Thatcher in England, beginning in 1979. It was soon reinforced

by Ronald Reagan in the United States in the 1980's, giving the straitjacket, and its rules, some real critical mass. It became a global fashion with the end of the Cold War, once the three democratizations blew away all the alternative fashions and all the walls that protected them.

The three democratizations he speaks of are Technology, Finance, and Information. By "democratization," he means that every country in the world had access to them once the Cold War had ended.

> The Thatcherite-Reaganite revolutions came about because popular majorities in these two major Western economies concluded that the old government-directed economic approaches simply were not providing sufficient levels of growth. Thatcher and Reagan combined to strip huge chunks of economic decision-making from the state, from the advocates of the Great Society and from traditional Keynesian economics, and hand them over to the free market.
>
> To fit into the Golden Straitjacket a country must either adopt, or be seen as moving toward, the following golden rules: making the private sector the primary engine of its economic growth, maintaining a low rate of inflation and price stability, shrinking the size of its state bureaucracy, maintaining as close to a balanced budget as possible, if not a surplus, eliminating and lowering tariffs on imported goods, removing restrictions on foreign investment, getting rid of quotas and domestic monopolies, increasing exports, privatizing state-owned industries and utilities, deregulating capital markets, making its currency convertible, opening its industries, stock and bond markets to direct foreign investment, deregulating its economy to promote as much domestic competition as possible, eliminating government corruption, subsidies and kickbacks as much as possible, opening its banking and telecommunications systems to private ownership and competition, and allowing its citizens to choose from an array of competing pension options and foreign-run pension and mutual funds. When you stitch all these pieces together you have the Golden Straitjacket.
>
> Unfortunately, this Golden Straitjacket is pretty much "one size fits all." So it pinches certain groups, squeezes others and keeps a society under pressure to constantly streamline its economic institutions and upgrade its performance. It leaves people behind quicker than ever if they shuck it off, and it helps them catch up quicker than ever if they wear it right. It is not pretty or gentle or comfortable. But it's here and it's the only model on the rack this season.

The Book of Mormon says we should not seek after wealth for its own sake and talks extensively about our responsibility to care for the poor. Democrats believe that redistribution of wealth through government action is the best way to do that. However, there can be no redistribution of something that doesn't exist in the first place, which brings us back, again, to the creation of wealth—an issue which has occupied the attention of thinkers from Adam Smith to Brigham Young to Tom Friedman.

The Lord believes in the creation of wealth. He instructed the Nephites to pray for their flocks and herds, "that they might increase," and promised them that they would prosper in the land if they kept the commandments. At the bedrock of any society, be it your family, the local Rotary Club, a company, a labor union or the Church of Jesus Christ of Latter-day Saints, if there is not enough money to sustain the legitimate needs of that society, it falls apart.

It is the wealth of a growing economy that generates the taxes that fill the government's coffers; without it there will be no government money available for education, or environmental protection, or law enforcement, or the military. There will certainly be no money available for redistribution to the poor, no matter what numbers are adopted in the federal budget. For all of the complaints about the benefits that accrue to the 1 percent, it is the poor who are helped the most by wealth creation.

Many don't believe this. When the American economy was booming in the manner described by Friedman, and the collective wealth of the richest Americans was growing much more rapidly than that of the poorest ones, one of my Democratic colleagues, hoping to highlight the message that this wealth wasn't being fairly distributed, asked then Fed Chairman Alan Greenspan, "Who is benefiting the most from our current economic boom?"

"Clearly," Greenspan replied, "it is the bottom quintile." (That's economics-speak for the poorest one-fifth of our population.)

The Senator immediately started arguing with him, citing figures showing how much new wealth was being amassed by the top quintile, but Greenspan stood his ground. He pointed out that the lifestyle of people at the top hadn't changed all that much. Adding an extra billion or two to the value of Bill Gates' stock portfolio might change the amount of money he gave to his foundation but did not alter the way he lived. However, the booming economy had made a huge difference to the previously unemployed, or the underemployed, or those with limited skills. Those in the bottom quintile weren't getting nearly as much money as those in the top, but their lives were being changed much more drastically and dramatically for the better.

When the recession hit and wealth was destroyed, the process worked in reverse. Warren Buffet and Oprah Winfrey stayed rich and kept their houses, but the construction worker who built houses for a living lost his, along with his job. Welfare programs to help the poor are fine, but the very best welfare program is a job.

Democrats sneeringly call my reasoning "trickle down economics," implying that the rich get gravy while the poor get stuck with nothing but a few scraps, or that one gets rich at the expense of the poor. That may have been true in times past—King Henry the Eighth amassed great wealth by taking it away from his subjects—but it isn't true today. Bill Gates, the college dropout, didn't get his money by taking it away from semi-skilled construction workers. The achievements for which he has been so handsomely rewarded have created hundreds of thousands of jobs that feed hundreds of thousand of families and pay hundreds of millions of dollars in taxes.

By supporting public policies that focus on creating wealth, which benefits everyone, very much including the poor, I believe I can face King Benjamin with as clear a conscience as any Democrat.

My Current Position

So, Bennett, sometimes the Democrats are right, but sometimes the Republicans are, too? Who are you, wishy-washy Charlie Brown? Pick a side!

I have.

The side I pick is whichever side has the solution to our nation's—nay, our world's—problems, by whatever process works best.

I am a Republican because I firmly believe in the "invisible hand" of which Adam Smith spoke, which allows free markets to do their magic in creating wealth, and I am suspicious of the efficacy of governmental power. However, if I can be convinced that the best solution to a problem happens to be one requiring governmental action in a form urged by the Democrats, so be it. I will support that as well. That's why many Republicans consider me "wishy-washy," to keep the language polite. They say I have no firm convictions.

On the contrary, my position is firmly rooted in the best tradition of American politics.

Thomas Jefferson had very firm convictions about the Constitution. He believed that it would be unconstitutional for him to make the Louisiana Purchase because nothing in Section I, Article 8 of the Constitution explicitly gives Congress the power to do such a thing. However, he realized that making the purchase would be of enormous benefit for the country. When Napoleon threatened to sell Louisiana to Spain, Jefferson stopped hesitating and made the deal. It was the most consequential thing he did as President.

Abraham Lincoln had very firm convictions about slavery. He was unalterably opposed to it. However, he said that his first responsibility, as a public official, was the preservation of the Union, and if allowing slavery to survive was the only way that could be done, he would acquiesce. Fortunately, the Union was saved without that becoming necessary.

I have already mentioned Dwight Eisenhower's decision to send federal troops into a state to override state laws, one which troubled him a great deal. However, he rose above his own doubts to make sure that Americans were given their rights, and history has vindicated him.

Then there is Ronald Reagan.

The first time I met Ronald Reagan, I was not particularly impressed. He was Governor of California at the time and I was taken into his office for a chat. I had hoped to engage him in a serious conversation about where American politics was going, but it didn't happen. There was virtually no dialogue; instead, he gave me what I was sure was a canned speech, full of Republican platitudes, and I left thinking that there was not much depth there. For years, I had no further contact with him.

Then I got a phone call. A good friend of mine, Dick Wirthlin, was Reagan's pollster and advisor, and involved in putting together Reagan's campaign team in 1976. That was the year he challenged President Ford for the nomination. Would I be willing to talk to Reagan's campaign manager about a job?

The real answer was no, but I felt I could not refuse to at least talk. At the appointed hour I went to Reagan's campaign headquarters. I expected to be thanked for coming and soon sent on my way, because I had no enthusiasm for the prospect of working for Reagan, and I was sure that that would show through during the interview.

It didn't. Instead, the interview went very well—so well, in fact, that it was clear that a firm job offer was in the offing. I decided to nip it in the bud.

"Before we go any further," I said, "I think I had better make one thing clear. I am not a true believer."

"That's OK," said the campaign manager, "neither is the Governor."

So we talked some more, in greater depth, and I got an insight into Ronald Reagan's view of the world. That changed my mind about him. He was not a kneejerk ideologue, as he had appeared to be in my first brief encounter. He was open to ideas that were not part of the canon of orthodox Republican beliefs. He really was more interested in solving problems than in ideology.

When the offer was made, I seriously considered it, but finally turned it down on family grounds. We had six children, the last two of which were newborn twins, and I simply could not be away from home as much as the job would have required.

After Reagan was elected in 1980—I helped in his campaign—I was offered and initially accepted a position in his administration at sub-cabinet level. I eventually had to turn that down as well, again for family reasons. I never got the opportunity to serve with him directly.

Nonetheless, I am a Reagan fan. He was firm in his convictions, but, like Jefferson, Lincoln, and Eisenhower before him, he was open to solutions that lay outside his preconceptions. He denounced the Soviet Union as an "evil empire"—which it was—but was willing to deal with Gorbachev as an equal. He fought hard for tax reform, but did so by sitting down with Democratic House Speaker Tip O'Neill and giving in to some of O'Neill's demands. He said, "It is better to get 80% of what you want than 100% of nothing." Forceful and flexible at the same time, he was my kind of Republican.

Jefferson, Lincoln, Eisenhower, Dirksen, and Reagan were men with firm ideological convictions that shaped the way they saw the world, but their strongest commitment was to find solutions to the problems they faced. Because they were less interested in being certain than in being right, I wonder how well they would be accepted in certain circles within the Republican Party today, circles where "compromise" is a dirty word.

It should not be. The Constitution, itself the product of compromises among people with very strong disagreements about what it should look like, deliberately created a system where compromise is required. Our government is not a Parliamentary system, where the majority party is all-powerful and compromise with the other side is unnecessary. Our Legislative Branch of government is only one of three, and there are two houses within it. Deals have to be made if anything is going to get through all the gates and become law. That's the way the Founders wanted it.

Conclusion

I am a Republican because I trust the markets more than I trust the government. I believe that the free exercise of individual initiative almost always produces more benefits for everyone, very much including the poor, than government programs do. I believe that the Republicans are right more often than the Democrats are.

But I am an American first. Like my historic fellow Republicans—Lincoln, Dirksen, Eisenhower, and Reagan—when faced with a political decision, I have an obligation to do my best to do the right thing, even if it means leaving my ideological comfort zone, listening to, and maybe even voting with the other side.

I have very firm political convictions, but, as the prophets have instructed, I am committed to embracing truth wherever it may be found.

In "Partisanship and the Gospel of Jesus Christ," Richard Davis argues against the unspoken if commonly held assumption that the Republican Party is most in line with Church teachings, asserting instead that in many ways the Democratic Party seeks a society founded on the Christian principles, including compassion and care for the destitute. The Church, and the gospel are decidedly non-partisan. But although "there is not a one true political agenda, party, or candidate," he writes, Latter-day Saints live in "nations where governments are formed and public policy must be made." He then examines the historical foundations for the dominance of the Republican Party among members of the Church in the United States, and considers how Saints should determine which party or candidate is closest to the Gospel of Jesus Christ. Choosing to focus on certain hot-button issues—such as abortion or same-sex marriage—may cause us to overlook other critical political issues that closely relate to Christ's teachings—teachings which, Davis believes, harmonize with many of the core tenets of the Democratic Party.

Fifteen

Partisanship and the Gospel of Jesus Christ

Richard Davis

The Gospel of Jesus Christ is about love for God and love for each other. It is not about politics. Our Heavenly Father does not have a political agenda. There is not a one true political agenda, party, or candidate. Yet, Church members do dwell in a temporal world. We live in nations where governments are formed and public policy must be made. In democratic societies, political parties endorsing various policy options form and vie for the ability to govern. Parties are not mandated in most democratic systems, but they form naturally as individuals realize majority rule requires organization with other like-minded people to canvass for broad-based support across the electorate.

Latter-day Saints, like other citizens in democratic nations, have the choice of which political party to support. That choice matters more in some countries—such as Germany or the United Kingdom—where parties are strong and candidates nearly always follow the party line. It matters less in the United States where parties are weaker and the differences across parties are less stark. In the United States there are liberal Republicans and conservative Democrats. Such diversity is less common elsewhere in the world where parties are more ideologically coherent.

In the United States today, LDS voters gravitate to the Republican Party. A survey by the Pew Research Center found that 74 percent of LDS voters self-identified as Republicans. Those figures are likely higher in the intermountain West where LDS voters are dominant or a significant electoral force (such as Utah, southeastern Idaho, and parts of Arizona). Republicans there usually win lopsided victories. Why does that lopsidedness exist? Is it because one party really represents the Church and its values while the other does not?

I want to pose two questions in this essay. Why do LDS voters so strongly identify with the Republican Party? And how should a Church member determine which candidate or party is closest to the Gospel of Jesus Christ?

Why Do LDS Voters Identify with Republicans?

It is important to remember that LDS voters did not always think of themselves as Republicans. The Republican Party did not even exist at the time of Joseph Smith. The choice for Latter-day Saints was between the Democrats and the Whigs. During the Nauvoo period, Joseph Smith had voiced support for Democratic candidates, although his political agenda was not partisan but mainly devoted to furthering the Church's rights in a hostile political environment. When neither party seemed particularly interested in the concerns of Latter-day Saints, a small, unpopular religious denomination in the West, Joseph Smith ran for president himself as an independent. He was in the midst of that campaign when he died at Carthage.

When the Republican Party formed in 1854, its main platform plank was to rid the country of the "twin relics of barbarism": polygamy and slavery. After the Civil War, Republicans governed the nation for a generation. Church members were not happy with Republicans because the party used its power to enact and then vigorously enforce anti-polygamy laws.

During the early years of Mormon settlement in the West, Latter-day Saints had little interest in national politics. By the end of the century, however, Utah became a state and individual Church members began to take sides. At that time, Latter-day Saints were predominantly Democrats, largely because the Democratic Party was more tolerant of the Church's plural marriage practices than were the Republicans. Democrats also were more supportive of Utah's statehood efforts and opposed national government dominance over state affairs. Utahns liked that approach since it meant they could follow their own religious practices without interference from others.

Efforts to win statehood altered Utah's political landscape. To win support among Republicans for statehood and to give the perception that Utah voters were not unlike those in the existing states, Church leaders urged some members to become Republicans. Stories have circulated about how wards were split down the middle of the chapel with one side asked to become Republicans, or of Church officials visiting every other house in a ward to call families to become Republicans in order to create a two-party church.

Church leaders themselves identified with both major parties. Wilford Woodruff and Joseph F. Smith were known as Republicans, but others such as Heber J. Grant and Hugh B. Brown were Democrats. And when they got involved in politics, they were not monolithic. While Reed Smoot was a Republican senator and an apostle, B. H. Roberts, a member of the Seventy, was elected to Congress as a Democrat.

Utah created a two-party system with both Republicans and Democrats alternating control of state offices and electing federal representatives. That system continued through most of the state's first century. Membership in either party was viewed by the vast majority of Latter-day Saints as a personal choice, not indicative of whether one was a faithful member.

That began to change in the 1970s. To date, the last Democrat elected Utah's governor left office in 1985. The last Democrat to serve as a US senator was defeated for re-election in 1976. The Utah state legislature has been firmly in Republican hands since the early 1980s. That situation is not likely to change anytime soon.

Why did LDS voters move to the Republican Party in droves in the 1970s and 1980s? The answer can be found in partisan political change in the United States. It also stems from the response of the Church to that change.

In the 1970s, quality of life issues competed for predominance with economics, which had been the primary issue for the generation of Americans who lived during the Great Depression. The vast majority of Americans were middle class by the 1970s. Unlike their parents, middle-aged and younger voters' views were not shaped by that economic downturn. They enjoyed a middle class socio-economic status and, unlike their parents and grandparents were not worried about becoming poor.

Other issues began to take precedence, particularly in light of social change brought about by the social upheaval of the 1960s. The first losing war in US history, youth rebellion, the civil rights movement, prominent assassinations, etc.—all combined to signal dramatic change in US society. For many, that change was scary and unwelcome. A conservative backlash in the 1970s attempted to undo societal changes by appealing to the public's unease about the future. The main struggle was a fight over the role of women in society. In the minds of many conservatives, abortion and the Equal Rights Amendment became symbols of the decline of traditional morals.

Elements of both major political parties tentatively supported both abortion reform and the Equal Rights Amendment early in the 1970s. But as the decade progressed, wings of the two parties polarized them. The Democratic Party moved to embrace these two social changes while the Republican Party went in the opposite direction.

Simultaneously, the Church became involved in national politics at an unprecedented level. While previously the Church often had taken stances on local issues related to Utah, it had not mobilized members to shape national public policy. That changed in the 1970s. The Church declared its opposition to both abortion-on-demand and the Equal Rights Amendment. These positions placed the Church in harmony with social conservatives who were taking control of the Republican Party. The emergence of Ronald Reagan as a Republican presidential candidate and then as president gave LDS voters a popular hero who voiced the same sentiments they were hearing in First Presidency statements and General Conference talks, firesides, sacrament meeting talks, class discussions, and even foyer conversations. The Church even took more aggressive steps in opposition to social change such as packing the International Women's conferences in 1977 to block resolutions regarding women and families and urging members to fight the Equal Rights Amendment. These actions accentuated the Church's preference in this new political cleavage.

Almost en masse, Church members believed they were being sent a message. In Utah, voting patterns shifted dramatically. While the two parties competed effectively in Utah politics up to that point, after the 1970s many Church members saw the Republican Party as the party that supported LDS values and the Democratic party as the one that did not.

A generation later, that one-party dominance has continued, despite the change in issues. The Equal Rights Amendment disappeared as an issue after it failed to be ratified by a sufficient number of states. Abortion also has receded somewhat. Today, conference talks or Church leader references to abortion are rare. Moreover, the Church's position on abortion is more liberal than that of the Catholic Church or the pro-life movement. And, unlike many evangelical and fundamentalist religious organizations, the Church explicitly does not endorse specific legislation on abortion.

But a new socially divisive issue took the place of these two earlier issues: same-sex marriage. For several years, it was a potent political issue energizing religious groups who, like their predecessors of a generation ago, treat this proposed social change as a symbol of serious moral decline. The Republican Party opposed same-sex marriage while the Democrats supported gay rights and, in 2012, voiced support for same-sex marriage as well.

The LDS Church actively worked to oppose same-sex marriage by mobilizing Latter-day Saints in various states to campaign for initiatives banning the practice. The Church continues to oppose same-sex marriage, although it has not been involved with anti-same-sex marriage campaigns in recent years. However, this issue became one more point of division between the Church and the Democratic Party.

The result has been a continuation of the Republican dominance among LDS voters, despite occasional efforts by Church leaders to communicate a different message. Not long after becoming prophet, President Gordon B. Hinckley told the National Press Club in Washington, DC that good Mormons could be Democrats. A First Presidency statement on the Utah caucuses in March 2006 added the line that principles of the Gospel were found in the platforms of both major political parties in the United States. And Elder Robert Wood of the Seventy gave a talk at the next conference urging more acceptance of others with differing political views, including those of contrasting partisan affiliations.

Which Party is the Church's Party?

Every presidential election year in the United States, the Church issues a neutrality and civic duty statement. The first part re-asserts the Church's neutrality in elections. The First Presidency reminds members that the Church does not endorse candidates or parties and that local Church leaders should not use Church facilities, meetings, directories, etc. to do so either. The second part of the statement urges members to participate in the political process and to choose wisely among candidates and ballot measures.

Members may conclude the neutrality stance is a legal requirement. Current US law does not allow tax-exempt charitable institutions to become electoral participants by endorsing parties or candidates. In other words, that's the "official" position. But just because the Church does not endorse a particular party or set of candidates does not mean that members assume there is not a preference. Rumors circulate about whom the prophet and the other Brethren really want members to vote for.

Members likely read tea leaves of Church leaders' pronouncements to discern where the Brethren stand in an election. They may watch which prominent politicians are quoted in General Conference or how Church leaders respond when politicians call on them. Is it perceived as a polite encounter or perhaps something more? Another example is when the Church issues a statement supporting a particular issue (such as a constitutional amendment on gay marriage) in the middle of an election year where one party has clearly endorsed the same position and the other opposes it. In that situation, members may read that as the closest thing to an endorsement the Church can give in an electoral campaign.

Such actions by Church leaders likely have an effect on members' voting decisions. In essence, the pump is primed. When members enter an electoral campaign and begin thinking about which candidate to support, what will have stimulated their thinking is the Church's recent statement on an issue. I know one student who said she was a Democrat and therefore should vote for the Democratic candidate for president. But since the Church had supported a constitutional amendment against gay marriage and the Republican presidential candidate had taken the same stance, she felt she was being told by Church leaders to vote for the Republican. It is highly unlikely she was alone in that thinking.

However, there is no indication that Church leaders actually are signaling such a thing to members. When the First Presidency endorsed a constitutional amendment to ban gay marriage in 2004 and again in 2006, it was because the Congress was voting on that issue at that time. The timing of the vote was not in the Church's hands, but in the hands of the Republican Party leadership. Republican Party officials knew this was a way to win the votes of evangelical and fundamentalist Christians who believe gay marriage would destroy the traditional family. Although members of Congress (including Republicans) knew full well that the amendment would not pass, the effort worked. In 2004, evangelicals turned out in large numbers helping George Bush and Republican candidates.

Whether such signals regarding candidates and parties are intentional on the part of Church leaders (and again there is no evidence they were), many members take them anyway. In fact, for a large percentage there is no real decision-making about which candidates to support. Their interpretation of a slew of Church statements on issues as well as other signs over the years has convinced them that they should vote Republican again and again. In fact, approximately 30 percent of Utah voters vote a straight Republican Party ticket.

Despite repeated statements by Church officials to study out the issues and contemplate which candidates would be best, many voters in Utah take a few seconds in the voting booth, pull one lever, and vote for every candidate who has an R by his or her name regardless of who the candidate really is. Some of these Republican candidates have had alcohol problems, morals charges, or hold extremist views opposing public education, a welfare system to aid the poor, or even government doing much more than running a police force. Yet, they get elected by voters who may perceive that they are doing the Church's (and therefore the Lord's) will by ignoring the Church's repeated counsel and voting by party election after election.

How to Decide Partisanship

So, if Church leaders are not necessarily signaling members to vote a certain way and, in fact, even urge thoughtful consideration of parties, candidates, and issues, what should be the approach of a Latter-day Saint to the question of partisanship? How does a member determine which party to support?

I believe my responsibility as a Latter-day Saint who seeks to live the Gospel of Jesus Christ requires me to act as a citizen and to choose wisely in that capacity. That choice is not based on divining whether a single First Presidency statement is intended to direct my voting for a certain candidate or party in a certain election. (I do not believe that is their intent anyway.) Instead, it is rooted in what I have been taught and believe about the nature of the Gospel of Jesus Christ and my obligation as a follower of Christ in a civil society.

As I look at the life of the Savior and His admonitions to me as one who wishes to be a disciple, I attempt to apply that example and doctrine in a secular world. As a result, I come to certain conclusions about what kind of society I would like to live in as a follower of Christ and what policy direction I should support to help create that kind of society.

First, I see each of us having a commitment to each other. The Savior's directive was to "love one another" and it has been repeated across generations and locations. How we treat each other in society becomes a mark of how well we follow that commandment. Our individual aim should not be selfishness and self-centeredness. We live in a society with others, sometimes others who are in need, and it is Christ-like to be focused on the needs of others rather than merely serving our own interests. This is true not only as individuals but also as groups of individuals, in other words, society as a whole. In a democratic society, government policy basically reflects the will of the society. Therefore, the government of a society that follows the Savior's admonition will be one that uses its power to serve the citizens of that society.

How is the society, through its government, to serve its citizens? One way to discern the answer is by looking at how the Savior acted and then attempting to follow that example. This admonition applies both to us as individuals and as citizens of democratic societies that we have the power to shape. A critical component of the Gospel of Jesus Christ is the intrinsic value of each individual in the society. "Remember the worth of souls is great in the sight of God" (D&C 18:10). Every individual is sent here to fulfill his or her individual mission. Society should not discard or neglect individuals.

As I think about that element of the Gospel, I wonder how that applies to the political choices I make today. I want to support parties and candidates that believe that children are precious and budding life should not be terminated because of inconvenience. Nor should children be exposed to rampant pornography or demeaning images that permeate today's advertising.

Jesus walked among the people of Israel through their crowded streets and marketplaces. He saw the lame, the sightless, the diseased sitting in corners and forgotten alleys. He did not ignore them or condemn them. He healed them. Soon, because of his reputation, people came to him to be healed. James, the brother of Jesus, said that this was pure religion: "to visit the fatherless and widows in their affliction, and to keep himself unspotted from the world" (James 1:27).

So it is with us today. Like Jesus, our obligation is to the most vulnerable in society—the poor, the widowed, the fatherless. The society I want to live in not only sees these people, but it comes to their aid. My responsibility is to support government policy that aids the poor and lifts them. That means supporting parties and candidates that do not ignore the poor (or worse ridicule or demean them) but instead seek to help them through programs that offer an opportunity for decent lives. That means voting for those who endorse a living wage, decent housing, health care benefits, and educational opportunities for every family in the society not just those who can afford it at the moment. That is one of the greatest family values—helping families succeed in a temporal world where the stakes are so often stacked against them.

Some Church members see these very government programs as antithetical to the Gospel. They point to scriptural examples from the Book of Mormon or the Bible of governments who taxed heavily and the Lord's subsequent disapproval of such practices. Then, they extrapolate to any government today that imposes taxes to run social welfare programs as similarly evil. But there are differences between today's governments that run social welfare programs and those scriptural examples of bad government: (1) Those regimes were dictatorships, not democracies. The people did not impose the taxes on themselves, either through their representatives or in direct referenda votes; (2) The taxes collected were not designed to serve the people but to enrich the dictator. Taxes collected today are used primarily for entitlement programs such as Social Security and Medicare that help the most vulnerable among us—the poor and the elderly—escape poverty and enjoy good health; (3) The interpretation of "heavy taxes" is a relative one. How does one define the term? When is a tax "heavy" and when is it not? For example, the United States is one of the lowest taxing nations among industrialized democracies. Relative to other nations, we have a low tax burden.

Also, in the minds of some people, it would seem taxes are bad if they are used to help individuals. So, taxes for a police force that arrests those who rob is justified, but taxes to give educational opportunities to the poor so they can earn their own income and not rob are not justified. That approach is not one of a Christian society.

Those who oppose taxes also argue that the tax system is a form of robbery. Taxes come from someone's hard-earned pay and it is not the business of government to take away that pay, particularly to give it to someone else. The argument can be appealing. However, there are certain commitments we make to be part of a society. In a democratic society, one of those agreements is to abide by majority rule. We make a choice to be part of a society, including a democratic society, and, by so doing, choose to live under the decisions of the majority.

I always wonder why some Church members object to taxes that help others, which is an obligation we all share as fellow citizens of the human race and particularly as disciples of Christ. When society as a whole acts in favor of its most vulnerable, we should applaud rather than complain about that demonstration of Christ-like behavior. That is the kind of society I want to live in, instead of one where there is a selfishness and self-centeredness that scoffs at giving for the common good, either by individuals in a private setting (such as churches or other charitable organizations) or by the society as a whole through its government.

Another trait of the Savior's is the embrace of all, not just certain peoples. It was the Savior who commanded Peter to accept the Gentiles as well as the Jews and called Paul to carry the Gospel beyond the borders of Israel. In more recent times, prophets have extended missionary work across the globe to assure that the Gospel is preached to all.

Already, most members of the Church live outside the United States. There will soon come a day when only a small percentage of Church members will speak English and have white faces and middle-class incomes. Instead, the Church will be a universal church with a wide array of racial, ethnic, language, and income backgrounds. Similarly, as a society in the United States we face changes in the demographic composition of our nation. Two hundred years ago, there was a dominance by white, English-speaking Protestants from the British Isles or northern Europe. Over time, we have welcomed people from across the globe including southern Europeans, Asians, Latin Americans, etc. They come with varying languages, cultures, physical appearance, and religious backgrounds—Catholics, Jews, Muslims, Buddhists, etc.

However, the welcome they have been given has not always been a warm one. Laws were passed to impose discrimination or mobs took over where the law fell short. LDS history is replete with examples of religious discrimination carried out by a majority that would not adjust to societal change and the presence of new residents seeking to live in peace.

My responsibility as a Latter-day Saint and as a citizen is to help create a society where discrimination based on race, religion, gender, and even sexual orientation is a thing of the past. Therefore, I want to support parties and candidates that seek to eradicate discrimination, not perpetuate it. If that is the society I wish to see—one that matches more nearly the Savior's example of love and compassion—then what can I do as a Latter-day Saint to bring about such a society? Are there parties and candidates who can help achieve that goal?

No specific current party exactly matches my views of the ideal society. I doubt there are many candidates who do either. Politics is not about finding the exact match, as wonderful as that might be. Instead, it is determining who and what best represents the majority of my views, and particularly those that are priorities. So the dilemma for me, as for many Latter-day Saints, is to support parties and candidates that come closest to my views as a disciple of Christ. Which party is more supportive of a just and fair society? Which is more inclined to look after the interests of the most vulnerable in society? Which seeks greater acceptance of others, particularly those who are discriminated against?

Overall, my answer today is the Democratic Party. I believe it is far more supportive than is the Republican Party of programs to help families to survive and succeed in society. It also has been at the forefront of civil rights legislation that limits discrimination against minorities.

Although most Church members in the United States would identify more with the Republican Party (which is not true in the rest of the world where members lean further to the left ideologically), I worry about the influence that association has had on Church members in the United States. The Republican Party consistently has favored large tax breaks for the wealthy while cutting social programs for the poor and vulnerable. Even worse, many Republican leaders over the last quarter century—beginning with Ronald Reagan—have demeaned the most vulnerable in society by focusing on "welfare queens." That is not Christian rhetoric, particularly when it is accompanied by the slashing of social programs that are designed to help the poor.

Another Republican mantra is that government is the enemy. The dismissal of a positive government role in society leads to actions that eventually hurt individuals. Not only is this true as it applies to cutting programs such as educational grants, veterans benefits, and health services, but we also see it in disaster relief when those in charge act slowly to handle emergencies and alleviate suffering. Senator William Cohen of Maine once remarked that "government is the enemy, until you need a friend." That narcissistic approach means that when government helps me with my needs (student loans and grants, Social Security, Medicare, etc.) that is justifiable, but when government helps someone else (welfare programs for the poor, Medicaid), then that is bad. The result is a self-absorption that permeates civil society. We are all inclined toward self-centeredness. The worst thing for our leaders to do is foster such an attitude. Instead, we need leaders who view government as a positive element in society—one that has a role in reflecting society's concerns for the welfare of the whole. Republicans, unfortunately, have turned away from such a conception of government. Democrats have embraced it.

Some members immediately will contend that the Democratic Party is not the party of the most vulnerable because it supports the *Roe v. Wade* decision that legalized abortion in the first trimester. My response is that, again, there is no perfect party. I want to change that aspect of the Democratic Party's position and have worked to do so to the extent that I can. However, it is important to note that the Church itself does not take a position in favor of legislation banning abortion. The position of the Church is more about counsel to members than a particular legislative agenda. Members who use that one issue to decide which party or candidates to support are on shaky ground since the Church has never advocated such a single-issue approach and has eschewed supporting a particular policy option on abortion.

Someone may respond to my issues emphases by saying that if these other areas are more important than gay marriage, abortion, or the Equal Rights Amendment, then why do not we hear more about them through the Church? I believe we do. Every time I read the scriptures I am reminded of the Lord's command for us to help create a Zion society, Christ's mission to the most vulnerable in society, and my obligation toward others. How can one read King Benjamin's address in Mosiah without wanting to reach out and help others in whatever way possible? Scriptural accounts of Jesus' example of his service to the forgotten, destitute, and cast out are not merely for our entertainment. They are for our application—both as individuals and as a society. Church lessons and talks repeat those themes constantly. General Conference is full of similar messages of outreach, acceptance, and ministering to others, particularly those in need.

Some people may respond that these messages from the Church are about individual efforts and not about government. Actually, the messages are about both. Doctrine and Covenants section 134 states: "We believe that governments were instituted of God for the benefit of man." Government is here to help us—all of us. It is not designed to benefit a few wealthy people who get massive tax cuts while social services to the poor are cut. Rather, it should be beneficial to all. Therefore, government has an explicit scriptural role in benefiting its citizens. As Church members, we should help government do that.

Also, the Constitution of the United States, which we believe to be inspired, has as its preface that the government was created, among other things, to "establish justice" and "promote the general welfare." Is it just and does it "promote the general welfare" when some are favored over others because of their wealth and the most vulnerable in society are discriminated against or are neglected? Does government policy "promote the general welfare" when it encourages people to think exclusively of themselves and their own financial situation and to disregard the needs of others?

Clearly, there is no reason government should be exempted as a vehicle for helping to create a Zion society. Government is one of many tools available to help create the kind of society where all can flourish in their God-given missions upon the earth. We can work as individuals, as groups of individuals in organizations, and as a whole society through our government.

There is no party that is the Church's party or the Lord's party. However, as citizens we have the obligation to determine which party is more likely to help construct the kind of society that fits the Savior's admonition that "inasmuch as ye have done it unto one of the least of these my brethren, ye have done it unto me" (Matt. 25:40) and also encourages us not to be selfish, but both individually and as a society to have "every man seeking the interest of his neighbor" (D&C 82:19).

In "Heaven and Earth: Thinking through Environmentalism," George Handley argues against the assumption that environmentalism is at odds with gospel teachings. He suggests that LDS teachings richly support careful environmental stewardship. For example, teachings on the close connection between the physical and the spiritual, the importance of stewardship, as well as our belief that the earth will ultimately be the celestial kingdom give great reason to better care for the physical condition of the earth. Although LDS environmentalists may take a different stance on some issues than those advocated by some versions of environmentalism (on severe population control, for example), many principles are not only compatible with but even supported by scripture. Too often Latter-day Saints have been unfairly critical of environmentalist efforts; environmentalists, for their part, have often been unduly harsh in their rejection of Christians in general and Mormons specifically as allies in their endeavors. Both parties lose under these circumstances. Instead of rejecting out of hand beliefs that may be different from our own, our belief in the restored gospel should encourage us to seek out and welcome truth from all sources, while still living with exactness "according to every word that proceedeth forth out of the mouth of God" (D&C 98:11), allowing, as Handley writes, "[our] joy to deepen on both the pew and the woods."

Sixteen

Heaven and Earth:
Thinking through Environmentalism

George B. Handley

When the Nobel-prize winning poet, Derek Walcott, published his first poem at the age of fourteen on his native Caribbean island of St. Lucia, he was hardly prepared for the reprimand that would come, in printed verse no less, from his town's local priest. The poem was a song of praise of nature, about finding God amidst "wanderings among the quiet woods," an experience he hoped would "be my first lesson from the Holy book." The priest chided him (in lines of his own that exhibited, ironically, an inferior skill for verse) for his youthful exuberance and foolish preference for sermons preached by "the tree, the ant, the sod" instead of heeding revelation. He wrote: "God wills that man should hear from man / the truths of faith that led above." That the priest insisted on a stark division between the revealed Word and nature's inspiration and was unwilling to build on the inspiration the boy poet had discovered was poor instruction. Fortunately Derek Walcott was not deterred and went on to become one of the greatest poets of the English language, one possessed of an exceptional devotion to the natural beauties of the Caribbean.

The priest, of course, was not wrong to teach that revelation through prophets must not be displaced by whatever portion of God's presence we might experience in the outdoors. It is, however, a penurious conception of revelation that insists on such mutual exclusion and cannot imagine a continuity of feeling, of imbued meaning, that we might experience on a pew and in the woods. Our understanding of God's revealed word today would be unthinkable if all fourteen-year-olds were prohibited from finding God in the woods! Joseph too was reprimanded for declaring what he had seen and felt among the trees near his home: a God whose body of flesh and bone challenged the prevailing view that heaven and earth, spirit and body, could not share the same space harmoniously.

My early teens were neither marked by signs of remarkable poetic nor prophetic gifts. Indeed, it would be closer to the truth to say that I can only look back on those years with a shudder! But what imbues those years with a softness and a holiness—despite my shameful awareness of myself as an earthy, embodied individual being—are my experiences in the woods of Connecticut and on the Long Island shore where I was raised. I can still feel the humid summer air sticking to my skin, hear the chorus of a million insects milling in the still air, and smell the brackish leaf mulch forming beds of loam around the banks of the small stream that provided a home for minnows and frogs in my backyard. Wordsworth once described himself as a young boy "in the hour / Of thoughtless youth" playing "like a roe /… o'er the mountains" of England's Lake District, and I think he accurately captures the anonymity a young adolescent can uniquely experience in such locales:

> The sounding cataract
> Haunted me like a passion: the tall rock,
> The mountain, and the deep and gloomy wood,
> Their colours and their forms, were then to me
> An appetite; a feeling and a love,
> That had no need of a remoter charm.

To my young mind, exploring nature—diving into the saline waters of the Sound, wandering through woods in search of sites for makeshift forts, catching frogs and salamanders and staring at their strange little eyes—all offered a balm for what C. S. Lewis once called "the wound of individuality" because it provided a way of communing with something greater than myself but something that was also embodied and thus not alien to my physical self. I had my adolescent difficulties in coming to understand the restored Gospel, but I intuited that a belief that rejected celibacy for its priesthood also potentially included the idea of the blessed state of physical existence. Nature seemed a holy extension of my body, and my senses seemed to be the portholes through which I communicated with my natural kin.

Unfortunately, so much of our modern technologically enhanced life has divorced us of this kinship, whether because of the virtual reality of television and the internet, our controlled climates, or because we no longer produce our own food. Because our alienation from nature begins so early, our exposure to it begins to fill us with a kind of nostalgia for something more, as if we were seeking something lost. And what specifically is it that we have lost? A purely ecological view of human existence would suggest that what we long for, what we vaguely recall in those moments of the disappearing self, is an understanding of our merely embodied, biological identity as physical beings who too easily succumb to the illusion of our separateness from the physical world; we must not be deceived, in other words, by what appears to be our distinct and exceptional capacity for conscious thought because our true and only home is the earth. A view of human existence that insists on our merely spiritual identity would argue that we long for a sense of belonging to God that nature only helps us to begin to intimate; we should not be deceived, in other words, by the appearance of things and by our sensual experience of our kinship with them because our true and only home is heaven.

Joseph Smith's vision suggests the possibility that this is simply a false dichotomy. His vision and subsequent revelations contained in the Doctrine and Covenants and the Pearl of Great Price consistently teach that we are both embodied and inspirited, biological and spiritual, and that these are not temporary contradictions that will be resolved in death's separation of the spirit and the body and of heaven and earth. Spirit is matter, the Prophet explained, and all physical life was created spiritually before it was physically on the earth; all things, therefore, hide beneath their tangible surface a spiritual entity that inhabits the same space. He taught: "the elements are eternal, and spirit and element [or physical matter], inseparably connected, receive a fullness of joy. And when separated, man cannot receive a fullness of joy" (D&C 93:33–34). Cannot receive a fullness of joy! Our happiness is limited if our physical experience is not enhanced by the spirit and if our spiritual experience is not enhanced by physical life. The Prophet's revelations make it clear that our eternal life will be an embodied one, like God's, and that the earth will become the site of the highest level of exaltation. Nature, then, provides a profoundly unique and valuable opportunity to understand the delicate balance between the spirit and the body, heaven and earth.

So it was that I attended my Sunday School classes, and despite my adolescent reluctance to throw myself wholly into my religion, I remember the doctrines that first grabbed my attention. I instinctively recognized the truth that animals and trees were "living souls" and were thus my kin (Moses 3:9). I hadn't always heard the voice of the Lord in my meetings, but I had spent enough time under the stars and floating in the sea to implicitly trust the idea that "all things denote there is a God" (Alma 30:44) and that "all things are created and made to bear record of [Christ]" (Moses 6:63). My young mind was being prepared to understand just how interfused all things were by the light of Christ, as the Prophet revealed in Doctrine and Covenants 88:12, but when I contemplate those words now—"as also he is in the sun . . . as also he is in the moon"—I can see my teenage self surrounded in His light even in the midst of my adolescent angst, my body glistening in the sun after a dip in the sea or bathed in moonlight on my lawn at night where I often sat to ponder life's purpose. Although I sought nature so I could be alone to sort out my choices, away from the instructions of family, church, and friends, on a jetty overlooking the Sound one night at the age of seventeen I finally came to realize that I was never alone, that I was surrounded by His love and light, that I could repent and follow Him, and that it would be my genuine choice.

I did not fully appreciate the broader global implications of these doctrines until I became aware of the extent of our contemporary environmental crisis. In college at Stanford University, in graduate school at UC Berkeley, and into my early thirties as a professor at Northern Arizona University, I learned about the frightening and increasing rates of species extinction worldwide. I remember hearing the early debates about global warming and have noticed the growth of what is now a remarkable consensus among scientists about its reality. Of course there were the disappearing rain forests, deforestation and soil erosion in poor countries, the millions who live without safe drinking water, the disasters of pollution, but closer to home I read about the disappearing water tables in the American West, even as I was part of the increasing growth. And I watched as our dependence on oil implicated us repeatedly in conflicts in the Middle East and threw us into war.

Throughout my education, I had always felt a respect for the environment and an instinctive belief in the need for restraint and conservation, but I wasn't able to formulate a way for me to act. As I reflect on this now, I can find at least three reasons this was the case: (1) I could not overcome my own inertia to change my life, the problems often seemed too complex to know exactly how to act, and in my undergraduate experience at Stanford it seemed environmental issues were always discussed in the context of population control; (2) you weren't a true environmentalist unless you committed to having no more than two children. I was frequently interrogated about how many children I planned to have (I have four, which is one more than I think I said at the time I wanted). Extreme restrictions on family size never sat comfortably with me, but I didn't know how to argue the issue. Besides, I didn't hear environmental lessons in church, and the scriptures seemed to indicate that alarmism was unwarranted since the fate of the earth was in the hands of the Lord; (3) I believed in principles of stewardship but stewardship over the fate of the earth in an age of global environmental problems challenged me to understand where and how I could enter into the fray. It didn't help that the general culture of environmentalism, as far as I could see while studying in California, didn't seem friendly to Christians. Christians of all stripes seemed easy targets for our belief in the millennial reign of Christ, our reluctance to unduly limit the size of our families, and our trust in divine providence.

At Northern Arizona University, however, I made friends with a small group of scholars who were intensely interested in broad questions about how we can define and use our quality of life, economic choices, and beliefs to benefit more effectively the well-being of the physical world now and in the future. I took the opportunity to attend a workshop aimed at helping professors in all fields to see the relevance of their disciplines to questions of sustainability. Sustainability was defined in terms of principles, not policies, and they included the notion that individual choices should be valued by their effect when we imagine that they are made by an entire society and over several generations. If one gum wrapper is left at a lakeside, it may not be measurable, but if we all individually assume that we only need to measure the individual effect of our puny acts, then we are all justified in throwing wrappers to the ground. A collective group acting with such impunity wouldn't take more than a few weeks to make an enormous mess, and if thousands do so on a weekly basis for several generations, worse still. As I heard these discussions, I couldn't help thinking that I had heard them before in LDS teachings about the law of consecration, the spirit of Elijah that inspires us to consider the effects of our actions on future generations and to measure them against the examples set by our ancestors, and Christ's teachings about moderation. It represented such a high standard that I also reflected on the need for patience and tolerance, since it didn't seem likely that anyone could live in such a way that nothing they did would cause harm if replicated worldwide. As Jesus had taught, "he who is without sin . . ."

One day while walking with a colleague, a Jewish scholar who studied Judaism's environmental values, I spoke of LDS beliefs about the spiritual creation that came before the physical one, the destiny of the earth as the site of the celestial kingdom, the Word of Wisdom and its emphasis on eating meat sparingly, and a variety of other doctrines that seemed relevant to environmental problems. She insisted that I research this further and publish something. She was sure people outside Mormonism were not aware of these unusual doctrines and that perhaps Mormons themselves would benefit from contemplating further what our scriptures teach about environmental stewardship. Thus began a wonderful journey of discovery.[1]

---

1. I did eventually publish an essay in response to this encouragement: "The Environmental Ethics of Mormon Belief." *BYU Studies* 40, no. 2 (Summer 2001): 187–211.

It seemed as if everything I had learned and come to believe in shone in a new light of understanding. As I read deeply in the formidable literature about religion and the environment and about environmental problems generally, and as I continued my personal study of the Gospel, it was hard not to feel excited by the answers it seemed the restored Gospel provided.

I learned that some scholars had argued that the Judeo-Christian tradition bore responsibility for the environmental crisis. Specifically these scholars saw the biblical injunction to assume dominion over the earth as a license to act without regard for the well-being of God's creations. They likewise pointed to Christianity's outright rejection of animism, the idea that all living things had spirits, as enabling this amoral view of our use of nature because, arguably, we are not likely to feel an ethical sense of responsibility toward something we view as dead matter. Furthermore, they insisted that Christianity's tendency to value the spirit over the body and heaven over the earth had led to an attitude of indifference toward the world's degradation. If the earth is going to be destroyed anyway and we will eventually depart it, why bother protecting it?

The logic of these criticisms made sense to me, but I knew that they only told part of the story. All religions can potentially become complicit with the evils of the status quo, since one of religion's ugliest distortions happens when it is mixed with seductive individualism. Believers emerge with that false confidence that as long as they get themselves to heaven, the rest of the world be damned. So although I had no doubts that many Christians were guilty as charged, I preferred the Christianity, for example, that had inspired the abolitionists to the Christianity that was used to justify the slave owner. Besides, it seems impractical at best and deeply prejudiced at worst to refuse to see the ethical potential of religion and to expect believers suddenly to drop worldviews they have held for generations. There is no place for chauvinism—either secular or religious—if we are going to solve environmental problems; the solution requires finding common ground and the reason is simple: environmental problems *are our common ground* and require shared, global solutions. This necessitates working together across distinct values and traditions with tolerance, in cultures of large and small families, among farmers and urban professionals, believers and non-believers, developed and developing nations, and so forth.

It is proving far more effective to rethink Christianity itself and all other religious traditions to find solutions to our contemporary problems. As one such critic put it wisely, "What we do about ecology depends on our ideas of the man-nature relationship. More science and more technology are not going to get us out of the present ecological crisis until we find a new religion, or rethink our old one."² In my research I was pleased to learn that an entire generation of Evangelicals, Baptists, Catholics, Muslims, Buddhists, Hindus, Jews, and other religious people the world over had responded to these criticisms in one of the most significant shifts in the history of religion, and they had given faith-based reason to the notion of a religiously motivated environmental stewardship.

This literature of ecotheology, as it is known, consistently argued that if the body is viewed as something alien and inherently hostile to the desires of our spirit, then we come to understand ourselves as beings whose real home is not earth nor whose real identity is physical. Concern for the well-being of the body or of the rest of creation is then viewed as an expression of faithlessness. Hence the logic concludes that there is no need for urgent action to save the planet, because we all know that the earth is going to die. Taken to its logical conclusion, this view completely privileges the spirit over the body and leads to a dangerous weakening of our capacity to be accountable moral agents. We become content with a panglossian view that reassures us that all that happens in this life, regardless of the damage done to the earth, is for the best. Environmental degradation, or any form of human evil, becomes a manifestation or sign of God's will since it is believed to fulfill prophecy. The Savior warned us about accountability in case we are tempted by such strange theology: "Woe unto the world because of offences! for it must needs be that offences come; but woe unto that man by whom the offence cometh!" (Matt. 18:7).

I had to admit to myself that despite the fact that we alone seemed to possess the most complete and explicitly stated doctrines that outlined these environmental principles, I had heard such apathetic thinking in my church meetings. I had heard that it apparently wasn't a good thing to be a "tree-hugger." Recycling, wilderness preservation, ethical and modest consumption, protection of endangered species, reduction of waste or of our use of water and gasoline—even just for the sake of living modestly—were never mentioned in our Sunday lessons or seemed to play a role in the planning of our ward activities. Indeed, they seemed implicitly absent in the doctrines we learned in the restored account of the creation, in temple worship, in our understanding of morality itself, and in our discussions of church welfare principles. While I heard plenty about the dangers of moral pollution, I scarcely heard a word of concern about any of the major environmental issues of our day; it was as if they did not exist. We spoke

---

2. Lynn White, "The Historical Roots of Our Ecological Crisis" in *This Sacred Earth: Religion, Nature, Environment* (New York: Routledge, 1996), 191–93.

often of the importance of watching our thoughts, of circumspection in all of our actions toward our fellow human beings, but nothing at all about our treatment of animals, our use of natural resources, or about the need to concern ourselves with where our goods and services came from. Most often I believe that this was due to apathy and lack of information, but it was surprising to me to learn of some members' outright opposition to any form of environmentalism. Although the vocal opponents were few, they were the only ones who seemed to address environmentalism at all. Hence, the impression was created, even if it was not fully articulated or justified, that a good Mormon would not make a good environmentalist and for good reason.

This was especially disappointing given our extraordinary doctrines about modest and consecrated living, trees and plants as living souls, and the sanctified earth as our eternal destination. Why, given the fact that the body's eventual resurrection does not justify our neglect of the body, would we conclude that an impending millennium justifies inaction in the face of the earth's mistreatment? Such apathy and commitment to inaction indeed seemed immoral. I went through the scriptures in search of any doctrines that would explain to me why I should not accept stewardship over the well-being of the environment. I could find none; I did find scriptures, however, that seemed to echo with the readings I had done among other religious traditions. In the Doctrine and Covenants I found strongly worded warnings against excess. In section 59, I read:

> Yea, all things which come of the earth, in the season thereof, are made for the benefit and the use of man, both to please the eye and to gladden the heart; Yea, for food and for raiment, for taste and for smell, to strengthen the body and to enliven the soul. And it pleaseth God that he hath given all these things unto man; for unto this end were they made to be used, with judgment, not to excess, neither by extortion. (vv. 18–22)

I had read these verses before merely in the context of this section's teachings on the Sabbath day, but nature appears here, as it does elsewhere in the scriptures, as both a resource to be used with moderation and as a sacred source of aesthetic pleasure. (See how in Moses 3:9, for example, the Lord states that trees were created so that we could behold them as well as use them as a resource.) What a wonderful principle of balance! The Lord instructs us to be responsive to his creations, to be fulfilled and awed by the simple fact of their existence. Once we have elevated our sensibilities to be able to do this, we are then permitted to take only what we need for our sustenance. This will endear to us the places we inhabit at the same time that we learn to use them judiciously. Consumption, when it is informed by this kind of spiritual and aesthetic capacity, will not corrupt us because our passions will be kept in check by a recognition of the Lord's gifts.

Another important consideration appears to be the needs of the poor. In Doctrine and Covenants 104, in a verse Mormons often cite in defense against those who argue for extreme population control measures, we read that "the earth is full and there is enough and to spare" (v. 17). What is not as frequently cited is how these verses explain that this promise is contingent upon our willingness to consume modestly. We are told that every man is "accountable, as a steward over earthly blessings" and that

> It must needs be done in mine own way; and behold this is the way that I, the Lord God, have decreed to provide for my saints, that the poor shall be exalted, in that the rich are made low. . . . Therefore if any man take of the abundance which I have made, and impart not his portion, according to the law of my gospel, unto the poor and the needy, he shall, with the wicked, lift up his eyes in hell, being in torment. (vv. 13–18)

In other words, the earth's capacity to support the human population depends on our willingness to live modestly. It is not a guarantee. Extreme poverty anywhere is a symptom of our wickedness as a human family. But because the emphasis is on our ingenuity and modesty, I have not felt the need to impose restrictions, and I have therefore never felt the need to impose restrictions on the size of my family *merely* on the basis of concerns about overpopulation. I do not mean to minimize the problems caused by growing populations, especially in areas of the world whose economies and environments are not currently able to sustain that growth or where women are not full partners in reproductive decision-making. I also understand well that my American patterns of consumption of all manner of natural resources is disturbingly disproportionate to the rest of the world, but I have always felt uncomfortable with the misanthropic and often racist attitudes that belief in population control fosters and the tendency it has had to create repressive forms of political power. I do not mean to suggest, in other words, that I see Mormon belief as indifferent to the responsibility of parents to plan their family size carefully. It is not well known outside of the Church, and sometimes within it, that the Church does not categorically oppose the use of birth control and that there is no overt policy that we are obligated to have the largest family possible.

The point is that if we wish to defend the right to exercise our own conscience and bring children into the world according to personal inspiration, we would do well to live up to the high standard of modest living imposed by these verses. I for one feel a persistent and nagging worry that my family and I do not exercise enough restraint on our spending and consumption. I suspect that the Lord wants us to have these worries. I would like to believe we might someday learn how to use a more fair proportion of the world's resources (something I am not convinced small families do better than large ones). I believe that the Lord cares more about what kind of children we are raising rather than how many, but I also emphatically believe that the kind he wants are not merely morally clean non-smokers and non-drinkers but also morally modest consumers, respectful toward all life and grateful users of His resources, and generous in their willingness to sacrifice so that others might have the same opportunities they enjoy.

Given the disparity of wealth in the world, it is foolish for the fortunate and very small fraction of God's children who have full educational and economic opportunities to be ungrateful. But it makes reason stare to conclude that such opportunities are providentially given merely so that these few can devote themselves to consuming at will the smorgasbord of First World amusements while millions go without the bare necessities of life. True gratitude requires more than saying "thank you"; it must be reflected in our willingness to make sacrifices and consecrate our gifts to bless others. We can't expect to pray for rain with impunity, for example, when we continue to use water recklessly. It is the height of folly to believe that First World living leaves no mark on the environment and has no consequences for future generations, and I believe it a desecration of religion itself to suppose that our God sanctions secular philosophies that justify indifference toward the suffering of people, animals, and the planet itself. This has never been the case in past societies, and although it is prophecy that the world will end, we would do well to avoid contributing to its death. I eventually came to understand in my teens the need to avoid the "eat, drink, and be merry" crowd, but sometimes I find myself part of the same crowd, only now we are eating and drinking fast food hamburgers and soda, throwing away our garbage with indifference, having no idea or even caring where our clothes and food come from, and generally bristling at any suggestion that there is something wrong with this picture.

Our doctrines of stewardship do not teach me which organizations I should join, whom I should vote for, or how many children I should have. They also do not tell me when to cut trees and when to preserve them, and they certainly do not seem to suggest that all use of natural resources is categorically wrong or that the protection of the environment should trump all other human concerns. But that does not free me of the responsibility to define proper and moderate use according to the principles of gospel living. As the scriptures above insist, I should deliberate carefully about use and my deliberations should be informed by a profound appreciation for the beauty and wonder of God's creations that I am contemplating using. I don't know why some Mormons therefore conclude that environmentalism should be viewed as the enemy. I might not like every version of environmentalism and I might not always come out on the environmentalist side of an issue as it is defined politically, but why should I disparage what environmentalists are trying to do? And why should I pretend that my religion gives me license to use nature however and whenever I please? Is it really more valuable to spend my time and words finding fault with environmentalism and justifying the status quo or to give my attention to changing my life to meet the high demands of stewardship as the gospel defines it?

Once possessed of the conviction that the gospel teaches environmental stewardship, it is a dangerous temptation for some to blame the Church and its leadership for giving inadequate attention to good stewardship and to see Mormons as a fallen and wayward people. Many people fall prey to the temptation to become a Johnny-one-note, playing the same monotonous theme over and over in their minds and only hearing messages that resonate with that theme. It might be a book or a radio program that has placed a new idea in the mind, and instead of experimenting on the word through diligent additional education, the idea becomes a slogan, a triumph over others. The messages of the restored gospel are so many and they create such wonderful and complexly beautiful and harmonious sounds. Why should I only listen for the bass line, or for notes in the key of C-sharp? Why should my concerns that we become better environmentalists mean that I refuse to be moved whenever I am called to repentance, reminded to do my home teaching (even if I must serve someone with different political beliefs, class background, or educational opportunities), or taught about service during General Conference? If it is spiritually debilitating to fear new knowledge and to sustain one's activity in the Church simply by shutting down curiosity and refusing to read widely, leaving the Church because one has only just begun an education on an issue that has created temporary dissonance hardly qualifies as an alternative. Thirst for righteousness and truth, forbearance, and the capacity to bear all things qualify us for the work of growing in our knowledge of what is true. Why anyone would turn away from what are arguably the richest environmental doctrines in the Christian world because of their environmental convictions is beyond me. But sometimes others in the Church feel uncomfortable with those who ask tough questions and lead the questioners to believe that their concerns are unfounded, unfaithful, morally suspect, even hedonistic. I don't mean to excuse those who leave, but they are just one example of many kinds of individuals with a viewpoint that with the right nurturing can find fertile ground in the church to benefit all of us.

Apparently we have not been listening to church teachings contained in restored scripture, the temple, and taught by our Church leaders. If we have the ears to hear, the sermon of environmental stewardship has been preached many times. President Gordon B. Hinckley has said "The earth is His creation. When we make it ugly we offend Him."[3] Elder Neal A. Maxwell observed:

> True disciples . . . would be consistent environmentalists—caring both about maintaining the spiritual health of a marriage and preserving a rain forest; caring about preserving the nurturing capacity of a family as well as providing a healthy supply of air and water. . . . Adam and Eve were to "dress the garden," not exploit it. Like them, we are to keep the commandments, so that we can enjoy all the resources God has given us, resources described as "enough and to spare" (D&C 104:17), if we use and husband them wisely.[4]

During the energy crisis of the 70s, which is starting to pale in comparison with current problems, the First Presidency said: "We urge Latter-day Saints and all citizens to join in efforts nationally and locally to conserve precious energy resources. Worshippers should walk to church meetings where it is feasible."[5] These are just a few samples of many similar Church teachings that are not rare or hard to find, just hard, I suppose, to hear.

What environmentally minded critics of the Church miss are the many unspoken environmental strengths of Mormon practice. Our scouting program teaches and promotes stewardship principles at the crucial age of adolescence when environmental awareness is just beginning. We have a history of creating a strong sense of place in our communities, which is no small accomplishment in an age of rapid movement and displacement that often renders people indifferent to the places they inhabit. We understand the need for sacred spaces in nature (usually nearby our places of residence) and often send our youth into the woods for Enos-like experiences of their own. We have a tradition of family gardening that serves to teach a relationship to the earth that grocery stores simply cannot provide. Our welfare system promotes modest use, recycling of clothing and other materials; church ranches and farms are developing sustainable practices;

---

3. Gordon B. Hinckley, "God So Loved the World," *New Era*, April 1983, 48.

4. Neal A. Maxwell, *A Wonderful Flood of Light* (Salt Lake City: Bookcraft, 1990), 103.

5. "First Presidency Supports Energy Conservation," *Ensign*, Aug. 1979, 78.

we sacrifice not only our tithing but our fast offerings to help keep in check our material ambitions.

Can we do better in these and other areas? Of course. But the point is that despite our failings, we are a resourceful, industrious, and conscientious people who know how to act collectively. We are, in other words, an important ally because of our tremendous potential, and so for some environmentalists to conclude that it would be better to disparage Mormons or any other Christians because of their shortcomings will only serve to weaken the collective force we all need to muster to solve our environmental problems. Sometimes it seems that critics of the Church and critics of environmentalism alike prefer to get in their jabs rather than to seek common ground so as to work cooperatively for solutions, and this unfortunately comes at the expense of the environment itself. It has always proved easier to find fault with others than to use our beliefs as a mirror for finding fault with ourselves. We certainly would not want to live without convictions, but it is important to remember that no matter how true, strongly held beliefs run the risk of becoming a part of our self-image before they have become a part of our character, and religious worship, like so much political propaganda, becomes a form of self-affirmation. Thus religious devotion leads to expending energy to be right instead of doing the self-questioning necessary to become good.

A few years ago now, I had the privilege of working with colleagues to hold a symposium at Brigham Young University to explore LDS perspectives on environmental stewardship.[6] Over three hundred people attended; Latter-day Saints participated from all walks of life: law, ranching, academia, public policy, wildlife management, and other fields. As the symposium was concluding, a man approached me and thanked me on behalf of his son, who had also attended the symposium. His son was a teenager still searching for his testimony of the gospel but already intensely interested in environmental stewardship. His son was beginning to feel that his fellow church members did not appreciate his interest, and this was slowly driving him out of the church. The father felt that the symposium had provided an important encouragement to the boy for having a strong conscience as well as an invitation to bring his convictions to the gospel table. I thought of similar students I had met at BYU, University of Utah, Utah State, and elsewhere, and other youth I had known, including the boy I once was. I

---

6. A subsequent book of the symposium proceedings was published. George B. Handley, Terry Ball, and Steven Peck, eds., *Our Stewardship and the Creation: LDS Perspectives on the Environment* (Provo: Religious Studies Center, 2006).

thought what a blessing it would be to congratulate them for caring about such serious topics at such a young age and to do all we can to bring them into the fold rather than unnecessarily alienating them.

As I serve in the Church, I hope that I am true to the generous impulses of the doctrines of the restoration, which unlike the attitude of Derek Walcott's priest, are the opposite of penurious. Instead of the priest's overly zealous orthodoxy, I prefer the generosity of vision expressed by one of our prophets:

> [The restoration of Christ's church and gospel] must be our great and singular message to the world. We do not offer it with boasting. We testify in humility but with gravity and absolute sincerity. We invite all, the whole earth, to listen to this account and take measure of its truth. God bless us as those who believe in His divine manifestations and help us to extend knowledge of these great and marvelous occurrences to all who will listen. To these we say in a spirit of love, bring with you all that you have of good and truth which you have received from whatever source, and come and let us see if we may add to it. This invitation I extend to men and women everywhere with my solemn testimony that this work is true, for I know the truth of it by the power of the Holy Ghost. In the name of Jesus Christ, Amen.[7]

The doctrines of the restoration, such as those pertaining to environmental stewardship, are like magnets or wide nets that draw in the many fragments of truth dispersed across the planet, expressed in innumerable philosophies and worldviews whose relationship to eternal verities is always worth exploring. We do this, as Alma instructed, by suspending disbelief and experimenting with the word so as to find out what fruit it bears. While the fundamental truths of the gospel, of God's nature and Christ's mission, and of the restoration are known, the truth of all things is yet to be known and therefore the world is always worth listening to and learning from. Our guide in the midst of potential confusion is, of course, the Holy Ghost. But it is more than this. It is also, according to Mormon, charity, or the true love of Christ in our own hearts, and as Mormon states, "if ye will lay hold of every good thing, ye certainly will be a child of Christ" (Moro. 7:19). Once possessed of this remarkable gift to desire the good, we learn to bear all things, even when all things don't always make sense, because we want to know all things, and we become possessed of an unquenchable thirst for all that is virtuous, lovely, of good report, or praiseworthy.

Over time we may find that our knowledge and sense of the good and true have become more broad, more generous, more faithful even at the same time that we have learned to live with more exactness "according to

---

7. Gordon B. Hinckley, "The Marvelous Foundation of Our Faith," *Ensign*, November 2002, 81.

every word that proceedeth forth out of the mouth of God" (D&C 98:11). My incipient environmentalism could have pulled me apart and away from the God of revelation but has instead helped me to hear God's inspired messages from His prophets as well as from good people in the world and from nature itself. This has allowed my joy to deepen on both the pew and in the woods, something I hope increases my chances for happiness on earth and in heaven, which I can only pray will be the same place.

In "An Argument against Embryonic Stem Cell Research," David Jensen argues that it is morally wrong to kill embryonic humans for the sake of research. While developing a substantive view on this topic, he also gives an example of how he integrates his LDS beliefs into his thinking on ethical matters. Jensen writes, "Sometimes our LDS beliefs will give us fairly direct guidance on matters of right and wrong. Other times—as in the case of embryonic stem cell research—they will give us points of departure which we may use in coming to a conclusion." Following this approach, he starts from the Church's position against abortion, and explores how that position might guide our reasoning on the ethical question of embryonic stem cell research.

Seventeen

An Argument Against Embryonic Stem Cell Research

David A. Jensen

Introduction

Advocates of embryonic stem cell research foresee significant and widespread medical benefits from the results of such research. These include cures or substantial treatments for intractable diseases such as Alzheimer's and Parkinson's disease. But is medical research on human embryos ("early humans" or "embryonic humans"[1])—in particular, research that provides these embryos with no benefit and costs them their lives—morally problematic? With regard to embryonic stem cell research, I will argue for a stronger and weaker conclusion. My stronger conclusion is that aspects of embryonic stem cell research are morally wrong; in particular, killing the embryonic human for the sake of research. My weaker conclusion is that those who endorse embryonic stem cell research in which embryonic humans are killed have a burden to show that the killing is not morally wrong. That stem cell research may provide important

---

1. Some will argue, incorrectly, that referring to a human embryo as an "early human" or "embryonic human" begs the question. The category of human, however, is not a moral category. Human is a biological category, and in that respect a developing embryo or fetus is a human, a member of a particular species. In contrast, the relevant moral category is *personhood*; it is to persons that we attribute rights, moral standing, duties, and responsibilities. The larger question regarding embryonic stem cell research (and abortion and similar issues) is whether all humans are persons, whether only those at a certain age or stage of development are persons, whether some non-human animals might also be persons or approach personhood adequately that they have some moral standing, and so forth. Thus, in using the biological category of "human," the question of moral standing is not being begged. See Michael Tooley, "Abortion and Infanticide," *Philosophy and Public Affairs* 2, no. 1 (1972): 37–65, for a critique of discussions which confuse this terminology. I shall use the terms "human embryo," "embryonic human," "very early human," and so forth interchangeably.

benefits to humanity does not automatically set aside moral concerns nor trump moral considerations.

I have several purposes in arguing for my conclusions. First, I want to bring my LDS beliefs openly into a discussion of broader ethical interest. My LDS beliefs always figure implicitly into any sincere argumentation of mine; here I make them explicit. Second, I want to show, by example, how I integrate LDS beliefs into ethical argumentation and, in doing so, demonstrate a harmony between LDS commitments and the practice of ethical inquiry. Finally, I want to develop a substantive view on the morality of embryonic stem cell research.[2]

Methodology

I will first consider some methodological points about ethical inquiry and LDS religious devotion that will elucidate how I attempt to integrate the two. To begin with, note that there are two kinds of questions we can ask with regard to someone's actions being morally right or morally wrong.

1. Is the action right or wrong?
2. Given a right or wrong action, what *makes* the action right or wrong, respectively?

The first question aims at knowing the moral status of an action. I call this a "what to do" question since it aims at knowing the rightness or wrongness of an action and, hence, whether one should or should not, prima facie, do the action. Suppose I return home from buying groceries and I discover that the clerk gave me an extra five cents. I'm faced with a *what to do* question: am I obligated to return the five cents? Given that it is such a small amount, and the grocery store is quite a distance away, is it wrong of me to keep the five cents? Questions of whether an action is right or wrong, what our duties or obligations are, are frequent and important ethical questions that we confront. My inquiry in this paper aims to answer a *what to do* question: is embryonic stem cell research, or some aspects of it, morally wrong?

Once we know or judge that a particular action is right or wrong, we might ask why it is right or wrong. I term this second kind of question a "why do" question? Consider, for example, killing an innocent person for personal gain. I'm as convinced of the prima facie wrongness of such an act as I am of anything. But why is it wrong? To ask this question is not to

---

2. A fuller treatment of these issues can be found in my "Abortion, Embryonic Stem Cell Research, and Waste," *Theoretical Medicine and Bioethics* 29, no. 1 (January 2008): 27–41.

be skeptical: I am not at all implying that perhaps it is not wrong to kill an innocent person for personal gain. I'm genuinely asking why in the sense of seeking further understanding. We ask these sorts of questions—*why do* questions—all the time. Upon learning that the space shuttle Columbia disintegrated on re-entry, it was very natural to ask why it disintegrated. But to ask this is not to deny or even doubt that it happened; it is only to seek further understanding about what made it happen. Even though we know, through revelation from ancient and modern prophets, that it is wrong to lie, for example, we can still ask why it is wrong; we can seek further understanding of this moral truth.

This brings us to my second methodological point: why do we need to ask *why do* questions about morality? Some might think that the answer to *why do* moral questions is obvious: what makes a wrong action wrong is that God commands us not to do it, and what makes a right action right is that God commands us to do it. This is certainly a tempting answer—especially to a Latter-day Saint who believes in God and continuing revelation—though an answer that I think we should resist. We should resist it because moral right and moral wrong explain why God commands much of what He commands, not the other way around. It is because murder is wrong that God commands us not to do it. It is because unkindness is wrong that we are commanded to be kind to and love one another.

I do not claim that all of God's commandments are reflections of moral right and wrong. God may command us to do something merely because it will benefit us and bless our life. In the case of Naaman, the prophet Elijah instructed Naaman to wash himself in the Jordan River seven times in order to cure his leprosy. It is not that there is something morally good about washing seven times in the Jordan River, nor something morally wrong with not doing it. Rather, Naaman would have lost out on a great blessing had he not obeyed.

The correct relationship, I believe, between moral right and wrong and God's commandments is something like the following: God's revealed commandments allow us to know what is right and wrong (and more generally, what we should and should not do). They answer both moral and amoral *what to do* questions. But something merely being commanded is not necessarily what makes it morally right or morally wrong, and so it does not answer *why do* questions (though commandments are often given with explanations that answer or help answer *why do* questions).[3] Consider

---

3. I am briefly considering here a very complex matter—the relationship between morality and God's commandments—and there is much more to be said and clarified

a gruesome moral wrong such as rape. Certainly what makes rape morally wrong is primarily something about the victim, something about what is done to him or her. Indeed, because of this, God commands against this act. And because of this wrongness an atonement is needed so God can be merciful on the one hand, but faithful to the principles of justice on the other. If what makes something right or wrong is that God commands it, then we get the odd result that what makes rape wrong is not that it hurts a person in a most brutal and depraved manner, but what makes it wrong is merely that God says not to do it.[4]

As Latter-day Saints, we are fortunate to have so many matters of moral right and wrong revealed to us. For many issues, there is no question about what we ought or ought not to do. But not all matters of right and wrong are revealed to us straightforwardly. Further, it is not always clear how to apply moral principles to particular situations we are faced with, especially situations that several moral principles bear on. But as we understand the principles which underlie our known cases of right and wrong, we can then apply these principles to less clear or unrevealed cases of moral indecision. In other words, answers to *why do* questions can help us answer *what to do* questions. I'll use this technique significantly in this paper: I'll examine cases of known right and wrong, partly in light of my LDS beliefs, in order to understand more general principles of what makes an action right or wrong. Then I'll apply these general principles to the specific case of embryonic stem cell research.

One concern might be raised at this point: if my reasoning depends in part on my LDS beliefs, what value will it be to one who is not of the LDS faith? This is a genuine concern. But when answering ethical questions, I believe that we must separate two tasks, only one of which this concern is related to. The first task in answering questions about what is right or wrong is to figure out *what the truth of the matter is*. Is embryonic stem

---

than is within the scope of this paper. For now, my primary concern is that in many cases, including the most important, there is something to the rightness and wrongness of moral behavior that underlies many of God's morally relevant commandments.

4. It is less clear on this view why an atonement is needed. If the ultimate authority on moral right and wrong is merely God's commanding it (and not his commanding it for some independent reason), then it is harder to understand in such circumstances that God's forgiving sin would not be adequate to satisfy the demands of justice. For in such a world God's command ultimately is justice. An atonement is needed by God so that he can be merciful while at the same time just (see Alma 42:13–15). But this implies that at least some fundamental aspects of justice are not decided by God.

cell research, for example, right or wrong, and why? In other words, the first task of moral inquiry is always a matter of discovering and convincing oneself of the truth of the matter. A second task involves how one might convince another person of this truth. This second task is subordinate to the first. Only in undertaking this second task do we need to worry explicitly about those who are not of our religious persuasion. This is not to deny that the second task is important, but the first task is fundamental. As we seek to understand the truth of some matter, especially matters of moral right and wrong behavior, we cannot set aside our deepest and most fundamental beliefs, our religious beliefs (especially given our commitment to the necessity of modern and continuing revelation). Once we have come to a knowledge of the truth, however—complemented by our knowledge of the gospel—then we can be concerned about how to present it to others in a way that will draw on truths we all accept.[5]

What's Not Wrong with Embryonic Stem Cell Research

In general, stem cells are relatively undifferentiated cells that can differentiate into specialized cells. Partially differentiated cells exist in adult humans ("adult stem cells"), which serve the valuable function of producing new cells when needed. Bone marrow, for example, contains (adult) stem cells which differentiate into red and white blood cells. Embryonic stem cells are the initial undifferentiated cells of a human embryo that develop into particular liver cells, kidney cells, and muscle cells; indeed, they differentiate into all the types of specialized cells a normal human is composed of.[6] Embryonic stem cell research involves experimentation on these cells and manipulation of them for potential therapeutic benefit. Because stem cells differentiate into specialized cells, they can perhaps be manipulated into growing new organs and repairing parts of the body damaged by disease, age, or injury.[7]

---

5. Of course, if we do not have enough beliefs in common, then any sort of persuasion or agreement may be impossible. Knowing the truth of something, moral or otherwise, does not imply that one can convince others of it.

6. For a more detailed discussion of the science of stem cells, see "Stem Cell Basics," National Institutes of Health, http://stemcells.nih.gov/info/basics/Pages/Default.aspx (accessed June 18, 2013).

7. See, for example, John McKenzie, "Doctors Use Patients' Own Stem Cells to Build New Blood Vessels," Abcnews.com, August 2, 2005, http://abcnews.go.com/WNT/print?id=1002059 (accessed June 18, 2013).

I do *not* argue that experimentation on stem cells themselves is morally wrong. Nothing appears morally objectionable about using stems cells to increase our understanding of the human body, to develop therapeutic techniques, or to administer therapy itself. We already make significant scientific and therapeutic use of our cells: I might donate some blood as part of a study for some new blood thinning medication. Cells of mine are, in effect, being experimented upon. When I have a mole removed and tested for cancer, cells of mine are removed and studied. In giving blood for a blood transfusion, I am giving cells of mine for the life of another.

In this important respect I have no objections to research embryonic stem cells themselves or to research cells in general. My objection (and the general controversy with stem cell research) concerns how we obtain the embryonic stem cells: they are obtained by killing the human embryo from which they are extracted. Presently this is an unavoidable consequence of extracting the stem cells. In typical medical research—say research on liver functioning—we do not kill persons in order to extract and study their livers. Only after a person has died (and not by our killing him), and if a certain standard of informed consent is met, do we then experiment on his body parts. Or we may take a biopsy of a living patient's liver, again with his consent, in a manner that does not harm him. I will not argue that it is wrong to kill someone for the sake of harvesting his cells and experimenting on them. I assume that this is morally wrong. But this reasonable assumption raises the question: why would it be okay to kill an embryonic human and harvest its cells for the sake of experimentation?

Perhaps there may be other ways to obtain embryonic stem cells. Perhaps we could induce an embryo to harmlessly "shed" a cell which could be collected for research. Or perhaps adult cells could be "reset" to their embryonic state.[8] There is also promising research on non-embryonic stem cells: adult stem cells and umbilical cord stem cells may provide all the benefits that embryonic stem cells are thought capable of providing.[9] I have no objections to these kinds of stem cell research, so long as, for example, the adult stem cells are not obtained by killing or harming the adult human. Only so far as the only way to obtain embryonic stem cells is

---

8. See, for example, Laurie Kellman, "GOP Probes Non-Destructive Cell Research," Abcnews.com, June 30, 2005, http://abcnews.go.com/Politics/print?id=894929 (accessed June 18, 2013).

9. See, for example, Byron Spice "Option to stem cells found: Pitt experts say placental cells offer palatable alternative," Pittsburgh Post-Gazette, August 5, 2005, http://www.post-gazette.com/stories/news/healthscience/option-to-stem-cells-found-594420/ (accessed June 18, 2013).

by killing an embryonic human, does it follow that I object to embryonic stem cell research.

Why Embryonic Stem Cell Research is Morally Wrong

Since my argument that embryonic stem cell research is morally wrong is not a challenge to embryonic stem cell research per se, but to certain aspects of it, I will limit my argument to that aspect. The argument is fairly straightforward:

1. Harvesting embryonic stem cells requires killing a human embryo.
2. It is wrong to kill human embryos.
3. Therefore, it is wrong to harvest embryonic stem cells.

If an instance of embryonic stem cell research requires harvesting embryonic stem cells, then it would follow that it is morally wrong.

As mentioned, we may develop techniques for obtaining embryonic stem cells without killing embryos. If this were the case, then (1) would be false. At the present time, however, (1) is true. Premise 2 brings in moral considerations, and is my primary focus. Implicit in the argument is that if it is wrong to do some action, and a certain practice requires that one do that action, then it is wrong to engage in that practice. To some extent this implicit premise can, and will be, questioned: perhaps certain practices are not wrong even though they necessarily involve actions that are wrong. Or perhaps, given the circumstances in which we perform the otherwise wrong action, the action is not wrong after all. This latter point is essentially a point about exceptions: moral rules—depending on how they are understood in general and in particular cases—generally have exceptions, and perhaps embryonic stem cell research is a circumstance in which an exception applies. If so, then it would not be wrong to kill embryonic humans for the sake of research. This line of argumentation will be discussed further on.

Why think that premise 2 is true, that it is wrong to kill embryonic humans? Here I bring my LDS beliefs to bear on this question, to explain why I believe it is wrong to kill an embryonic human even for the sake of medical research. As a Latter-day Saint, I believe that abortion is wrong.[10] There may be exceptions to this as with most moral principles; for example,

---

10. See "Abortion," Newsroom: An Official Website of The Church of Jesus Christ of Latter-day Saints, http://www.mormonnewsroom.org/ldsnewsroom/eng/public-issues/abortion (accessed June 18, 2013), for a statement of the Church's position on abortion.

perhaps abortion is justified when the mother will die as a result of maintaining the pregnancy. Nevertheless, the principle that abortion is wrong strongly implies that there is something about an early human—an embryonic human—such that it is wrong to kill it. That is, there is something valuable about early humans such that it is wrong to kill them or even harm them. Given that abortion is wrong, it follows that the embryonic human is something of value such that it ought not to be killed. Thus premise 2 is true.

This argument for premise 2 relies on my LDS belief that abortion is wrong. Without my LDS beliefs, it would be difficult to appeal to the wrongness of abortion so easily since it is a topic of intense and varied argument. The challenge that abortion brings to this issue is simply the following: if it is wrong to kill in the case of abortion, why would it be morally permissible to kill in the case of embryonic stem cell research? After all, many pregnant women have very good reasons for not wanting to be pregnant, for not wanting to have children. Further, there are many pregnant women that we generally agree should not be pregnant or rearing children (thirteen-year-old girls, for example). But for all this, abortion is still morally wrong. The most likely answer to why it is wrong is that there is something about the human, even in its earliest stages, that it ought not to be killed.

Note the application of the distinction between what I termed *what to do* questions and *why do* questions. In talking about abortion, I am not asking a *what to do* question. I already know, based on my LDS teachings, that abortion is wrong. The kind of question I am asking with regard to abortion is a *why do* question: what makes abortion wrong? My view, to which I'll consider objections momentarily, is the rather obvious view that the human, at any stage of development, is something of intrinsic value such that it ought not to be killed or harmed. Much more may be said about this view, but it is a start. And it is enough of a start, enough of an answer, that we can then apply the answer to the *what to do* question of the morality of killing human embryos for the sake of stem cell research.

One might, however, object to this understanding of why abortion is wrong. Perhaps what makes abortion wrong is not that there is something valuable about humans, including early, pre-birth humans. If this were the case, then we could maintain the view that abortion is wrong but that early humans can nevertheless be killed for the sake of experimentation. But what else could it be that would make abortion wrong? Here is one line of thought: the reason we, as Latter-day Saints, consider abortion to be morally wrong is because most cases of abortion follow a person's engaging in violations of the law of chastity; abortion becomes a quick method of avoiding the consequences of sinful behavior, a way of covering up one's wrong. This, and not any special status of early humans, is the reason why abortion is wrong. And if this is the reason why abortion is wrong, then nothing about the wrongness of abortion implies that killing embryonic humans is wrong.

However, if this is a correct account of the wrongness of abortion, then it would follow that it is morally permissible for a married woman who becomes pregnant (from her husband) to have an abortion since, after all, her getting pregnant was not a violation of the law of chastity. This seems plainly false given our LDS view of abortion, yet it is implied by the preceding account of abortion. And so we must reject the view that what makes abortion wrong is that it is typically associated with violations of the law of chastity.

Another line of thought on the wrongness of abortion could be as follows: what makes abortion wrong is not that it involves the killing of an early human, but the reason why one is killing the early human; one kills the early human for convenience. For example, a woman becomes pregnant much earlier than she wants to start having children, and so she chooses to abort. Stem cell research does not involve this sort of convenience, and so the prohibition against abortion does not count against killing embryonic humans since in the case of stem cell research it is done for the sake of medical progress and medical therapy.

This line of thought reveals an interesting strategy since, after all, we do believe that some instances of killing are morally permissible. For example, if I'm brutally and unjustifiably attacked and the only way to defend myself is by taking the life of my attacker, it may very well be morally permissible for me to kill him. My killing would be a case of justified self-defense.

Likewise, soldiers in war are not morally liable, in principle, for the killings they commit in combat situations. If what makes abortion wrong is that one kills for convenience, then perhaps the wrongness of abortion does not imply that the early human has a special status—like humans at other stages—and so ought not, in general, to be killed.

As an explanation for why abortion is wrong, however, this account also has serious problems. First of all, it is surely not convenience alone that makes abortion wrong; after all, there is nothing morally wrong with buying pre-grated cheese because of the convenience that it holds over block cheese that has not been grated. Convenience alone is not sufficient to make some action morally wrong. While I agree that it is wrong to kill someone for the sake of convenience, it is because there is something about the nature of a human being, including an early human being, that makes it wrong to kill it for convenience. So this explanation for the wrongness of abortion does not sidestep my explanation that the wrongness of abortion implies some status to the embryonic human; on the contrary it relies on the embryonic human's having some special status. For that matter, it would be difficult to maintain that all cases of abortion are cases of convenience killing; thus, though convenience as a reason for aborting may be a sufficient condition for its wrongness, it is surely not a necessary condition.

New Avenues for the Justification of Killing Human Embryos

Thus far I've argued that the wrongness of abortion implies that early humans have the same sort of status as post-birth humans, and so it is wrong to kill the former even for the sake of stem cell research. I've also considered objections to this account of the wrongness of abortion. I want to continue this strategy essentially but with a shift in emphasis by leaving behind the attempt to find an alternate explanation for the wrongness of abortion. Frankly, the alternate explanations seem fruitless. Given my LDS commitment to the wrongness of abortion, and killing in general, it is difficult not to concede that because of some moral standing held by human beings, it is wrong to kill humans at any stage: the embryonic, fetal, neonatal, teen, adult, elderly, and so forth. Rather, I will focus on why stem cell research might provide an exception. This is a shift in emphasis because instead of trying to challenge the obvious implication of the wrongness of abortion, I accept the general implication and consider ways in which stem cell research involves an exception to it.

The subject of exceptions warrants explicit discussion. Moral rules are generalizations: they are broad characterizations of how we should act. To claim that they may have exceptions is not to do damage to their truth. Consider the principle that it is wrong to break a promise. Suppose I make a promise to my son that I will come home early from work and play catch with him. But as I walk to my car, a co-worker who is also walking to his car collapses with a heart attack. If I administer CPR, call the paramedics, and stay with him until the paramedics arrive, I will be late getting home and so break my promise to my son. But if I don't help him out—being the only person in the parking lot with him—he will likely die. Surely this is a situation in which it is morally permissible, if not morally good, to break a promise. But this does not mean that the moral rule—it is wrong to break promises—is not true. Part of understanding moral rules is understanding the exceptions they may have. Killing is no different. It is usually considered morally permissible to kill in self-defense if one has no other reasonable means of defending oneself from unjust attack. And so we can grant that it is wrong to kill humans while conceding that there are some exceptions to this. The challenge for killing embryonic humans for the sake of stem cell research, then, is to demonstrate that this is a case of a legitimate exception.

So why might killing an embryonic human for the sake of stem cell research be an exception? One quick argument is that it promises great benefits to humankind; it involves a small sacrifice for the sake of the many; it will relieve the suffering and disability of countless individuals. Certainly this is a motivation to do embryonic stem cell research. But does it justify killing? There are two problems with maintaining that it does. First, it is not clear that it will deliver these great benefits. There is speculation that it will, but it is far from certain. (Consider gene therapy from not so many years ago; it had a similar sort of intense enthusiasm as stem cell research does today, but has failed to deliver on its promises.) I'm not claiming that this alone makes the argument bad—nor am I claiming that we must be absolutely certain that it will provide benefits—but we would have to ensure that there is adequate evidence that it will likely produce significant results before we could make an argument on the basis of benefits. I will not consider this further because there is a more serious problem: normally, we don't think it is morally permissible to kill someone because it will bring benefits to others. Surely medical researchers could move forward the pace of medical advances if we forced persons into medical experiments, including experiments that were likely to cause harm and death to otherwise healthy individuals. That the promise of benefits is morally inadequate to justify experimenting on normal, healthy humans implies that it is inadequate in the case of early humans. In some respects this is one of the more disturbing aspects of the current societal dialogue on the morality embryonic stem cell research: many proponents of embryonic stem cell research advocate the practice merely on the basis of the supposed benefits it will bring, with no mention of who bears the cost of these benefits. But all sorts of immoral practices can bring great benefits to some at the expense of others. In this respect the argument from benefits is not unlike the convenience argument discussed previously. There will have to be something about the early human such that, given that we can get benefits from killing it, it is okay to kill it and experiment on it (though not abort it). But what could this be?

Abandoned Early Humans

One possibility is abandoned human embryos: some human embryos are created and abandoned, and perhaps their being abandoned is the quality that makes permissible death-inducing experimentation on embryonic humans. To put the case of abandoned early humans in a larger context, let's return to cases of morally acceptable cases of experimentation on and use of mature humans. Though I reject abandonment as adequate justification for killing an embryonic human, considering abandonment in this larger context will show that abandoned embryonic humans are the best possible case for justified killing of embryonic humans.

One accepted type of adult human medical experimentation and use of human parts involves the dead; for example, we remove organs from the dead for research (eventually leading to improved medical care). Sometimes the dead can even be used therapeutically: cadaver skin is used on burn victims. This type of human experimentation and use of human parts is problematic in the case of an embryonic human since stem cells need to be alive for embryonic stem cell research. Once the embryonic human is dead, his cells are useless for the research or therapeutic purposes that embryonic stem cell research envisions.

Another accepted type of adult human medical experimentation and use of human parts involves the living, for example, donation of an organ to a person in need, or donation of blood or other tissue samples for a study. Sometimes the tissues are donated by living subjects, and sometimes they are donated just before death where the donor has previously specified that his organs can be harvested if needed. This latter case allows for the donation of essential organs such as the heart.

Here again there appears to be no corresponding cases at the embryonic level. First, embryonic humans cannot merely donate some tissue and yet continue living the way I can when I donate blood. Second, it is simply not clear, empirically, that harvesting cells from a naturally dying (i.e., not being killed by a researcher) embryonic human is even possible. Dying adult humans who have their organs harvested die in circumstances where harvesting is possible: they are in a hospital and their death is sufficiently (perhaps artificially) slow that the organs can be removed and preserved as needed. But typically an embryonic human dies in its mother's uterus. The circumstances of its death—and short embryonic life—just do not allow us, at the last moments of life, to take one or more of its stem cells.

So morally acceptable experimentation on and use of adult humans does not correspond feasibly to embryonic humans and embryonic stem cell research. But the case of embryonic stem cell research opens up possibilities that do not exist at the adult level. For example, while we cannot in any immediate and straightforward sense create, in a controlled environment, an adult human, we can do this very thing with an embryonic human. Using donor sperm and a donor egg, we can create an embryonic human *in vitro*. This artificially created embryonic human could then, in the controlled setting of a laboratory, have its stem cells harvested.

This is one of the more morally troublesome cases of killing embryonic humans for the sake of embryonic stem cell research since it involves creating life with the purpose of killing it to obtain something it has.[11] The first two cases of experimentation (on mature humans) were interesting because the harvested persons were not created for harvesting, and in some cases were naturally expiring or expired; thus the harvesting was not harming them in any way. Where the harvesting or experimentation was a harm, it at least involved the consent of the harvested subject. At present, some embryonic stem cell researchers do in fact create humans *in vitro* for the sake of embryonic stem cell research, and then proceed to harvest their stem cells, thereby killing them. I won't consider this case of obtaining embryonic stem cells, however, because there is a less morally problematic way of obtaining them that also does not correspond to our methods of experimentation on mature humans. This less problematic case involves the use of abandoned embryonic humans.

As it turns out, women who undergo *in vitro* fertilization (IVF) will often create more embryos than are needed for implantation, and the remaining embryos are left frozen.[12] A couple might create a dozen embryos, implant five of them, have a child, and decide they do not want to have any other children. The remaining seven embryos are left frozen. In essence, they are abandoned embryonic humans. They have not been created for the sake of harvesting. But they are not dead (they are preserved, in a state of suspended growth, until they are to be implanted, discarded, or die). This seems like the most likely case for the permissibility of killing embryonic humans since these embryos were created for the very purpose that *in utero* embryos are created (when created purposely), for procreation.

---

11. Many proponents of killing embryos for the sake of stem cell research reject, on moral grounds, creating embryos for the sake of killing them. Instead, they limit themselves to using abandoned embryos.

12. Fertility clinics practice a wide variety of methods for disposing of or caring for left-over embryos. Typically, however, embryos which are created for implantation are frozen (ceasing their development) until the time of implantation. Those which are not implanted, thus abandoned, frequently remain frozen.

As one who values human life at any stage, an initial reaction might be that it is wrong in the first place to create a human without the intent to provide it the opportunity for normal development; this would mean implantation in the case of IVF. (In fact, some fertility clinics will only make as many embryos as the woman intends to implant.) Thus, abandoning embryos that one has created is already to commit a moral wrong. While conception is no guarantee of reaching birth or adult status, artificial conception without implantation is a guarantee of no possibility.

I do not want to consider this issue in detail. In the end, I don't think it matters to the embryonic stem cell debate. Even if it is wrong to create more embryos than one intends to implant, this alone doesn't imply that using the left over embryos for research is wrong. In general, though a certain action may be morally wrong, benefitting from its consequences is not thereby necessarily wrong also (though it may be wrong for other reasons). Consider a scientist who develops a drug that eliminates all cancers and does so with no side effects. However, it turns out that he developed this by forcing over 1000 people into medical experiments, which painfully and unnecessarily cost them their lives. Surely, his behavior was immoral. But it does not follow that we could not use the knowledge he obtained to treat and cure cancer. We might have to take measures to ensure that our using his cure did not further encourage immoral experimentation. But it is difficult to accept that we would have to throw away his work and rediscover the cure for cancer before we could use the results of his experimentation. Likewise, if an embryonic human has been killed and his stem cells harvested, I do not object to experimentation on those stem cells. But I do assert that the act which brought it about was immoral, and any similar such acts to obtain further stem cells would also be immoral.

So even if it is wrong to create more embryos than one will implant, that alone does not make it wrong to use them once they have been created. And given that persons do create more embryos than they use, and in effect abandon them, the embryonic stem cell researcher may have an opportunity to morally obtain embryonic stem cells. That the embryonic human has been abandoned could be that feature which makes for an exception to the principle that it is wrong to kill.

But this view still has serious problems. Even though the embryonic human in this kind of case has been abandoned, we still must kill it in the process of extracting its stem cells. Its being abandoned is not equivalent to its being dead or dying. But one might object: doesn't the fact that the embryo has been abandoned mean that it is *as good as dead*? By using it for its stem cells, we are not depriving it of some future that it will have since it has been abandoned in an embryonic state. It is not as if it has better options; it is not clear that its being in a freezer is a better option. Coming back to the case of abortion, we might think that when a human is aborted it is losing out on its life: it would have been born, raised either by its mother or adoptive parents, had a family of its own, and so forth. But in the case of abandoned embryonic humans, they have no future that they are losing out on by being killed and experimented upon.

But suppose a mother does abandon, as sometimes happens, her baby after birth. Does this alter its moral standing? And suppose a medical researcher finds this baby. Does this mean, being abandoned, that he can now experiment upon it? After all, if left to itself it would quickly die; it has no future without years' worth of help from others. Suppose the baby is so malnourished and sick from being abandoned that it will only live a few more days; we are able to determine that it has no chance of recovery. Since, like the abandoned embryonic human, it will not have any sort of meaningful life, can we use those last few days to experiment upon it?

Intuitively, experimenting on either an abandoned but well baby or an abandoned but dying baby is morally outrageous. But if abandonment of newborns does not allow death-inducing experimentation, why does it do so in the case of abandoned embryonic humans? One might argue: the difference is that we can find a home for the abandoned neonatal, we can find someone who will want to adopt it. In the case of embryonic humans, we don't have persons who want to adopt and implant them. But suppose, for whatever reason, we couldn't find someone to adopt an abandoned neonate: would this really mean, morally, that we could experiment on it? The abandoned but dying baby is perhaps an apt analogy to our responsibility to abandoned embryonic humans. Intuitively, in the case of an abandoned but dying newborn, our responsibility is to comfort it in its death in the same way we would an aged adult human whose life is expiring. Why not view the status of abandoned embryonic humans in the same way? Because we allow them to die without hastening their death for the sake of experimentation.

In the end, abandonment is not enough to justify experimentation, nor is the lack of a meaningful future. There will have to be something about the status of an early human—as opposed to a neonatal human, or elderly human—such that when they are abandoned, it is okay to kill them and do research on them. But given the strong view against abortion that I am accepting in this discussion—and the implication that early humans have a moral standing similar to adult humans—it is hard to see what this could be. One difference in cases of experimentation on adults is consent. The human experimented upon, or who donates his tissues or parts for another, gives his informed consent. Informed consent allows one to be experimented upon notwithstanding one's moral standing. But as with infants and children, informed consent is not something that can happen in the case of embryonic humans. Of course at times experimental procedures are used on infants and children. But this is done when it is in the best interest of the subject: other treatments have failed and the experimental treatment, if successful, will benefit the subject. We can't assume that embryonic humans would consent to being the subjects of embryonic stem cell research since they obviously do not benefit from it.

This concludes my stronger argument against embryonic stem cell research. Essentially, given our beliefs about abortion, it follows that the embryonic human has a moral status such that it ought not to be killed.[13] As for the impermissibility of killing in general, there may be exceptions. But killing for the sake of research does not appear to be one of them. To the extent that some kinds of embryonic stem cell research depend on killing embryonic humans, then those particular undertakings are morally wrong.[14]

A Weaker Argument Against Killing Embryonic Humans

In this section I argue for a weaker conclusion against embryonic stem cell research. It draws heavily on my argument for the stronger conclusion

---

13. One might raise the objection that the LDS view against abortion allows for exceptions such as rape or the likely death of the mother. Thus, if some killings are permissible, one might argue that the wrongness of abortion cannot be based on some moral standing of the early human since these exceptional cases of abortion would likewise be impermissible. The problem, however, is that these exceptional cases provide clear instances of conflicts of (moral) rights. The mother who will die if she carries her baby to term may be justified in having an abortion because even though the baby has a moral standing, that is, a moral right to life, so does the mother. Since the mother's life is threatened, and she is capable of preventing it, it is permissible for her to stop the one causing the death, even though it has a moral standing and even though it will bring about the death of the child. The problem for stem cell research, however, is that abandoned embryos are in no way threatening the lives or livelihood of anyone.

14. This does not imply, as I've tried to clarify, that it would necessarily be wrong to experiment on embryonic stem cells that one took no part in obtaining. (This is the reasoning underlying the federal government's current policy on funding for research on embryonic stem cells.) Though the wrongness of the killing does not necessarily imply that it would be wrong to use the stem cells that such killing makes available, it would certainly prohibit one's encouraging or indirectly bring about such killings.

but does so in a way that constructs a more positive account of the status of early humans. In general, I've assumed that it is wrong to kill humans. And given LDS views on abortion, this principle appears to extend to early humans.[15] There are some exceptions to this principle, but I don't see that experimentation—even for good purposes on abandoned subjects—is one of them. The resulting positive view is that it is wrong to kill humans at any stage for the sake of medical experimentation. Although medical experimentation is important and has brought and will yet bring many great and widespread benefits and the relief of significant suffering, there is a limit to what can morally be done in its pursuit. That there are limits should come as no surprise, for we readily accept that it would be wrong to force adult humans into life-threatening experiments. Though IVF has made the opportunity for experimentation on embryonic humans possible, this does not mean that such experimentation does not cross the line for morally acceptable research.

Still, there may be more arguments, more possible exceptions to consider. I do grant that the principle that it is wrong to kill has exceptions, and perhaps I have simply not found the right one. My weaker conclusion, then, is that the burden of proof is on one who accepts the wrongness of abortion and wants to kill embryonic humans to show that it is justified. Given the importance of life, and given the importance of the principle of not killing, the burden must be fulfilled with some degree of definitiveness. In particular, the following claims must be reconciled:

1. Abortion is morally wrong.
2. It is wrong to kill adults, children, infants for experimentation, even when they have been abandoned or may be dying.
3. Nothing about the status of embryonic humans makes it wrong to kill abandoned ones for the sake of experimentation that will not benefit them.

Two things can make it difficult to see this burden of proof. One is our great excitement at the promise of medical advancement. In the case of stem cell research, publicly this excitement often takes the form of the spouse or parent of the infirm urging the need for stem cell research (to the exclusion of other considerations). But our moral health and well-being is just as important, indeed, more important, than our physical health and well-being. Though the benefits may be great, they should not distort our assessment of the moral issues that may be relevant. That benefits may ob-

---

15. See footnote 13 for a discussion of exceptions.

scure relevant moral concerns is certainly not unique to issues of health, but they do seem particularly strong in these cases.

Two, early humans are an easy target. It would be far more difficult to force experimentation on adult humans. Those with a voice, and with power in a community, can speak out against abuse. Abandoned early humans, and even newborns, infants, and children, have no voice of their own. But defense of the innocent may be one of our most important ethical responsibilities. I'm not claiming that the appearance of innocence or the lack of a voice imply moral standing, only that such cases require especial prudence.

One might object to the preceding claims as grossly impractical, or merely "academic." After all, as many have said, we are talking about a "clump of cells," not a human, not a person; merely a bunch of cells that, if manipulated, may provide great benefits to the many. Further, it is simply difficult, perhaps impossible, to see that there is something wrong with using an abandoned clump of cells in a freezer; indeed, we might think it is a waste not to use them for something good. There are two responses to this. First, this objection brings us back to where we started: if we accept that abortion is wrong, then we cannot dismiss early humans as mere clumps of cells with no moral standing (otherwise, "what is wrong with abortion? It's just a clump of cells that's growing in your body?"). As a Latter-day Saint, my most fundamental beliefs about my life, my place in the universe, and what I am to be doing (and not doing) are not impractical or academic; indeed, they define who I am, and the ideal community for which I strive.

Second, we engage in so-called "wasteful" and "impractical" behavior already, and we do so for moral reasons. Consider the case of the elderly infirm.

An increasing number of our population ages to the point where their life continues in otherwise undesirable circumstances, experiencing a significant loss of independence, physical, and mental capacity. What are we to do with them? One practice is to put them in convalescence homes—at great expense and, from some perspectives, at great waste. Why do this? Why not use them—their bodies, their organs—for some good? The ideal entity with moral standing—the ideal characterization of a person—is the healthy, well-behaved, rational adult human with a meaningful future. The severely infirm elderly fall short of this standard, but we accord them moral standing because we recognize their connection with this ideal.

Consider also the severely mentally retarded and others who are severely handicapped. They too will, in many cases, fall short of any meaningful standard of personhood. Yet, our practice is to accord them the same rights and privileges as healthy, well-developed persons. Add to these groups the clinically insane: those who have so declined in their rational, mental capacity that they must be institutionalized. Is it a waste to prolong and provide for their lives in institutions that most of us never see or experience? I suppose in some sense it appears to be a waste. But from another point of view it shows respect for their being part of the human species, part of the group to which we accord moral standing even though not all members meet, as individuals, the standard of personhood. We can add to these groups much of the prison population: groups of persons whose immoral and antisocial behavior leads us to strip them of many of the rights that most persons enjoy. Is it a waste to lock someone up for life in prison, without the possibility of parole? Would it be better to kill them, to save the money, to harvest their body parts, to use them for experiments? From a certain point of view this seems enticing. But as with all these examples, our practice is to accord them adequate moral standing that we do not take their lives.

The standard of personhood, and hence moral standing, has been extensively debated among philosophers and done so without clear consensus. The ideal standard of personhood is something like the well-developed rational creature, such as an adult human. But how, then, do we integrate infants, adolescences, the elderly, and so forth? Our current practice, with the exception of abortion in many countries, is to grant any human moral standing. While this does not show that killing embryos is wrong, it shows that the claims of waste are hardly unique or out of the ordinary. Further, it shows a consistency in respecting the lives of abandoned embryos, the violation of which requires significant argument for why it should not apply to other categories of marginalized humans.

Conclusion

I began this paper with the express purpose of considering the matter of embryonic stem cell research and, in particular, the ethics of killing an embryonic human for the sake of stem cell research. More broadly, however, I wanted to give an example of how I integrate my LDS beliefs into my thinking about ethical matters. Aside from the correctness or incorrectness of my conclusion, I've hoped to show the relative ease by which this integration can occur. In fact, attempting to ignore or exclude my LDS beliefs from some matter of ethical import would seem to be more difficult and problematic. Sometimes our LDS beliefs will give us fairly direct guidance on matters of right and wrong. Other times—as in the case of embryonic stem cell research—they will give us points of departure which we may use in coming to a conclusion.

Having made these arguments on the ethics of embryonic stem cell research, none of this should be taken to imply that I believe myself to have complete or irrefutable knowledge on these matters. Further, my appeal to LDS beliefs should not be taken to imply doctrinal conclusions: in no way am I claiming that, even if my argument is correct, my conclusions should be considered canonical since they draw on established doctrine. My claims and my methods are far more ordinary. We make judgments and act according to the light and knowledge we acquire through our study and faith: if confronted with a question about the ethics of some behavior, we do our best to think through it and come to a conclusion. And yet, we may learn more that is relevant to the question, and God may reveal other information indirectly or directly relevant to it, including knowledge that will show our original conclusion, or my argument and conclusion in this case, to be problematic. This same attitude of openness by which we think through our revealed beliefs to come to a decision on a matter of morality should lead us in a spirit of openness to further light and knowledge on any of these matters.

In "Becoming a Person," Sariah Cottrell and Steven Peck use scientific and medical practice as well as church teachings to examine stem cell research. Since the creation and the completion of life are two of the most important and beautiful events in earthly existence, as a church we have strong commitments toward related issues and should approach them with great care. "Embryonic stem cell research" is unique because it "involves both the giving and taking of life; it encompasses both ends of the spectrum of earthly existence." If researching cells from embryos were the same as murder in the name of science, this research would clearly be wrong. But they claim that "to say 'Stem cell research is murder' is too simplistic, [failing to] address the myriad of questions within this field of research." Since embryos for embryonic stem cell research primarily come from donations from *in vitro* fertilization, they discuss the ethical permissibility of stem cell research from an LDS perspective in light of the things that may be done to or with the embryos. They argue that "donating embryos is far preferable to discarding embryos or allowing embryos to remain frozen indefinitely" and may "have a permanent effect on the wellbeing of mankind." Since the question largely hinges on the point at which the embryo becomes a person, they discuss several different options in light of LDS teachings and conclude that "embryos used in embryonic stem cell research come from cells fertilized in a test tube, and [without a mother's womb] have no potential to become anything other than cells. These embryos are bodies without spirits: they are not human souls. It is not murder to harvest cells from these embryos. No potential is destroyed; in fact, potential is being created, for these cells hold numerous possibilities for bettering the life of mankind."

Eighteen

Becoming a Person: Stem Cells and LDS Teachings

Sariah Cottrell and Steven L. Peck

Toying with life and death is a dangerous business. Recent scholarship demonstrates how deeply Mormon views are conditioned by our understanding of life and death and its relation to the eternities.[1] Be it creating life or ending it, it is a weighty thing when we attempt to influence the existence or non-existence of a child of God outside of His system and direction. We know that the creation of life and the completion of life are two of the most important and beautiful events in earthly existence. Two of the Ten Commandments are dedicated to these ideas: "Thou shalt not commit adultery" and "Thou shalt not kill." Is it any wonder, then, that as a church we have very strong commitments toward anything that might involve either of these great themes? Is it any surprise that we meet issues of this kind with anxiety?

Because of the blessings we enjoy as our knowledge of the world increases, we have many difficult issues unique to our day. The issue of embryonic stem cell research is one of these. Interestingly, this issue involves both the giving and taking of life; it encompasses both ends of the spectrum of earthly existence. At first glance, some conclude that researching cells from embryos is the same as murder in the name of science. If this is right, then this research would certainly be wrong. That makes us hesitate. Fortunately, such is not likely the case. Embryonic stem cell research is a much, much bigger issue than this, and to say "Stem cell research is murder" is too simplistic, because it does not address the myriad of questions within this field of research. Here we will explain what embryonic stem cell research is, why it is an issue, and investigate how we can reconcile the resulting moral questions with our unique Latter-day Saint perspective.

---

1. Samuel M. Brown, *In Heaven as It Is on Earth: Joseph Smith and the Early Mormon Conquest of Death* (New York: Oxford University Press, 2012).

What Are Stem Cells? What Does "Embryonic" Mean?

Cells are the smallest unit of life, and every living thing consists of one or more cells. In this article, "cells" will refer exclusively to "human cells." There are different types of cells in humans, and they all have different tasks: a muscle cell's task is to contract, a neuron's task is to pass along information, etc. A neuron cannot contract like a muscle cell because it is already specialized (or differentiated) for its specific function in the nervous system.

Stem cells are unspecialized, which means they have the ability to develop into many different types of cells. Our bodies use stem cells constantly: in our intestines and bone marrow, stem cells regularly divide to repair and replace worn-out or damaged tissues.

The two main sources of stem cells we will discuss here are embryonic stem cells and somatic (or adult) stem cells. *Embryonic* stem cells come from an embryo, meaning the beginning stages of development after an egg is fertilized. Embryonic stem cells are remarkable because they can become any of the more than two hundred types of cells found in humans; the same embryonic stem cell has the potential to become a cell in the heart, brain, taste bud, or kneecap. Somatic (adult) stem cells have significantly less potential than embryonic stem cells, because they can each only specialize into a limited handful of cell types. These include bone marrow, cord blood, and intestinal cells, among others. Somatic stem cells are commonly applied in medical procedures to replace or regenerate tissues that are damaged as a regenerative therapy. Although somatic stem cells are routinely used safely and effectively, they do not have the same broad potential as embryonic stem cells for future medical advancements.

What Do We Use Stem Cells For? What Potential Do They Hold?

We study stem cells not only because we hope to learn about cellular processes, we also use these cells to treat diseases and provide regenerative therapy. The remarkable potential of embryonic stem cells renders them more useful than somatic stem cells for achieving these goals. Embryonic stem cells have an especially promising role in therapies for the treatment of major human diseases and disorders.[2] The evidence indicates that, at

---

2. Mi. Stojkovic, M. Lako, T. Strachan, and A. Murdoch, "Derivation, Growth and Applications of Human Embryonic Stem Cells," *Reproduction* 128, no. 3 (September 2004): 259–67.

this time, research on embryonic stem cells holds a great deal more promise than research on adult stem cells.[3]

Embryonic stem cell research has three specific areas of promise: (1) the study of human biological development, (2) testing of new and existing drugs and compounds, and (3) the cultivation of different types of cells, tissues, and organs.[4] Each has great potential to impact our lives, but the third area of promise causes the most excitement. If we were able to cultivate artificial human tissue, this would open up possibilities for reducing rejection of transplanted tissues and deal with shortages of necessary tissues for those needing organ or tissue transplants, as well as provide a means to repair significant damage that might otherwise result in severe disabilities or death.[5]

Literally billions of lives could be affected, improved, or saved through advances achieved through embryonic stem cell research. Many scientists agree that stem cell therapies will be critical for treating heart disease, cancer, and degenerative diseases of aging, including Parkinson's disease. Over half the world's population "will suffer at some point in life with one of these three conditions. . . . Stem cell research is a pursuit of known and important moral goods."[6] To arrive at these promising ends, scientists must take and use cells from embryos. Some perceive this as "killing" a person (i.e., the person the embryo can no longer become). However, this initial perception is neither reasonable nor true.

Stem cells have a great potential for helping humans fulfill Christ's directive to clothe the naked and visit the sick (Matt. 25:34–36), which has always been one of the guiding tenets of our church. Mankind as a whole has likewise held service and compassion in the highest regard, as seen in the Hippocratic Oath. Both "the Western ethic of rescue and the practical structure of contemporary health care and other social institutions make it clear that among the deepest moral habits of human life is that of compassion for the sick and vulnerable."[7] It is our duty as Christians to be

---

3. *Congressional Record*, 2006, p. S7659.

4. O. Baune, et al., "The Moral Status of Human Embryos with Special Regard to Stem Cell Research and Therapy," in *Stem Cells, Human Embryos and Ethics: Interdisciplinary Perspectives*, ed. L. Ostnor (New York: Springer, 2008), 1–18.

5. M. Bobbert, "Human Embryos and Embryonic Stem Cells - Ethical Aspects," in *Stem Cells, Human Embryos and Ethics: Interdisciplinary Perspectives*, ed. L. Ostnor (New York: Springer, 2008), 237–50.

6. G. McGee and A. Caplan, "The Ethics and Politics of Small Sacrifices in Stem Cell Research," *Kennedy Institute of Ethics Journal* 9, no. 2 (1999): 154.

7. Ibid., 153.

charitable. The Hippocratic Oath sworn by Western doctors includes the obligation to "respect the hard-won scientific gains of those physicians in whose steps I walk" and the promise to "apply, for the benefit of the sick, all measures [that] are required . . . [and to] prevent disease whenever I can, for prevention is preferable to cure."[8] These last two obligations reflect the modern medical ethics of beneficence (promoting the wellbeing of others) and non-maleficence (doing no harm). This oath means that doctors must respect and cannot dismiss scientific knowledge of the medical field, much of which has and likely will result from stem cell research. It also means that doctors support preventative medicine and methods, which stem cell research will certainly lead to. And most importantly, it means that doctors will do all that they can to help those in their care. These obligations are heavy indeed if one views stem cell research as unethical; it invites the utilitarian question of greater good: which is more important, all the good that can be done through the research, or the potential for harm to the embryo? Of course, if there are reasons to believe that real harm is being done in this research to living persons, the question of its benefits will be outweighed by the rights of that being. So the question must be answered: who or what is harmed, and in what way? It is to that question we now turn.

What Exactly Is the Issue?

The cells being researched in embryonic stem cell research come from an embryo. The conflict comes from the question of whether embryos are people, and whether it is killing a person to take embryonic cells for research. To understand the answers to this, it is important to understand and investigate the implications of: (1) the source of the embryos providing the stem cells, (2) when life begins, and (3) if scientists are killing people when researching embryonic stem cells.

1. Where Do Embryos Come From?

Embryos for embryonic stem cell research primarily come from donations from IVF (*in vitro* fertilization) clinics. Embryos used in stem cell research coming from IVF clinics do *not* come from aborted fetuses or

---

8. Peter Tyson, "The Hippocratic Oath Today," *NOVA beta*, March 27, 2001, http://www.pbs.org/wgbh/nova/body/hippocratic-oath-today.html (accessed June 19, 2013).

from eggs fertilized in a woman's body;[9] they come from surplus embryos slated for destruction at IVF clinics.

Infertile couples who want to have children have several options available to them, including IVF treatments to help the couple conceive. *In vitro* literally means "in glass," meaning in a test tube or an artificial environment *outside* of a living organism. *In vitro* fertilization is a technique where an egg is fertilized in a lab, an artificial and external environment. The fertilized eggs are then transferred into the mother's uterus. IVF is expensive: including medications, the simplest IVF process runs around $10,000,[10] and this is excluding any of the other diagnostic or analytical processes the couple will have already undergone prior to commencing IVF.

Pregnancy is not guaranteed through IVF, so several eggs are fertilized for each couple during IVF treatment in the event that either the attempt is unsuccessful or should patients want additional children in the future. Couples may preserve these embryos for future use by freezing and then storing them through embryo cryopreservation, with a starting rate of $1,000, and an annual cost of about $400 after the first year.[11] While this is expensive, it is much cheaper than undergoing the entire IVF process again should the couple want more children later. In 2002 there were nearly 400,000 frozen embryos in storage in the United States.[12] Occasionally, genetic screening tests on these test tube embryos reveal severe genetic disorders, and the couple selects another embryo. These embryos in particular will never be used by the couple for children—the purpose of the IVF clinic was to exclude embryos of this kind. These embryos, as well as other unneeded embryos, provide the couple with an ethical dilemma. When people have a surplus of embryos they do not need or want, they must choose between donating the embryos to other couples, discarding them, donating them for stem cell research, or paying to keep them frozen in storage indefinitely.[13]

---

9. "Stem Cell Basics," National Institutes of Health, http://stemcells.nih.gov/info/basics/Pages/Default.aspx (accessed June 18, 2013).

10. "Pricing Guidelines," University of Utah Healthcare, http://healthcare.utah.edu/ucrm/pricing/index.php (accessed November 14, 2011).

11. Ibid.

12. D.I. Hoffman, et al., "Cryopreserved Embryos in the United States and their Availability for Research," *Fertility and Sterility* 79, no. 5 (2003): 1063–69.

13. S. Bangsboll, et al., "Patients' Attitudes Towards Donation of Surplus Cryopreserved Embryos for Treatment or Research," *Human Reproduction* 19, no. 10 (2004): 2415–19.

Viewpoints opposing embryonic stem cell research overlook the significance of the origin of these cells. Some say that donating these embryos to research equates to murder, and is the equivalent of abortion, but abortion deals with fetuses (more developed than embryos) inside a woman's womb, while stem cells donations involve embryos that were never and will never be in a womb. These IVF embryos slated for destruction do not have the potential to become people because they will never be transferred to a uterus. Former Senator Connie Mack, a pro-life Catholic, said: "For me, as long as that fertilized egg is not destined to be placed in a uterus, it cannot become life."[14] In fertility treatments, there will inevitably be test tube embryos that are not needed and which will never be placed in a uterus. These embryos do not have the potential to become people if left in a test tube where there is no place for them to grow and develop, so of their own accord, these embryos lack all potential to become persons.

Let's investigate the above listed three alternatives for surplus embryos. Donating an embryo to another couple could be a way to avoid destroying the embryos outright, possibly seen as a form of adoption, but the LDS Church Handbook "strongly discourages in vitro fertilization using semen from anyone but the husband or an egg from anyone but the wife."[15] So while donating embryos is a definite and real option, it is not necessarily consistent with church standards. Discarding embryos is to destroy them permanently as biohazardous waste. Discarding one's embryos seems to be the worst of these options: the embryo has no promise to ever become a person nor to ever be useful to mankind if it is disposed of. Keeping embryos frozen indefinitely may seem like postponing the couple's decision, but during the time the couple is not using those embryos it is just as surely preventing the embryos from becoming people as discarding them. There is far less controversy against the costly freezing of embryos than there is against stem cell research, yet arguably, cryopreservation is no more ethical.

If, instead of discarding embryos or preventing embryonic development, couples donate those embryos to research, those cells that will never become people have a great potential to be of permanent, lasting use to mankind. There is good reason to believe that this research is "necessary to develop

---

14. M. Z. Wahrman, *Brave New Judaism: When Science and Scripture Collide* (Hanover, N.H.: University Press of New England for Brandeis University Press, 2002), 59.

15. "Selected Church Policies and Guidelines," in *Handbook 2: Administering the Church*, 21.4.7, https://www.lds.org/handbook/handbook-2-administering-the-church/selected-church-policies?lang=eng#21.4 (accessed June 19, 2013).

cures for life-threatening or severely debilitating diseases . . . when appropriate protections and oversight are in place in order to prevent abuse."[16]

To argue against embryonic stem cell research is, in part, to argue against IVF treatment. We, as a church, clearly do not contend that IVF is an immoral practice. Senator Orrin Hatch, an LDS Senator from Utah, reported to the Senate in 2006 that at that time, "over 200,000 Americans [had] been born through this technique [IVF] that is widely accepted today."[17] Hundreds of thousands of Americans exist *because* of this process. Our church is known for our emphasis on families, and accordingly, Utah has a high number of fertility clinics to help couples conceive, many of which provide IVF. In 2011, in just one of the IVF infertility clinics in Utah, 513 cycles were started, meaning that process of IVF (medications, egg and sperm retrieval, fertilization, and embryo transfer) was begun 513 times.[18] Clearly, using fertility clinics is not found immoral by the Church or even America, as seen in these levels of IVF activity. Since the IVF process is designed to produce excess embryos, any evaluation of IVF needs to address the use of all embryos produced. Senator Hatch told the Senate, "It seems to me that you would have to believe that the in vitro fertilization process was unethical to begin with if you believe that it is unethical to use spare embryos that would never be used for fertility purposes and were slated for routine destruction."[19]

Donating embryos for research actually "lend[s] permanence to the embryo" because the only unique part of an embryo, in terms of its cellular components, is the recombined DNA from the father and mother.[20] In an embryo conceived naturally, if it survives to birth, the DNA of that embryo is what directs and defines the identity of that person. The stem cells harvested to form cell lines each contain "in dormant form, the full component of embryonic DNA. The DNA in the cell lines has a much greater chance of continuing to exist through many years than does the DNA of a frozen embryo (which in most cases already will have been slated for destruction by the IVF clinic that facilitated the donation, and which would have no bet-

---

16. *Ethical Issues in Human Stem Cell Research*, Vol. 1 (Rockville, Md.: National Bioethics Advisory Commission, 1999), 52.
17. *Congressional Record*, 2006, p. S7659.
18. "Clinic Summary Report: Reproductive Care Center (Sandy, Utah)," Society for Assisted Reproductive Technology, https://www.sartcorsonline.com/rptCSR_PublicMultYear.aspx?ClinicPKID=2080 (accessed June 19, 2013).
19. *Congressional Record*, 2006, p. S7660.
20. McGee and Caplan, "Ethics and Politics," 154–55.

ter than a 5–10 percent chance of successful implantation in any event)."[21] Donating embryos to research not only prevents permanent destruction of the genetic identity of that individual, but provides that unique genetic material with a far greater chance for existing indefinitely as a contribution to the quality and length of human life. Donating embryos is far preferable to discarding embryos or allowing embryos to remain frozen indefinitely because the embryo's identity will not be lost, but may rather have a permanent effect on the wellbeing of mankind.

Part of the question about the use of embryos centers around the question of when life begins. A brief exploration of this shows that LDS thought contains no fixed doctrine on this issue that might be used as a pivot point for considering how this question is answered.

2. When Does Life Begin?

The National Bioethics Advisory Commission presented a thorough review of the ethical issues of human stem cell research to President Clinton in 1998, wherein they determined:

> The fundamental argument of those who oppose the destruction of human embryos is that these embryos are human beings and, as such, have a right to life. The very humanness of the embryo is thus thought to confer the moral status of a person. . . . Although it is not clear that those who advance this view are able to establish the point at which, if ever, embryos first acquire the moral status of persons, those who oppose the destruction of embryos likewise fail to establish, in a convincing manner, why society should ascribe the status of persons to human embryos.[22]

We can safely say, then, that the main point of this controversy is rooted in this question: *when does life begin*? But that question is confusing. Are we asking at what stage we are dealing with living matter? The answer is: we are dealing with living matter at all stages. All cells are living. The egg and the sperm that formed the embryo were living. At no point was the embryo or its constituents not living. In that case, are we asking at what stage does the embryo become a human? Again, the answer is at all stages. The egg and sperm themselves were human, came from a human, contained one copy of a human genome; the cellular material and DNA never stopped being human. So the question becomes, when does the life of *what* begin?[23]

---

21. Ibid., 155.
22. *Ethical Issues in Human Stem Cell Research*, 50–51.
23. A. Kenny, "The Beginning of Individual Human Life," in *Stem Cells, Human*

The question here is not a question about being human or a question of being alive: it is about personhood. We want to know when living human cells become a person.

This question has had variety of answers in different areas of the world and in different religions. Historically, in some cultures, you were not a person until you had been alive for a year or more. An important rabbinic text in Judaism indicates that the individual human life begins when a child's head emerges from the womb.[24] Some Stoics believed that just as life ends when we draw our last breath, it begins when we draw our first breath. A statement of the Prophet Muhammad is understood by Muslim scholars to mean that the soul is breathed into the embryo at 120 days, at which point the embryo becomes a person.[25] Since 1869, the dominant position of Roman Catholics has been that life begins at conception. Further study of the history of the topic "makes it abundantly clear that there is no such thing as *the* Christian consensus on the timing of the origin of the human individual."[26] Most of Western society believes it is somewhere between conception and birth.

The Church has unique doctrine surrounding what is meant by "life," as regarding the essence of a soul. We believe that our soul is our spirit and our body together. Neither the body without the spirit, nor the spirit without the body, as it were. Both the Old Testament and the Pearl of Great Price tell us that God "formed man from the dust of the ground, and breathed into his nostrils the breath of life; and man became a living soul" (Gen. 2:7, Moses 3:7). For us, personhood is the creation of a soul, or the union of the spirit and body. We existed long before conception or birth, and our existence does not cease after physical death. We are eternal spirit children of God; one of the purposes for our mortality is to obtain a body. For members of the Church of Jesus Christ of Latter-day Saints, the question is not *when does life begin*, but more specifically, *when does the spirit enter the body?*

Unfortunately, this question cannot easily be answered by a simple appeal to statements by Church leaders. Just as there were a number of

---

Embryos and Ethics: Interdisciplinary Perspectives, ed. L. Ostnor (New York: Springer, 2008), 167–76.

24. Ibid.

25. T. Eich, "Decision-Making Processes Among Contemporary 'Ulama': Islamic Embryology and the Discussion of Frozen Embryos," in *Muslim Medical Ethics: From Theory to Practice*, ed. J. E. Brockopp and T. Eich (Columbia, S.C.: University of South Carolina Press, 2008), 298.

26. Kenny, "The Beginning of Individual Human Life," 169.

answers to the beginning of life question outside the Church, there are also many answers within the Church. A deeper investigation of the issue in Church history and revelation reveals many answers which seem to fall into three main categories. The words of Church leaders support three main possibilities for when "life begins," or when the spirit enters the body: at conception, at or immediately prior to birth, or at some point in between the two.

At Conception. Personhood beginning at conception is the most relevant of these options in terms of the embryonic stem cell issue. If life begins at birth, or significantly after conception (i.e., when the embryo has developed into a fetus and is no longer an embryo), then the issue is closed: it is not killing a person if an embryo is not a person. It is only *if* personhood begins at or very close to conception (or fertilization) that embryonic stem cell research is problematic. We will therefore spend more time investigating the implications of personhood beginning at fertilization than the other options.

The idea of personhood beginning at conception has unreasonable implications. This position of personhood is supported by Elder Nelson, of the Quorum of the Twelve Apostles, who wrote: "I learned that a new life begins when two special cells unite to become one cell, bringing together 23 chromosomes from the father and 23 from the mother."[27] We do not disagree with Elder Nelson's statement: at conception, an embryo is a living cell. However, if this were the time when personhood absolutely and unequivocally began, what does that mean for miscarriages? It is estimated that approximately half of all pregnancies will result in miscarriage, largely before the mother even knows she's pregnant. This can occur before or after implantation of the embryo in the uterus.[28] That means that if personhood begins at conception, approximately *half* of God's children have never had an earthly existence. The two main purposes for our mortal experience are to get a body and to be tested; we might ask, would God have designed a plan that excluded this many of his children from participating?

The other unnerving implication of fertilization is the commencement of life involves our own responsibilities for the lives of others. Some forms of contraception do not prevent fertilization, but rather prevent implanta-

---

27. Russell M. Nelson, "Abortion: An Assault on the Defenseless," *Ensign*, October 2008, 35–36.

28. A. J. Wilcox, D. D. Baird, and C. R. Wenberg, "Time of Implantation of the Conceptus and Loss of Pregnancy," *New England Journal of Medicine* 340, no. 23 (1999): 1796–99.

tion of the zygote (the one cell resulting from fertilization) into the uterine wall. If personhood begins when sperm and egg unite, then deliberately acting in a way that will prevent that embryo from developing into a full human body could be considered murder. Additionally, most miscarriages (also known as spontaneous abortions) are caused by chromosomal problems that make development of the embryo impossible, but other miscarriages result from either physiological or behavioral traits of the mother. Physiological maternal factors include hormonal imbalances, problems with reproductive organs, maternal age, or disease. Behavioral factors contributing to miscarriages include substance abuse as well as other lifestyles more commonly engaged in by Church members: malnutrition, obesity, excessive exposure to certain toxic substances, or extreme physical activities that would result in trauma to the mother or the fetus. If a woman miscarries because she has been eating unhealthily or she engages in extreme activity, and if personhood begins at conception, is she guilty of destroying a person? Since most miscarriages happen very early on in pregnancy, a mother could not even know she is pregnant and be killing unknowingly.

Fortunately, Heavenly Father does not trick us into sin. It is not reasonable to think he would allow us to be responsible for such a grand scale of "killing" without it having been a choice on our part. Agency is key in his plan; would he allow such a great number of us to ignorantly commit and be held accountable for one of the most serious sins? If these are the consequences of personhood beginning at fertilization, then surely that is not the time when personhood truly begins. Embryos from IVF fall into this category, and if naturally conceived embryos are not persons at conception, then neither are artificially fertilized embryos persons at fertilization.

At or Immediately Prior to Birth. The second option is that life begins at birth or just prior to birth, which is supported by some of the Brethren, but opposed by others. Theodore M. Burton of the first Quorum of the Seventy said that "when the body is prepared and the spirit enters the body, a living soul is created ready for birth. Without that spirit . . . the creation process would not be complete."[29] This means that a body must be prepared prior to the spirit entering that body, so an embryo is not a person because it is not a body yet; it is a mass of cells. The creation process of a person is not complete without the spirit.

---

29. Theodore M. Burton, "A Born-Again Christian," in *Speeches* (Provo, Utah: Brigham Young University, 1982), 3.

In the Church, temple ordinances are not performed for stillborn children.[30] This is different than the temple ordinances that are not performed for children who died before the age of eight; in the case of stillborn children, though we still keep records of them in our family history, these children are not sealed to their families. While some Church leaders have stated that parents will get to raise their stillborn children in the future, the Church's stance on temple ordinances suggests that stillborn children did not have their spirits enter their bodies and are therefore not complete souls nor are complete persons. This also forestalls the idea that personhood began any time at all before birth: if this is true, then embryos are certainly safe from the potential to be killed because they are definitely not persons if personhood begins at birth.[31]

At Some Point Between Conception and Birth. The third option is that life begins somewhere between conception and birth, perhaps the most vague and yet prevalent opinion. Instead of a specific point, this opinion encompasses anywhere within the many months of pregnancy. This opinion provides a slippery slope because it is easy to hedge back to the personhood at conception idea: if we do not know at what point embryos become people, we can avoid crossing that line if we assume life begins at conception. Fortunately, while some Church leaders are extremely vague about at what point this is, some leaders give opinions that still exclude embryos from personhood.

Bruce R. McConkie and Joseph Fielding Smith both give quotes to support a vague sense of post-conception, pre-birth personhood, while Brigham Young is more specific. Elder McConkie advocates "the concept that the eternal spirit enters the body prior to a normal birth."[32] In 1954, Joseph Fielding Smith stated in his controversial book, *Man: His Origin and Destiny*, that "the body of a man enters upon its career as a tiny germ or embryo, which becomes an infant, quickened at a certain stage by the spirit whose tabernacle it is, and the child, after being born, develops into a man."[33] Brigham Young's more detailed, yet inexact statement is: "When

---

30. *Member's Guide to Temple and Family History Work* (Salt Lake City: Church of Jesus Christ of Latter-day Saints, 2009), 31.

31. The conclusions of this option also include the possibility of a spirit being increasingly inside a fetus as birth approaches but not being permanently tied to a body until its birth.

32. Bruce R. McConkie, *Mormon Doctrine*, 2nd ed. (Salt Lake City: Bookcraft, 1966), 768.

33. Joseph Fielding Smith, *Man: His Origin and Destiny* (Salt Lake City: Deseret News Press, 1954), 354.

the mother feels life come to her infant, it is the spirit entering the body preparatory to the immortal existence."[34] Many today agree with this idea that when the infant's movements are perceptible, it is then a distinct individual separate from the mother, and the spirit has entered that body.

In the world today, many people consider the beginning of personhood to be fourteen days after conception. Philosophically, this has a great deal of merit. In its early days, the cells of a zygote or embryo can become something that is not a human being (the placenta arises from the fertilized egg alongside the embryo), something that is one human being, or something that may be more than one human being (identical twins). It is therefore difficult to say that the fertilized egg itself is an individual, because it is at least also the placenta (not a person) and possibly could become more than one person. Before the placenta and zygote are separated, you cannot say that an embryo is "a person" because it is a person and a placenta. Up until day 14, a zygote may still split to become identical twins, so it is impossible to say that before day 14 an embryo is "a person" because it may well be two or three people. After day 14, this is no longer an option, so the earliest you could say an embryo is, for sure, *a person*, is at that point, which excludes personhood beginning at the time of fertilization. Counting embryos is not the same as counting human beings.[35]

Embryos from IVF clinics are far too "young" to be considered people, according to these ideas of personhood beginning between conception and birth.

3. Are Scientists Killing People When Researching Embryonic Stem Cells?

It appears that the argument for the beginning of personhood at fertilization is the only definition that would qualify such research as killing. This is not consistent with the Plan of Salvation. But even if we were to proceed with the assumption that personhood *did* begin at conception, the principle does not necessarily apply to the embryos involved in stem cell research because of where they come from. These discussions of when personhood begins generally refer to naturally conceived individuals, but embryonic stem cells come from surplus IVF clinic embryos, so the differences between natural conception and artificial fertilization is an additional factor in deciding whether scientists are killing people when researching embryonic stem cells.

---

34. As quoted in McConkie, *Mormon Doctrine*, 354.
35. Kenny, "The Beginning of Individual Human Life."

Senator Hatch succinctly describes the relevancy of the origin of embryonic stem cells when considering the ethics of this research:

> When I considered the question of the moral status of stem cells created for, but no longer needed in, the in-vitro fertilization process, I did so from a long and fervently held pro-life philosophy.
>
> After much thought, reflection, and prayer, I concluded that life begins in, and requires, a nurturing womb.
>
> Human life does not begin in a Petri dish. I do not question that an embryo is a living cell. But I do not believe that a frozen embryo in a fertility clinic freezer constitutes human life.
>
> I cannot imagine, for example, that many Americans would view an employee of a fertility clinic whose job it is to destroy unneeded embryos as a criminal. Yet this is a task that is performed thousands of times each and every year by hundreds of fertility clinic employees.
>
> I find both fertility treatment and embryonic stem cell research to be ethical. I believe that being pro-life involves helping the living. Regenerative medicine is pro-life and pro-family; it enhances, not diminishes human life.[36]

Any consideration of personhood applies only to embryos that can continue to develop and have the potential to become people. Embryos generated by IVF clinics have no such potential unless actively transferred to a womb. Embryos donated from IVF that would otherwise have been discarded have absolutely no potential to become people. In the womb, an embryo's potential comes from the possibility for implantation, nourishment, and development, but outside of the womb, an embryo will never become a person. There is no chance that an embryo fertilized externally will become a person if it remains external. The embryos being donated to research are never going to be transferred into a uterus; they will be discarded if not researched. Embryos from which we extract stem cells have no potential to become people. Their "life" did not begin at conception; they have yet to even be considered as having the potential of becoming persons. Senator Hatch quotes Senator Gordon Smith, a former LDS Senator from Oregon (now an Area Seventy), who powerfully and simply captures the heart of this issue:

> When does life begin? Some say it is at conception. Others say it is at birth. For me in my quest to be responsible and to be as right as I know how to be, I turn to what I regard as sources of truth. I find this: "And the Lord God formed man of the dust of the ground and breathed into his nostrils the breath of life, and man became a living soul." This allegory of creation describes a two-step process to life, one of the flesh, the other of the spirit. . . . Cells, stem cells,

---

36. *Congressional Record*, 2006, p. S7660.

adult cells, are, I believe, the dust of the earth. They are essential to life, but standing alone will never constitute life. A stem cell in a petri dish or frozen in a refrigerator will never, even in 100 years, become more than stem cells. They lack the breath of life. An ancient apostle once said: "For the body without the spirit is dead." I believe that life begins in the mother's womb, not in a scientist's laboratory. Indeed, scientists tell me that nearly one-half of fertilized eggs never attach to a mother's womb, but naturally slough off. Surely, life is not being taken here by God or by anyone else.[37]

Applying our LDS theology to this idea, we appreciate the difference between a living body and a living soul—the difference is inhabitation by a spirit. Embryos used in embryonic stem cell research come from cells fertilized in a test tube, and they have no potential to become anything other than cells. These embryos are bodies without spirits: they are not human souls. It is not murder to harvest cells from these embryos. No potential is destroyed; in fact, potential is being created, for these cells hold numerous possibilities for bettering the life of mankind. Their potential can only be brought forth by using the technological and scientific blessings unique to our time. Indeed, embryonic stem cells themselves are a blessing unique to these latter days.

Beyond Religion:
Implications of the Moral Status of Embryos

It is important to note that, in America, embryos are not constitutionally protected persons, and legally, do not have rights: in a court case in 1973, the Supreme Court determined that "the word 'person,' as used in the Fourteenth Amendment, does not include the unborn."[38] One problem with ethical issues that involve a party "without a voice," such as embryos, is that the silent party often gets overrepresented. Those who argue against embryonic stem cell research "make the assumption that an embryo has not only the moral status of human person, but also a sort of super status that outweighs the needs of others in the human community."[39] Embryos should never have a higher moral or legal status in our country than adult citizens. The National Bioethics Advisory Commission concurred, agree-

---

37. Ibid.
38. R. Rao, "Equal Liberty: Assisted Reproductive Technology and Reproductive Equality," *George Washington Law Review* 76, no. 6 (2008): 1457–89.
39. McGee and Caplan, "Ethics and Politics," 152.

ing that while an embryo does merit "respect as a form of human life," it does not merit "the same level of respect accorded persons."[40]

Many complications arise if embryos are legally defined as persons, and if personhood legally begins at conception. One such complication is found in the biological fact that nearly 50 percent of all fertilized embryos are aborted from the female human body naturally.[41] Should these be given the status of personhood, we would be under an ethical mandate to do all we can to save these "persons." It would require monumental efforts to identify and save all of these embryos, and no one makes an argument for doing that. It is clear that conferring the status of personhood on embryos is extremely problematic, and biological evidence and LDS religious perspectives suggest they are not yet persons.

Conclusion

When dealing with difficult issues surrounding life and death, we naturally seek to be ethical and follow Church policy, yet it seems apparent that Latter-day Saints have no clear doctrine on when personhood begins. Moreover, there is an implicit assumption within LDS culture that fertilization clinics provide a needed service for infertile LDS couples seeking to follow the mandate of the Church to create families. This holds true despite the creation of large numbers of embryos that will be disposed of. If that disposal can provide blessings to living persons, then it seems clear that this use of embryos is ethically justified from a LDS position. Just as Heavenly Father gave us our bodies so we could become living souls, He also gave us blessings of technology and modern medicine that help us enhance and protect our physical bodies. In embryonic stem cell research, we have an opportunity to increase our knowledge of our bodies and use medical advances to improve the quality of our mortal lives.

---

40. *Ethical Issues in Human Stem Cell Research*, 50.
41. T. Ord, "The Scourge: Moral Implications of Natural Embryo Loss," *American Journal of Bioethics* 8, no. 7 (2008): 12–19.

In "Evolution: From Naiveté to Understanding," Daniel Fairbanks explores the common perception that faith and evolution are irreconcilable, noting that quite a few people agree that the two are so polar that to accept one requires rejection of the other. There are, however, notable exceptions to this view, among them prominent scientists such as Henry Eyring, Francis Collins, and Theodosius Dobzhansky. Fairbanks then asks how those who perceive an apparent conflict between faith and evolution can reconcile it. This question, he believes, may be the "wrong question because it hinges too strongly on the need for reconciliation. The idea that faith and evolution can be reconciled presumes that we know enough to craft assumptions and twist logic until the two neatly fit together in a way that intellectually satisfies us." Instead, he opts for another formulation—"How can we integrate what we learn through science with knowledge from all academic disciplines, including religion, to better understand the world in which we live and our place in it?"—and then offers three keys to that pursuit. First, "we should always approach learning with humility, recognizing that we do not know everything and much still remains undiscovered. . . . Second, we need to recognize science and religion for what they are—and what they are not. . . . Third, the means we use to seek understanding through science and religion are different."

Nineteen

Evolution: From Naiveté to Understanding[1]

Daniel Fairbanks

I've often tried to remember when I first heard about evolution. My elementary and junior high-school science teachers never mentioned it, or if they did, they didn't teach it forcefully enough to leave an impression of it on my mind. And I was not one to miss anything about science in school. From the time I was a child, nature fascinated me more than anything else. During summer vacation, while other children participated in sports, played games, or watched TV, I spent hours each day lying in the tall grass by a pond near our home spying on turtles, fish, frogs, snakes, muskrats, and insects as they emerged from their hiding places. My mind often wandered in school but never during science.

My first memories of evolution are from my high school years. I was raised in a strong Latter-day Saint family and I knew the scriptural stories of the creation and the Garden of Eden. I recall being taught, even by some of my university professors who were not scientists, that organisms could change from one generation to the next, but that one species could not change into another. I was also taught that each species has its own unique number of chromosomes that no other species has, so for one species to change into another, the number of chromosomes would have to change, and that did not happen. Evolution within species was fine, but species themselves were fixed. Thus, Darwin was wrong and the theory of evolution had to be false.

Ironically, decades later, while conducting research comparing cultivated and wild species of olives, I came across the fact that olive trees have exactly the same number of chromosomes as humans, 46 in each cell—and we and olives are obviously very different species. Also, as a part of my own research, I have studied many instances when chromosome numbers changed in nature and new species arose. Scores of scientific studies comparing chromosomes among closely related species have revealed in remarkable detail how

---

1. Portions of this essay are adapted from my book, *Relics of Eden: The Powerful Evidence of Evolution in Human DNA* (Amherst, N.Y.: Prometheus Books, 2007).

the chromosomes have changed as species diverged from common ancestry. The chromosomal basis of evolution is one of the best documented and most prolific areas of research in evolutionary science.

I have the greatest admiration for the many dedicated teachers I had from grade school through graduate school, who kindled the passion of scientific inquiry in my mind. Many were not well versed in the sciences, but they took a special interest in my scientific curiosity and inspired me to crave learning, lessons for which I will always be grateful. I treasure the way they strengthened the minds and hearts of their students, including me.

As a child, I loved dinosaurs. I found it odd that most adults seemed uncomfortable whenever the topic came up. As I grew older, I realized why. Was there a time when people lived alongside these magnificent creatures? Were dinosaurs in the Garden of Eden along with all of the other animals that are now extinct? I posed these questions to my mother, who gave me an answer that satisfied me at the time. No, she did not think that dinosaurs were in the Garden of Eden. But, remember, she said, that God made this earth from other worlds where dinosaurs probably lived. Thus, dinosaur fossils probably came from the remnants of those other worlds.

As an undergraduate student, I took a geology course, which was one of the most insightful experiences of my education. There were only three students in the class, so our professor canceled the classroom and reserved a car for us to drive through the deserts and mountains, studying geology firsthand. I soon discovered that my mother's explanation of dinosaur fossils was completely inconsistent with the abundant geological evidence we discussed and observed in our class. Before long, I recognized the wisdom of James Talmage when, referring to the countless fossils of plants and animals, he wrote "these lived and died, age after age, while the earth was yet unfit for human habitation."[2]

My mother was as close to being perfect as any person could be. No one taught me the value of integrity through words and example better than she, and her love for me was boundless. I later learned that her understanding of geology was lacking. But the pure and unconditional love my angelic mother showered on my siblings and me far outweighs any misunderstandings she may have had about science.

After graduating from high school I went to BYU for a semester, and to no one's surprise I declared a major in zoology. When I returned from my mission, I enrolled in a vertebrate zoology class. Naively, I expected my

---

2. James E. Talmage, *Earth and Man* (Salt Lake City, Utah: The Church of Jesus Christ of Latter-day Saints, 1931).

professor, who happened to be a world-class expert in his field, to show me solid scientific evidence against evolution. After all, evolution was "just a theory," and a shaky one at that, because, according to much of what I had been taught, it had to be wrong—or so I thought. I remember being shocked on the first day of class. Not only was the entire course based on evolution, it seemed to me that my professor actually accepted it! Day by day, the evidence I read in my textbook and heard in class eroded my neatly crafted view of how the world came to be. I felt puzzled and deflated. It seemed to me that if evolution were right, and an enormous body of evidence suggested that it was, then much of what I had learned from people whom I greatly admired must be wrong. I spent quite a few sleepless nights struggling with this newfound conflict.

I was too shy to approach the professor with my dilemma. Fortunately, other students were not. About three weeks into the semester, a group of students met with him to express their concerns. In response, he took an entire lecture period to discuss his insights about science and religion. He told us how we gain scientific understanding through study and that we can test scientific conclusions experimentally. He also told us how we gain religious understanding through study and inspiration, and we do not test that understanding experimentally in the way we do scientific conclusions. He encouraged us to withhold judgment when confronting an apparent conflict between science and religion because we don't have the whole of knowledge before us now, nor are we likely to ever obtain it within our lifetimes. He then shared differing viewpoints on evolution written by several scientific and religious scholars.

I was on the edge of my seat throughout the lecture, and the class applauded him when the bell rang. I stayed after to thank him personally. Fortunately, he perceived that I had some personal concerns, so he invited me to come to his office where he spent more than an hour sharing his understanding, feelings, and convictions with me, and he then introduced me to another professor, whose specialty was evolution, and he did the same. I walked away from their offices a changed person. I recorded the experience and the date in my journal: January 30, 1979.

I will forever be grateful to those two professors who took the time to share their insights with me. From that point on, evolution never troubled me. I studied evolutionary biology in depth in graduate school, and as a geneticist I continue to research it and publish on it. I also look on January 30, 1979, as the day I truly began to think as a scientist.

All too often, university students do not have a caring professor to help them through an intellectual dilemma. They perceive their religious upbringing and the overwhelming evidence of evolution to be hopelessly in conflict. They may convince themselves that their past experiences and upbringing have lost meaning, displaced by a more enlightened scientific understanding.

Sometimes a well-meaning parent, leader, or teacher, who knows little about biology, may unintentionally intensify the conflict by citing supposed evidences against evolution touted by advocates of the Creationism and Intelligent Design movements. These movements are elaborate and well-funded attempts to discredit evolution, giving the impression that evolution is a "theory in crisis."[3] They have produced numerous books, articles, and websites that on the surface seem to raise serious doubts about the scientific validity of evolution. Most students who have taken a general biology class, as well as many well-informed people, can readily identify the inaccuracies and misinformation in these materials. Though craftily written, they are scientifically flawed and are the product of either ignorance or, all too often, intentional attempts to mislead.

Even worse, some people encourage university students to altogether avoid learning of evolution, something that is neither desirable nor possible at most universities. Evolution is the central theme of modern biology. For us to exclude it from a university education, or even a high-school biology class, and claim that we are teaching biology, would be blatantly dishonest. Most scientists agree with the title of a famous article written in 1973 by Theodosius Dobzhansky, one of the foremost biologists of the twentieth century: "Nothing in biology makes sense except in the light of evolution."[4] The preface of a 1998 report by the National Academy of Sciences, the most prestigious group of scientists in the United States, includes this statement: "It is no longer possible to sustain scientifically the view that living things did not evolve from earlier forms or that the human species was not produced by the same evolutionary mechanisms that apply to the rest of the living world."[5] When Dobzhansky published his article in 1973, most biologists considered evolution as the core of modern biology. No one could have anticipated, however, the explosive pace at which evidence of evolution would accumulate in the ensuing years.

In light of the overwhelming evidence of evolution, students often struggle to reconcile what they learn in biology classes with their faith.

---

3. This phrase is taken from the title of a popular creationist book: Michael Denton, *Evolution: A Theory in Crisis*, (Bethesda, Md.: Adler and Adler, 1986).

4. Theodosius Dobzhansky, "Nothing in Biology Makes Sense Except in the Light of Evolution," *American Biology Teacher* 35 (1973): 125–29.

5. *Teaching About Evolution and the Nature of Science* (Washington, D.C.: National Academy Press, 1998), 16.

Those who oppose evolution often espouse the view that reconciliation between faith and evolution is impossible. In their minds, the two are so polar that to accept one *requires* rejection of the other. According to Phillip Johnson, a University of California at Berkeley law professor and founder of the Intelligent-Design movement:

> The story of salvation by the cross makes no sense against a background of evolutionary naturalism. The evolutionary story is a story of humanity's climb from animal beginnings to rationality, not a story of a fall from perfection. It is a story about recognizing gods as illusions, not a story about recognizing God as the ultimate reality we are always trying to escape. It is a story about learning to rely entirely on human intelligence, not a story of the helplessness of that intelligence in the face of the inescapable fact of sin.
>
> There is no satisfactory way to bring two such fundamentally different stories together, although various bogus intellectual systems offer a superficial compromise to those who are willing to overlook a logical contradiction or two. A clear thinker simply has to go one way or another.[6]

Must we accept such a dichotomy, and if so, what are the options? Questioning the scientific validity of evolution is not plausible; the evidence is far too abundant and powerful, especially evidence that has accumulated in recent years. For instance, many of the so-called gaps in the fossil record have been closed, such as the gradual transition from reptiles to mammals, which is now exceptionally well documented, as is the fish-amphibian transition. The emergence of large-scale DNA sequencing, coincident with the genome projects, has produced an enormous body of information repeatedly confirming the broad evolutionary relationships established through traditional means and clarifying many of the questions that were unanswered before large-scale DNA analysis was available. Today's scientific evidence supporting evolution, including human evolution, is so vast, so consistent, and so overwhelming that to reject it is to reject science itself.

Some people, when confronted with this evidence, explain it as God's way of testing our faith. In other words, they claim, God placed countless fossils throughout the earth, arranged geological formations, organized the myriad forms of life, and designed the DNA of all living things to give the impression of an earth that is several billion years old with more than a billion years of evolution—to test our willingness to reject all of that evidence as a demonstration of our faith. Leaders of the Creationism movement, especially its founder, the late Henry Morris, have often resorted to this no-

---

6. Phillip E. Johnson, *Defeating Darwinism by Opening Minds* (Downer's Grove, Ill.: InterVarsity Press, 1997), 111.

tion to explain how so many lines of scientific evidence point to evolution. Kenneth Miller, a professor and cell biologist at Brown University, and a practicing Roman Catholic, emphasized the danger of such a view:

> In order to defend God against the challenge from evolution, they [the creationists] have had to make Him into a schemer, a trickster, even a charlatan. Their version of God is one who intentionally plants misleading clues beneath our feet and in the heavens themselves. Their version of God is one who has filled the universe with so much bogus evidence that the tools of science can give us nothing more than a phony version of reality. In other words, their God has negated science by rigging the universe with fiction and deception. To embrace that God we must reject science and worship deception itself.[7]

Like Miller, several prominent biologists have openly shared their views on the compatibility of evolution and religion. One of the most respected is Francis Collins, former Director of the Human Genome Project and currently Director of the National Institutes of Health. As a physician, Collins was so impressed with the power of faith in sustaining some of his patients in the face of tremendous adversity that he decided to study Christianity. He eventually was converted and is now a practicing Evangelical Christian, while adamantly reaffirming the reality of evolution. Standing in the East Room of the White House while announcing completion of the first draft of the human genome, he invoked his religious faith: "It's humbling for me, and awe inspiring, to realize that we have caught the first glimpse of our own instruction book, previously known only to God."[8]

Theodosius Dobzhansky, one of history's most respected evolutionary biologists, wrote the article whose title I mentioned earlier: "Nothing in biology makes sense except in the light of evolution." Few people reading the title realize that one of the purposes of his article was to express his view of the harmony between evolution and religion. Near its conclusion, he stated,

> It is wrong to hold creation and evolution as mutually exclusive alternatives. I am a creationist *and* an evolutionist. Evolution is God's, or Nature's method of creation.[9]

Henry Eyring was one of the world's most respected scientists. Among the many prestigious positions he held were Professor at Princeton

---

7. Kenneth R. Miller, *Finding Darwin's God: A Scientist's Search for Common Ground Between God and Evolution* (New York: Harper Perennial, 2002), 80.

8. Francis S. Collins, *The Language of God: A Scientist Presents Evidence for Belief* (New York: Free Press, 2006), 3.

9. Dobzhansky, "Nothing in Biology," 125–29.

University and the University of Utah, and President of the American Association for the Advancement of Science, the largest body of scientists in the United States. He was also a faithful and prominent Latter-day Saint. In his book, *Reflections of a Scientist*, he wrote,

> God has left messages all over in the physical world that scientists have learned to read. These messages are quite clear, well-understood, and accepted in science. That is, the theories that the earth is about four-and-one-half billion years old and that life evolved over the last billion years or so are as well established scientifically as many theories ever are.[10]

Addressing the situation university students often face, Stephens and Meldrum, in their book, *Evolution and Mormonism: A Quest for Understanding*, summarized it well:

> There is a relatively common experience among LDS students who enter colleges and universities. Some, perhaps many, of these students have been taught that evolution is false and, even more, that it is evil and not God's way. Enrolled in a college biology course, these students become confused when faced with a body of well-established evidence that supports the theory of evolution and seemingly contradicts previous religious education. Students who pursue a health-sciences profession or attend a graduate biology program often major in biology as undergraduates. They are required to take advanced courses in genetics and evolution and become acquainted with even more compelling evidence for evolution. Such a student is then faced with a difficult dilemma: "Do I believe what I've been previously taught in spite of what seems to be convincing evidence, or do I accept the evidence of science and discount the ideas of my family and former teachers? If I discount what they have told me about evolution, what about other church teachings?" Must students be forced to choose between science and their faith? We think not.[11]

So how can those who struggle with evolution and religion reconcile the apparent conflict? I pose this question because it is one students frequently ask themselves (often leaving out the word "apparent"). However, I have come to realize that perhaps it is the wrong question because it hinges too strongly on the need for reconciliation. The idea that faith and evolution can be reconciled presumes that we know enough to craft assumptions and twist logic until the two neatly fit together in a way that intellectually satisfies us. Instead, I prefer to rephrase the question: How can we integrate what we learn through science with knowledge from all academic disci-

---

10. Henry Eyring, *Reflections of a Scientist* (Salt Lake City: Deseret Book Co., 1983), 61.

11. Trent D. Stephens and D. Jeffrey Meldrum, *Evolution and Mormonism: A Quest for Understanding* (Salt Lake City: Signature Books, 2001), xv–xvi.

plines, including religion, to better understand the world in which we live and our place in it?

In my mind, there are three keys to answering this question. First, we should always approach learning with humility, recognizing that we do not know everything and much still remains undiscovered. When there is a conflict between religious belief and science, we do not always need to reconcile the two because resolution of the conflict may well reside in what we do not know. Trying to reconcile the two with current information may require speculation, which can lead to error. Learning to suspend judgment and live with unresolved conflict is one of the hallmarks of intellectual humility.

Second, we need to recognize science and religion for what they are—and what they are not. Both science and religion are ways of seeking understanding. But the types of understanding we seek through them are different. Modern science is inextricably grounded in the natural universe. Scientists seek natural explanations for the phenomena we observe around us day-to-day, and the phenomena that we cannot see but can measure with scientific instruments. They use the information they have gathered through observation and experimentation to derive the most reasonable explanations of the natural phenomena they study. Those explanations must be based entirely on natural laws and observations. Supernatural explanations are by definition beyond the realm of science.

Religion, on the other hand, is not a means for determining how the earth and everything on it originated. If we turn to religion to tell us the details of how we and the rest of life came to be, we must admit that the available information is very meager. On the other hand, religion offers abundant explanations of the purpose of life and provides a moral compass to guide our actions.

Third, the means we use to seek understanding through science and religion are different. Scientists carefully observe nature and design experiments to test hypotheses. They use increasingly sophisticated instruments to measure phenomena that are beyond our ability to see, even with the most powerful microscopes or telescopes. Their observations and interpretations allow them to refine hypotheses and eventually derive detailed and well-supported explanations of how nature works. These explanations are always open to modification as new evidence is discovered, so scientific explanations are never absolute. Religious understanding, by contrast, is based on authoritative writings (both ancient and modern), teachings, and inspiration, which typically are not testable in the same sense as scientific explanations.

These views on the separate domains of science and religion are not mine alone; numerous scientists and theologians have expressed them in one form or another, most pointedly in recent years. Stephen Jay Gould, a Harvard evolutionary biologist and one of the most popular and prolific science writers and speakers in the late twentieth century, articulated them well in the following passage from a 1997 article he titled "Nonoverlapping Magisteria":

> Magister is Latin for "teacher." We may, I think, adopt this word and concept to express . . . the principled resolution of supposed "conflict" or "warfare" between science and religion. No such conflict should exist because each subject has a legitimate magisterium, or domain of teaching authority—and these magisteria do not overlap (the principle that I would like to designate as NOMA or "nonoverlapping magisteria").
>
> The net of science covers the empirical universe: what it is made of (fact) and why does it work this way (theory). The net of religion extends over questions of moral meaning and value. These two magisteria do not overlap, nor do they encompass all inquiry. . . .
>
> This resolution might remain all neat and clean if the nonoverlapping magisteria (NOMA) of science and religion were separated by an extensive no man's land. But, in fact, the two magisteria bump right up against each other, interdigitating in wondrously complex ways along their joint border. Many of our deepest questions call upon aspects of both for different parts of a full answer—and the sorting of legitimate domains can become quite complex and difficult.[12]

This interdigitation of magisteria reaches perhaps its greatest intensity when it touches on the questions evolution poses for religious belief. Much of the conflict, in my view, is a direct consequence of the tendency some people have to impose a strictly literal interpretation on scriptural accounts of creation. In my book, *Relics of Eden: The Powerful Evidence of Evolution in Human DNA*, I posed what I believe is the principal source of this apparent conflict and its most reasonable solution:

> Modern science is absolutely incompatible with the creationist views of a universe less than ten thousand years old, a worldwide flood that obliterated all terrestrial life except that preserved on an ark, and the special creation of all species, including humans. For those who insist on such a narrow interpretation of religious texts, there is indeed a dichotomy. . . . If instead, however, we view religious texts as spiritual guiding documents rather than literal historical records, the perceived dichotomy fades. Religion and science become complementary ways to interpret our world.[13]

---

12. Stephen Jay Gould, "Nonoverlapping Magisteria," *Natural History* 106 (March 1997): 16–22.

13. Fairbanks, *Relics of Eden*, 168–69.

To me, science is a treasured gem that glistens whenever I have the chance to observe nature. In my current research, I spend countless hours sorting through the digital information of DNA sequences, and I repeatedly discover new evidence of evolution that no one before has seen. Each of these new discoveries elicits feelings of wonder and awe that envelop my soul, much like the feelings I had as a child hiding in the tall grass, entranced with the events of nature that surrounded me. In this sense, science is not entirely separate from the spiritual realm but rather a part of it. As Darwin has so beautifully affirmed in his closing words from *Origin of Species*, "there is grandeur in this view of life."

In "Genesis and Darwin: Finding Common and Uncommon Ground," David Grandy explores the relationship of Darwin and other evolutionary accounts to Christianity. Starting with Darwin himself, then moving to subsequent thinkers as varied as Thomas Huxley, Charles Hartshorne, Richard Dawkins, Daniel Dennett, Kenneth Miller, John Haught, and Holmes Rolston, Grandy examines some of the assumptions and consequences of certain approaches to these issues—ranging from the atheistic and agnostic to a theology of evolution. Some prominent attempts to apply Darwin to religion—either positively or negatively—have led to, as Grandy puts it, "what has now become a familiar occurrence: a brilliant scientist oversteps the scientific evidence at hand to make sweeping claims about reality and the human condition." In his essay, though, Grandy finds both common and uncommon ground. Regarding the uncommon ground, he writes, "What I am proposing is that the creation story and modern science are not fully commensurable. Implied within each is a different yardstick against which truth is measured." Yet he adds, "Notwithstanding this discontinuity, there is, I think, a thread that runs through any earnest treatment of life's origins and our cosmic beginnings. Michael Ruse, an agnostic evolutionist, identifies this thread when he insists that 'All of these people are simply overwhelmed by the glory of creation,'" from Darwin to Dawkins to "the author(s) of the Genesis creation story for whom the pristine earth is blessed by God and pronounced 'very good.'"

Twenty

Genesis and Darwin: Finding Common and Uncommon Ground

David Grandy

For many LDS thinkers Charles Darwin's theory of organic evolution—known loosely as natural selection—offers a stiff challenge to religious faith. Moreover, there does not seem to be a consistent way of talking about the theory among Latter-day Saints. Sometimes it is summarily dismissed, occasionally out of rancor but more often out of the sincere but naïve belief that it is an anti-God manifesto against which the Church is unalterably opposed, because it contradicts the sacred creation narratives found in the books of Genesis, Moses, and Abraham. And yet natural selection is routinely taught at LDS universities, at least by biologists, anthropologists, and other scientists who appreciate its explanatory power.

Like many who have grown up in the faith, my introduction to this complex topic was haphazard and unsystematic. I was first compelled to think about it as a young missionary. One day an investigator informed my companion and me that she could not join a church that opposed evolution. Assuming that she was right about the Church's stance on evolution, we proposed that while Adam was not the first man on the earth, he was the first to receive a spirit from our Heavenly Father. Adam's primacy, in other words, consisted in his spiritual kinship with God; his physical body, by contrast, may have been the product of a long and perhaps even random evolutionary process.

While this response temporarily appeased our investigator (she eventually lost interest in the Church), I felt at the time that there was something incongruous about it. I nevertheless kept it handy for future use until, toward the end of my mission, I purchased a copy of Joseph Fielding Smith's *Man: His Origin and Destiny*. Later I would learn that Elder Smith's unconditional condemnation of organic evolution was not Church doctrine; at the time, however, I assumed it was and tried to conform my thinking to it. My post-mission BYU experience did little to clarify the issue.

Granted, I did not actively seek clarification but I was alert to what my professors said. In a private conversation, a zoology professor told me that his belief in evolution did not disturb his religious faith. When he did not elaborate, I inferred that he was content to leave the matter—apparent contradictions and all—in the Lord's hands. Across campus in a religion class, another professor explained fossils as bits of matter from other planets on which dinosaurs once lived. Since the earth was organized from cosmic material, he reasoned, it was natural that such vestiges would occasionally show up. Another religion teacher, also concerned with dinosaurs, proposed that they died out when left behind by Noah's ark.

It is ironic that I did not begin to understand the issue more deeply until reintroduced to it while taking graduate courses at a secular university. At Harvard University, I. B. Cohen, a prominent historian of science, remarked during a lecture that he had many friends who had no difficulty reconciling their religious convictions with a belief in evolution. His point was that evolutionary theory was not innately irreligious, although it could be misconstrued as such. I kept this point in mind when, later on, I took a class entitled "The Darwinian Revolution." In the class we read Darwin's *The Origin of Species* (1859). What surprised me about the book was its literary dimension. I had expected a dry, carefully reasoned disquisition. Much of the book fit this expectation, but many of the central arguments relied on metaphor and personification.

I still marvel at Darwin's personification of Natural Selection. (He often capitalized the term.) I understood the analogy on which it was based: just as human agents—farmers, pigeon breeders, and so forth—select certain traits for propagation and development, so does nature. The difference, it would seem, is that humans do so intelligently while nature does so blindly. But Darwin minimized this difference and, in fact, sometimes reversed it by portraying nature, by dint of its longevity and ubiquity, as "infinitely wise" compared to man.[1] How could natural selection, I asked myself while reading *The Origin*, be anything other than nature? How could it also be, as Darwin seemed to portray it, a principle of intelligence governing nature's operation?

My questions were not dismissive, for I felt they were introducing me to a previously unsuspected aspect of science. Dawning on me was the sense that scientific theories are complex mixtures of fact, logic, *and* poetic imagination. What is more, even before the mixing, no ingredient is fully distinct from the others. The sharp divide between science and the humanities—one that I had embraced while growing up—began to blur, and with this blurring came a new way of thinking about science in general and

---

1. Charles Darwin and A. R. Wallace, *Evolution by Natural Selection* (Cambridge: Cambridge University Press, 1958), 58.

natural selection in particular. Continuing my graduate studies at Indiana University, I noted that most good scientists—Darwin included—realized that scientific theories partly rely on metaphysical leaps of faith that cannot be scientifically justified. Thus, to follow Stephen Toulmin, "Science is not an intellectual computing machine: it is a slice of life."[2]

This makes plausible Albert Einstein's claim that "physical [scientific] concepts are free creations of the human mind, and are not, however it may seem, uniquely determined by the external world."[3] Although science is a method for understanding reality truthfully, it is not a *privileged* method for generating uniquely truthful maps of reality; nature also yields to other modes of inquiry and apprehension. And so there is a creative aspect to science that rescues it from those who naively depict it as an unbiased or "objective" reading of the text of nature. One problem with that naïve view is that there is no clear point at which the so-called text of nature leaves off and we the readers begin. Again, things get blurred.

Given science's creative or arbitrary aspect, it should not surprise us that there is also a dramatic aspect to science, and this point often gets overlooked in our discussions of Darwinian biology. More than any other modern scientific theory, natural selection has been dramatized in various ways—sometimes to promote the theory itself, sometimes to add scientific luster to an ideology that cannot stand on its own merits, and sometimes to promote the theory and ideology in lockstep. I do not necessarily decry this dramatization; indeed in the first instance—where it is used to promote the theory itself—I find it compelling. Such promotion is part of the excitement of science. Nevertheless, I believe that it is important to recognize such dramatization where it occurs. This recognition can do much to alleviate tension in the Church between those who affirm evolution and those who reject it.

Momentarily leaving aside, then, the question of whether natural selection is true, let us consider the different ways people have taken poetic or philosophical license with it. We will eventually circle back to the question of truth, but I hope with a heightened appreciation of how extra-scientific—poetic, religious, and philosophical—intuitions play into Darwin's theory. With this background in place, we will be able to find some common—and uncommon—ground between natural selection and Genesis.

---

2. Stephen Toulmin, *Foresight and Understanding: An Enquiry into the Aims of Science* (Bloomington, Ind.: Indiana University Press, 1961), 99.

3. Albert Einstein and Leopold Infeld, *The Evolution of Physics* (New York: Simon & Schuster, 1961), 31.

Darwin's *Origin*

Few ideas antagonize Christian believers more than the proposition that the present world came about through a long series of random accidents. While this idea may prevail in some quarters, it cannot be unequivocally attributed to Darwin. Although Darwin sometimes talked as if nature bumbled along in a blind and mindless way, more often he endowed nature with rare creative and intellectual powers. In *The Origin* he stated that "Natural Selection . . . is a power incessantly ready for action, and is as immeasurably superior to man's feeble efforts, as the works of Nature are to those of Art."[4] Elsewhere he took the man-nature comparison further by portraying nature as "infinitely more sagacious than man" and as an "all-seeing being" that is ever "rigid and scrutinizing."[5] Being long-lived and ever-present, nature had a vast advantage over humankind when it came to shaping the environment. As I suggested earlier, there is a problem here: Darwin personifies the very thing—nature—he seeks to explain, thereby ending up with a kind of self-superintending world.

The problem is not as serious as it seems, at least from a religious point of view, for Darwin allowed that God *might* stand behind the whole enterprise. His complaint was against those who portrayed God as micromanaging nature. Chief among these was William Paley, whose *Natural Theology*—a work the youthful Darwin all but memorized—insisted that science can read God's book of nature and therein find countless illustrations of his loving intelligence and care. Introducing his central argument, Paley offered a now familiar analogy that drove home the probability of a God-designed world. A man walking across a heath stumbles on a rock but takes no note of it. He then notices a clock, picks it up and inspects it. Unlike the rock, the clock, with its many interacting parts, betokens a designer. Similarly, nature with its many intricacies and harmonies betokens a Designer or Creator.

When I first heard this analogy as a young boy in sacrament meeting, I was deeply impressed—it seemed almost irrefutable. A good question to ask about it, however, is this: Is God directly involved in the smallest details of nature or did he enact physical laws that, over immense stretches of time, have brought about the world we now survey? In either case, God stands behind his creation, but the second possibility, in Darwin's mind, was more reverential than the first. "It is derogatory," he wrote, "that the Creator of countless systems of worlds should have created each of the myriads of creeping parasites and slimy worms which have swarmed each

---

4. Charles Darwin, *The Origin of Species* (London: Penguin Books, 1985), 115.
5. Darwin and Wallace, *Evolution by Natural Selection*, 45–48.

day of life on this globe."⁶ In other words, God is not directly responsible for all the seeming inequities and cruelties of nature. Queen bees kill their female offspring, ants make slaves of other ants, cuckoos trick other birds into hatching their eggs and rearing their young, certain wasps paralyze their prey and store them as live fodder for their larvae, and species pass out of existence. Would a loving Creator conceive and directly implement all this, asked Darwin, or might he, having set the world in motion, merely suffer it to occur for some higher purpose?

My intent is not to decide the issue but to indicate how religious considerations play into Darwin's argument. Unlike many Christians of his day, Darwin preferred the long miracle of creation rather than the short one. He felt the long, not fully pre-scripted miracle, with God—assuming He exists—in a *laissez-faire* rather than micromanaging mode, invested the life adventure with tremendous depth and possibility. Part of the cost of this new outlook, of course, involved giving up traditional beliefs about the past and humankind's relationship with other species. An old earth—one stretching back millions of years—caused the first moment of creation ("In the beginning . . .") to recede from historical sight, upset Biblical chronology, and set the mind reeling as it tried to assimilate the Genesis creation story to the naturalistic account of humankind's evolutionary ascent. Even more disturbing was Darwin's handling of other species, which had traditionally been cordoned off from the human species. The prevailing metaphor before Darwin was the Great Chain of Being, a static hierarchy of life forms reaching upward to humankind, each species occupying a distinct and permanent niche (species did not become extinct) in the hierarchy. Darwin offered a different metaphor, one connoting ongoing change and interdependency among species.

Unlike the Great Chain or Ladder of Being, Darwin's metaphor is organic: it draws upon one of nature's multifaceted productions. At the close of *The Origin*, Darwin unveils the metaphor:

> It is interesting to contemplate an entangled bank, clothed with many plants of many kinds, with birds singing on the bushes, with various insects flitting about, and with worms crawling through the damp earth, and to reflect that these elaborately constructed forms, so different from each other, and dependent on each other in so complex a manner, have all been produced by laws acting around us.⁷

---

6. Ibid., 86.
7. Darwin, *Origin*, 459.

After enumerating those laws, which for him could be the secondary means by which the Creator accomplishes his purposes, Darwin proposes that the entangled bank—a richly diverse but deeply interdependent biological world in microcosm—complicates the question of good and evil. After all, goodness arises from difference or opposition: "Thus, from the war of nature, from famine and death, the most exalted object which we are capable of conceiving, namely the production of the higher animals, directly follows."[8] Put differently, one species cannot hold itself aloof—morally, biologically, or otherwise—from any other, for the life adventure is a mutually shared and mutually entangled experience.

Darwin's next sentence—the last of the book—is too good to pass up. Note the biblical imagery and the oblique reference to Isaac Newton, whom Darwin wished to emulate in the field of biology:

> There is a grandeur in this view of life, with its several powers, having originally been breathed into a few forms or into one; and that, whilst this planet has gone cycling on according to the fixed law of gravity, from so simple a beginning endless forms most beautiful and most wonderful have been, and are being, evolved.[9]

I confess that on one level I find this outlook compelling. My oldest daughter graduated in anthropology from Brigham Young University. She once remarked that she found the theory of evolution beautiful. That may seem a strange way to describe it, but I think it captures Darwin's sentiment. He brought forth an aspect of the world that had previously received little emphasis: the interdependency of life forms and the way seemingly insignificant, bothersome, or even harmful creatures enhance the human experience with beauty as well as hardship. The following passage from *The Origin* comes readily to mind whenever I look at flowers and marvel at what Darwin called nature's "prodigality" in giving us so many diverse and beautiful species.

> Flowers rank amongst the most beautiful productions of nature; but they have been rendered conspicuous in contrast with the green leaves, and in consequence at the same time beautiful, so that they may be easily observed by insects. I have come to this conclusion from finding it an invariable rule that when a flower is fertilised by the wind it never has a gaily-coloured corolla. Several plants habitually produce two kinds of flowers: one kind open and coloured so as to attract insects; the other closed, not coloured, destitute of nectar, and never visited by insects. Hence we may conclude that, if insects

---

8. Ibid.
9. Ibid., 459–60.

had not been developed on the face of the earth, our plants would not have been decked with beautiful flowers.[10]

At least for me, the varied beauty of flowers is rendered all the more striking by the buzzing, creeping, and sometimes creepy insects that play into their production. This is not to refute the scriptural point that God brings forth "all things which come of the earth . . . for the benefit and the use of man, both to please the eye and to gladden the heart" (D&C 59:18). The question again is whether God attends to every detail of nature or only to broad developments. What is more, there is the additional question of whether scripture and scientific explanation are comparable modes of expression: the two may reflect different casts of mind. In Darwin's view, the "dignified language" of scripture, more concerned with description and prescription, often stopped short of explanation.[11] Science could therefore offer an explanation that kept God from handing down edicts on every twist and turn of nature. And while this explanation was a naturalistic way of making sense of the world, it need not be taken as proof against God's existence. Darwin never said or implied that, but he did want to clear space for scientific explanation among those who reflexively interpreted every natural event, no matter how trivial, as a matter of divine intervention. After all, as Steven Weinberg insists, "the only way that any sort of science can proceed is to assume that there is no divine intervention and to see how far one can get with this assumption."[12]

Given its scientific detail, literary appeal, and advocacy of a new historical attitude, *The Origin* merits study. It valorized the evolutionary outlook, but that outlook has since lent itself to many expressions or dramatizations, some darker and some brighter than Darwin intended. That is to say the theory of evolution now comes in many metaphysical flavors.

Agnostic and Atheistic Evolution

In addition to challenging traditional religious belief, Darwinian biology has exerted a religious appeal of its own. I first noticed this while reading the works of Thomas Huxley, Darwin's colleague and advocate. Huxley invented the word *agnosticism* after having decided that theology and phi-

---

10. Darwin, *Origin*, 210.
11. Ibid., 217. Later (p. 453) Darwin writes: "It is so easy to hide our ignorance under such expressions as the 'plan of creation,' 'unity of design,' &c., and to think that we give an explanation when we only restate a fact."
12. Steven Weinberg, *Dreams of a Final Theory* (New York: Vintage Book, 1993), 247.

losophy were incapable of proving God's existence. Science could not prove his existence either, but, unlike theology and philosophy, it did not pretend that it could. There was, then, a certain intellectual modesty about science that one could embrace in the interest of moral development. Shortly after coming to terms with the death of one of his children, Huxley wrote:

> Science seems to me to teach in the highest and strongest manner the great truth which is embodied in the Christian conception of entire surrender to the will of God. Sit down before fact as a little child, be prepared to give up every preconceived notion, follow humbly wherever and to whatever abysses nature leads, or you shall learn nothing. I have only begun to learn contentment and peace of mind since I have resolved at all risks to do this.[13]

Huxley was particularly enamored with Darwinian evolution. For him, as for others, Darwin had unlocked the "mystery of mysteries"[14] and had solved "the great riddle of existence"[15] pertaining to life and its various manifestations. Newton had shown that insofar as inanimate processes were concerned, physical law was indifferent to distinctions between stellar and terrestrial locations. Now it appeared that this finding had been extended to animate processes as well, a circumstance that further suggested that "organic and inorganic nature are two inseparably connected realms of an undivided universe."[16] Huxley credited such sweeping generalizations when he spoke of evolution as a cosmic law to whose operation could be ascribed all the pain, beauty, and terror of the universe.

It was a powerful vision, capable of transporting one to higher planes of sympathy and understanding. Huxley meant it as a vision of life's meaning because evolution was fully synonymous with nature's operation. "[T]he cosmic process," he stated, "is evolution; . . . it is full of wonder, full of beauty, and, at the same time, full of pain."[17] This, of course, was not empirical fact, but Huxley had found in the theory something more than fact; he had found a new expression of the "tragic ambivalence of life and death."[18] Darwin had

---

13. T. H. Huxley, *Life and Letters of Thomas Henry Huxley*, ed. Leonard Huxley (New York: D Appleton, 1900), 1:235. Original wording is "content," which I have changed to "contentment." Some of the material in this section is taken from my book *Leo Szilard: Science as a Mode of Being* (Lanham, Md.: University Press of America, 1996).

14. Darwin, *Origin*, 65.

15. Ernst Haeckel, *Die Welträtsel* (Leipzig: Alfred Kröner Verlag, 1924), 388.

16. Ibid., 486.

17. T. H. Huxley, *Evolution and Ethics and Other Essays* (London: Macmillan, 1893-94), 53.

18. Stanley Edgar Hyman, *The Tangled Bank: Darwin, Marx, Frazer, and Freud*

already embraced this ambivalence and, like Huxley, he neither asserted nor denied God's existence. We should note also that Darwin, the doting father of ten children, like Huxley suffered a loss of Christian faith on the death of one of his children. Both men struggled with the setback, wondering if the seemingly random cruelty they regularly observed in nature applied also to human circumstance. It was a short leap to agnosticism and the likelihood of an impersonal God—or no God at all.

With Huxley one glimpses the cost of turning scientific theories into omni-explanatory worldviews—dramatizing the theories in the interest of settling or shutting down age-old religious and philosophical questions. Religion is a vote of confidence in the ultimate goodness of things, but Huxley's vision offers no such vote. While he felt that science embodies ethical truth, he also felt that the evolutionary process was blind and amoral. Therefore, despite our high aspirations, "the cosmos works through the lower nature of man, not for righteousness, but against it."[19] Thanks to science, however, there was a way out. Citing Pascal, Huxley argued that though man is a "fragile reed" in the universe, he is a "thinking reed" and therein lay his power to first blunt and then master the evolutionary process. This might take several centuries but in Huxley's mind there "was no limit to the extent to which intelligence and will, guided by sound principles of investigation, and organized in common effort, may modify the conditions of existence . . . and . . . change the nature of man himself."[20]

I find this outlook appalling, both as a recipe for humankind's survival and as a scientific mandate. It is an early instance of what has now become a familiar occurrence: a brilliant scientist oversteps the scientific evidence at hand to make sweeping claims about reality and the human condition. Science thus becomes a handy weapon in worldview warfare. As I noted earlier, creativity inevitably plays into the construction of scientific theories, but those theories do not license unbridled metaphysical speculation. The irony, of course, is that Huxley dismissed theology and philosophy for their lack of intellectual modesty and then used science to fill the void.

But along with irony there was dissonance in Huxley's outlook. Without a Divine Creator to stand behind nature, one wonders if anything, science included, really goes anywhere. That is, it would seem that the world's tragic ambivalence—what a believing Christian might call its fallen state—goes unredeemed. The problem was that science at the turn of the

---

as Imaginative Writers (New York: Atheneum, 1962), 29–30.

19. Huxley, *Evolution and Ethics*, 76.

20. Ibid., 83, 85.

twentieth century offered little ground for religious hope. Writing in 1902 William James remarked that "nature has no one distinguishable ultimate tendency with which it is possible to feel a sympathy. In the vast rhythm of her processes, as the scientific mind now follows them, she appears to cancel herself."[21] The proposition, then, of surviving in an uncaring, self-canceling cosmos struck an odd and empty note. To what larger end would human survival be directed?

One occasionally hears this note in the writings of H. G. Wells, Huxley's most famous student. Wells championed evolution with great vigor, feeling that it was a unifying paradigm, a higher perspective that would eventually interconnect all facets of human endeavor. It was also a torch illuminating the future, and in 1902 he wrote of the "great unmanageable, disturbing fact" that the human species is not the final term of the evolutionary drama. One day beings, as different from us as our fossil-record predecessors but already "latent in our thoughts and hidden in our loins, shall stand upon this earth as one stands upon a footstool, and shall laugh and reach out their hands amid the stars."[22] But there was another side to the evolutionary coin, and counterbalancing Wells's optimism was a despair born of the possibility that humankind might fall short of the high destiny he foresaw. For one thing, only the most quixotic believer could envisage a successful campaign against the principle of entropy or second law of thermodynamics with its implication of universal heat death. As early as 1891, in perhaps his "first flash of [. . .] true genius,"[23] Wells suggested that science might not be able to deliver on its promise of comprehensive understanding and material comfort. Note the religious imagery.

> Science is a match that man has just got alight. He thought he was in a room—in moments of devotion, a temple—and that his light would be reflected from and display walls inscribed with wonderful secrets and pillars carved with philosophical systems wrought in harmony. It is a curious sensation, now that the preliminary sputter is over and the flame burns up clear, to see his hands lit and just a glimpse of himself and the patch he stands on

---

21. William James, *The Varieties of Religious Experience* (New York: Vintage, 1990), 440.

22. H. G. Wells, *The Discovery of the Future* (New York: B.W. Huebsch, 1914), 60–61.

23. Lovat Dickson, *H. G. Wells: His Turbulent Life and Times* (New York: Atheneum, 1969), 48. On page 68 Dickson writes: "Already at the age of twenty-nine the beginnings of a religion which might be called Wellsianity was taking vague shape in [Wells's] mind, with science as its god, evolution its history, nature—including man—its congregation."

visible, and around him, in place of all that human comfort and beauty he had anticipated—darkness still.[24]

The point I want to stress—and this informs much of what follows—is the incongruity between science as an instrument of salvation and its bleak depiction of the cosmos. Early in his career Wells stated that he intended to "reconcile a scientific faith in evolution with optimism."[25] But he never accomplished this. *The Time Machine* ends in seeming vindication of the Time Traveler, who "thought but cheerlessly of the Advancement of Mankind, and saw in the growing pile of civilization only a foolish heaping that must inevitably fall back upon and destroy its makers in the end." And the best Wells can do to mitigate this dreary prognosis is to add: "If that is so, it remains for us to live as though it were not so."[26]

This platitude—to fight on against a senseless, uncaring cosmos—has become a trademark sentiment among those who have dramatized atheistic outlooks as worldviews. Indeed, it has become a kind of religious response celebrating the ultimate futility of things and humankind's stoically unflinching reaction thereto. But, as Mary Midgley points out, "Low-temperature rhetoric proves nothing; people are proud of their ability to withstand this kind of cold."[27] Moreover, the rhetoric steps beyond science. Witness Bertrand Russell's pronouncement that "the whole temple of Man's achievement must inevitably be buried beneath the debris of a universe in ruins"[28] or Steven Weinberg's claim that "the more the universe seems comprehensible, the more it seems pointless."[29] Both statements borrow authority from science but only as scientific fact is warped to serve a larger-than-science purpose. That is, an ideological purpose.

Richard Dawkins is a contemporary ideologue who routinely warps biological science to his anti-religious ends. Given his brilliance it may be puzzling that he does not seem to realize that his science cannot do everything he says it does. It cannot, for instance, rule out God's existence—it simply lacks the tools. I suspect that Dawkins knows there is a certain inco-

---

24. H. G. Wells, "The Rediscovery of the Unique," *The Fortnightly Review* (July 1891): 111.
25. H. G. Wells, "Human Evolution: An Artificial Process," *The Fortnightly Review* (Oct. 1896): 590–95; excerpts reprinted in *Review of Reviews* (Nov. 1896): 605–6.
26. H. G. Wells, *The Time Machine* (Mahwah, N.J.: Watermill Press, 1980), 147.
27. Mary Midgley, *Science as Salvation: A Modern Myth and its Meaning* (London: Routledge, 1992), 137.
28. Bertrand Russell, "A Free Man's Worship," in *Mysticism and Logic* (Garden City, N.Y.: Doubleday, 1918). 45.
29. Weinberg, *Dreams of a Final Theory*, 255.

herence and duplicity to his argument but nevertheless chooses to fight fire with a religiously-tinged fire of his own, all the while presenting himself as the humble servant of scientific truth. This truth, he declares, now precludes the need "to resort to superstition when faced with the deep problems: Is there meaning to life? What are we for? What is man?" With regard to this last question, Dawkins cites with approval G. G. Simpson's claim that "all attempts to answer that question before 1859 [the year Darwin's *Origin* was published] are worthless and . . . we will be better off if we ignore them completely." No need, in other words, to consult the world's sacred and philosophical literature regarding humankind's purpose and origin.

Dawkins's answer to the deep problems is the "selfish gene," the locus at which natural selection initiates evolutionary change. Our bodies, says Dawkins, are the means by which genes achieve immortality. Organisms and even species die out, but not before their genes, having rigged their hosts with a need to reproduce, transfer themselves to new bodies. Thus, genes cleverly tumble from one generation to the next, unscathed by the evolutionary agonies and ecstasies they instigate. To follow Dawkins, they are "immortal replicators" who "swarm in huge colonies, safe inside gigantic lumbering robots."[30]

Dawkins' argument, which he buttresses with many subplots and analogies, is plausible if one does not pry too deeply. Trying to keep things fully naturalistic, he insists that genes arose through random or meaningless processes. How then did replication become meaningful to them? This is a creation *ex nihilo* that Dawkins fails to address. Yet another, it seems to me, is implicit in his proposal that, now that we are aware of our selfish genes, we might be able to "upset their designs" and teach ourselves "generosity and altruism."[31] This is a nice sentiment, but it calls for a discussion of the question of whether a "survival machine" (the human body) could bootstrap itself into a realm of possibility beyond the imaginative reach of its wholly selfish creators. A related problem here is that Dawkins treats the gene as a distinct entity and something existing in dichotomous opposition to its biological milieu. But contrary to Dawkins and popular treatments in general, genes are not stable, self-contained units cleanly detachable from the body's other forms and functions. Instead, they are expansively and dy-

---

30. Richard Dawkins, *The Selfish Gene*, 2nd ed., (Oxford: Oxford University Press, 1989), 19, 266.

31. Ibid., 3.

namically distributed throughout the body; that is, not easily demarcated and not invulnerable to biological disruption.[32]

Another high profile purveyor of atheistic evolution is Daniel Dennett. His 1995 best seller *Darwin's Dangerous Idea* takes on the question of life's meaning and settles it through an explication of Design Space. An updated, high-powered version of an old argument, Design Space allows Dennett to revel in the proposition that everything of significance has insignificant evolutionary origins. That is, significance or meaning arises from a teleological vacuum. This may seem a stretch, but only because, according to Dennett, our minds have not been sufficiently stretched by Darwin's revolutionary insights. Granted, one monkey typing for eons probably could not reproduce a single line from Shakespeare, but what about an innumerable crowd of monkeys? Dennett gets a great deal of mileage out of the old monkey-at-the-typewriter argument simply by expanding its parameters. If one universe is not enough Design Space, try more. There is, after all, no conceivable limit to the number of universes that may have failed before things happened to click in this one.

Is this an explanation or a circular argument? Would not unlimited Design Space entail the conclusion that everything that has happened was eventually bound to happen? And yet Dennett insists that this is not one of those "remarkably persuasive Darwinian explanations that evaporate on closer inspection."[33] I submit that it is, but not because the theory of evolution is wrong. Dennett is using Darwinian biology to market atheism and failing to acknowledge that Design Space is his way of assimilating science to his own ideological fantasies.

Theistic Evolution

By now I hope it is clear that atheism or agnosticism is not an implicit dimension of evolution theory but rather pre-calculated ways of elaborating or spinning the theory. It is true that evolution requires belief in an old earth; the theory also requires an open mind regarding a host of interrelated issues such as physical law or necessity, chance, speciation, and mechanisms of organic development and adaptation. But an open mind is

---

32. Evelyn Fox Keller, *The Century of the Gene* (Cambridge: Harvard University Press, 2000).

33. Daniel C. Dennett, *Darwin's Dangerous Idea: Evolution and the Meanings of Life* (New York: Touchstone, 1995), 521.

just that, and none of these issues, which are far from decided themselves, decide anything of religious consequence.

Still, the theory of evolution clashes in some respects with Genesis and so it is natural to wonder if the two can be reconciled. Darwin, devoted as a youth to his native Anglican faith, settled into agnosticism toward the end of his life. During his middle years, however, he occasionally professed a belief in God. This belief, he wrote,

> follows from the extreme difficulty or rather impossibility of conceiving this immense and wonderful universe, including man with his capacity of looking far backwards and far into futurity, as the result of blind chance or necessity. When thus reflecting I feel compelled to look to a First Cause having an intelligent mind in some degree analogous to that of man, and I deserve to be called a Theist.[34]

But of course Darwin's theism (or perhaps, more correctly, deism) did not entail biblical fundamentalism, and neither do most theistic or providential accounts of evolution today. Like the godless versions of evolution it opposes, theistic evolution interprets or slants events and evidence toward a particular metaphysical outlook. One such outlook, already illustrated in Darwin's thinking, involved restricting God's role in the world to that of a First Cause. This kept him in the background and ruled out the possibility of divine intervention *after* the Creation. Such intervention, Darwin reasoned, would compromise the laws of nature and the integrity of science. Not surprisingly, many Christians find this outlook unacceptable, for it suggests an impersonal, ultimately uncaring God. Even Paley's God—the one who lavished loving care on the smallest details of nature—could be so construed if he were not *always* attending to nature's operation. After all, the clockwork universe, no matter how marvelous, was just a divine artifact, not Divinity itself. What is more—and this is where the God as Clockmaker analogy fully backfires in a religious sense—if the world were a perfect clock or machine fashioned by the perfect Craftsman and then left to its perfectly lawful operation, would it not be a deterministic system? What then of human freedom, the sense that we are making real choices from moment to moment?

In thinking through these issues, Darwin "thought more cogently than the bishops mostly did."[35] That is the judgment of Charles Hartshorne, a

---

34. Charles Darwin, *Autobiographies*, ed. Michael Neve and Sharon Messenger (London: Penguin Books, 2002), 53.

35. Charles Hartshorne, "Creation through Evolution," in *Omnipotence and Other Theological Mistakes* (Albany, N.Y.: SUNY Press, 1984), 70.

well-known process philosopher who sees Darwinian evolution as a partial answer to theological problems pertaining to traditional Christianity's definition of God as an absolutely omnipotent and omniscient Being. This definition, says Hartshorne, rules out creaturely or human freedom. But Darwin, upon offering a plausible theory of terrestrial life under the tacit assumption that God does not intervene in nature, makes freedom a real possibility. Indeed Darwin's outlook prompts the suggestion that life is a voluntary response to God's love—not a mechanical reaction to his all-arranging power. As Hartshorne puts it: "God charms every creature irresistibly to whatever extent is compatible with that creature's level of freedom." Further, "Because God loves each creature better than it or its fellows can love it, the creature, even though it is partly self-creative, cannot but make some response to the divine love."[36] Hartshorne's aim is to realign Christian theology with what life feels like, and that entails freedom, chance or risk, and a sense of self-determination or self-creativity. Given this realignment and Darwinian biology's amenability thereto, Hartshorne ventures that by means of evolution God "makes things partly make themselves."[37]

Today, it seems to me, the tendency among theistic evolutionists is to eliminate the break between Creation as a moment of divine origination and creation as the natural order. God's creative work is ever in process and below the radar of scientific observation. Moreover, God does not contravene the laws of nature; he finesses them to accomplish his purposes, all the while preserving the world's dignity and freedom. How he does this is, of course, a matter of opinion. Kenneth Miller proposes that God slips into the world through quantum uncertainty, thereby nudging things ever so slightly toward religiously promising ends.[38] This strikes me as a God-of-the-gaps argument, but if the Copenhagen Interpretation of quantum physics is right, the gaps—events not fully determined by prior causes—are deep ontological fixtures that therefore cannot be closed by human understanding.

Rather than trying to summarize the many varieties of theistic evolution, let me mention two contemporary thinkers who, along with Miller and Hartshorne, have mined Darwinian biology for religious meaning. When Darwin remarked that "there is a grandeur in this view of life," he was, I believe, letting his mind expand across eons of evolutionary history and feeling sympathetic kinship with barnacles, trilobites, dinosaurs and

---

36. Ibid., 81.
37. Ibid., 80.
38. Kenneth R. Miller, *Finding Darwin's God: A Scientist's Search for Common Ground Between God and Evolution* (New York: Cliff Street Books, 2000), 192–219.

other vanished and extant species. True, most had no capacity to ponder their condition, but, like Darwin himself, all instinctively embraced life and recoiled from death. All were intimate with birth, life, pain, and the prospect of death, and Darwin saw this intimacy as shared initiation into the world's tragic ambivalence.[39]

Earlier I suggested that agnostic and atheistic evolution goes no further than this. It targets a world in which the perpetuation of physical life necessitates death. If I am to grow and live, I must regularly feed upon other species and contribute directly or indirectly to their harvest or innocent slaughter. Inured as we are to this world and the demands it makes of us, we rarely stop to question these practices. Moreover, given our relative material comfort, we perhaps overlook what Darwin saw: the impress of suffering upon nature. I think it wrong to deny or trivialize this suffering just because most of it belongs to other species. It can be for them, as for us, terrifyingly real. But it is not senseless within the wider frame of Christian belief. Holmes Rolston reminds us that while Darwinian biology throws the harshness of nature into stark relief, the Christian gospel confers sacramental meaning on that harshness. Nature, he says, is a *via dolorosa* whereby we walk a few halting steps with Christ in his last hours before death.[40] So in its reaffirmation and intensification of the problem of suffering, evolutionary biology may give us fresh eyes with which to witness the sacrificial love of God. The evolutionary landscape, stretching back billions of years and accommodating the painful coming and going of countless organisms, is one part of the redemptive drama, and one whose bleakness renders the miracle of redemption all the more striking and marvelous.

Thinking along these lines, John Haught has developed a "theology of evolution." He asserts that, thanks to Darwin, we now have "an account of life whose depth, beauty, and pathos—when seen in the context of the larger cosmic epic of evolution—expose us afresh to the raw reality of the sacred and to a resoundingly meaningful universe."[41] I do not expect that all Latter-day Saints will find Haught's theology persuasive, but it is a full-

---

39. In one of his notebooks Darwin wrote: "If we choose to let conjecture run wild, then animals, our fellow brethren in pain, disease, death, suffering and famine—our slaves in the most laborious works, our companions in our amusements—they may partake [of] our origin in one common ancestor—we may all be melted together." Cited in Darwin and Wallace, *Evolution by Natural Selection*, 5.

40. Holmes Rolston, *Science and Religion: A Critical Survey* (Philadelphia: Temple University Press, 1987), 146.

41. John F. Haught, *God After Darwin: A Theology of Evolution* (Boulder, Co.: Westview Press, 2000), 2.

scale religious dramatization of evolution theory that has provoked much discussion. I keep it in mind because it puts the redemptive spotlight on *all* species, and it does this not just by recalling that God loves all his creatures, but also by assuming that human experience is enabled and enriched by difference and opposition—by biodiversity. When Adam named the animals in the Garden of Eden, he was also naming or discovering himself.

What about Genesis?

We now arrive at the crucial question: is evolution theory compatible with Genesis? Some versions of evolution theory definitely are not but others are, in the sense that they, like Genesis, see nature as a stage for the display, however nuanced, of God's purposes. But, one may ask, what does science proper—evolution theory trimmed of ideological motivations—say about Genesis? As noted earlier, science seeks to explain the world naturalistically. It consequently does not pronounce for or against God. Unless, of course, it is dramatized beyond its factual content, and then it is not science proper.

Having said this, we must acknowledge that the Genesis creation story still poses questions to theistic evolutionists. What, for example, are we to believe about the age of the earth? Has it been around for billions of years or only several thousand? Here I think we must not falsely oppose the two outlooks. Genesis is not concerned with historical chronology. Of course the narrative is chronological in that certain events occur before others, but those events are not marked off against some pre-established timeline. That timeline—stretching back into the past in a perfectly linear fashion—had not yet been conceptualized. What is more, the creation events narrated in Genesis are sacred; they therefore, at least by ancient canons of understanding, cannot be squeezed down to single historical moments.[42] Trying to so squeeze them is something moderns reflexively do, conditioned as we are by the scientific assumption that every event occurs at a precise location in time and space.

To put the matter differently, *what* happens in Genesis is far more important than *when* it happens. But even with the what, modern proclivities can steer us in the wrong direction. Inclined as we are to reach for historical facts and "hard data," we may stare past all-important dimensions of the story. According to Michael Welker, understanding of Genesis

---

42. Mircea Eliade, *The Sacred and the Profane: The Nature of Religion*, trans. Willard R. Trask (San Diego: Harcourt Brace & Co., 1959).

begins with the realization that "Creation connects diverse processes and domains of life and orders them in such a way that they can be known by human beings and that human beings can enter into communication with God."[43] The emphasis, in other words, is on relationship, integration, and communion: humankind is not an afterthought or accident—as in, say, the *Enuma Elish*—but preciously worked into the created order. Moreover, a single transcendent Being is the ultimate point of linkage or source from which all originates. That is, divinity is not, as it was for surrounding nations, polytheistic and coincidental with natural phenomena like rivers, stars, and various life forms.

If we are not alert to these ancient concerns—which are mostly resolved issues for us—the Genesis creation story can spark different thoughts for us than it did anciently. Unthreatened by polytheism, I may never be struck by the fact that nature—the primordial waters, say—is not itself divine but under the governance of a Being who transcends nature. And secure in the belief that I am precious to that Being, I may never breathe a sigh of gratitude upon learning that humankind is made in the image and likeness of God. Instead I will probably assimilate the Genesis creation story to my own modern concerns and to my inclination to view the past through a scientific lens. I will, that is, tend to read the story as a scientifically primitive account of the earth's formation.

What I am proposing is that the creation story and modern science are not fully commensurable. Implied within each is a different yardstick against which truth is measured. This may sound like a concession to relativism but only if one very important religious fact gets overlooked: the Creation occurred before the Fall, before humankind's descent into toil, aging, sickness, and death. If there is radical discontinuity between what happened before and after the Fall, we should expect a similar discontinuity upon comparing respective accounts. Indeed the Book of Genesis, taken as a whole, embodies this discontinuity. As Donald Gowan points out, the chapters of Genesis "depict movement from a world none of us has ever known toward the real world of human history."[44]

---

43. Michael Welker, "Creation: Big Bang or the World of Seven Days?" *Theology Today* 52, no. 2 (Jul 1995): 186.

44. Donald E. Gowan, *From Eden to Babel: A Commentary on the Book of Genesis 1–11* (Grand Rapid, Mich.: Wm. B. Eerdmans Publishing Co., 1988), 3. Even in modern cosmology, which, like Genesis, takes up the question of cosmic origins, there is a similar rupture or discontinuity, although I do not want to equate it with the Fall. The laws of physics break down at the Big Bang singularity, the primeval moment of creation, and so it becomes impossible to connect before and after. As

Notwithstanding this discontinuity, there is, I think, a thread that runs through any earnest treatment of life's origins and our cosmic beginnings. Michael Ruse, an agnostic evolutionist, identifies this thread when he insists that "All of these people are simply overwhelmed by the glory of creation."[45] That includes Darwin, Huxley, Dawkins, Hartshorne, Rolston, and, of course, the author(s) of the Genesis creation story for whom the pristine earth is blessed by God and pronounced "very good." How that glory came into existence is, of course, much disputed, but its continuing presence is a necessary condition for both science and religion. Even a fallen world provokes astonishment, and to his credit Darwin came under its spell more than most. I believe he saw things clearly but not completely. He did not look over the horizon of natural law to see with the eye of faith the redemption of nature from its fallen state. That redemption marks a newness of life beyond the ken of our best thinking. As Paul wrote: "Eye hath not seen, nor ear heard, neither have entered into the heart of man, the things which God hath prepared for them that love him" (1 Cor. 2:9).

Stephen Hawking puts it: "At a singularity, all the laws of physics would have broken down. This means that the state of the universe, after the Big Bang, will not depend on anything that may have happened before, because the deterministic laws that govern the universe will break down in the Big Bang. The universe will evolve from the Big Bang, completely independently of what it was like before." Stephen W. Hawking, "The Beginning of Time," Stephen Hawking: The Official Website, http://www.hawking.org.uk/the-beginning-of-time.html (accessed June 21, 2013).

45. Michael Ruse, *Darwin and Design* (Cambridge: Harvard University Press, 2003), 334.

The Authors

Robert Bennett was born in Salt Lake City and educated at the University of Utah. He has worked as a legislative staffer, a lobbyist, a public relations executive, and the CEO of numerous businesses. From 1993 to 2011, he served as a United States Senator for the state of Utah.

Kent Brooks, PhD, was born in Provo, Utah and raised in Utah, Texas, and California. He has been a Religious Educator for thirty-four years and has maintained a private practice in Marriage and Family Therapy for over thirty years.

Sariah Cottrell is from Denver, Colorado, and she studies bioethics as a graduate student at Brigham Young University. Her research interests focus on cloning and personhood.

Richard Davis is a professor of political science at Brigham Young University. He is the author of several books on American politics.

Eric A. Eliason is a professor of folklore at Brigham Young University. From 2002 to 2008 he served as chaplain for the 1st Battalion, 19th Special Forces Group (Airborne) in the Utah Army National Guard. He served in Afghanistan, the Philippines, and at Arlington National Cemetery. He developed the first training program for Afghan Security Forces chaplains and worked closely with Afghan religious and community leaders on peacemaking and reconstruction projects.

Daniel J. Fairbanks is Associate Dean of Science and Health and Professor of Biology at Utah Valley University, a research geneticist, author, and artist. He is author of the books *Relics of Eden: The Powerful Evidence of Evolution in Human DNA*, *Evolving: the Human Effect and Why It Matters*, and the coauthor of *Ending the Mendel-Fisher Controversy* (with A. Franklin, A. W. F. Edwards, D. L. Hartl, and T. Seidenfeld), in addition to numerous scientific articles. For more information see his website at www.danielfairbanks.net.

James E. Faulconer is a professor of philosophy and a Richard L. Evans Professor of Religious Understanding at Brigham Young University, where he has taught since 1975. His professional work is in LDS thought and contemporary European philosophy. His books include *The Life of Holiness: Romans 1, 5–8* and *Transcendence in Philosophy and Religion*. He and Janice Allen Faulconer are the parents of four and the grandparents of eleven.

Robert L. Gleave, PhD, ABPP, CGP is a psychologist and clinical professor at Brigham Young University. He has a joint appointment with Counseling and Psychological Services and the Counseling Psychology Doctoral Program. He also maintains a small private practice.

David Grandy is a professor of philosophy at Brigham Young University. He has a special interest in the history and philosophy of science. He has published *Everyday Quantum Reality*, *The Speed of Light: Constancy and Cosmos*, and *Leo Szilard: Science as a Mode of Being*, and he is the co-author of *Magic, Mystery, and Science: The Occult in Western Civilization*.

Kristine Haglund is editor of *Dialogue: A Journal of Mormon Thought*. She holds degrees in German Studies and German Literature from Harvard and the University of Michigan. Her research interests include gender and religion, Mormon women's and children's history, and religious publications in new media. She lives in Massachusetts with her three children, and blogs at www.bycommonconsent.com.

George Handley is a professor of Interdisciplinary Humanities and chair of the department of Humanities, Classics, and Comparative Literature at BYU where he has taught since 1998. His publications include *New World Poetics: Nature and the Adamic Imagination of Whitman, Neruda and Walcott* and an environmental autobiography, *Home Waters: A Year of Recompenses on the Provo River*.

David A. Jensen is Associate Professor of philosophy at Brigham Young University. His research interests include all areas of ethics including current issues in medical ethics. He and his spouse, Ashley Heilner Jensen, have four children.

Robert L. Millet is Abraham O. Smoot University Professor and Professor of Religious Education at Brigham Young University. Since joining the BYU faculty in 1983, Professor Millet has served as chair of the department of Ancient Scripture, dean of Religious Education, Richard L. Evans Professor of Religious Understanding, and Director of Publications for the BYU Religious Studies Center.

Nathan Oman is a professor of law at the College of William & Mary. He was educated at Brigham Young University and Harvard Law School. A life-long Latter-day Saint, he currently lives in Williamsburg, Virginia with his family.

Steven L. Peck is Associate Professor of Biology at Brigham Young University where he teaches History and Philosophy of Biology and Bioethics.

Taylor G. Petrey is the Lucinda Hinsdale Stone Assistant Professor of Religion at Kalamazoo College in Kalamazoo, Michigan and Director of the Women, Gender, and Sexuality Program. He holds a Doctorate of Theology and Masters of Theological Studies from Harvard Divinity School in New Testament and Early Christianity.

Justin F. White is a graduate student in philosophy at the University of California, Riverside. He studied philosophy and English at Brigham Young University. His current research focuses on nineteenth- and twentieth-century European philosophy. He and his wife, Anna Snyder White, are the parents of three children.

Camille Stilson Williams completed a BA and MA in English, and a JD, all at Brigham Young University. She has taught reading and writing, and family law for undergraduates at BYU, and has also published articles related to women and the family and law in national magazines, online magazines, specialized journals, and chapters in books. Her work covers issues related to women, feminism, religion, and law. She and her husband, Richard, have five children and twenty grandchildren.

Marleen S. Williams, PhD, is a clinical professor of counseling psychology at Brigham Young University. Her research has focused on women's mental health, spirituality and mental health, disabilities and the effects of trauma on mental health.

Richard N. Williams is a professor of psychology at Brigham Young University. His specialty areas include the philosophical, theoretical, and historical foundations of psychology, with concentration on issues related to human agency, as well as the science of psychology and research methods and statistics. Williams has authored, co-authored, and edited numerous journals, articles, and books. Williams and his wife, Camille, have five children and twenty grandchildren.

Larry T. Wimmer is Dusenberry University Professor of Economics, Emeritus, at Brigham Young University. He has been a member of the economics department since 1963, having received his PhD in economics from the University of Chicago. His essay, "Presiding in Our Homes: Are We Doing Too Much or Too Little?" is derived from a talk given while serving as a member of the Stake Presidency in the BYU Eighth Stake of young married students.

Bruce W. Young is Associate Professor of English at Brigham Young University, where he has taught since 1983. His teaching and research interests include Shakespeare, C. S. Lewis, world literature, and the philosophy of Emmanuel Levinas. Among his publications are a book (*Family Life in the Age of Shakespeare*), articles, reviews, poetry, and personal essays. He and his wife, Margaret Blair Young, live in Provo, Utah.

Margaret Blair Young has focused her studies primarily on race issues in Mormonism for the past fifteen years. With Darius Gray, she has co-authored a trilogy of fully documented historical novels on black Mormon pioneers, and has made three documentaries, the best known being *Nobody Knows: The Untold Story of Black Mormons*.

Subject Index

Abbot, Douglas, 101
Abel, Elijah, 182
abortion, 265, 292–94
Abu Ghraib, 227–28
abuse, 142
adoption, 93–96
Afghanistan, 219–31
agency, 9, 66, 116–17, 121
Alcott, Louisa May, 146
Ammonites, 199
animism, 274
Anthony, Susan B., 164
anti-Mormonism, 18, 23–24
atheism, 343–49
atomic bomb, 203
Atonement, 4, 67–68
Austin, John, 38
authority, viii, 37–39, 42–43
Ballard, M. Russell, 16
Ballard, Melvin J., 64
Beck, Julie, 150
Benson, Ezra Taft, 55, 69, 96, 211
blacks. *See* priesthood ban.
bodies, 153, 155–56, 271
Book of Mormon, 166
  and racism, 180
  and war, 196–200, 208
Brown, Hugh B., 32
Brown, Samuel, 94
Burns, Lucy, 164
Byrd, A. Dean, 101
Cain. *See* curse of Cain.
Cannon, Martha Hughes, 166
Catholicism, 35–36
Chesterton, C. K., 219
Christofferson, D. Todd, 191
Church leaders, 18, 54. *See also* prophets.

Clark, J. Reuben, 203
Cohen, J. B., 338
Cohen, William, 265
Collins, Francis, 330
Coltrin, Zebedee, 185
conception, 316
Conroy, Pat, 221
consecration, 273
Constitution, 252
Creation, 353–55
curse of Cain, 183, 186, 188, 191
Darwin, Charles, 340–45
Dawkins, Richard, 347–48
Democratic Party, 245–47, 256
determinism, 112–16
Dirksen, Everett, 247
disagreements, x
divine command, 287–88
divine embodiment, 89. *See also* bodies.
DNA, 313
Dobzhansky, Theodosius, 328
doctrine, 13–51
duty, 3, 6
Dworkin, Ronald, 45–46
economics, 249–50
education, viii
Einstein, Albert, 339
Eisenhower, Dwight, 251
embryos, 291–92, 295, 310–13
England, Eugene, 187
environmentalism, 272–83
Equal Rights Amendment, 132–33, 257–58
ethics, 4
evolution, theistic, 349–55
Eyring, Henry, 330–31
Eyring, Henry B., 69
fall of Adam, 67

"Family: A Proclamation to the World," 54, 57, 63–64, 71–74, 76, 97, 102, 124–25, 149–50, 225–26
Faust, James E., 81
feminism, 134, 151, 154–60
  first wave, 163–68
  second wave, 168
feminist theology, 142
freedom. *See* agency.
Frieden, Betty, 168
Friedman, Tom, 247–48
Fuller, Margaret, 159
Gantt, Edwin E., 112
gender, 63–64, 70–71, 124
  eternal, 97–104
gender roles, 54, 71–72, 82, 97, 102–3, 132–33, 137–40, 149–53, 225–26
Glaze, Jamie, 228
Goldwater, Barry, 247
Gould, Stephen Jay, 333
Great Chain of Being, 341
Great Depression, 257
Great Santini, The, 221
guilt, 4
Hafen, Bruce C., 83
Hales, Robert D., 15
Hall, G. Stanley, 164
happiness, 65
Hart, H. L. A., 41–42
Hartshorne, Charles, 350–51
Haught, John, 352
heavenly parents, 88
Hinckley, Gordon B., 21–22, 70, 74, 189, 204–6, 212, 259, 280, 282
Hiroshima, 203
Holland, Jeffrey R., 15, 77, 188, 191
homosexual relationships, 286
homosexuality, 100, 133
Hübner, Helmuth, 212
human experimentation, 296
husbands, 53–56
Hussein, Saddam, 228
Huxley, Thomas, 343–45
Hyde, Orson, 94
integrity, 49–50
intelligence, 87
Intelligent Design, 328–30
in vitro fertilization, 297–98, 310–12, 320
Jefferson, Thomas, 250

Jesus Christ, 7, 66–67, 165, 200–201, 261–62
Johnson, Greg, 24
Johnson, Phillip, 329
Johnson, Sonia, 170–71
just war, 202, 206–10
killing, 294–96, 319–21
Kimball, Spencer W., 187
King Follett Discourse, 29–30, 94
kinship, 92–97, 270
Lee, Harold B., 21, 30–31
legal positivism, 41
Levinas, Emmanuel, 7, 178
Lewis, C. S., 270
Lewis, Q. Walker, 182–83
life, 314–19
Light of Christ, 124
Lincoln, Abraham, 211, 251
marriage, 69–82, 114–15, 124–25
Maxwell, Neal A., 14, 31–33, 79–80, 135, 244
McConkie, Bruce R., 20–21, 28–29, 42, 188
McConkie, Joseph Fielding, 22
McFague, Sallie, 153
McKay, David O., 20, 207–8
Meldrum, Jeffrey, 331
Midgley, Mary, 347
mission, 5
modesty, 154
morality, 78, 286–89
Mormon Doctrine, 42
Moroni (captain), 197
Morris, Henry, 329–30
motherhood, 136–39, 151
Moynihan, Pat, 246
mullah, 231
"N word," 179
Nagasaki, 203
natural law, 40–41, 121–22
Natural Selection, 338
Nelson, Russell M., 82–83, 316
nihilism, 112
nurturing, 138
Oaks, Dallin H., 15, 27–28, 31, 65–66, 68, 173
obedience, 3, 5
Packer, Boyd K., 14, 67, 76, 78–79, 172
parable of the five Samaritans, 234–35
parenting, 73
patriarchy, 141–42, 159
patriotism, 210–13
Paul, Alice, 164

Penrose, Charles W., 30
Persian Gulf War, 205
personhood, 316, 319, 321–22
Pesch Valley, 230
political neutrality, 259–60
politics, ix, 243–66
poor, 248, 262
Popenoe, David, 81–82
population control, 277
pornography, 154
Pratt, Parley P., 94
preexistence, 64, 87–88
pregnancy, 136, 316–19
presiding, 53–54
priesthood, 58–59, 91, 133–34
priesthood ban, 28–29, 179, 182–92
procreation, 79, 87–92, 124
prophets, 13, 19–22, 132, 135
 fallibility, 20–22, 25, 191
racism, 179–82, 189
Raz, Joseph, 37
Reagan, Ronald, 251, 258
Relief Society, 165
Republican Party, 243–53, 255
revelation, 16
Reynolds, Emily, 112
Richards, Louisa Greene, 147
rights, 73
Roosevelt, Franklin, 203
Russell, Bertrand, 347
sacrifice, 10
same-sex marriage, 69–82, 93, 114–15, 118, 120–23, 258
science, viii
science and religion, 327, 330–34, 343–52
Scott, Richard G., 172
scriptures, 15, 43
service, 58
sexual revolution, 113, 172–73
sexuality, 111–27, 152, 155
sin, 153
Smith, Gordon, 320–21

Smith, Joseph, 14, 16, 19–20, 26, 40, 44, 164, 166, 183, 189, 210, 271
Smith, Joseph Fielding, 16, 210
Snow, Lorenzo, 19, 189–90
society, 78
Sorokin, Pitirim A., 79
spirit birth, 87–88
spirits, 271, 318
Spooner, Lysander, 232–33
Stanton, Elizabeth Cady, 164
stem cells, 289–90, 308–10
Stephens, Trent, 331
stewardship, 278–82
Swain, Louisa, 146
Talmage, James E., 90
Tanner, N. Eldon, 55
taxes, 262–63
Taylor, John, 184
testimony, 6
Thirteenth Amendment, 246
trials, 65
truth, 7, 40–41, 167, 253, 288–89
Ulrich, Laurel, 159
Walcott, Derek, 269
war, 219–40
weakness, 65
wealth, 249
wealth disparity, 278
welfare, 249
Welker, Michael, 353–54
Wells, H. G., 346–47
Wickman, Lance, 215
Wirthlin, Dick, 251
Wirthlin, Richard B., 15
wives, 53–56
Wollstonecraft, Mary, 164
Wood, Robert, 259
Woodruff, Wilford, 104–5
Word of Wisdom, 40–41, 43–44, 47–48
World War II, 201
Young, Brigham, 40, 184

Scripture Index

Old Testament

Genesis 1:1 — 19
Genesis 1:27 — 71-72, 91
Genesis 1-2 — 90, 353
Genesis 2:7 — 315
Genesis 9:25 — 186
Genesis 19:5 — 78
Genesis 19:24 — 78
Genesis 25:29-34 — 129
Genesis 27:38 — 130
Num. 12:10 — 178
Ezra 7:10 — 78
Isaiah 1:18 — 67
Isaiah 2:4 — 206
Isaiah 28:9-10 — 26
Isaiah 28:10 — 23
Jeremiah 20:11 — 221

New Testament

Matthew 5:48 — 29
Matthew 7:11 — 209
Matthew 10:34 — 222
Matthew 10:34-36 — 201
Matthew 15:28 — 165
Matthew 18:7 — 275
Matthew 19:8 — 74
Matthew 22:37-39 — 83
Matthew 24:12 — 214
Matthew 25:34-36 — 309
Matthew 25:40 — 266
Matthew 26:52 — 201
Matthew 27:56 — 165
Mark 4:41 — 165
Mark 10:6-9 — 43
Mark 10:7-9 — 74
Mark 14:3-9 — 165
Luke 9:55-56 — 215
Luke 10:38-41 — 165
Luke 11:46 — 37
Luke 21:19 — 129
Luke 21:26 — 214
John 4:25-26 — 165
John 6:68 — 143
John 9:1-4 — 192
John 12:3-8 — 165
John 15:13 — 222
John 17:11 — ix
John 20:11-17 — 165
Acts 10:34 — 191
Acts 17:4 — 165
Acts 9:36 — 165
Romans 1:24-27 — 78
Romans 8:17 — 29
1 Corinthians 2:9 — 355
1 Corinthians 2:10 — 32
1 Corinthians 2:16 — 29
1 Corinthians 6:18 — 77
1 Corinthians 6:19-20 — 77
1 Corinthians 11:11 — 71
1 Corinthians 15:1-3 — 14
Galatians 3:28 — 105
Galatians 3:28-29 — 187
Ephesians 6:11-18 — 235
1 Timothy 4:6 — 33
1 Timothy 4:13 — 33
2 Timothy 1:2-5 — 146
2 Timothy 1:7 — 146
2 Timothy 3:16 — 13
2 Timothy 3:16-17 — 15
Hebrews 6:6 — 77
Hebrews 11:35 — 165
James 1:5-6 — 62
James 1:27 — 262
James 5:17 — 19

1 Peter 3:5 — 165
1 Peter 3:15 — vii, 32
2 Peter 1:4 — 29
1 John 3:2 — 29
Revelation 22:21 — 19

Book of Mormon

1 Nephi 11:17 — 63, 132
1 Nephi 12:15-16 — 197
1 Nephi 13:20-29 — 19
2 Nephi 1:4 — 68
2 Nephi 2:8 — 67
2 Nephi 2:11 — 64
2 Nephi 2:13 — 125
2 Nephi 2:16 — 65
2 Nephi 2:25 — 167
2 Nephi 2:27 — 65
2 Nephi 2:28 — 63
2 Nephi 5:21 — 181
2 Nephi 5:27 — 63
2 Nephi 23:25 — 67
2 Nephi 26:24 — 63
2 Nephi 26:33 — 105, 129, 166, 192
2 Nephi 28:30 — 23, 26, 62
2 Nephi 29:7 — 210
2 Nephi 30:6 — 181
Jacob 2:7-11 — 166
Jacob 2:8 — 14
Enos 1:23 — 17
Mosiah 3:19 — 64, 65
Mosiah 18:8-9 — x
Mosiah 18:9 — 70
Mosiah 18:18-19 — 15
Mosiah 23:28-29 — 199
Mosiah 25:21-22 — 15
Mosiah 28:2 — 199
Mosiah 28:3 — 198
Alma 2:30 — 214
Alma 4:3 — 198
Alma 6:63 — 271
Alma 7:8 — 63
Alma 10:27 — 37
Alma 13:3 — 64
Alma 24:27 — 200
Alma 26:23-25 — 199
Alma 26:26 — 199
Alma 26:31-34 — 199
Alma 30:44 — 271
Alma 31:5 — 14, 197
Alma 34:13 — 67
Alma 39:5 — 79
Alma 42:8 — 63
Alma 42:16 — 63
Alma 43:37-38 — 197
Alma 43:47 — 207
Alma 44:20 — 197
Alma 46:12-13 — 166
Alma 48:14 — 207
Alma 48:15-16 — 207
Alma 48:21-23 — 199
Alma 48:24 — 199
Alma 54:11 — 166
Alma 56:46 — 198
Alma 62:41 — 198
Helaman 4:5 — 197
Helaman 6:37 — 197
3 Nephi 3:20-21 — 208
3 Nephi 11:28-29 — 50
3 Nephi 27:13-16 — x
3 Nephi 27:29 — 62
4 Nephi 1:13-18 — 198
4 Nephi 1:17 — 182
4 Nephi 1:20 — 182
Mormon 2:8 — 197
Mormon 3:9 — 198
Mormon 3:9-11 — 208
Mormon 3:14-15 — 209
Mormon 4:4 — 208
Mormon 4:5 — 201
Mormon 4:11 — 197-98
Mormon 4:12-15 — 166
Mormon 5:8 — 197
Ether 8:19 — 215
Ether 12:27 — 65, 67
Ether 14:21 — 197
Ether 14:22 — 198
Ether 15:22 — 198
Moroni 7:19 — 282
Moroni 8:27 — 211
Moroni 9:5 — 198
Moroni 9:8-10 — 166
Moroni 9:18 — 198
Moroni 9:23 — 198
Moroni 10:5 — 135
Moroni 10:32 — 67

Doctrine and Covenants

Doctrine and Covenants 1:30 — 18
Doctrine and Covenants 2:3 — 77
Doctrine and Covenants 4:7 — 62
Doctrine and Covenants 10:37 — 209
Doctrine and Covenants 18:10 — 261
Doctrine and Covenants 21:4-5 — 69
Doctrine and Covenants 25:4 — 143
Doctrine and Covenants 30:2 — x
Doctrine and Covenants 38:27 — x
Doctrine and Covenants 38:39 — 211
Doctrine and Covenants 41:2 — x
Doctrine and Covenants 42:61 — 62
Doctrine and Covenants 45:27 — 214
Doctrine and Covenants 46:8 — 133
Doctrine and Covenants 49:15-17 — 72
Doctrine and Covenants 49:26 — 62
Doctrine and Covenants 52:9 — 15
Doctrine and Covenants 52:36 — 15
Doctrine and Covenants 59:6 — 77
Doctrine and Covenants 59:18-22 — 276
Doctrine and Covenants 63:31 — 215
Doctrine and Covenants 63:33 — 201, 215
Doctrine and Covenants 64:10 — 82
Doctrine and Covenants 68:3-4 — 15, 22
Doctrine and Covenants 76:40-42 — 14
Doctrine and Covenants 76:58 — 29
Doctrine and Covenants 82:19 — 266
Doctrine and Covenants 84:53-58 — 209
Doctrine and Covenants 88:7-12 — 271
Doctrine and Covenants 88:63 — 62
Doctrine and Covenants 88:69 — 62
Doctrine and Covenants 88:77-78 — 13
Doctrine and Covenants 88:91 — 214
Doctrine and Covenants 88:118 — 62
Doctrine and Covenants 89:12-13 — 43
Doctrine and Covenants 89:18 — 48
Doctrine and Covenants 90:3-5 — 18
Doctrine and Covenants 93 — 87
Doctrine and Covenants 93:29 — 124
Doctrine and Covenants 93:29-33 — 88
Doctrine and Covenants 93:33-34 — 271
Doctrine and Covenants 98:11 — 268, 283
Doctrine and Covenants 98:11-12 — 26
Doctrine and Covenants 98:16 — 196, 201
Doctrine and Covenants 98:23 — 207
Doctrine and Covenants 98:30-31 — 207
Doctrine and Covenants 98:33 — 207
Doctrine and Covenants 98:36 — 207
Doctrine and Covenants 101:38 — 129
Doctrine and Covenants 101:45 — 57
Doctrine and Covenants 101:78-80 — 233
Doctrine and Covenants 104:13-18 — 277
Doctrine and Covenants 104:17 — 277, 280
Doctrine and Covenants 109:43-44 — 215
Doctrine and Covenants 109:77 — 30
Doctrine and Covenants 121:26 — 31
Doctrine and Covenants 121:37 — 57-58
Doctrine and Covenants 121:39 — 55
Doctrine and Covenants 121:41 — 166, 227
Doctrine and Covenants 121:41-43 — 55
Doctrine and Covenants 121:46 — 166
Doctrine and Covenants 123:7 — 209
Doctrine and Covenants 124:41 — 31
Doctrine and Covenants 124:61 — 69
Doctrine and Covenants 128 — 125
Doctrine and Covenants 128:18 — 31
Doctrine and Covenants 130:22 — 29
Doctrine and Covenants 131:1-3 — 76
Doctrine and Covenants 131:1-4 — 86, 125
Doctrine and Covenants 131:7 — 156
Doctrine and Covenants 132:5-6 — 74
Doctrine and Covenants 132:9-11 — 74
Doctrine and Covenants 132:12-15 — 75
Doctrine and Covenants 132:19 — 88
Doctrine and Covenants 132:19-20 — 29
Doctrine and Covenants 132:46 — 85
Doctrine and Covenants 134:10 — 17
Doctrine and Covenants 138:56 — 64
Official Declaration 2 — 192

Pearl of Great Price

Moses 1:39 — 76, 123, 167, 178
Moses 1:40-41 — 19
Moses 3:7 — 90, 315
Moses 3:9 — 271, 276
Moses 4:1-4 — 224
Moses 5:1-5 — 167
Moses 5:8 — 67
Moses 5:9-12 — 167
Moses 5:11 — 67
Moses 5:11-12 — 167
Moses 5:16 — 167
Moses 6:6 — 167
Moses 6:9 — 167
Moses 6:54 — 27

Moses 6:57 — 29
Moses 6:60 — 8
Moses 7:33 — 178
Moses 7:44 — 140
Abraham 1:2 — 142
Abraham 3:18 — 124
Abraham 3:22-25 — 124
Abraham 3:22-28 — 167

Abraham 3:24-26 — 123
Abraham 4-5 — 90
Joseph Smith—History 1:11-12 — 44
Articles of Faith 2 — 27
Articles of Faith 8 — 19
Articles of Faith 9 — 31
Articles of Faith 11 — 227

Also available from
GREG KOFFORD BOOKS

"This is My Doctrine": The Development of Mormon Theology

Charles R. Harrell

Hardcover, ISBN: 978-1-58958-103-6

The principal doctrines defining Mormonism today often bear little resemblance to those it started out with in the early 1830s. This book shows that these doctrines did not originate in a vacuum but were rather prompted and informed by the religious culture from which Mormonism arose. Early Mormons, like their early Christian and even earlier Israelite predecessors, brought with them their own varied culturally conditioned theological presuppositions (a process of convergence) and only later acquired a more distinctive theological outlook (a process of differentiation).

In this first-of-its-kind comprehensive treatment of the development of Mormon theology, Charles Harrell traces the history of Latter-day Saint doctrines from the times of the Old Testament to the present. He describes how Mormonism has carried on the tradition of the biblical authors, early Christians, and later Protestants in reinterpreting scripture to accommodate new theological ideas while attempting to uphold the integrity and authority of the scriptures. In the process, he probes three questions: How did Mormon doctrines develop? What are the scriptural underpinnings of these doctrines? And what do critical scholars make of these same scriptures? In this enlightening study, Harrell systematically peels back the doctrinal accretions of time to provide a fresh new look at Mormon theology.

"*This Is My Doctrine*" will provide those already versed in Mormonism's theological tradition with a new and richer perspective of Mormon theology. Those unacquainted with Mormonism will gain an appreciation for how Mormon theology fits into the larger Jewish and Christian theological traditions.

Mormon Women Have Their Say: Essays from the Claremont Oral History Collection

Edited by Claudia L. Bushman and Caroline Kline

Paperback, ISBN: 978-1-58958-494-5

The Claremont Women's Oral History Project has collected hundreds of interviews with Mormon women of various ages, experiences, and levels of activity. These interviews record the experiences of these women in their homes and family life, their church life, and their work life, in their roles as homemakers, students, missionaries, career women, single women, converts, and disaffected members. Their stories feed into and illuminate the broader narrative of LDS history and belief, filling in a large gap in Mormon history that has often neglected the lived experiences of women. This project preserves and perpetuates their voices and memories, allowing them to say share what has too often been left unspoken. The silent majority speaks in these records.

This volume is the first to explore the riches of the collection in print. A group of young scholars and others have used the interviews to better understand what Mormonism means to these women and what women mean for Mormonism. They explore those interviews through the lenses of history, doctrine, mythology, feminist theory, personal experience, and current events to help us understand what these women have to say about their own faith and lives.

Praise for *Mormon Women Have Their Say*:

"Using a variety of analytical techniques and their own savvy, the authors connect ordinary lives with enduring themes in Latter-day Saint faith and history." --Laurel Thatcher Ulrich, author of *Well-Behaved Women Seldom Make History*

"Essential. . . . In these pages, Mormon women will find *ourselves*." --Joanna Brooks, author of *The Book of Mormon Girl: A Memoir of an American Faith*

"The varieties of women's responses to the major issues in their lives will provide many surprises for the reader, who will be struck by how many different ways there are to be a thoughtful and faithful Latter-day Saint woman." --Armand Mauss, author of *All Abraham's Children: Changing Mormon Conceptions of Race and Lineage*

War & Peace in Our Time: Mormon Perspectives

Edited by Patrick Q. Mason, J. David Pulsipher, and Richard L. Bushman

Paperback, ISBN: 978-1-58958-099-2

"This provocative and thoughtful book is sure both to infuriate and to delight.... The essays demonstrate that exegesis of distinctly Latter-day Saint scriptures can yield a wealth of disputation, the equal of any rabbinical quarrel or Jesuitical casuistry. This volume provides a fitting springboard for robust and lively debates within the Mormon scholarly and lay community on how to think about the pressing issues of war and peace." - ROBERT S. WOOD, Dean Emeritus, Center for Naval Warfare Studies, Chester W. Nimitz Chair Emeritus, U.S. Naval War College

"This is an extraordinary collection of essays on a topic of extraordinary importance.... Whatever your current opinion on the topic, this book will challenge you to reflect more deeply and thoroughly on what it means to be a disciple of Christ, the Prince of Peace, in an era of massive military budgets, lethal technologies, and widespread war." - GRANT HARDY, Professor of History and Religious Studies, University of North Carolina, Asheville, Author, *Understanding the Book of Mormon: A Reader's Guide*

"Mormons take their morality seriously. They are also patriotic. Tragically, the second trait can undermine the first. When calls for war are on the horizon, it is possible for well-intended Saints to be too sure of our selective application of scripture to contemporary matters of life and death, too sure that we can overcome evil by force, that we can control the results of military conflict, that war is the only option for patriots. Yet pacifism has its own critics. This collection of differing views by thoughtful scholars comprises a debate. Reading it may save us in the future from enacting more harm than good in the name of God, country, or presumption." - PHILIP BARLOW, Arrington Chair of Mormon History and Culture, Utah State University, Author, *Mormons and the Bible: The Place of the Latter-day Saints in American Religion*

"Let the Earth Bring Forth" Evolution and Scripture

Howard C. Stutz

Paperback, ISBN: 978-1-58958-126-5

A century ago in 1809, Charles Darwin was born. Fifty years later, he published a scientific treatise describing the process of speciation that launched what appeared to be a challenge to the traditional religious interpretation of how life was created on earth. The controversy has erupted anew in the last decade as Creationists and Young Earth adherents challenge school curricula and try to displace "the theory of evolution."

This book is filled with fascinating examples of speciation by the well-known process of mutation but also by the less well-known processes of sexual recombination and polyploidy. In addition to the fossil record, Howard Stutz examines the evidence from the embryo stages of human beings and other creatures to show how selection and differentiation moved development in certain favored directions while leaving behind evidence of earlier, discarded developments. Anatomy, biochemistry, and genetics are all examined in their turn.

With rigorously scientific clarity but in language accessible to a popular audience, the book proceeds to its conclusion, reached after a lifetime of study: the divine map of creation is one supported by both scientific evidence and the scriptures. This is a book to be read, not only for its fascinating scientific insights, but also for a new appreciation of well-known scriptures.

www.ingramcontent.com/pod-product-compliance
Lightning Source LLC
Chambersburg PA
CBHW031325230426
43670CB00006B/238